DRACULA'S
BROOD

THE IRISH "VAMPIRE."

Illustration by John Tenniel, from *Punch* (24 October 1885).

DRACULA'S BROOD

**Neglected Vampire Classics by
Sir Arthur Conan Doyle,
Algernon Blackwood, M. R. James, and Others**

Selected and Introduced by
RICHARD DALBY

BARNES
&NOBLE
BOOKS
NEW YORK

To all admirers of *Dracula*
and connoisseurs of vampire literature
everywhere

CONTENTS

Introduction   9

William Gilbert
  The Last Lords of Gardonal (1867)   13

Eliza Lynn Linton
  The Fate of Madame Cabanel (1880)   43

Phil Robinson
  The Man-Eating Tree (1881)   55

Vasile Alecsandrai
  The Vampyre (1886)   62

Anne Crawford
  A Mystery of the Campagna (1887)   64

Julian Hawthorne
  Ken's Mystery (1888)   92

Sir Arthur Conan Doyle
  The Parasite (1894)   111

Mary E. Braddon
  Good Lady Ducayne (1896)   145

Mary Cholmondeley
  Let Loose (1898)   171

Vincent O'Sullivan
  Will (1899)   185

H. B. Marriott Watson
  The Stone Chamber (1899)   190

Hume Nisbet
  The Vampire Maid (1900)   217
  The Old Portrait (1900)   222

Vernon Lee
  Marsyas in Flanders (1900)   226

Louise J. Strong
An Unscientific Story (1903)   238

Sabine Baring-Gould
A Dead Finger (1904)   249

Horacio Quiroga
The Feather Pillow (1907)   264

Algernon Blackwood
The Singular Death of Morton (1910)   268

Alice and Claude Askew
Aylmer Vance and the Vampire (1914)   276

Ulric Daubeny
The Sumach (1919)   293

M. R. James
Wailing Well (1927)   304

E. Heron-Allen
Another Squaw? (1934)   313

E. R. Punshon
The Living Stone (1939)   321

Frederick Cowles
Princess of Darkness (1940)   330

Acknowledgements   349

INTRODUCTION

THE chief aim of this anthology is to demonstrate the wide interest shown in Victorian England for the genre of vampire literature, the influence of these works on Bram Stoker, and the impetus given by *Dracula* to this form of horror fiction in the first half of the twentieth century.

The name 'Dracula' has been synonymous with horror for over five hundred years. His exploits were fully described in an English 'best-seller' at the end of the Tudor era by Richard Knolles in *The Generall Historie of the Turkes* (1603), a giant folio of 1190 pages which passed through copious editions during the next three centuries. Knolles described the family of Draculas in some detail: 'Dracula, of Valachia, a man of great experience in martiall affaires', and his sons 'Wladus Dracula' and 'Dracula, the younger brother of Wladus'—known today respectively as Vlad ('Dracul'), Vlad (the 'Impaler'), and Radu (the 'Handsome'). Dracula's 'cruell manner' in dealing with his 'mortall enemies' is covered in full—'twentie thousand dead carkases of men, women and children . . . sticking upon sharpe stakes . . .'. We know from Stoker's working notes for *Dracula* that one of his sources for his classic novel was the *Account of the Principalities of Wallachia and Moldavia* (1820) by the British consul at Bucharest, William Wilkinson. And Wilkinson himself acknowledged that his book was based, in turn, on the writings of Richard Knolles.

Other writers, including Horace Walpole, Samuel Johnson, Shelley, and Byron, had known of Dracula through Knolles. Johnson wrote in the *Rambler*: 'None of our writers can in my opinion justly contest the superiority of Knolles, who in his History of the Turks has displayed all the excellencies that narration can admit.' And shortly before his death at Missolonghi, Byron wrote: 'Old Knolles was one of the first books that gave me pleasure when a child; and I believe it had much influence on my future wishes to visit the Levant, and gave perhaps the oriental colouring which is observed in my poetry.'

Seventy years later, Knolles and Wilkinson were vital aids for Stoker during his researches on Dracula, together with the assistance provided by the Hungarian professor Arminius Vambery (referred to as 'my friend Arminius of Buda-Pesth University' by Van Helsing, in *Dracula*) and his colleague Ion Bogdan, biographer of Vlad Tepes (1896).

Articles on vampires proliferated in the popular weekly and monthly magazines of the Victorian era. One of these, entitled 'Vampyres and Ghouls' (in *All the Year Round*, 20 May 1871), describes several cases from the most widely affected areas of the Danubian and Greek countries. The final conclusion reached was that 'all the stories of vampyres, ghouls, and were-wolves, can find their solution in a combination of three causes—a sort of epidemic superstition among ignorant persons; some of the phenomena of trance or epileptic sleep; and special monomaniac diseases which it is the province of the physician to study'.

The Romany scholar Francis Hindes Groome discussed gypsy beliefs in real vampires in his volume *Gypsy Folk-Tales*. Their word *ciohano*, meaning 'vampire', is identical with the Turkish-Romani *tchovekhano*, a 'revenant' or spectre.

Many famous names have had no doubts about the credibility of vampires. Horace Walpole (in his *Letters*, vol. 1, p. cix) revealed that King George I was a firm believer in the vampire superstition. In a special preface to *Dracula* (deleted from the British edition, but later added to the Icelandic edition), Stoker himself wrote: 'I am quite convinced that there is no doubt whatever that the events here described really took place, however unbelievable and incomprehensible they might appear at first sight . . . I state yet again that this mysterious tragedy which is here described is completely true in all its external respects, though naturally I have reached a different conclusion on certain points than those involved in the story.' (His friends' reactions are not recorded!)

'True' records of vampires have continued to appear up to the present day. One of the most intriguing 'plagues' is said to have occurred on Cagayan Sulu, a remote island in the Philippines. Ethelbert Skertchley's account (in 1896) was adapted by Andrew Lang in his book *The Disentanglers*, and later was a great favourite of M. R. James (as recorded by Commander R. T. Gould in his fascinating essay on the subject).

This anthology intentionally avoids all the most celebrated classics in the genre, which are readily available elsewhere and have constantly been reprinted: Polidori's 'The Vampyre', Le Fanu's 'Carmilla', Tieck's 'To Wake the Dead', Crawford's 'For the Blood is the Life', Loring's 'The Tomb of Sarah', Benson's 'Mrs Amworth' and 'The Room in the Tower', Stoker's 'Dracula's Guest', and excerpts from the mammoth novel *Varney the Vampire* (written anonymously, but credited to the 'author of *Grace Rivers*', i.e. James Malcolm Rymer).

Instead I have gone to some of the more neglected examples of the vampire genre, including pieces by some very distinguished names: Arthur Conan Doyle, Algernon Blackwood, Julian Hawthorne, Vernon Lee, Eliza Lynn Linton, Sabine Baring-Gould, Mary Braddon and Mary Cholmondeley; together with unjustly neglected writers: Ulric Daubeny, Anne Crawford (sister of F. Marion Crawford), Frederick Cowles, William Gilbert (father of W. S. Gilbert), Edward Heron-Allen, and Vincent O'Sullivan. Several of these were friends of Stoker, including Doyle, Gilbert, Heron-Allen, Hawthorne, and Braddon. Classic and traditional vampires can be found in the stories by Gilbert, Crawford, Hawthorne, Nisbet, Blackwood, Cowles, the Askews, and others; but a wide choice of other bloodthirsty and vampiric manifestations are described in the other stories, from stakes to trees, from stones to a fish and a feather pillow.

Apart from the blood-seeking creatures, there are the 'human' vampires or parasites whose prey is the soul, or the old needing strength from the young. Winifred Graham, in her autobiography, quoted her friend—the great vampire-authority Montague Summers—on this subject:

The phenomenon [of 'psychic vampires'] is very well known to me. Often they are excellent good souls, but they do (often unconsciously and unwittingly) drain and exhaust the mental vitality of their companions. They are not bores, as you clearly point out. I know a man, a witty and clever individual, kindly and good, who is one of these folk. After a visit from him I have literally had to go to bed and rest. He has not the slightest idea of this. I have known these vampires for years and many times have I heard this problem discussed. I do not think there is a 'scientific' explanation, but there is a psychological explanation. Merely they are psychic vampires. There are also far more terrible beings, men and women who deliberately tap the life-stream of others and feed their own vitality by preying on others. This borders on witchcraft.

One of the best examples of the latter in English literature is *The Parasite* by Arthur Conan Doyle, which appears in this anthology. (It appeared in the Acme Library series with Bram Stoker's *The Watter's Mou'*.)

Psychic vampires are almost as numerous in late Victorian and Edwardian fiction as the traditional variety. Among them may be counted Frank Stockton's 'A Borrowed Month' (1886), E. Heron-Allen's 'The Princess Daphne' (1888), A. Quiller-Couch's 'Old Aeson' (1891), Florence Marryat's 'The Blood of the Vampire' (1897), and Mary Wilkins's 'Luella Miller' (1903). The word 'vampire' meaning 'parasite' in political terms was frequently used in Victorian periodicals and cartoons; e.g. The Irish 'Vampire' portrayed by John Tenniel in

Punch, 24 October 1885 (see frontispiece). The face of the bat looks amazingly like Stoker's!

For suggestions and helpful advice with this selection, I am very grateful to Doris Cowles, Brian Frost, David Simeon, and Jessica Amanda Salmonson.

RICHARD DALBY

THE LAST LORDS OF GARDONAL

William Gilbert

William Gilbert (1804–90) is now known only as the father of William Schwenk Gilbert of 'Gilbert and Sullivan' fame; but he was once an important novelist in the 1860s and 1870s. Many of his novels were in the Dickensian mould, dealing with the contrast between the lots of the rich and the poor. He also wrote a series of occult and supernatural tales for the *Argosy* magazine featuring a strange Italian wizard and astrologer known as the Innominato, an oracle figure consulted by various characters in the stories. 'The Last Lords of Gardonal', one of the best of the mid-nineteenth-century tales to feature a vampire, first appeared in the *Argosy* as a serial from July to September 1867; it was reprinted in Gilbert's collection *The Wizard of the Mountain* for Christmas that year. Bram and Florence Stoker were well acquainted with both Gilberts, father and son, and they were later regular visitors to W. S. Gilbert's beautiful house at Harrow, Grim's Dyke. W. S. Gilbert, in his early years, illustrated several of his father's works.

I

ONE of the most picturesque objects of the valley of the Engadin is the ruined castle of Gardonal, near the village of Madaline. In the feudal times it was the seat of a family of barons, who possessed as their patrimony the whole of the valley, which with the castle had descended from father to son for many generations. The two last of the race were brothers; handsome, well-made, fine-looking young men, but in nature they more resembled fiends than human beings—so cruel, rapacious, and tyrannical were they. During the earlier part of his life their father had been careful of his patrimony. He had also been unusually just to the serfs on his estates, and in consequence they had attained to such a condition of comfort and prosperity as was rarely met with among those in the power of the feudal lords of the country; most of whom were arbitrary and exacting in the extreme. For several years in the latter part of his life he had been subject to a severe illness, which had confined him to the castle, and the management of his possessions and the government of his serfs had thus fallen into the hands of his sons. Although the old baron had placed so much power in their hands, still he was far from resigning his own authority. He exacted a strict account from them of the manner in which they performed the different duties he had intrusted to them; and having a strong suspicion of their character, and the probability of their endeavouring to conceal their misdoings, he caused agents to watch them secretly, and to report to him as to the correctness of the statements they gave. These agents, possibly knowing that the old man had but a short time to live, invariably gave a most favourable description of the conduct of the two young nobles, which, it must be admitted, was not, during their father's lifetime, particularly reprehensible on the whole. Still, they frequently showed as much of the cloven foot as to prove to the tenants what they had to expect at no distant day.

At the old baron's death, Conrad, the elder, inherited as his portion the castle of Gardonal, and the whole valley of Engadin; while to Hermann, the younger, was assigned some immense estates belong to his father in the Bresciano district; for even in those early days, there was considerable intercourse between the inhabitants of that northern portion of Italy and those of the valley of the Engadin. The old baron had also willed, that should either of his sons die without children his estates should go to the survivor.

Conrad accordingly now took possession of the castle and its territory, and Hermann of the estates on the southern side of the Alps; which, although much smaller than those left to his elder brother, were still of great value. Notwithstanding the disparity in the worth of the legacies bequeathed to the two brothers, a perfectly good feeling existed between them, which promised to continue, their tastes being the same, while the mountains which divided them tended to the continuance of peace.

Conrad had hardly been one single week feudal lord of the Engadin before the inhabitants found, to their sorrow, how great was the difference between him and the old baron. Instead of the score of armed retainers his father had kept, Conrad increased the number to three hundred men, none of whom were natives of the valley. They had been chosen with great care from a body of Bohemian, German, and Italian outlaws, who at that time infested the borders of the Grisons, or had found refuge in the fastnesses of the mountains—men capable of any atrocity and to whom pity was unknown. From these miscreants the baron especially chose for his body-guard those who were ignorant of the language spoken by the peasantry of the Engadin, as they would be less likely to be influenced by any supplications or excuses which might be made to them when in the performance of their duty. Although the keeping of so numerous a body of armed retainers might naturally be considered to have entailed great expense, such a conclusion would be most erroneous, at least as far as regarded the present baron, who was as avaricious as he was despotic. He contrived to support his soldiers by imposing a most onerous tax on his tenants, irrespective of his ordinary feudal imposts; and woe to the unfortunate villagers who from inability, or from a sense of the injustice inflicted on them, did not contribute to the uttermost farthing the amount levied on them. In such a case a party of soldiers was immediately sent off to the defaulting village to collect the tax, with permission to live at free quarters till the money was paid; and they knew their duty too well to return home till they had succeeded in their errand. In doing this they were frequently merciless in the extreme, exacting the money by torture or any other means they pleased; and when they had been successful in obtaining the baron's dues, by way of further punishment they generally robbed the poor peasantry of everything they had which was worth the trouble of carrying away, and not unfrequently, from a spirit of sheer mischief, they spoiled all that remained. Many were the complaints which reached the ears of the baron of the cruel behaviour of his retainers; but in no case did they receive any redress; the baron making it a portion of his policy that no crimes committed by those under his command should be invested, so long as those crimes took place when employed in collecting taxes which he had imposed, and which had remained unpaid.

But the depredations and cruelties of the Baron Conrad were not confined solely to the valley of the Engadin. Frequently in the summer-time when the snows had melted on the mountains, so as to make the road practicable for his soldiers and their plunder, he would make a raid on the Italian side of the Alps. There they would rob and commit every sort of atrocity with impunity; and when they had collected sufficient booty they returned with it to the castle. Loud indeed were the complaints which reached the authorities of Milan. With routine tardiness, the government never took any energetic steps to punish the offenders until the winter had set in; and to cross the mountains in that season would have been almost an impossibility, at all events for an army. When the spring returned, more prudential reasons prevailed, and the matter, gradually diminishing in interest, was at last allowed to die out without any active measures being taken. Again, the districts in which the atrocities had been committed were hardly looked upon by the Milanese government as being Italian. The people themselves were beginning to be infected by a heresy which approached closely to the Protestantism of the present day; nor was their language that of Italy, but a patois of their own. Thus the government began to consider it unadvisable to attempt to punish the baron, richly as he deserved it, on behalf of those who after all were little worthy of the protection they demanded. The only real step they took to chastise him was to get him excommunicated by the Pope;

which, as the baron and his followers professed no religion at all, was treated by them with ridicule.

It happened that in one of his marauding expeditions in the Valteline, the baron, when near Bormio, saw a young girl of extraordinary beauty. He was only attended at the time by two followers, else it is more than probable he would have made her a prisoner and carried her off to Gardonal. As it was he would probably have made the attempt had she not been surrounded by a number of peasants, who were working in some fields belonging to her father. The baron was also aware that the militia of the town, who had been expecting his visit, were under arms, and on an alarm being given could be on the spot in a few minutes. Now as the baron combined with his despotism a considerable amount of cunning, he merely attempted to enter into conversation with the girl. Finding his advances coldly received, he contented himself with inquiring of one of the peasants the girl's name and place of abode. He received for reply that her name was Teresa Biffi, and that she was the daughter of a substantial farmer, who with his wife and four children (of whom Teresa was the eldest) lived in a house at the extremity of the land he occupied.

As soon as the baron had received this information, he left the spot, and proceeded to the farmer's house, which he inspected externally with great care. He found it was of considerable size, strongly built of stone, with iron bars to the lower windows, and a strong well-made oaken door which could be securely fastened from the inside. After having made the round of the house (which he did alone), he returned to his two men, whom, in order to avoid suspicion, he had placed at a short distance from the building, in a spot where they could not easily be seen.

'Ludovico,' he said to one of them who was his lieutenant, and invariably accompanied him in all his expeditions, 'mark well that house; for some day, or more probably night, you may have to pay it a visit.'

Ludovico merely said in reply that he would be always ready and willing to perform any order his master might honour him with; and the baron, with his men, then left the spot.

The hold the beauty of Teresa Biffi had taken upon the imagination of the baron actually looked like enchantment. His love for her, instead of diminishing by time, seemed to increase daily. At last he resolved on making her his wife; and about a month after he had seen her, he commissioned his lieutenant Ludovico to carry to Biffi an offer of marriage with his daughter; not dreaming, at the moment, of the possibility of a refusal. Ludovico immediately started on his mission, and in due time arrived at the farmer's house and delivered the baron's message. To Ludovico's intense surprise, however, he received from Biffi a positive refusal. Not daring to take back so uncourteous a reply to his master, Ludovico went on to describe the great advantage which would accrue to the farmer and his family if the baron's proposal were accepted. Not only, he said, would Teresa be a lady of the highest rank, and in possession of enormous wealth both in gold and jewels, but that the other members of her family would also be ennobled, and each of them, as they grew up, would receive appointments under the baron, besides having large estates allotted to them in the Engadin Valley.

The farmer listened with patience to Ludovico, and when he had concluded, he replied—

'Tell your master I have received his message, and that I am ready to admit that great personal advantages might accrue to me and my family by accepting his offer. Say, that although I am neither noble nor rich, that yet at the same time I am not poor; but were I as poor as the blind mendicant whom you passed on the road in coming hither, I would spurn such an offer from so infamous a wretch as the baron. You say truly that he is well known for his power and his wealth; but the latter has been obtained by robbing both rich and poor, who had not the means to resist him, and his power has been greatly strengthened by engaging in his service a numerous band of robbers and cut-throats, who are ready and willing to murder any one at his bidding. You have my answer, and the sooner you quit this neighbourhood the better, for I can assure you that any one known to be in the service of the Baron Conrad is likely to meet with a most unfavourable reception from those who live around us.'

'Then you positively refuse his offer?' said Ludovico.

'Positively, and without the slightest reservation,' was the farmer's reply.

'And you wish me to give him the message in the terms you have made use of?'

'Without omitting a word,' was the farmer's reply. 'At the same time, you may add to it as many of the same description as you please.'

'Take care,' said Ludovico. 'There is yet time for you to reconsider your decision. If you insist on my taking your message to the baron, I must of course do so; but in that case make your peace with heaven as soon as you can, for the baron is not a man to let such an insult pass. Follow my advice, and accept his offer ere it is too late.'

'I have no other answer to give you,' said Biffi.

'I am sorry for it,' said Ludovico, heaving a deep sigh; 'I have now no alternative,' and mounting his horse he rode away.

Now it must not be imagined that the advice Ludovico gave the farmer, and the urgent requests and arguments he offered, were altogether the genuine effusions of his heart. On the contrary, Ludovico had easily perceived, on hearing the farmer's first refusal, that there was no chance of the proposal being accepted. He had therefore occupied his time during the remaining portion of the interview in carefully examining the premises, and mentally taking note of the manner in which they could be most easily entered, as he judged, rightly enough, that before long he might be sent to the house on a far less peaceable mission.

Nothing could exceed the rage of the baron when he heard the farmer's message.

'You cowardly villain!' he said to Ludovico, 'did you allow the wretch to live who could send such a message to your master?'

'So please you,' said Ludovico. 'What could I do?'

'You could have struck him to the heart with your dagger, could you not?' said the baron. 'I have known you do such a thing to an old woman for half the provocation. Had it been Biffi's wife instead you might have shown more courage.'

'Had I followed my own inclination,' said Ludovico, 'I would have killed the fellow on the spot; but then I could not have brought away the young lady with me, for there were too many persons about the house and in the fields at the time. So I thought, before acting further, I had better let you hear his answer. One favour I hope your excellency will grant me, that if the fellow is to be punished you will allow me to inflict it as a reward for the skill I showed in keeping my temper when I heard the message.'

'Perhaps you have acted wisely, Ludovico,' said the baron, after a few moments' silence. 'At present my mind is too much ruffled by the villain's impertinence to think calmly on the subject. Tomorrow we will speak of it again.'

Next day the baron sent for his lieutenant, and said to him—

'Ludovico, I have now a commission for you to execute which I think will be exactly to your taste. Take with you six men whom you can trust, and start this afternoon for Bormio. Sleep at some village on the road, but let not one word escape you as to your errand. Tomorrow morning leave the village—but separately—so that you may not be seen together, as it is better to avoid suspicion. Meet again near the farmer's house, and arrive there, if possible, before evening has set in, for in all probability you will have to make an attack upon the house, and you may thus become well acquainted with the locality before doing so; but keep yourselves concealed, otherwise you will spoil all. After you have done this, retire some distance, and remain concealed till midnight, as then all the family will be in their first sleep, and you will experience less difficulty than if you began later. I particularly wish you to enter the house without using force, but if you cannot do so, break into it in any way you consider best. Bring out the girl and do her no harm. If any resistance is made by her father, kill him; but not unless you are compelled, as I do not wish to enrage his daughter against me. However, let nothing prevent you from securing her. Burn the house down or anything you please, but bring her here. If you execute your mission promptly and to my satisfaction, I promise you and those with you a most liberal reward. Now go and get ready to depart as speedily as you can.'

Ludovico promised to execute the baron's mission to the letter, and shortly afterwards left the castle accompanied by six of the greatest ruffians he could find among the men-at-arms.

Although on the spur of the moment Biffi had sent so defiant a message to the baron, he afterwards felt considerable uneasiness as to the manner in which it would be received. He did not repent having refused the proposal, but he knew that the baron was a man of the most cruel and vindictive disposition, and would in all probability seek some means to be avenged. The only defence he could adopt was to make the fastenings of his house as secure as possible, and to keep at least one of his labourers about him whom he could send as a messenger to Bormio for assistance, and to arouse the inhabitants in the immediate vicinity, in case of his being attacked. Without any hesitation all promised to aid Biffi in every way in their power, for he had acquired great renown among the inhabitants of the place for the courage he had shown in refusing so indignantly the baron's offer of marriage for his daughter.

About midnight, on the day after Ludovico's departure from the castle, Biffi was aroused by some one knocking at the door of his house, and demanding admission. It was Ludovico, for after attempting in vain to enter the house secretly, he had concealed his men, determining to try the effect of treachery before using force. On the inquiry being made as to who the stranger was, he replied that he was a poor traveller who had lost his way, and begged that he might be allowed a night's lodging, as he was so weary he could not go a step further.

'I am sorry for you,' said Biffi, 'but I cannot allow you to enter this house before daylight. As the night is fine and warm you can easily sleep on the straw under the windows, and in the morning I will let you in and give you a good breakfast.'

Again and again did Ludovico plead to be admitted, but in vain; Biffi would not be moved from his resolution. At last, however, the bravo's patience got exhausted, and suddenly changing his manner he roared out in a threatening tone, 'If you don't let me in, you villain, I will burn your house over your head. I have here, as you may see, plenty of men to help me to put my threat into execution,' he continued, pointing to the men, who had now come up, 'so you had better let me in at once.'

In a moment Biffi comprehended the character of the person he had to deal with; so, instead of returning any answer, he retired from the window and alarmed the inmates of the house. He also told the labourer whom he had engaged to sleep there to drop from a window at the back and run as fast as he could to arouse the inhabitants in the vicinity, and tell them that his house was attacked by the baron and his men. He was to beg them to arm themselves and come to his aid as quickly as possible, and having done this, he was to go on to Bormio on the same errand. The poor fellow attempted to carry out his master's orders; but in dropping from the window he fell with such force on the ground that he could only move with difficulty, and in trying to crawl away he was observed by some of the baron's men, who immediately set on him and killed him.

Ludovico, finding that he could not enter the house either secretly or by threatenings, attempted to force open the door, but it was so firmly barricaded from within that he did not succeed; while in the meantime Biffi and his family employed themselves in placing wooden faggots and heavy articles of furniture against it, thus making it stronger than ever. Ludovico, finding he could not gain an entrance by the door, told his men to look around in search of a ladder, so that they might get to the windows on the first floor, as those on the ground floor were all small, high up, and well barricaded, as was common in Italian houses of the time; but in spite of all their efforts no ladder could be found. He now deliberated what step he should next take. As it was getting late, he saw that if they did not succeed in effecting an entrance quickly the dawn would break upon them, and the labourers going to their work would raise an alarm. At last one man suggested that as abundance of fuel could be obtained from the stacks at the back of the house they might place a quantity of it against the door and set fire to it; adding that the sight of the flames would soon make the occupants glad to effect their escape by the first-floor windows.

The suggestion was no sooner made than acted upon. A quantity of dry fuel was piled up against the house door to the height of many feet, and a light having been procured by striking a flint stone against the hilt of a sword over some dried leaves, fire was set to the pile. From the dry nature of the fuel, the whole mass was in a blaze in a few moments. But the scheme did not have the effect Ludovico had anticipated. True, the family rushed towards the windows in the front of the house, but when they saw the flames rising so fiercely they retreated in the utmost alarm. Meanwhile the screams from the women and children—who had now lost all self-control—mingled with the roar of the blazing element, which, besides having set fire to the faggots and furniture placed within the door, had now reached a quantity of fodder and Indian corn stored on the ground floor.

Ludovico soon perceived that the whole house was in flames, and that the case was becoming desperate. Not only was there the danger of the fire alarming the inhabitants in the vicinity by the light it shed around, but he also reflected what would be the rage of his master if the girl should perish in the flames, and the consequent punishment which would be inflicted on him and those under his command if he returned empty-handed. He now called out to Biffi and his family to throw themselves out of the window, and that he and his men would save them. It was some time before he was understood, but at last Biffi brought the two younger children to the window, and, lowering them as far as he could, he let them fall into the arms of Ludovico and his men, and they reached the ground in safety.

Biffi now returned for the others, and saw Teresa standing at a short distance behind him. He took her by the hand to bring her forward, and they had nearly reached the window, when she heard a scream from her mother, who being an incurable invalid was confined to her bed. Without a moment's hesitation, the girl turned back to assist her, and the men below, who thought that the prey they wanted was all but in their hands, and cared little about the fate of the rest of the family, were thus disappointed. Ludovico now anxiously awaited the reappearance of Teresa—but he waited in vain. The flames had gained entire mastery, and even the roof had taken fire. The screams of the inmates were now no longer heard, for if not stifled in the smoke they were lost in the roar of the fire; whilst the glare which arose from it illumined the landscape far and near.

It so happened that a peasant, who resided about a quarter of a mile from Biffi's house, had to go a long distance to his work, and having risen at an unusually early hour, he saw the flames, and aroused the inmates of the other cottages in the village, who immediately armed themselves and started off to the scene of the disaster, imagining, but too certainly, that it was the work of an incendiary. The alarm was also communicated to another village, and from thence to Bormio, and in a short time a strong band of armed men had collected, and proceeded together to assist in extinguishing the flames. On their arrival at the house, they found the place one immense heap of ashes—not a soul was to be seen, for Ludovico and his men had already decamped.

The dawn now broke, and the assembled peasantry made some attempt to account for the fire. At first they were induced to attribute it to accident, but on searching around they found the dead body of the murdered peasant, and afterwards the two children who had escaped, and who in their terror had rushed into a thick copse to conceal themselves. With great difficulty they gathered from them sufficient to show that the fire had been caused by a band of robbers who had come for the purpose of plundering the house; and their suspicion fell immediately on Baron Conrad, without any better proof than his infamous reputation.

As soon as Ludovico found that an alarm had been given, he and his men started off to find their horses, which they had hidden among some trees about a mile distant from Biffi's house. The daylight was just breaking, and objects around them began to be visible, but not so clearly as to allow them to see for any distance. Suddenly one of the men pointed to an indistinct figure in white some little way in advance of them. Ludovico halted for a moment to see what it might be, and, with his men, watched it attentively as it appeared to fly from them.

'It is the young girl herself,' said one of the men. 'She has escaped from the fire; and that was exactly as she appeared in her white dress with her father at the window. I saw her well, and am sure I am not mistaken.'

'It is indeed the girl,' said another. 'I also saw her.'

'I hope you are right,' said Ludovico; 'and if so, it will be fortunate indeed, for should we return without her we may receive but a rude reception from the baron.'

They now quickened their pace, but, fast as they walked, the figure in white walked quite as rapidly. Ludovico, who of course began to suspect that it was Teresa attempting to escape from them, commanded his men to run as fast as they could in order to reach her. Although they tried their utmost, the figure, however, still kept the same distance before them. Another singularity about it was, that as daylight advanced the figure appeared to become less distinct, and ere they had reached their horses it seemed to have melted away.

II

Before mounting their horses, Ludovico held a consultation with his men as to what course they had better adopt; whether they should depart at once or search the neighbourhood for the girl. Both suggestions seemed to be attended with danger. If they delayed their departure, they might be attacked by the peasantry, who by this time were doubtless in hot pursuit of them; and if they returned to the baron without Teresa, they were almost certain to receive a severe punishment for failing in their enterprise. At last the idea struck Ludovico that a good round lie might possibly succeed with the baron and do something to avert his anger, while there was little hope of its in the slightest manner availing with the enraged peasantry. He therefore gave the order for his men to mount their horses, resolving to tell the baron that Teresa had escaped from the flames, and had begged their assistance, but a number of armed inhabitants of Bormio chancing to approach, she had sought their protection. A great portion of this statement could be substantiated by his men, as they still fully believed that the figure in white which they had so indistinctly seen was the girl herself. Ludovico and his men during their homeward journey had great difficulty in crossing the mountains, in consequence of a heavy fall of snow (for it was now late in the autumn). Next day they arrived at the castle of Gardonal.

It would be difficult to describe the rage of the baron when he heard that his retainers had been unsuccessful in their mission. He ordered Ludovico to be thrown into a dungeon, where he remained for more than a month, and was only then liberated in consequence of the baron needing his services for some expedition requiring special skill and courage. The other men were also punished, though less severely than their leader, on whom, of course, they laid all the blame.

For some time after Ludovico's return, the baron occupied himself in concocting schemes, not only to secure the girl Teresa (for he fully believed the account Ludovico had given of her escape), but to revenge himself on the inhabitants of Bormio for the part they had taken in the affair; and it was to carry out these schemes that he liberated Ludovico from prison.

The winter had passed, and the spring sun was rapidly melting the snows on the mountains, when one morning three travel-stained men, having the appearance of respectable burghers, arrived at the Hospice, and requested to be allowed an interview with the Innominato. A messenger was despatched to the castle, who shortly afterwards returned, saying that his master desired the visitors should immediately be admitted into his presence. When they arrived at the castle they found him fully prepared to receive them, a handsome repast being spread out for their refreshment. At first the travellers seemed under some restraint; but this was soon dispelled by the friendly courtesy of the astrologer. After partaking of the viands which had been set before them, the Innominato inquired the object of their visit. One of them, who had been evidently chosen as spokesman, then rose from his chair, and addressed their host as follows:

'We have been sent to your excellency by the inhabitants of Bormio, as a deputation, to ask your advice and assistance in a strait we are in at present. Late in the autumn of last year, the Baron Conrad, feudal lord of the Engadin, was on some not very honest expedition in our neighbourhood, when by chance he saw a very beautiful girl, of the name of Teresa Biffi, whose father occupied a large farm about half a league from the town. The baron, it appears, became so deeply enamoured of the girl that he afterwards sent a messenger to her father with an offer of marriage for his daughter. Biffi, knowing full well the infamous reputation of the baron, unhesitatingly declined his proposal, and in such indignant terms as to arouse the tyrant's anger to the highest pitch. Determining not only to possess himself of the girl, but to avenge the insult he had received, he sent a body of armed retainers, who in the night attacked the farmer's house, and endeavoured to effect an entrance by breaking open the door. Finding they could not succeed, and after murdering one of the servants who had been sent to a neighbouring village to give the alarm, they set fire to the house, and with the exception of two children who contrived to escape, the whole family, including the young girl herself, perished in the flames. It appears, however, that the baron (doubtless through his agents) received a false report that the young girl had escaped, and was taken under the protection of some of the inhabitants of Bormio. In consequence, he sent another body of armed men, who arrived in the night at the house of the podesta, and contrived to make his only son, a boy of about fifteen years old, a prisoner, bearing him off to the baron's castle. They left word, that unless Teresa Biffi was placed in their power before the first day of May, not only would the youth be put to death, but the baron would also wreak vengeance on the whole town. On the perpetration of this last atrocity, we again applied to the government of Milan for protection; but although our reception was most courteous, and we were promised assistance, we have too good reason to doubt our receiving it. Certainly up to the present time no steps have been taken in the matter, nor has a single soldier been sent, although the time named for the death of the child has nearly expired. The townsmen therefore, having heard of your great wisdom and power, your willingness to help those who are in distress, as well as to protect the weak and oppressed, have sent us to ask you to take them under your protection; as the baron is not a man to scruple at putting such a threat into execution.'

The Innominato, who had listened to the delegate with great patience and attention, told him that he had no soldiers or retainers at his orders; while the baron, whose wicked life was known to him, had many.

'But your excellency has great wisdom, and from all we have heard, we feel certain that you could protect us.'

'Your case,' said the Innominato, 'is a very sad one, I admit, and you certainly ought to be protected from the baron's machinations. I will not disguise from you that I have the power to help you. Tell the unhappy podesta that he need be under no alarm as to his son's safety, and that I will oblige the baron to release him. My art tells me that the boy is still alive, though confined in prison. As for your friends who sent you to me, tell them that the baron shall do them no harm. All you have to do is, to contrive some means by which the baron may hear that the girl Teresa Biffi has been placed by me where he will never find her without my permission.'

'But Teresa Biffi,' said the delegate, 'perished with her father; and the baron will wreak his vengeance both on you and us, when he finds you cannot place the girl in his power.'

'Fear nothing, but obey my orders,' said the Innominato. 'Do what I have told you, and I promise you shall have nothing to dread from him. The sooner you carry out my directions the better.'

The deputation now returned to Bormio, and related all that had taken place at their interview with the Innominato. Although the result of their mission was scarcely considered satifactory, they determined, after much consideration, to act on the astrologer's advice. But how to carry it out was a very difficult matter. This was, however, overcome by one of the chief inhabitants of the town—a man of most determined courage—offering himself as a delegate to the baron, to convey to him the Innominato's message. Without hesitation the offer was gratefully accepted, and the next day he started on his journey. No sooner had he arrived at the castle of Gardonal, and explained the object of his mission, than he was ushered into the presence of the baron, whom he found in the great hall, surrounded by a numerous body of armed men.

'Well,' said the baron, as soon as the delegate had entered, 'have your townspeople come to their senses at last, and sent me the girl Teresa?'

'No, they have not, baron,' was the reply; 'for she is not in their custody. All they can do is to inform you where you may possibly receive some information about her.'

'And where may that be?'

'The only person who knows where she may be found is the celebrated astrologer who lives in a castle near Lecco.'

'Ah now, you are trifling with me,' said the baron sternly. 'You must be a great fool or a very bold man to try such an experiment as that.'

'I am neither the one nor the other, your excellency; nor am I trifling with you. What I have told you is the simple truth.'

'And how did you learn it?'

'From the Innominato's own lips.'

'Then you applied to him for assistance against me,' said the baron, furiously.

'That is hardly correct, your excellency,' said the delegate. 'It is true we applied to him for advice as to the manner in which we should act in case you should attack us, and put your threat into execution respecting the son of the podesta.'

'And what answer did he give you?'

'Just what I have told you—that he alone knows where Teresa Biffi is to be found, and that you could not remove her from the protection she is under without his permission.'

'Did he send that message to me in defiance?' said the baron.

'I have no reason to believe so, your excellency.'

The baron was silent for some time; he then inquired of the delegate how many armed retainers the Innominato kept.

'None, I believe,' was the reply. 'At any rate, there were none to be seen when the deputation from the town visited him.'

The baron was again silent for some moments, and seemed deeply absorbed in thought. He would rather have met with any other opponent than the Innominato, whose reputation was well known to him, and whose learning he dreaded more than the power of any nobleman—no matter how many armed retainers he could bring against him.

'I very much suspect,' he said at last, 'that some deception is being practised on me. But should my suspicion be correct I shall exact terrible vengeance. I shall detain you,' he continued, turning abruptly and fiercely on the delegate, 'as a hostage while I visit the Innominato; and if I do not succeed with him, you shall die on the same scaffold as the son of your podesta.'

It was in vain that the delegate protested against being detained as a prisoner, saying that it was against all rules of knightly usage; but the baron would not listen to reason, and the unfortunate man was immediately hurried out of the hall and imprisoned.

Although the baron by no means liked the idea of an interview with the Innominato, he immediately made preparations to visit him, and the day after the delegate's arrival he set out on his journey, attended by only four of his retainers. It should here be mentioned, that it is more than probable the baron would have avoided meeting the Innominato on any other occasion whatever, so great was the dislike he had to him. He seemed to be acting under some fatality; some power seemed to impel him in his endeavours to obtain Teresa which it was impossible to account for.

The road chosen by the baron to reach the castle of the Innominato was rather a circuitous one. In the first place, he did not consider it prudent to pass through the Valteline; and in the second, he thought that by visiting his brother on his way he might be able to obtain some particulars as to the character of the mysterious individual whom he was about to see, as his reputation would probably be better known among the inhabitants of the Bergamo district than by those in the valley of the Engadin.

The baron arrived safely at his brother's castle, where the reports which had hitherto indistinctly reached him of the wonderful power and skill of the astrologer were fully confirmed. After remaining a day with his brother, the baron started for Lecco. Under an assumed name he stayed here for two days, in order that he might receive the report of one of his men, whom he had sent forward to ascertain whether the Innominato had any armed men in his castle; for, being capable of any act of treachery himself, he naturally suspected treason in others. The man in due time returned, and reported that, although he had taken great pains to find out the truth, he was fully convinced, that not only were there no soldiers in the castle, but that it did not, to the best of his belief, contain an arm of any kind—the Innominato relying solely on his occult power for his defence.

Perfectly assured that he had no danger to apprehend, the baron left Lecco, attended by his retainers, and in a few hours afterwards he arrived at the Hospice, where his wish for an interview was conveyed to the astrologer. After some delay a reply was sent that the Innominato was willing to receive the baron on condition that he came alone, as his retainers would not be allowed to enter the castle. The baron hesitated for some moments, not liking to place himself in the power of a man who, after all, might prove a very dangerous adversary, and who might even use treacherous means. His love for Teresa Biffi, however, urged him to accept the invitation, and he accompanied the messenger to the castle.

The Innominato received his guest with stern courtesy; and, without even asking him to be seated, requested to know the object of his visit.

'Perhaps I am not altogether unknown to you,' said the baron. 'I am lord of the Engadin.'

'Frankly,' said the Innominato, 'your name and reputation are both well known to me. It would give me great satisfaction were they less so.'

'I regret to hear you speak in that tone,' said the baron, evidently making great efforts to repress his rising passion. 'A person in my position is not likely to be without enemies, but it rather surprises me to find a man of your reputation so prejudiced against me without having investigated the accusations laid to my charge.'

'You judge wrongly if you imagine that I am so,' said the Innominato. 'But once more, will you tell me the object of your visit?'

'I understood,' said the baron, 'by a message sent to me by the insolent inhabitants of Bormio, that you know the person with whom a young girl, named Teresa Biffi, is at present residing. Might I ask if that statement is correct?'

'I hardly sent it in those words,' said the Innominato. 'But admitting it to be so, I must first ask your reason for inquiring.'

'I have not the slightest objection to inform you,' said the baron. 'I have nothing to conceal. I wish to make her my wife.'

'On those terms I am willing to assist you,' said the astrologer. 'But only on the condition that you immediately release the messenger you have most unjustly confined in one of your dungeons, as well as the young son of the podesta, and that you grant them a safe escort back to Bormio; and further, that you promise to cease annoying the people of that district. Do all this, and I am willing to promise you that Teresa Biffi shall not only become your wife, but shall bring with her a dowry and wedding outfit sufficiently magnificent even for the exalted position to which you propose to raise her.'

'I solemnly promise you,' said the baron, 'that the moment the wedding is over, the delegate from Bormio and the son of the podesta shall both leave my castle perfectly free and unhampered with any conditions; and moreover that I will send a strong escort with them to protect them on their road.'

'I see you are already meditating treachery,' said the Innominato. 'But I will not, in any manner, alter my offer. The day week after their safe return to Bormio Teresa Biffi shall arrive at the castle of Gardonal for the wedding ceremony. Now you distinctly know my conditions, and I demand from you an unequivocal acceptance or refusal.'

'What security shall I have that the bargain will be kept on your side?' said the baron.

'My word, and no other.'

The baron remained silent for a moment, and then said—

'I accept your offer. But clearly understand me in my turn, sir astrologer. Fail to keep your promise, and had you ten times the power you have I will take my revenge on you; and I am not a man to threaten such a thing without doing it.'

'All that I am ready to allow,' said the Innominato, with great coolness; 'that is to say, in case you have the power to carry out your threat, which in the present instance you have not. Do not imagine that because I am not surrounded by a band of armed cut-throats and miscreants I am not the stronger of the two. You little dream how powerless you are in my hands. You see this bird,' he continued, taking down a common sparrow in a wooden cage from a nail in the wall on which it hung,—'it is not more helpless in my hands than you are; nay more, I will now give the bird far greater power over you than I possess over it.'

As he spoke he unfastened the door of the cage, and the sparrow darted from it through the window into the air, and in a moment afterwards was lost to sight.

'That bird,' the astrologer went on to say, 'will follow you till I deprive it of the power. I bear you no malice for doubting my veracity. Falsehood is too much a portion of your nature for you to disbelieve its existence in others. I will not seek to punish you for the treachery which I am perfectly sure you will soon be imagining against me without giving you fair warning; for, a traitor yourself, you naturally suspect treason in others. As soon as you entertain a thought of evading your promise to release your prisoners, or conceive any treason or ill feeling against me, that sparrow will appear to you. If you instantly abandon the thought no harm will follow; but if you do not a terrible punishment will soon fall upon you. In whatever position you may find yourself at the moment, the bird will be near you, and no skill of yours will be able to harm it.'

The baron now left the Innominato, and returned with his men to Lecco, where he employed himself for the remainder of the day in making preparations for his homeward journey. To return by the circuitous route he had taken in going to Lecco would have occupied too much time, as he was anxious to arrive at his castle, that he might without delay release the prisoners and make preparations for his wedding with Teresa Biffi. To pass the Valteline openly with his retainers—which was by far the shortest road—would have exposed him to too much danger; he therefore resolved to divide his party and send three men back by his brother's castle, so that they could return the horses they had borrowed. Then he would disguise himself and the fourth man (a German who could not speak a word of Italian, and from whom he had nothing therefore to fear on the score of treachery) as two Tyrolese merchants returning to their own country. He also purchased two mules and some provisions for the journey, so that they need not be obliged to rest in any of the villages they passed through, where possibly they might be detected, and probably maltreated.

Next morning the baron and his servant, together with the two mules, went on board a large bark which was manned by six men, and which he had hired for the occasion, and in it they started for Colico. At the commencement of their voyage they kept along the eastern side of the lake, but after advancing a few miles the wind, which had hitherto been moderate, now became so strong as to cause much fatigue to the rowers, and the captain of the bark determined on crossing the lake, so as to be under the lee of the mountains on the other side. When half way across they came in view of the turrets of the castle of the Innominato. The sight of the castle brought to the baron's mind his interview with its owner, and the defiant manner in which he had been treated by him. The longer he gazed the stronger became his anger against the Innominato, and at last it rose to such a point that he exclaimed aloud, to the great surprise of the men in the boat, 'Some day I will meet thee again, thou insolent villain, and I will then take signal vengeance on thee for the insult offered me yesterday.'

The words had hardly been uttered when a sparrow, apparently driven from the shore by the wind, settled on the bark for a moment, and then flew away. The baron instantly remembered what the Innominato had said to him, and also the warning the bird was to give. With a sensation closely resembling fear, he tried to change the current of his thoughts, and was on the point of turning his head from the castle, when the rowers in the boat simultaneously set up a loud shout of warning, and the baron then perceived that a heavily-laden vessel, four times the size of his own, and with a huge sail set, was running before the wind with great velocity, threatening the next moment to strike his boat on the beam; in which case both he and the men would undoubtedly be drowned. Fortunately, the captain of the strange bark had heard the cry of the rowers, and by rapidly putting down his helm, saved their lives; though the baron's boat was struck with so much violence on the quarter that she nearly sank.

The Baron Conrad had now received an earnest that the threat of the Innominato was not a vain one, and feeling that he was entirely in his power, resolved if possible not to offend him again. The boat continued on her voyage, and late in the evening arrived safely at Colico, where the baron, with his servant and the mules, disembarked, and without delay proceeded on their journey. They continued on their road till nightfall, when they began to consider how they should pass the night. They looked around them, but they could perceive no habitation or shelter of any kind, and it was now raining heavily. They continued their journey onwards, and had almost come to the conclusion that they should be obliged to pass the night in the open air, when a short distance before them they saw a low cottage, the door of which was open, showing the dim light of a fire burning within. The baron now determined to ask the owner of the cottage for permission to remain there for the night; but to be certain that no danger could arise, he sent forward his man to discover whether it was a house standing by itself, or one of a village; as in the latter case he would have to use great caution to avoid being detected. His servant accordingly left him to obey orders, and shortly afterwards returned with the news that the house was a solitary one, and that he could not distinguish a trace of any other in the neighbourhood. Satisfied with this information, the baron proceeded to the cottage door, and begged the inmates to afford him shelter for the night, assuring them that the next morning he would remunerate them handsomely. The peasant and his wife—a sickly-looking, emaciated old couple—gladly offered them all the accommodation the wretched cabin could afford. After fastening up the mules at the back of the house, and bringing in the baggage and some dry fodder to form a bed for the baron and his servant, they prepared some of the food their guests had brought with them for supper, and shortly afterwards the baron and his servant were fast asleep.

Next morning they rose early and continued on their journey. After they had been some hours on the road, the baron, who had before been conversing with his retainer, suddenly became silent and absorbed in thought. He rode on a few paces in advance of the man, thinking over the conditions made by the Innominato, when the idea struck him whether it would not be possible in some way to evade them. He had hardly entertained the thought, when the sparrow flew rapidly before his mule's head, and then instantly afterwards his servant, who had ridden up to him, touched him on the shoulder and pointed to a body of eight or ten armed men about a quarter of a mile distant, who were advancing towards them. The baron, fearing lest they might be some of the armed inhabitants of the neighbourhood who were banded together against him, and seeing that no time was to be lost, immediately plunged, with his servant, into a thick copse where, without being seen, he could command a view of the advancing soldiers as they passed. He perceived that when they came near the place where he was concealed they halted, and evidently set about examining the traces of the footsteps of the mules. They communed together for some time as if in doubt what course they should adopt, and finally, the leader giving the order, they continued their march onwards, and the baron shortly afterwards left his place of concealment.

Nothing further worthy of notice occurred that day; and late at night they passed through Bormio, fortunately without being observed.

They afterwards arrived safely at the foot of the mountain pass, and at dawn began the ascent. The day was fine and calm, and the sun shone magnificently. The baron, who now calculated that the dangers of his journey were over, was in high spirits, and familiarly conversed with his retainer. When they had reached a considerable elevation, the path narrowed, so that the two could not ride abreast, and the baron went in advance. He now became very silent and thoughtful, all his thoughts being fixed on the approaching wedding, and in speculations as to how short a time it would take for the delegate and the youth to reach Bormio. Suddenly the thought occurred to him, whether the men whom he should send to escort the hostages back, could not, when they had completed their business, remain concealed in the immediate neighbourhood till after the celebration of the wedding, and then bring back with them some other hostage, and thus enable him to make further demands for compensation for the insult he considered had been offered him. Although the idea had only been vaguely formed, and possibly with but little intention of carrying it out, he had an immediate proof that the power of the astrologer was following him. A sparrow settled on the ground before him, and did not move until his mule was close to it, when it rose in the air right before his face. He continued to follow its course with his eyes, and as it rose higher he thought he perceived a tremulous movement in an immense mass of snow, which had accumulated at the base of one of the mountain peaks. All thought of treachery immediately vanished. He gave a cry of alarm to his servant, and they both hurried onwards, thus barely escaping being buried in an avalanche, which the moment afterwards overwhelmed the path they had crossed.

The baron was now more convinced than ever of the tremendous power of the Innominato, and so great was his fear of him, that he resolved for the future not to contemplate any treachery against him, or entertain any thoughts of revenge.

The day after the baron's arrival at the castle of Gardonal, he ordered the delegate and the podesta's son to be brought into his presence. Assuming a tone of much mildness and courtesy, he told them he much regretted the inconvenience they had been put to, but that the behaviour of the inhabitants of Bormio had left him no alternative. He was ready to admit that the delegate had told him the truth, although from the interview he had with the Innominato, he was by no means certain that the inhabitants of their town had acted in a friendly manner towards him, or were without blame in the matter. Still he did not wish to be harsh, and was willing for the future to be on friendly terms with them if they promised to cease insulting him—what possible affront they could have offered him it would be difficult to say. 'At the same time, in justice to myself,' he continued (his natural cupidity gaining the ascendant at the moment), 'I hardly think I ought to allow you to return without the payment of some fair ransom.'

He had scarcely uttered these words when a sparrow flew in at the window, and darting wildly two or three times across the hall, left by the same window through which it had entered. Those present who noticed the bird looked at it with an eye of indifference—but not so the baron. He knew perfectly well that it was a warning from the astrologer, and he looked around him to see what accident might have befallen him had he continued the train of thought. Nothing of an extraordinary nature followed the disappearance of the bird. The baron now changed the conversation, and told his prisoners that they were at liberty to depart as soon as they pleased; and that to prevent any misfortune befalling them on the road, he would send four of his retainers to protect them. In this he kept his promise to the letter, and a few days afterwards the men returned, reporting that the delegate and the son of the podesta had both arrived safely at their destination.

III

Immediately after the departure of his prisoners, the baron began to make preparations for his wedding, for although he detested the Innominato in his heart, he had still the fullest reliance on his fulfilling the promise he had made. His assurance was further confirmed by a messenger from the astrologer to inform him that on the next Wednesday the affianced bride would arrive with her suite, and that he (the Innominato) had given this notice, that all things might be in readiness for the ceremony.

Neither expense nor exertion was spared by the baron to make his nuptials imposing and magnificent. The chapel belonging to the castle, which had been allowed to fall into a most neglected condition, was put into order, the altar redecorated, and the walls hung with tapestry. Preparations were made in the inner hall for a banquet on the grandest scale, which was to be given after the ceremony; and on a dais in the main hall into which the bride was to be conducted on her arrival were placed two chairs of state, where the baron and his bride were to be seated.

When the day arrived for the wedding, everything was prepared for the reception of the bride. As no hour had been named for her arrival, all persons who were to be engaged in the ceremony were ready in the castle by break of day; and the baron, in a state of great excitement, mounted to the top of the watch-tower, that he might be able to give orders to the rest the moment her cavalcade appeared in sight. Hour after hour passed, but still Teresa did not make her appearance, and at last the baron began to feel considerable anxiety on the subject.

At last a mist, which had been over a part of the valley, cleared up, and all the anxiety of the baron was dispelled; for in the distance he perceived a group of travellers approaching the castle, some mounted on horseback and some on foot. In front rode the bride on a superb white palfrey, her face covered with a thick veil. On each side of her rode an esquire magnificently dressed. Behind her were a waiting woman on horseback and two men-servants; and in the rear were several led mules laden with packages. The baron now quitted his position in the tower and descended to the castle gates to receive his bride. When he arrived there, he found one of the esquires, who had ridden forward at the desire of his mistress, waiting to speak to him.

'I have been ordered,' he said to the baron, 'by the Lady Teresa, to request that you will be good enough to allow her to change her dress before she meets you.'

The baron of course willingly assented, and then retired into the hall destined for the reception ceremony. Shortly afterwards Teresa arrived at the castle, and being helped from her palfrey, she proceeded with her lady in waiting and a female attendant (who had been engaged by the baron) into her private apartment, while two of the muleteers brought up a large trunk containing her wedding dress.

In less than an hour Teresa left her room to be introduced to the baron, and was conducted into his presence by one of the esquires. As soon as she entered the hall, a cry of admiration arose from all present—so extraordinary was her beauty. The baron, in a state of breathless emotion, advanced to meet her, but before he had reached her she bent on her knee, and remained in that position till he had raised her up. 'Kneel not to me, thou lovely one,' he said. 'It is for all present to kneel to thee in adoration of thy wonderful beauty, rather than for thee to bend to any one.' So saying, and holding her hand, he led her to one of the seats on the daîs, and then, seating himself by her side, gave orders for the ceremony of introduction to begin. One by one the different persons to be presented were led up to her, all of whom she received with a grace and amiability which raised her very high in their estimation.

When the ceremony of introduction was over the baron ordered that the procession should be formed, and then, taking Teresa by the hand, he led her into the chapel, followed by the others. When all were arranged in their proper places the marriage ceremony was performed by the priest, and the newly-married couple, with the retainers and guests, entered into the banqueting hall. Splendid as was the repast which had been prepared for the company, their attention seemed for some time more drawn to the baron and his bride than to the duties of the feast. A handsomer couple it would have been impossible to find. The baron himself, as has been stated already, had no lack of manly beauty either in face or form; while the loveliness of his bride appeared almost more than mortal. Even their splendid attire seemed to attract little notice when compared with their personal beauty.

After the surprise and admiration had somewhat abated, the feast progressed most satisfactorily. All were in high spirits, and good humour and conviviality reigned throughout the hall. Even on the

baron it seemed to produce a kindly effect, so that few who could have
seen him at that moment would have imagined him to be the stern,
cold-blooded tyrant he really was. His countenace was lighted up with
good humour and friendliness. Much as his attention was occupied
with his bride, he had still a little to bestow on his guests, and he rose
many times from his seat to request the attention of the servants to their
wants. At last he cast his eye over the tables as if searching for some
person whom he could not see, and he then beckoned to the major
domo, who, staff of office in hand, advanced to receive his orders.

'I do not see the esquires of the Lady Teresa in the room,' said the
baron.

'Your excellency,' said the man, 'they are not here.'

'How is that?' said the baron, with some impatience. 'You ought to
have found room for them in the hall. Where are they?'

'Your excellency,' said the major domo, who from the expression of
the baron's countenance evidently expected a storm, 'they are not here.
The whole of the suite left the castle immediately after the mules were
unladen and her ladyship had left her room. I was inspecting the places
which I had prepared for them, when a servant came forward and told
me that the esquires and attendants had left the castle. I at once hurried
after them and begged they would return, as I was sure your excellency
would feel hurt if they did not stay to the banquet. But they told me
they had received express orders to leave the castle directly after they
had seen the Lady Teresa lodged safely in it. I again entreated them to
stay, but it was useless. They hurried on their way, and I returned by
myself.'

'The ill-bred hounds!' said the baron, in anger. 'A sound scourging
would have taught them better manners.'

'Do not be angry with them,' said Teresa, laying her hand gently on
that of her husband's; 'they did but obey their master's orders.'

'Some day, I swear,' said the baron, 'I will be revenged on their
master for this insult, miserable churl that he is!'

He had no sooner uttered these words than he looked round him for
the sparrow, but the bird did not make its appearance. Possibly its
absence alarmed him even more than its presence would have done, for
he began to dread lest the vengeance of the astrologer was about to fall
on him, without giving him the usual notice. Teresa, perceiving the
expression of his countenance, did all in her power to calm him, but for
some time she but partially succeeded. He continued to glance anxiously about him, to ascertain, if posible, from which side the blow might
come. He was just on the point of raising a goblet to his lips, when the
idea seized him that the wine might be poisoned. He declined to touch
food for the same reason. The idea of being struck with death when at
the height of his happiness seemed to overwhelm him. Thanks,
however, to the kind soothing of Teresa, as well as the absence of any

visible effects of the Innominato's anger, he at last became completely reassured, and the feast proceeded.

Long before the banquet had concluded the baron and his wife quitted the hall and retired through their private apartments to the terrace of the castle. The evening, which was now rapidly advancing, was warm and genial, and not a cloud was to be seen in the atmosphere. For some time they walked together up and down on the terrace; and afterwards they seated themselves on a bench. There, with his arm round her waist and her head leaning on his shoulder, they watched the sun in all his magnificence sinking behind the mountains. The sun had almost disappeared, when the baron took his wife's hand in his.

'How cold thou art, my dear!' he said to her. 'Let us go in.'

Teresa made no answer, but rising from her seat was conducted by her husband into the room which opened on to the terrace, and which was lighted by a large brass lamp which hung by a chain from the ceiling. When they were nearly under the lamp, whose light increased as the daylight declined, Conrad again cast his arm round his wife, and fondly pressed her head to his breast. They remained thus for some moments, entranced in their happiness.

'Dost thou really love me, Teresa!' asked the baron.

'Love you?' said Teresa, now burying her face in his bosom. 'Love you? Yes, dearer than all the world. My very existence hangs on your life. When that ceases my existence ends.'

When she had uttered these words, Conrad, in a state of intense happiness, said to her—

'Kiss me, my beloved.'

Teresa still kept her face pressed on his bosom; and Conrad, to overcome her coyness, placed his hand on her head and gently pressed it backwards, so that he might kiss her.

He stood motionless, aghast with horror, for the light of the lamp above their heads showed him no longer the angelic features of Teresa, but the hideous face of a corpse that had remained some time in the tomb, and whose only sign of vitality was a horrible phosphoric light which shone in its eyes. Conrad now tried to rush from the room, and to scream for assistance—but in vain. With one arm she clasped him tightly round the waist, and raising the other, she placed her clammy hand upon his mouth, and threw him with great force upon the floor. Then seizing the side of his neck with her lips, she deliberately and slowly sucked from him his life's blood; while he, utterly incapable either of moving or crying, was yet perfectly conscious of the awful fate that was awaiting him.

In this manner Conrad remained for some hours in the arms of his vampire wife. At last faintness came over him, and he grew insensible. The sun had risen some hours before consciousness returned. He rose from the ground horror-stricken and pallid, and glanced fearfully around him to see if Teresa were still there; but he found himself alone in the room. For some minutes he remained undecided what step to take. At last he rose from his chair to leave the apartment, but he was so weak he could scarcely drag himself along. When he left the room he bent his steps towards the courtyard. Each person he met saluted him with the most profound respect, while on the countenance of each was visible an expression of intense surprise, so altered was he from the athletic young man they had seen him the day before. Presently he heard the merry laughter of a number of children, and immediately hastened to the spot from whence the noise came. To his surprise he found his wife Teresa, in full possession of her beauty, playing with several children, whose mothers had brought them to see her, and who stood delighted with the condescending kindness of the baroness towards their litle ones.

Conrad remained motionless for some moments, gazing with intense surprise at his wife, and the idea occurred to him that the events of the last night must have been a terrible dream and nothing more. But he was at a loss how to account for his bodily weakness? Teresa, in the midst of her gambols with the children, accidentally raised her head and perceived her husband. She uttered a slight cry of pleasure when she saw him, and snatching up in her arms a beautiful child she had been playing with, she rushed towards him, exclaiming—

'Look, dear Conrad, what a little beauty this is! Is he not a little cherub?'

The baron gazed wildly at his wife for a few moments, but said nothing.

'My dearest husband, what ails you?' said Teresa. 'Are you not well?'

Conrad made no answer, but turning suddenly round staggered hurriedly away, while Teresa, with an expression of alarm and anxiety on her face, followed him with her eyes as he went. He still hurried on till he reached the small sitting-room from which he was accustomed each morning to issue his orders to his dependants, and seated himself in a chair to recover if possible from the bewilderment he was in. Presently Ludovico, whose duty it was to attend on his master every morning for instructions, entered the room, and bowing respectfully to the baron, stood silently aside, waiting till he should be spoken to, but during the time marking the baron's altered appearance with the most intense curiosity. After some moments the baron asked him what he saw to make him stare in that manner.

'Pardon my boldness, your excellency,' said Ludovico, 'but I was afraid you might be ill. I trust I am in error.'

'What should make you think I am unwell?' inquired the baron.

'Your highness's countenance is far paler than usual, and there is a small wound on the side of your throat. I hope you have not injured yourself.'

The last remark of Ludovico decided the baron that the events of the evening had been no hallucination. What stronger proof could be required than the marks of his vampire wife's teeth still upon him? He perceived that some course of action must be at once decided upon, and the urgency of his position aided him to concentrate his thoughts. He determined on visiting a celebrated anchorite who lived in the mountains about four leagues distant, and who was famous not only for the piety of his life, but for his power in exorcising evil spirits. Having come to this resolution, he desired Ludovico immediately to saddle for him a sure-footed mule, as the path to the anchorite's dwelling was not only difficult but dangerous.

Ludovico bowed, and after having been informed that there were no other orders, he left the room, wondering in his mind what could be the reason for his master's wishing a mule saddled, when he generally rode only the highest-spirited horses. The conclusion he came to was, that the baron must have been attacked with some serious illness, and was about to proceed to some skilful leech.

As soon as Ludovico had left the room, the baron called to one of the servants whom he saw passing, and ordered breakfast to be brought to him immediately, hoping that by a hearty meal he should recover sufficient strength for the journey he was about to undertake. To a certain extent he succeeded, though possibly it was from the quantity of wine he drank, rather than from any other cause, for he had no appetite and had eaten but little.

He now descended into the courtyard of the castle, cautiously avoiding his wife. Finding the mule in readiness, he mounted it and started on his journey. For some time he went along quietly and slowly, for he still felt weak and languid, but as he attained a higher elevation of the mountains, the cold breeze seemed to invigorate him. He now began to consider how he could rid himself of the horrible vampire he had married, and of whose real nature he had no longer any doubt. Speculations on this subject occupied him till he had entered on a narrow path on the slope of an exceedingly high mountain. It was difficult to keep footing, and it required all his caution to prevent himself from falling. Of fear, however, the baron had none; and his thoughts continued to run on the possibility of separating himself from Teresa, and on what vengeance he would take on the Innominato for the treachery he had practised on him, as soon as he should be fairly freed. The more he dwelt on his revenge, the more excited he became, till at last he exclaimed aloud, 'Infamous wretch! Let me be but once fairly released from the execrable fiend you have imposed upon me, and I swear I will burn thee alive in thy castle, as a fitting punishment for the sorcery thou hast practised.'

Conrad had hardly uttered these words, when the pathway upon which he was riding gave way beneath him, and glided down the incline into a tremendous precipice below. He succeeded in throwing himself from his mule, which, with the *débris* of the rocks, was hurried over the precipice, while he clutched with the energy of despair at each object he saw likely to give him a moment's support. But everything he touched gave way, and he gradually sank and sank towards the verge of the precipice, his efforts to save himself becoming more violent the nearer he approached to what appeared certain death. Down he sank, till his legs actually hung over the precipice, when he succeeded in grasping a stone somewhat firmer than the others, thus retarding his fall for a moment. In horror he now glanced at the terrible chasm beneath him, when suddenly different objects came before his mind with fearful reality. There was an unhappy peasant, who had without permission killed a head of game, hanging from the branch of a tree, still struggling in the agonies of death, while his wife and children were in vain imploring the baron's clemency.

This vanished and he saw a boy with a knife in his hand, stabbing at his own mother for some slight offence she had given him.

This passed, and he found himself in a small village, the inhabitants of which were all dead within their houses; for at the approach of winter he had, in a fit of ill-temper, ordered his retainers to take from them all their provisions; and a snowstorm coming on immediately afterwards, they were blocked up in their dwellings, and all perished.

Again his thoughts reverted to the position he was in, and his eye glanced over the terrible precipice that yawned beneath him, when he saw, as if in a dream, the house of Biffi the farmer, with his wife and children around him, apparently contented and happy.

As soon as he had realized the idea, the stone which he had clutched began to give way, and all seemed lost to him, when a sparrow suddenly flew on the earth a short distance from him, and immediately afterwards darted away. 'Save but my life!' screamed the baron, 'and I swear I will keep all secret.'

The words had hardly been uttered, when a goatherd with a long staff in his hand appeared on the incline above him. The man perceiving the imminent peril of the baron, with great caution, and yet with great activity, descended to assist him. He succeeded in reaching a ledge of rock a few feet above, and rather to the side of the baron, to whom he stretched forth the long mountain staff in his hand. The baron clutched it with such energy as would certainly have drawn the goatherd over with him, had it not been that the latter was a remarkably powerful man. With some difficulty the baron reached the ledge of the rock, and the goatherd then ascended to a higher position, and in like manner drew the baron on, till at last he had contrived to get him to a place of safety. As soon as Conrad found himself out of danger, he gazed wildly around him for a moment, then dizziness came over him, and he sank fainting on the ground.

When the baron had recovered his senses, he found himself so weak that it would have been impossible for him to have reached the castle that evening. He therefore willingly accompanied the goatherd to his hut in the mountains, where he proposed to pass the night. The man made what provision he could for his illustrious guest, and prepared him a supper of the best his hut afforded; but had the latter been composed of the most exquisite delicacies, it would have been equally tasteless; for Conrad had not the slightest appetite. Evening was now rapidly approaching, and the goatherd prepared a bed of leaves, over which he threw a cloak, and the baron, utterly exhausted, reposed on it for the night, without anything occurring to disturb his rest.

Next morning he found himself somewhat refreshed by his night's rest, and he prepared to return to the castle, assisted by the goatherd, to whom he had promised a handsome reward. He had now given up all idea of visiting the anchorite, dreading that by so doing he might excite the animosity of the Innominato, of whose tremendous power he had lately received more than ample proof. In due time he reached home in safety, and the goatherd was dismissed after having received the promised reward. On entering the castle-yard the baron found his wife in a state of great alarm and sorrow, and surrounded by the retainers. No sooner did she perceive her husband, than, uttering a cry of delight and surprise, she rushed forward to clasp him in her arms; but the baron pushed her rudely away, and hurrying forwards, directed his steps to the room in which he was accustomed to issue his orders. Ludovico, having heard of the arrival of his master, immediately waited on him.

'Ludovico,' said the baron, as soon as he saw him, 'I want you to execute an order for me with great promptitude and secrecy. Go below, and prepare two good horses for a journey; one for you, the other for myself. See that we take with us provisions and equipments for two or three days. As soon as they are in readiness, leave the castle with them without speaking to any one, and wait for me about a league up the mountain, where in less than two hours I will join you. Now see that you faithfully carry out my orders, and if you do so, I assure you you will lose nothing by your obedience.'

Ludovico left the baron's presence to execute his order, when immediately afterwards a servant came into the room, and inquired if the Lady Teresa might enter.

'Tell your mistress,' said the baron, in a tone of great courtesy and kindness, 'that I hope she will excuse me for the moment, as I am deeply engaged in affairs of importance; but I shall await her visit with great impatience in the afternoon.'

The baron now left to himself, began to draw out more fully the plan for his future operations. He resolved to visit his brother Hermann, and consult him as to what steps he ought to take in this horrible emergency; and in case no better means presented themselves, he determined on offering to give up to Hermann the castle of Gardonal and the whole valley of the Engadin, on condition of receiving from him an annuity sufficient to support him in the position he had always been accustomed to maintain. He then intended to retire to some distant country, where there would be no probability of his being followed by the horrible monster whom he had accepted as his wife. Of course he had no intention of receiving Teresa in the afternoon, and he had merely put off her visit the purpose of allowing himself to escape with greater convenience from the castle.

About an hour after Ludovico had left him, the baron quitted the castle by a postern, with as much haste as his enfeebled strength would allow, and hurried after his retainer, whom he found awaiting him with the horses. The baron immediately mounted one, and followed by Ludovico, took the road to his brother's, where in three days he arrived in safety. Hermann received his brother with great pleasure, though much surprised at the alteration in his appearance.

'My dear Conrad,' he said to him, 'what can possibly have occurred to you? You look very pale, weak, and haggard. Have you been ill?

'Worse, a thousand times worse,' said Conrad. 'Let us go where we may be by ourselves, and I will tell you all.'

Hermann led his brother into a private room, where Conrad explained to him the terrible misfortune which had befallen him. Hermann listened attentively, and for some time could not help doubting whether his brother's mind was not affected; but Conrad explained everything in so circumstantial and lucid a manner as to dispel that idea. To the proposition which Conrad made, to make over the territory of the Engadin Valley for an annuity, Hermann promised to give full consideration. At the same time, before any further steps were taken in the matter, he advised Conrad to visit a villa he had, on the sea-shore, about ten miles distant from Genoa; where, in quiet and seclusion, he would be able to recover his energies.

Conrad thanked his brother for his advice, and willingly accepted the offer. Two days afterwards he started on the journey, and by the end of the week arrived safely, and without difficulty, at the villa.

On the evening of his arrival, Conrad, who had employed himself during the afternoon in visiting the different apartments as well as the grounds surrounding the villa, was seated at a window overlooking the sea. The evening was deliciously calm, and he felt such ease and security as he had not enjoyed for some time past. The sun was sinking in the ocean, and the moon began to appear, and the stars one by one to shine in the cloudless heavens. The thought crossed Conrad's mind that the sight of the sun sinking in the waters strongly resembled his own position when he fell over the precipice. The thought had hardly been conceived when some one touched him on the shoulder. He turned

round, and saw standing before him, in the full majesty of her beauty—his wife Teresa!

'My dearest Conrad,' she said, with much affection in her tone, 'why have you treated me in this cruel manner? It was most unkind of you to leave me suddenly without giving the slightest hint of your intentions.'

'Execrable fiend,' said Conrad, springing from his chair, 'leave me! Why do you haunt me in this manner?'

'Do not speak so harshly to me, my dear husband,' said Teresa. 'To oblige you I was taken from my grave; and on you now my very existence depends.'

'Rather my death,' said Conrad. 'One night more such as we passed, and I should be a corpse.'

'Nay, dear Conrad,' said Teresa; 'I have the power of indefinitely prolonging your life. Drink but of this,' she continued, taking from the table behind her a silver goblet, 'and tomorrow all ill effects will have passed away.'

Conrad mechanically took the goblet from her hand, and was on the point of raising it to his lips when he suddenly stopped, and with a shudder replaced it again on the table.

'It is blood,' he said.

'True, my dear husband,' said Teresa; 'what else could it be? My life is dependent on your life's blood, and when that ceases so does my life. Drink then, I implore you,' she continued, again offering him the goblet. 'Look, the sun has already sunk beneath the wave; a minute more and daylight will have gone. Drink, Conrad, I implore you, or this night will be your last.'

Conrad again took the goblet from her hand to raise it to his lips; but it was impossible, and he placed it on the table. A ray of pure moonlight now penetrated the room, as if to prove that the light of day had fled. Teresa, again transformed into a horrible vampire, flew at her husband, and throwing him on the floor, fastened her teeth on the half-healed wound in his throat. The next morning, when the servants entered the room, they found the baron a corpse on the floor; but Teresa was nowhere to be seen, nor was she ever heard of afterwards.

Little more remains to be told. Hermann took possession of the castle of Gardonal and the Valley of the Engadin, and treated his vassals with even more despotism than his brother had done before him. At last, driven to desperation, they rose against him and slew him; and the valley afterwards became absorbed into the Canton of the Grisons.

THE FATE OF
MADAME CABANEL

Eliza Lynn Linton

Eliza Lynn Linton (1822–98) was, in Rider Haggard's opinion, 'one of the very ablest and keenest intellects of her time, and will, I think be reckoned in its history'. She was equally renowned for her novels and her journalism, and was chiefly concerned with the position of the modern woman, writing many essays on women's place in society. 'The Fate of Madame Cabanel' appeared in her collection of tales *Within a Silken Thread* (1880), and is a cogent study of primitive superstitions. Belief in witches and vampires was still very wide-spread in the nineteenth century, especially in remote backwaters. A similar case occurred in Ireland fifteen years *after* this story was published when Bridget Cleary was tortured and murdered by her own family, who thought she had been possessed by a demon or 'fairy changeling'.

PROGRESS had not invaded, science had not enlightened, the little hamlet of Pieuvrot, in Brittany. They were a simple, ignorant, superstitious set who lived there, and the luxuries of civilization were known to them as little as its learning. They toiled hard all the week on the ungrateful soil that yielded them but a bare subsistence in return; they went regularly to mass in the little rock-set chapel on Sundays and saints' days; believed implicitly all that monsieur le curé said to them, and many things which he did not say; and they took all the unknown, not as magnificent, but as diabolical.

The sole link between them and the outside world of mind and progress was Monsieur Jules Cabanel, the proprietor, par excellence, of the place; *maire, juge de paix,* and all the public functionaries rolled into one. And he sometimes went to Paris whence he returned with a cargo of novelties that excited envy, admiration, or fear, according to the degree of intelligence in those who beheld them.

Monsieur Jules Cabanel was not the most charming man of his class in appearance, but he was generally held to be a good fellow at bottom. A short, thickset, low-browed man, with blue-black hair cropped close like a mat, as was his blue-black beard, inclined to obesity and fond of good living, he had need have some virtues behind the bush to compensate for his want of personal charms. He was not bad, however; he was only common and unlovely.

Up to fifty years of age he had remained the unmarried prize of the surrounding country; but hitherto he had resisted all the overtures made by maternal fowlers, and had kept his liberty and his bachelorhood intact. Perhaps his handsome housekeeper, Adèle, had something to do with his persistent celibacy. They said she had, under their breath as it were, down at *la Veuve Prieur's*; but no one dared to so much as hint the like to herself. She was a proud, reserved kind of woman; and had strange notions of her own dignity which no one cared to disturb. So, whatever the underhand gossip of the place might be, neither she nor her master got wind of it.

Presently and quite suddenly, Jules Cabanel, who had been for a longer time than usual in Paris, came home with a wife. Adèle had only twenty-four hours' notice to prepare for this strange home-coming; and the task seemed heavy. But she got through it in her old way of silent determination; arranged the rooms as she knew her master would wish them to be arranged; and even supplemented the usual nice adornments by a voluntary bunch of flowers on the salon table.

'Strange flowers for a bride,' said to herself little Jeannette, the goose-girl who was sometimes brought into the house to work, as she noticed heliotrope—called in France *la fleur des veuves*—scarlet poppies, a bunch of belladonna, another of aconite—scarcely, as even ignorant little Jeannette said, flowers of bridal welcome or bridal significance. Nevertheless, they stood where Adèle had placed them; and if Monsieur Cabanel meant anything by the passionate expression of disgust with which he ordered them out of his sight, madame seemed to understand nothing, as she smiled with that vague, half-deprecating look of a person who is assisting at a scene of which the true bearing is not understood.

Madame Cabanel was a foreigner, and an Englishwoman; young, pretty and fair as an angel.

'*La beauté du diable*,' said the Pieuvrotines, with something between a sneer and a shudder; for the words meant with them more than they mean in ordinary use. Swarthy, ill-nourished, low of stature and meagre in frame as they were themselves, they could not understand the plump form, tall figure and fresh complexion of the Englishwoman. Unlike their own experience, it was therefore more likely to be evil than good. The feeling which had sprung up against her at first sight deepened when it was observed that, although she went to mass with praiseworthy punctuality, she did not know her missal and signed herself *à travers*. La beauté du diable, in faith!

'*Pouf!*' said Martin Briolic, the old gravedigger of the little cemetery; 'with those red lips of hers, her rose cheeks and her plump shoulders, she looks like a vampire and as if she lived on blood.'

He said this one evening down at *la Veuve Prieur's*; and he said it with an air of conviction that had its weight. For Martin Briolic was reputed the wisest man of the district; not even excepting Monsieur le curé who was wise in his own way, which was not Martin's—nor Monsieur Cabanel who was wise in his, which was neither Martin's nor the curé's. He knew all about the weather and the stars, the wild herbs that grew on the plains and the wild shy beasts that eat them; and he had the power of divination and could find where the hidden springs of water lay far down in the earth when he held the baguette in his hand. He knew too, where treasures could be had on Christmas Eve if only you were quick and brave enough to enter the cleft in the rock at the right moment and come out again before too late; and he had seen with his own eyes the White Ladies dancing in the moonlight; and the little imps, the Infins, playing their prankish gambols by the pit at the edge of the wood. And he had a shrewd suspicion as to who, among those black-hearted men of La Crèche-en-bois—the rival hamlet—was a loup-garou, if ever there was one on the face of the earth and no one had doubted that! He had other powers of a yet more mystic kind; so that Martin Briolic's bad word went for something, if, with the illogical injustice of ill-nature his good went for nothing.

Fanny Campbell, or, as she was now Madame Cabanel, would have excited no special attention in England, or indeed anywhere but at such a dead-alive, ignorant, and consequently gossiping place as Pieuvrot. She had no romantic secret as her background; and what history she had was commonplace enough, if sorrowful too in its own way. She was simply an orphan and a governess; very young and very poor; whose employers had quarrelled with her and left her stranded in Paris, alone and almost moneyless; and who had married Monsieur Jules Cabanel as the best thing she could do for herself. Loving no one else, she was not difficult to be won by the first man who showed her kindness in her hour of trouble and destitution; and she accepted her middle-aged suitor, who was fitter to be her father than her husband, with a clear conscience and a determination to do her duty cheerfully and faithfully—all without considering herself as a martyr or an interesting victim sacrificed to the cruelty of circumstances. She did not know however, of the handsome househeeper Adèle, nor of the housekeeper's little nephew—to whom her master was so kind that he allowed him to live at the Maison Cabanel and had him well taught by the curé. Perhaps if she had she would have thought twice before she put herself under the same roof with a woman who for a bridal bouquet offered her poppies, heliotrope and poison-flowers.

If one had to name the predominant characteristic of Madame Cabanel it would be easiness of temper. You saw it in the round, soft, indolent lines of her face and figure; in her mild blue eyes and placid,

unvarying smile; which irritated the more petulant French temperament and especially disgusted Adèle. It seemed impossible to make
madame angry or even to make her understand when she was insulted,
the housekeeper used to say with profound disdain; and, to do the
woman justice, she did not spare her endeavours to enlighten her. But
madame accepted all Adèle's haughty reticence and defiant continuance
of mistress-hood with unwearied sweetness; indeed, she expressed
herself gratified that so much trouble was taken off her hands, and that
Adèle so kindly took her duties on herself.

The consequences of this placid lazy life, where all her faculties were
in a manner asleep, and where she was enjoying the reaction from her
late years of privation and anxiety, was, as might be expected, an
increase in physical beauty that made her freshness and good condition
still more remarkable. Her lips were redder, her cheeks rosier, her
shoulders plumper than ever; but as she waxed, the health of the little
hamlet waned, and not the oldest inhabitant remembered so sickly a
season, or so many deaths. The master too, suffered slightly; the little
Adolphe desperately.

This failure of general health in undrained hamlets is not uncommon
in France or in England; neither is the steady and pitiable decline of
French children; but Adèle treated it as something out of all the lines of
normal experience; and, breaking through her habits of reticence spoke
to every one quite fiercely of the strange sickliness that had fallen on
Pieuvrot and the Maison Cabanel; and how she believed it was
something more than common; while as to her little nephew, she could
give neither a name nor find a remedy for the mysterious disease that
had attacked him. There were strange things among them, she used to
say; and Pieuvrot had never done well since the old times were
changed. Jeannette used to notice how she would sit gazing at the
English lady, with such a deadly look on her handsome face when she
turned from the foreigner's fresh complexion and grand physique to
the pale face of the stunted, meagre, fading child. It was a look, she said
afterwards, that used to make her flesh get like ice and creep like
worms.

One night Adèle, as if she could bear it no longer, dashed down to
where old Martin Briolic lived, to ask him to tell her how it had all
come about—and the remedy.

'Hold, Ma'am Adèle,' said Martin, as he shuffled his greasy tarot
cards and laid them out in triplets on the table; 'there is more in this
than one sees. One sees only a poor little child become suddenly sick;
that may be, is it not so? and no harm done by man? God sends sickness
to us all and makes my trade profitable to me. But the little Adolphe
has not been touched by the Good God. I see the will of a wicked
woman in this. Hein!' Here he shuffled the cards and laid them out with
a kind of eager distraction of manner, his withered hands trembling and

his mouth uttering words that Adèle could not catch. 'Saint Joseph and all the saints protect us!' he cried; 'the foreigner—the Englishwoman—she whom they call Madame Cabanel—no rightful madame she!—Ah, misery!'

'Speak, Father Martin! What do you mean!' cried Adèle, grasping his arm. Her black eyes were wild; her arched nostrils dilated; her lips, thin, sinuous, flexible, were pressed tight over her small square teeth.

'Tell me in plain words what you would say!'

'Broucolaque!' said Martin in a low voice.

'It is what I believed!' cried Adèle. 'It is what I knew. Ah, my Adolphe! woe on the day when the master brought that fair-skinned devil home!'

'Those red lips don't come by nothing, Ma'am Adèle,' cried Martin nodding his head. 'Look at them—they glisten with blood! I said so from the beginning; and the cards, they said so too. I drew "blood" and a "bad fair woman" on the evening when the master brought her home, and I said to myself, "Ha, ha, Martin! you are on the track, my boy—on the track. Martin!"—and, Ma'am Adèle, I have never left it! Broucolaque! that's what the cards say, Ma'am Adèle. Vampire. Watch and see; watch and see; and you'll find that the cards have spoken true.'

'And when we have found, Martin?' said Adèle in a hoarse whisper.

The old man shuffled his cards again. 'When we have found, Ma'am Adèle?' he said slowly. 'You know the old pit out there by the forest?—the old pit where the lutins run in and out, and where the White Ladies wring the necks of those who come upon them in the moonlight? Perhaps the White Ladies will do as much for the English wife of Monsieur Cabanel; who knows?'

'They may,' said Adèle, gloomily.

'Courage, brave woman!' said Martin. 'They will.'

The only really pretty place about Pieuvrot was the cemetery. To be sure there was the dark gloomy forest which was grand in its own mysterious way; and there was the broad wide plain where you might wander for a long summer's day and not come to the end of it; but these were scarcely places where a young woman would care to go by herself; and for the rest, the miserable little patches of cultivated ground, which the peasants had snatched from the surrounding waste and where they had raised poor crops, were not very lovely. So Madame Cabanel, who, for all the soft indolence that had invaded her, had the Englishwoman's inborn love for walking and fresh air, haunted the pretty little graveyard a good deal. She had no sentiment connected with it. Of all the dead who laid there in their narrow coffins, she knew none and cared for none; but she liked to see the pretty little flower-beds and the wreaths of immortelles, and the like; the distance too, from her own home was just enough for her; and the view over the plain to the dark belt of forest and the mountains beyond, was fine.

The Pieuvrotines did not understand this. It was inexplicable to them that any one, not out of her mind, should go continually to the cemetery—not on the day of the dead and not to adorn the grave of one she loved—only to sit there and wander among the tombs, looking out on to the plain and the mountains beyond when she was tired.

'It was just like—' The speaker, one Lesouëf, had got so far as this, when he stopped for a word.

He said this down at *la Veuve Prieur's* where the hamlet collected nightly to discuss the day's small doings, and where the main theme, ever since she had come among them, three months ago now, had been Madame Cabanel and her foreign ways and her wicked ignorance of her mass-book and her wrong-doings of a mysterious kind generally, interspersed with jesting queries, banded from one to the other, of how Ma'am Adèle liked it?—and what would become of le petit Adolphe when the rightful heir appeared?—some adding that monsier was a brave man to shut up two wild cats under the same roof together; and what would become of it in the end? Mischief of a surety.

'Wander about the tombs just like what, Jean Lesouëf?' said Martin Briolic. Rising, he added in a low but distinct voice, every word falling clear and clean: 'I will tell you like what, Lesouëf—like a vampire! La femme Cabanel has red lips and red cheeks; and Ma'am Adèle's little nephew is perishing before your eyes. La femme Cabanel has red lips and red cheeks; and she sits for hours among the tombs. Can you read the riddle, my friends? For me it is as clear as the blessed sun.'

'Ha, Father Martin, you have found the word—like a vampire!' said Lesouëf with a shudder.

'Like a vampire!' they all echoed with a groan.

'And I said vampire the first,' said Martin Briolic. 'Call to mind I said it from the first.'

'Faith! and you did,' they answered; 'and you said true.'

So now the unfriendly feeling that had met and accompanied the young Englishwoman ever since she came to Pieuvrot had drawn to a focus. The seed which Martin and Adèle had dropped so sedulously had at last taken root; and the Pieuvrotines would have been ready to accuse of atheism and immorality any one who had doubted their decision, and had declared that pretty Madame Cabanel was only a young woman with nothing special to do, a naturally fair complexion, superb health—and no vampire at all, sucking the blood of a living child or living among the tombs to make the newly buried her prey.

The little Adolphe grew paler and paler, thinner and thinner; the fierce summer sun told on the half-starved dwellers within those foul mud-huts surrounded by undrained marshes; and Monsieur Jules Cabanel's former solid health followed the law of the rest. The doctor, who lived at Crèche-en-bois, shook his head at the look of things; and said it was grave. When Adèle pressed him to tell her what was the matter with the child and with monsieur, he evaded the question; or gave her a word which she neither understood not could pronounce. The truth was, he was a credulous and intensely suspicious man; a viewy man who made theories and then gave himself to the task of finding them true. He had made the theory that Fanny was secretly poisoning both her husband and the child; and though he would not give Adèle a hint of this, he would not set her mind at rest by a definite answer that went on any other line.

As for Monsieur Cabanel, he was a man without imagination and without suspicion; a man to take life easily and not distress himself too much for the fear of wounding others; a selfish man but not a cruel one; a man whose own pleasure was his supreme law and who could not imagine, still less brook, opposition or the want of love and respect for himself. Still, he loved his wife as he had never loved a woman before. Coarsely moulded, common-natured as he was, he loved her with what strength and passion of poetry nature had given him; and if the quantity was small, the quality was sincere. But that quality was sorely tried when—now Adèle, now the doctor—hinted mysteriously, the one at diabolical influences, the other at underhand proceedings of which it behoved him to be careful, especially careful what he eat and drank and how it was prepared and by whom; Adèle adding hints about the perfidiousness of English women and the share which the devil had in fair hair and brilliant complexions. Love his young wife as he might, this constant dropping of poison was not without some effect. It told much for his steadfastness and loyalty that it should have had only so small effect.

One evening however, when Adèle, in an agony, was kneeling at his feet—madame had gone out for her usual walk—crying: 'Why did you leave me for such as she is?—I, who loved you, who was faithful to you, and she, who walks among the graves, who sucks your blood and our child's—she who has only the devil's beauty for her portion and who loves you not?'—something seemed suddenly to touch him with electric force.

'Miserable fool that I was!' he said, resting his head on Adèle's shoulders and weeping. Her heart leapt with joy. Was her reign to be renewed? Was her rival to be dispossessed?

From that evening Monsieur Cabanel's manner changed to his young wife but she was too easy-tempered and unsuspicious to notice anything, or if she did, there was too little depth in her own love for him—it was so much a matter of untroubled friendliness only—that she did not fret but accepted the coldness and brusqueness that had crept into his manner as good-naturedly as she accepted all things. It would have been wiser if she had cried and made a scene and come to an open fracas with Monsieur Cabanel. They would have understood each other better; and Frenchmen like the excitement of a quarrel and a reconciliation.

Naturally kind-hearted, Madame Cabanel went much about the
village, offering help of various kinds to the sick. But no one among
them all, not the very poorest—indeed, the very poorest the least—
received her civilly or accepted her aid. If she attempted to touch one of
the dying children, the mother, shuddering, withdrew it hastily to her
own arms; if she spoke to the adult sick, the wan eyes would look at her
with a strange horror and the feeble voice would mutter words in a
patois she could not understand. But always came the same word,
'broucolaque!'

'How these people hate the English!' she used to think as she turned
away, perhaps just a little depressed, but too phlegmatic to let herself be
uncomfortable or troubled deeply.

It was the same at home. If she wanted to do any little act of kindness
to the child, Adèle passionately refused her. Once she snatched him
rudely from her arms, saying as she did so: 'Infamous broucolaque!
before my very eyes?' And once, when Fanny was troubled about her
husband and proposed to make him a cup of beef-tea à l'Anglaise, the
doctor looked at her as if he would have looked through her; and Adèle
upset the saucepan; saying insolently—but yet hot tears were in her
eyes—'Is it not fast enough for you, madame? Not faster, unless you
kill me first!'

To all of which Fanny replied nothing; thinking only that the doctor
was very rude to stare so fixedly at her and that Adèle was horribly
cross; and what an ill-tempered creature she was; and how unlike an
English housekeeper!

But Monsieur Cabanel, when he was told of the little scene, called
Fanny to him and said in a more caressing voice than he had used to her
of late: 'Thou wouldst not hurt me, little wife? It was love and
kindness, not wrong, that thou wouldst do?'

'Wrong? What wrong could I do?' answered Fanny, opening her blue
eyes wide. 'What wrong should I do to my best and only friend?'

'And I am thy friend? thy lover? thy husband? Thou lovest me dear?'
said Monsieur Cabanel.

'Dear Jules, who is so dear; who so near?' she said kissing him, while
he said fervently:

'God bless thee!'

The next day Monsieur Cabanel was called away on urgent business.
He might be absent for two days, he said, but he would try to lessen the
time; and the young wife was left alone in the midst of her enemies,
without even such slight guard as his presence might prove.

Adèle was out. It was a dark, hot summer's night, and the little
Adolphe had been more feverish and restless than usual all the day.
Towards evening he grew worse; and though Jeannette, the goose-girl,
had strict commands not to allow madame to touch him, she grew
frightened at the condition of the boy; and when madame came into the

small parlour to offer her assistance, Jeannette gladly abandoned a charge that was too heavy for her and let the lady take him from her arms.

Sitting there with the child in her lap, cooing to him, soothing him by a low, soft nursery song, the paroxysm of his pain seemed to her to pass and it was as if he slept. But in that paroxysm he had bitten both his lip and tongue; and the blood was now oozing from his mouth. He was a pretty boy; and his mortal sickness made him at this moment pathetically lovely. Fanny bent her head and kissed the pale still face;—and the blood that was on his lips was transferred to hers.

While she still bent over him—her woman's heart touched with a mysterious force and prevision of her own future motherhood—Adèle, followed by old Martin and some others of the village, rushed into the room.

'Behold her!' she cried, seizing Fanny by the arm and forcing her face upwards by the chin—'behold her in the act! Friends, look at my child—dead, dead in her arms; and she with his blood on her lips! Do you want more proofs? Vampire that she is, can you deny the evidence of your own senses?'

'No! no!' roared the crowd hoarsely. 'She is a vampire—a creature cursed by God and the enemy of man; away with her to the pit. She must die as she has made others to die!'

'Die, as she has made my boy to die!' said Adèle; and more than one who had lost a relative or child during the epidemic echoed her words, 'Die, as she has made mine to die!'

'What is the meaning of all this?' said Madame Cabanel, rising and facing the crowd with the true courage of an Englishwoman. 'What harm have I done to any of you that you should come about me, in the absence of my husband, with these angry looks and insolent words?'

'What harm hast thou done?' cried old Martin, coming close to her. 'Sorceress as thou art, thou hast bewitched our good master; and vampire as thou art, thou nourishest thyself on our blood! Have we not proof of that at this very moment? Look at thy mouth—cursed broucolaque; and here lies thy victim, who accuses thee in his death!'

Fanny laughed scornfully, 'I cannot condescend to answer such folly,' she said lifting her head. 'Are you men or children?'

'We are men, madame,' said Legros the miller; 'and being men we must protect our weak ones. We have all had our doubts—and who more cause than I, with three little ones taken to heaven before their time?—and now we are convinced.'

'Because I have nursed a dying child and done my best to soothe him!' said Madame Cabanel with unconscious pathos.

'No more words!' cried Adèle, dragging her by the arm from which she had never loosed her hold. 'To the pit with her, my friends, if you would not see all your children die as mine has died—as our good Legros' have died!'

A kind of shudder shook the crowd; and a groan that sounded in itself a curse burst from them.

'To the pit!' they cried. 'Let the demons take their own!'

Quick as thought Adèle pinioned the strong white arms whose shape and beauty had so often maddened her with jealous pain; and before the poor girl could utter more than one cry Legros had placed his brawny hand over her mouth. Though this destruction of a monster was not the murder of a human being in his mind, or in the mind of any there, still they did not care to have their nerves disturbed by cries that sounded so human as Madame Cabanel's. Silent then, and gloomy, that dreadful cortège took its way to the forest, carrying its living load; gagged and helpless as if it had been a corpse among them. Save with Adèle and old Martin, it was not so much personal animosity as the instinctive self-defence of fear that animated them. They were executioners, not enemies; and the executioners of a more righteous law than that allowed by the national code. But one by one they all dropped off, till their numbers were reduced to six; of whom Legros was one, and Lesouëf, who had lost his only sister, was also one.

The pit was not more than an English mile from the Maison Cabanel. It was a dark and lonesome spot, where not the bravest man of all that assembly would have dared to go alone after nightfall, not even if the curé had been with him; but a multitude gives courage, said old Martin Briolic; and half a dozen stalwart men, led by such a woman as Adèle, were not afraid of even lutins or the White Ladies.

As swiftly as they could for the burden they bore, and all in utter silence, the cortège strode over the moor; one or two of them carrying rude torches; for the night was black and the way was not without its physical dangers. Nearer and nearer they came to the fatal bourn; and heavier grew the weight of their victim. She had long ceased to struggle; and now lay as if dead in the hands of her bearers. But no one spoke of this or of aught else. Not a word was exchanged between them; and more than one, even of those left, began to doubt whether they had done wisely, and whether they had not better have trusted to the law. Adèle and Martin alone remained firm to the task they had undertaken; and Legros too was sure; but he was weakly and humanly sorrowful for the thing he felt obliged to do. As for Adèle, the woman's jealousy, the mother's anguish and the terror of superstition, had all wrought in her so that she would not have raised a finger to have lightened her victim of one of her pains, or have found her a woman like herself and no vampire after all.

The way got darker; the distance between them and their place of execution shorter; and at last they reached the border of the pit where this fearful monster, this vampire—poor innocent Fanny Cabanel—was to be thrown. As they lowered her, the light of their torches fell on her face.

'Grand Dieu!' cried Legros, taking off his cap; 'she is dead!'

'A vampire cannot die,' said Adèle, 'It is only an appearance. Ask Father Martin.'

'A vampire cannot die unless the evil spirits take her, or she is buried with a stake thrust through her body,' said Martin Briolic sententiously.

'I don't like the look of it,' said Legros; and so said some others.

They had taken the bandage from the mouth of the poor girl; and as she lay in the flickering light, her blue eyes half open; and her pale face white with the whiteness of death, a little return of human feeling among them shook them as if the wind had passed over them.

Suddenly they heard the sound of horses' hoofs thundering across the plain. They counted two, four, six; and they were now only four unarmed men, with Martin and Adèle to make up the number. Between the vengeance of man and the power and malice of the wood-demons, their courage faded and their presence of mind deserted them. Legros rushed frantically into the vague darkness of the forest; Lesouëf followed him; the other two fled over the plain while the horsemen came nearer and nearer. Only Adèle held the torch high above her head, to show more clearly both herself in her swarthy passion and revenge and the dead body of her victim. She wanted no concealment; she had done her work, and she gloried in it. Then the horsemen came plunging to them—Jules Cabanel the first, followed by the doctor and four gardes champêtres.

'Wretches! murderers!' was all he said, as he flung himself from his horse and raised the pale face to his lips.

'Master,' said Adèle; 'she deserved to die. She is a vampire and she has killed our child.'

'Fool!' cried Jules Cabanel, flinging off her hand. 'Oh, my loved wife! thou who did no harm to man or beast, to be murdered now by men who are worse than beasts!'

'She was killing thee,' said Adèle. 'Ask monsieur le docteur. What ailed the master, monsieur?'

'Do not bring me into this infamy,' said the doctor looking up from the dead. 'Whatever ailed monsieur, she ought not to be here. You have made yourself her judge and executioner, Adèle, and you must answer for it to the law.'

'You say this too, master?' said Adèle.

'I say so too,' returned Monsieur Cabanel. 'To the law you must answer for the innocent life you have so cruelly taken—you and all the fools and murderers you have joined to you.'

'And is there to be no vengeance for our child?'

'Would you revenge yourself on God, woman?' said Monsieur Cabanel sternly.

'And our past years of love, master?'

'Are memories of hate, Adèle,' said Monsieur Cabanel, as he turned again to the pale face of his dead wife.

'Then my place is vacant,' said Adèle, with a bitter cry. 'Ah, my little Adolphe, it is well you went before!'

'Hold, Ma'am Adèle!' cried Martin.

But before a hand could be stretched out, with one bound, one shriek, she had flung herself into the pit where she had hoped to bury Madame Cabanel; and they heard her body strike the water at the bottom with a dull splash, as of something falling from a great distance.

'They can prove nothing against me, Jean,' said old Martin to the garde who held him. 'I neither bandaged her mouth nor carried her on my shoulders. I am the gravedigger of Pieuvrot, and, *ma foi*, you would all do badly, you poor creatures, when you die, without me! I shall have the honour of digging madame's grave, never doubt it; and, Jean,' he whispered, 'they may talk as they like, those rich aristos who know nothing. She is a vampire, and she shall have a slatte through her body yet! Who knows better than I? If we do not tie her down like this, she will come out of her grave and suck our blood; it is a way these vampires have.'

'Silence there!' said the garde, commanding the little escort. 'To prison with the assassins; and keep their tongues from wagging.'

'To prison with martyrs and the public benefactors,' retorted old Martin. 'So the world rewards its best!'

And in this faith he lived and died, as a forçat at Toulon, maintaining to the last that he had done the world a good service by ridding it of a monster who else would not have left one man in Pieuvrot to perpetuate his name and race. But Legros and also Lesouëf, his companion, doubted gravely of the righteousness of that act of theirs on that dark summer's night in the forest; and though they always maintained that they should not have been punished, because of their good motives, yet they grew in time to disbelieve old Martin Briolic and his wisdom, and to wish that they had let the law take its own course unhelped by them—reserving their strength for the grinding of the hamlet's flour and the mending of the hamlet's sabots—and the leading of a good life according to the teaching of monsieur le curé and the exhortations of their own wives.

THE MAN-EATING TREE

Phil Robinson

Philip Stewart Robinson (1847–1902), a leading naturalist and author born at Chunar (India), always signed his work as 'Phil Robinson'. He was a pioneer of Anglo–Indian literature and his many books include *In My Indian Garden,* *Tigers at Large, The Valley of Teetotum Trees,* etc. Several of his stories contained vampiric elements, including 'The Man–Eating Tree', 'Medusa', and 'The Last of the Vampires' (*Contemporary Review*, 1892). 'The Man–Eating Tree' first appeared in his collection *Under the Punkah* in 1881. It was one of the earliest tales in the subgenre dealing with bloodthirsty plants and vegetation, of which later examples include Fred M. White's 'The Purple Terror' and E. Nesbit's 'The Pavilion'.

[Before committing this paper to the ridicule of the Great Mediocre—for many, I fear, will be inclined to regard this story as incredible—I would venture on the expression of an opinion regarding credulity, which I do not remember to have met before. It is this. Placing supreme Wisdom and supreme Unwisdom at the two extremes, and myself in the exact mean between them, I am surprised to find that whether I travel towards the one extreme or the other, the credulity of those I meet increases. To put it as a paradox—*whether a man be foolisher or wiser than I am, he is more credulous*. I make this remark to point out to those of the Great Mediocre whose notice it may have escaped, that credulity is not of itself shameful or contemptible, and that it depends upon the manner rather than the matter of their belief, whether they gravitate towards the sage or the reverse way. According, therefore, to the incredibility found in the following, the reader may measure, as pleases him, his wisdom or his unwisdom.—Z. ORIEL.]

PEREGRINE ORIEL, my maternal uncle, was a great traveller, as his prophetical sponsors at the font seemed to have guessed he would be. Indeed he had rummaged in the garrets and cellars of the earth with something more than ordinary diligence. But in the narrative of his travels he did not, unfortunately, preserve the judicious caution of Xenophon between 'the thing seen' and 'the thing heard', and thus it came about that the town-councillors of Brunsbüttel (to whom he had shown a duck-billed platypus, caught alive by him in Australia, and who had him posted for 'an importer of artificial vermin') were not alone in their scepticism of some of the old man's tales.

Thus, for instance, who could hear and believe the tale of the man-sucking tree from which he had barely escaped with life? He called it himself 'more terrible than the Upas'—'This awful plant, that rears its splendid deathshade in the central solitude of a Nubian fern forest, sickens by its unwholesome humours all vegetation from its immediate vicinity, and feeds upon the wild beasts that, in the terror of the chase, or the heat of noon, seek the thick shelter of its boughs; upon the birds that, flitting across the open space, come within the charmed circle of its power, or innocently refresh themselves from the cups of its great waxen flowers; upon even man himself when, an infrequent prey, the savage seeks its asylum in the storm, or turns from the harsh foot-wounding sword-grass of the glade, to pluck the wondrous fruit that hang plumb down among the wondrous foliage.' And such fruit!—'glorious golden ovals, great honeydrops, swelling by their own weight into pear-shaped translucencies. The foliage glistens with a strange dew, that all day long drips on to the ground below, nurturing a rank growth of grasses, which shoot up in places so high that their spikes of fierce blood-fed green show far up among the deep-tinted foliage of the terrible tree, and, like a jealous body-guard, keep concealed the fearful secret of the charnel-house within, and draw round the black roots of the murderous plant a decent screen of living green.'

Such was his description of the plant; and the other day, looking up in a botanical dictionary, I find that there is really known to naturalists a family of 'carnivorous' plants; but I see that they are most of them very small, and prey upon litle insects only. My maternal uncle, however, knew nothing of this, for he died before the days of the discovery of the sun dew and pitcher plants, and grounding his knowledge of the man-sucking tree simply on his own terrible experience of it, explained its existence by theories of his own. Denying the fixity of all the laws of nature except one, that the stronger shall endeavour to consume the weaker, and 'holding even this fixity to be itself only a means to a greater general changefulness,' he argued that—since any partial distribution of the faculty of self-defence would presume an unworthy partiality in the Creator, and since the sensual instincts of beast and vegetable and manifestly analogous—'the world must be as percipient as sentient throughout.' Carrying on his theory (for it was something more than 'hypothesis' with him) a stage or two further, he arrived at the belief that, 'given the necessity of any imminent danger or urgent self-interest, every animal or vegetable could eventually revolutionize its nature, the wolf feeding on grass or nesting in trees, and the violet arming herself with thorns or entrapping insects.'

'How?' he would ask, 'can we claim for man the consequence of perceptions to sensations, and yet deny to beasts that hear, see, feel, smell, and taste, a percipient principle co-existent with their senses? And if in the whole range of the "animate" world there is this gift of self-defence against extirpation and offence against weakness, why is the "inanimate" world, holding as fierce a struggle for existence as the other, to be left defenceless and unarmed? And I deny that it is. The Brazilian epiphyte strangles the tree and sucks out its juices. The tree, again, to starve off its vampire parasite, withdraws its juices into its roots, and piercing the ground in some new place, turns the current of its sap into other growths. The epiphyte then drops off the dead boughs on to the fresh green sprouts springing from the ground beneath it—and so the fight goes on. Again, look at the Indian peepul tree; in what does the fierce yearning of its roots towards the distant well differ from the sad struggling of the camel to the oasis or of Sennacherib's army to the saving Nile?

'Is the sensitive plant unconscious! I have walked for miles through plains of it, and watched, till the watching almost made me afraid lest the plants should pluck up courage and turn upon me, the green carpet paling into silver grey before my feet, and fainting away all round me as I walked. So strangely did I feel the influence of this universal aversion, that I would have argued with the plant; but what was the use? If only I stretched out my hands, the mere shadow of the limb terrified the vegetable to sickness; shrubs crumbled up at every commencement of my speech; and at my periods great sturdy-looking bushes, to whose robustness I had foolishly appealed, sank in pallid supplication. Not a leaf would keep me company. A breath went forth from me that sickened life. My mere presence paralyzed life, and I was glad at last to come out among a less timid vegetation, and to feel the resentful spear-grass retaliating on the heedlessness that would have crushed it. The vegetable world, however, has its revenges. You may keep the guinea-pig in a hutch, but how will you pet the basilisk? The little sensitive plant in your garden amuses your children (who will find pleasure also in seeing cockchafers spin round on a pin), but how could you transplant a vegetable that seizes the running deer, strikes down the passing bird, and once taking hold of him, sucks the carcase of man himself, till his matter becomes as vague as his mind, and all his "animate" capabilities cannot snatch him from the terrible embrace of—God help him!—an "inanimate" tree?'

'Many years ago,' said my uncle, 'I turned my restless steps towards Central Africa, and made the journey from where the Senegal empties itself into the Atlantic to the Nile, skirting the Great Desert, and reaching Nubia on my way to the eastern coast. I had with me then three native attendants, two of them brothers, the third, Otona, a young savage from the Gaboon uplands, a mere lad in his teens; and one day, leaving my mule with the two men, who were pitching my tent for the night, I went on with my gun, the boy accompanying me, towards a fern forest, which I saw in the near distance. As I approached it I found the forest was cut into two by a wide glade, and seeing a small herd of the common antelope, an excellent beast in the pot, browsing their way along the shaded side, I crept after them. Though ignorant of their real danger, the herd was suspicious, and slowly trotting along before me, enticed me for a mile or more along the verge of the fern growths. Turning a corner I suddenly became aware of a solitary tree growing in the middle of the glade—one tree alone. It struck me at once that I had never seen a tree exactly like it before; but being intent upon venison for my supper, I looked at it only long enough to satisfy my first surprise at seeing a single plant of such rich growth flourishing luxuriantly in a spot where only the harsh fern-canes seemed to thrive.

'The deer meanwhile were midway between me and the tree, and looking at them I saw they were going to cross the glade. Exactly opposite them was an opening in the forest, in which I should certainly have lost my supper; so I fired into the middle of the family as they were filing before me. I hit a young fawn, and the rest of the herd, wheeling round in their sudden terror, made off in the direction of the tree, leaving the fawn struggling on the ground. Otona,' the boy, ran forward at my order to secure it, but the little creature seeing him coming, attempted to follow its comrades, and at a fair pace held on their course. The herd had meanwhile reached the tree, but suddenly, instead of passing under it, swerved in their career, and swept round it at some yards distance.

'*Was I mad? or did the plant really try to catch the deer?* On a sudden I saw, or thought I saw, the tree violently agitated, and while the ferns all round were standing motionless in the dead evening air, its boughs were swayed by some sudden gust towards the herd, and swept in the force of their impulse almost to the ground. I drew my hand across my eyes, closed them for a moment, and looked again. The tree was as motionless as myself!

'Towards it, and now close to it, the boy was running in excited pursuit of the fawn. He stretched out his hands to catch it. It bounded from his eager grasp. Again he reached forward, and again it escaped him. There was another rush forward, and the next instant boy and deer were beneath the tree.

'And now there was no mistaking what I saw.

'The tree was convulsed with motion, leaned forward, swept its thick foliaged boughs to the ground, and enveloped from my sight the pursuer and the pursued! I was within a hundred yards, and the cry of Otona from the midst of the tree came to me in all the clearness of its agony. There was then one stifled, strangling scream, and except for the agitation of the leaves where they had closed upon the boy, there was not a sign of life!

'I called out "Otona"! No answer came. I tried to call out again, but my utterance was like that of some wild beast smitten at once with sudden terror and its death wound. I stood there, changed from all semblance of a human being. Not all the terrors of earth together could have made me take my eye from the awful plant, or my foot off the ground. I must have stood thus for at least an hour, for the shadows had crept out from the forest half across the glade before that hideous paroxysm of fear left me. My first impulse then was to creep stealthily away lest the tree should perceive me, but my returning reason bade me approach it. The boy might have fallen into the lair of some beast of prey, or perhaps the terrible life in the tree was that of some great serpent among its branches. Preparing to defend myself, I approached the silent tree—the harsh grass crisping beneath my feet with a strange loudness—the cicadas in the forest shrilling till the air seemed throbbing round me with waves of sound. The terrible truth was soon before me in all its awful novelty.

'The vegetable first discovered my presence at about fifty yards distance. I then became aware of a stealthy motion among the thick-lipped leaves, reminding me of some wild beast slowly gathering itself up from long sleep, a vast coil of snakes in restless motion. Have you ever seen bees hanging from a bough—a great cluster of bodies, bee clinging to bee—and by striking the bough, or agitating the air, caused that massed life to begin sulkily to disintegrate, each insect asserting its individual right to move? And do you remember how, without one bee leaving the pensile cluster, the whole became gradually instinct with sullen life and horrid with a multitudinous motion?

'I came within twenty yards of it. The tree was quivering through every branch, muttering for blood, and, helpless with rooted feet, yearning with every branch towards me. It was that Terror of the Deep Sea which the men of the northen fiords dread, and which, anchored upon some sunken rock, stretches into vain space its longing arms, pellucid as the sea itself, and as relentless—maimed Polypheme groping for his victims.

'Each separate leaf was agitated and hungry. Like hands they fumbled together, their fleshy palms curling upon themselves and again unfolding, closing on each other and falling apart again, thick, helpless, fingerless hands—rather lips or tongues than hands—dimpled closely with little cup-like hollows. I approached nearer and nearer, step by step, till I saw that these soft horrors were all of them in motion, opening and closing incessantly.

'I was now within ten yards of the farthest reaching bough. Every part of it was hysterical with excitement. The agitation of its members was awful—sickening yet fascinating. In an ecstasy of eagerness for the food so near them, the leaves turned upon each other. Two meeting would suck together face to face, with a force that compressed their joint thickness to a half, thinning the two leaves into one, now grappling in a volute like a double shell, writhing like some green worm, and at last faint with the violence of the paroxysm, would slowly separate, falling apart as leeches gorged drop off the limbs. A sticky dew glistened in the dimples, welled over, and trickled down the leaf. The sound of it dripping from leaf to leaf made it seem as if the tree was muttering to itself. The beautiful golden fruit as they swung here and there were clutched now by one leaf, and now by another, held for a moment close enfolded from the sight, and then as suddenly released. Here a large leaf, vampire-like, had sucked out the juices of a smaller one. It hung limp and bloodless, like a carcase of which the weasel has tired.

'I watched the terrible struggle till my starting eyes, strained by intense attention, refused their office, and I can hardly say what I saw. But the tree before me seemed to have become a live beast. Above me I felt conscious was a great limb, and each of its thousand clammy hands reached downwards towards me, fumbling. It strained, shivered, rocked, and heaved. It flung itself about in despair. The boughs, tantalized to madness with the presence of flesh, were tossed to this side and to that, in the agony of a frantic desire. The leaves were wrung together as the hands of one driven to madness by sudden misery. I felt the vile dew spurting from the tense veins fall upon me. My clothes began to give out a strange odour. The ground I stood on glistened with animal juices.

'Was I bewildered by terror? Had my senses abandoned me in my need? I know not—but the tree seemed to me to be alive. Leaning over towards me, it seemed to be pulling up its roots from the softened ground, and to be moving towards me. A mountainous monster, with myriad lips, mumbling together for my life, was upon me!

'Like one who desperately defends himself from imminent death, I made an effort for life, and fired my gun at the approaching horror. To my dizzied senses the sound seemed far off, but the shock of the recoil partially recalled me to myself, and starting back I reloaded. The shots had torn their way into the soft body of the great thing. The trunk as it received the wound shuddered, and the whole tree was struck with a sudden quiver. A fruit fell down—slipping from the leaves, now rigid with swollen veins, as from carven foliage. Then I saw a large arm slowly droop, and without a sound it was severed from the juice-fattened bole, and sank down softly, noiselessly, through the glistening leaves. I fired again, and another vile fragment was powerless—*dead*. At each discharge the terrible vegetable yielded a life. Piecemeal I attacked it, killing here a leaf and there a branch. My fury increased with the slaughter till, when my ammunition was exhausted, the splended giant was left a wreck—as if some hurricane had torn through it. On the ground lay heaped together the fragments, struggling, rising and falling, gasping. Over them drooped in dying languor a few stricken boughs, while upright in the midst stood, dripping at every joint, the glistening trunk.

'My continued firing had brought up one of my men on my mule. He dared not, so he told me, come near me, thinking me mad. I had now drawn my hunting-knife, and with this was fighting—*with the leaves*. Yes—but each leaf was instinct with a horrid life; and more than once I felt my hand entangled for a moment and seized as if by sharp lips. Ignorant of the presence of my companion I made a rush forward over the fallen foliage, and with a last paroxysm of frenzy drove my knife up to the handle into the soft bole, and, slipping on the fast congealing sap, fell, exhausted and unconscious, among the still panting leaves.

'My companions carried me back to the camp, and after vainly searching for Otona awaited my return to consciousness. Two or three hours elapsed before I could speak, and several days before I could approach the terrible thing. My men would not go near it. It was quite dead; for as we came up a great-billed bird with gaudy plumage that had been securely feasting on the decaying fruit, flew up from the wreck. We removed the rotting foliage, and there, among the dead leaves still limp with juices, and piled round the roots, we found the ghastly relics of many former meals, and—its last nourishment—the corpse of little Otona. To have removed the leaves would have taken too long, so we buried the body as it was with a hundred vampire leaves still clinging to it.'

Such, as nearly as I remember it, was my uncle's story of the Man-eating Tree.

THE VAMPYRE
(*Strigoiul*)

Vasile Alecsandri

Translated into English
by Wm. Beatty-Kingston

Vampire poetry was widespread in Eastern Europe, especially Moldavia, Roumania, and Hungary, throughout the nineteenth century. Occasionally some of this poetry found its way into the British popular magazines, of which 'The Vampyre' is a classic example. Vasile Alecsandrai (1821–90) was a Romanian lyric poet, born in Moldavia, and the first important collector of Romanian popular songs. 'The Vampyre' was published in the *English Illustrated Magazine* (November 1886). Bram Stoker would certainly have read this piece, as his elder sister (Matilda) contributed an article on 'Sheridan and Miss Linley' to the same volume.

NEAR the cliff's sharp edge, on high
Standing out against the sky,
Dost thou see a ruined cross
Weatherstained, o'ergrown by moss,
Gloomy, desolate, forsaken,
By unnumbered tempests shaken?

Not a blade of grass grows nigh it,
Not a peasant lingers by it.
E'en the sombre bird of night
Shuns it in her darksome flight,
Startled by the piteous groan
That arises from the stone.

All around, on starless nights,
Myriad hosts of livid lights
Flicker fretfully, revealing
At its foot a phantom, kneeling
Whilst it jabbers dismal plaints,
Cursing God and all the saints.

Tardy traveller, beware
Of that spectre gibbering there;
Close your eyes, and urge your steed
To the utmost of his speed;—

For beneath that cross, I ween,
Lies a Vampyre's corpse obscene!

*　　*　　*　　*　　*

Though the night is black and cold
Love's fond story, often told,
Floats in whispers through the air.
Stalwart youth and maiden fair
Seal sweet vows of ardent passion
With their lips, in lovers' fashion.

Restless, pale, a shape I see
Hov'ring nigh; what may it be?
'Tis a charger, white as snow,
Pacing slowly to and fro
Like a sentry. As he turns
Haughtily the sward he spurns.

'Leave me not, beloved, tonight!
Stay with me till morning's light!'
Weeping, thus besought the maid;
'Love, my soul is sore afraid!
Brave not the dread Vampyre's
　　power,
Mightiest at this mystic hour!'

Not a word he spake, but prest
The sobbing maiden to his breast;
Kissed her lips and cheeks and eyes
Heedless of her tears and sighs;
Waved his hand, with gesture gay,
Mounted—smiled—and rode away.

   *   *   *   *   *

Who rides across the dusky plain
Tearing along with might and main
Like some wild storm-fiend, in his
   flight
Nursed on the ebony breast of Night?
'Tis he, who left her in her need—
Her lover, on his milk-white steed!

The blast in all its savage force
Strives to o'erthrow the gallant horse
That snorts defiance to his foe
And struggles onward. See! below
The causeway, 'long the river-side
A thousand flutt'ring flamelets glide!

Now they approach, and now
   recede,
Still followed by the panting steed;
He nears the ruined cross! A crash,
A piteous cry, a heavy splash,
And in the rocky river-bed
Rider and horse lie crushed and
   dead.

Then from those dismal depths arise
Blaspheming yells and strident cries
Re-echoing through the murky air.
And, like a serpent from its lair,
Brandishing high a blood-stained
   glaive
The Vampyre rises from his grave!

A MYSTERY OF THE CAMPAGNA

Anne Crawford

F. Marion Crawford's classic 'For the Blood is the Life' (1905) is one of the best-known tales of vampirism, but 'A Mystery of the Campagna', written by his eldest sister Anne almost twenty years earlier, has rarely been reprinted. Anne Crawford, Baroness Von Rabe, did not pursue a literary career with the same diligence as her siblings Francis Marion Crawford and Mary Crawford (Mrs Hugh Fraser, author of *A Diplomatist's Wife in Many Lands* and several novels, including *The Satanist*, a notable study of devil-worship in Italy). 'A Mystery of the Campagna' was first published in *Unwin's Annual* (1887) under the pseudonym 'Von Degen', together with her brother's story 'By the Waters of Paradise'. Four years later T. Fisher Unwin reissued Anne's story (with another novella, 'A Shadow on a Wave') in the Pseudonym Library series, still under the 'Von Degen' alias. It is undoubtedly one of the most artistic and interesting vampire tales to be published in the decade preceding *Dracula* and deserves to be better known.

I

Martin Detaille's Account
of What Happened at the Vigna Marziali

MARCELLO'S voice is pleading with me now, perhaps because after years of separation I have met an old acquaintance who had a part in his strange story. I have a longing to tell it, and have asked Monsieur Sutton to help me. He noted down the circumstances at the time, and he is willing to join his share to mine, that Marcello may be remembered.

One day, it was in spring, he appeared in my little studio amongst the laurels and green alleys of the Villa Medici. 'Come *mon enfant*,'he said, 'put up your paints;' and he unceremoniously took my palette out of my hand. 'I have a cab waiting outside, and we are going in search of a hermitage.' He was already washing my brushes as he spoke, and this softened my heart, for I hate to do it myself. Then he pulled off my velvet jacket and took down my respectable coat from a nail on the wall. I let him dress me like a child. We always did his will, and he knew it, and in a moment we were sitting in the cab, driving through the Via Sistina on our way to the Porta San Giovanni, whither he had directed the coachman to go.

I must tell my story as I can, for though I have been told by my comrades, who cannot know very well, that I can speak good English, writing it is another thing. Monsieur Sutton has asked me to use his tongue, because he has so far forgotten mine that he will not trust himself in it, though he has promised to correct my mistakes, that what I have to tell you may not seem ridiculous, and make people laugh when they read of Marcello. I tell him I wish to write this for my countrymen, not his; but he reminds me that Marcello had many English friends who still live, and that the English do not forget as we do. It is of no use to reason with him, for neither do they yield as we do, and so I have consented to his wish. I think he has a reason which he does not tell me, but let it go. I will translate it all into my own language for my own people. Your English phrases seem to me to be always walking sideways, or trying to look around the corner or stand upon their heads, and they have as many little tails as a kite. I will try not to have recourse to my own language, but he must pardon me if I forget myself. He may be sure I do not do it to offend him. Now that I have explained so much, let me go on.

When we had passed out of the Porta San Giovanni, the coachman drove as slowly as possible; but Marcello was never practical. How could he be, I ask you, with an Opera in his head? So we crawled along, and he gazed dreamily before him. At last, when we had reached the part where the little villas and vineyards begin, he began to look about him.

You all know how it is out there; iron gates with rusty names or initials over them, and beyond them straight walks bordered with roses and lavender leading up to a forlorn little casino, with trees and a wilderness behind it sloping down to the Campagna, lonely enough to be murdered in and no one to hear you cry. We stopped at several of these gates and Marcello stood looking in, but none of the places were to his taste. He seemed not to doubt that he might have whatever pleased him, but nothing did so. He would jump out and run to the gate, and return saying, 'The shape of those windows would disturb my inspiration,' or, 'That yellow paint would make me fail my duet in the second Act'; and once he liked the air of the house well enough, but there were marigolds growing in the walk, and he hated them. So we drove on and on, until I thought we should find nothing more to reject. At last we came to one which suited him, though it was terribly lonely, and I should have fancied it very *agaçant* to live so far away from the world with nothing but those melancholy olives and green oaks—

ilexes, you call them—for company.

'I shall live here and become famous!' he said, decidedly, as he pulled the iron rod which rang a great bell inside. We waited, and then he rang again very impatiently and stamped his foot.

'No one lives here, *mon vieux*! Come, it is getting late, and it is so damp out here, and you know that the damp for a tenor voice—' He stamped his foot again and interruped me angrily.

'Why, then, have you got a tenor? You are stupid! A bass would be more sensible; nothing hurts it. But you have not got one, and you call yourself my friend! Go home without me.' How could I, so far on foot? 'Go and sing you lovesick songs to your lean English misses! They will thank you with a cup of abominable tea, and you will be in Paradise! This is *my* Paradise, and I shall stay until the angel comes to open it!'

He was very cross and unreasonable, and those were just the times when one loved him most, so I waited and enveloped my throat in my pocket-handkerchief and sang a passage or two just to prevent my voice from becoming stiff in that damp air.

'Be still! silence yourself!' he cried. 'I cannot hear if anyone is coming.'

Someone came at last, a rough-looking sort of keeper, or *guardiano* as they are called there, who looked at us as though he thought we were mad. One of us certainly was, but it was not I. Marcello spoke pretty good Italian, with a French accent, it is true, but the man understood him, especially as he held his purse in his hand. I heard him say a great many impetuously persuasive things all in one breath, then he slipped a gold piece into the *guardiano*'s horny hand, and the two turned towards the house, the man shrugging his shoulders in a resigned sort of way, and Marcello called out to me over his shoulder—

'Go home in the cab, or you will be late for your horrible English party! I am going to stay here tonight.' *Ma foi*! I took his permission and left him; for a tenor voice is as tyrannical as a jealous woman. Besides, I was furious, and yet I laughed. His was the artist temperament, and appeared to us by turns absurd, sublime, and intensely irritating; but this last never for long, and we all felt that were we more like him our pictures would be worth more. I had not got as far as the city gate when my temper had cooled, and I began to reproach myself for leaving him in that lonely place with his purse full of money, for he was not poor at all, and tempting the dark *guardiano* to murder him. Nothing could be easier than to kill him in his sleep and bury him away somewhere under the olive trees or in some old vault of a ruined catacomb, so common on the borders of the Campagna. There were sure to be a hundred convenient places. I stopped the coachman and told him to turn back, but he shook his head and said something about having to be in the Piazza of St Peter at eight o'clock. His horse began to go lame, as though he had understood his master and was his accomplice. What could I do? I said to myself that it was fate, and let him take me back to the Villa Medici, where I had to pay him a pretty sum for our crazy expedition, and then he rattled off, the horse not lame at all, leaving me bewildered at this strange afternoon.

I did not sleep well that night, though my tenor song had been applauded, and the English misses had caressed me much. I tried not to think of Marcello, and he did not trouble me much until I went to bed; but then I could not sleep, as I have told you.

I fancied him already murdered, and being buried in the darkness by the *guardiano*. I saw the man dragging his body, with the beautiful head thumping against the stones, down dark passages, and at last leaving it all bloody and covered with earth under a black arch in a recess, and coming back to count the gold pieces. But then again I fell asleep, and dreamed that Marcello was standing at the gate and stamping his foot; and then I slept no more, but got up as soon as the dawn came, and dressed myself and went to my studio at the end of the laurel walk. I took down my painting jacket, and remembered how he had pulled it off my shoulders. I took up the brushes he had washed for me; they were only half cleaned after all, and stiff with paint and soap. I felt glad to be angry with him, and *sacré'd* a little, for it made me sure that he was yet alive if I could scold at him. Then I pulled out my study of his head for my picture of Mucius Scaevola holding his hand in the flame, and then I forgave him; for who could look upon that face and not love it?

I worked with the fire of friendship in my brush, and did my best to endow the features with the expression of scorn and obstinacy I had seen at the gate. It could not have been more suitable to my subject! Had I seen it for the last time? You will ask me why I did not leave my work and go to see if anything had happened to him, but against this there were several reasons. Our yearly exhibition was not far off and my picture was barely painted in, and my comrades had sworn that it would not be ready. I was expecting a model for the King of the Etruscans; a man who cooked chestnuts in the Piazza Montanara, and who had consented to stoop to sit to me as a great favour; and then, to tell the truth, the morning was beginning to dispel my fancies. I had a good northern light to work by, with nothing sentimental about it, and I was not fanciful by nature; so when I sat down to my easel I told myself that I had been a fool, and that Marcello was perfectly safe: the smell of the paints helping me to feel practical again. Indeed, I thought every moment that he would come in, tired of his caprice already, and even was preparing and practising a little lecture for him. Some one knocked at my door, and I cried 'Entrez!' thinking it was he at last, but no, it was Pierre Magnin.

'There is a curious man, a man of the country, who wants you,' he said. 'He has your address on a dirty piece of paper in Marcello's handwriting, and a letter for you, but he won't give it up. He says he must see 'il Signor Martino.' He'd make a superb model for a murderer! Come and speak to him, and keep him while I get a sketch of his head.'

I followed Magnin through the garden, and outside, for the porter had not allowed him to enter, I found the *guardiano* of yesterday. He showed his white teeth, and said, 'Good day, signore,' like a Christian; and here in Rome he did not look half so murderous, only a stupid, brown, country fellow. He had a rough peasant-cart waiting, and he had tied up his shaggy horse to a ring in the wall. I held out my hand for the letter and pretended to find it difficult to read, for I saw Magnin standing with his sketch-book in the shadow of the entrance hall. The note said this: I have it still and I will copy it. It was written in pencil on a leaf torn from his pocketbook:

Mon vieux! I have passed a good night here, and the man will keep me as long as I like. Nothing will happen to me, except that I shall be divinely quiet, and I already have a famous *motif* in my head. Go to my lodgings and pack up some clothes and all my manuscripts, with plenty of music paper and a few bottles of Bordeaux, and give them to my messenger. Be quick about it!

Fame is preparing to descend upon me! If you care to see me, do not come before eight days. The gate will not be opened if you come soner. The *guardiano* is my slave, and he has instructions to kill any intruder who in the guise of a friend tries to get in uninvited. He will do it, for he has confessed to me that he has murdered three men already.

(Of course this was a joke. I knew Marcello's way.)

When you come, go to the *poste restante* and fetch my letters. Here is my card to legitimate you. Don't forget pens and a bottle of ink! Your Marcello.

There was nothing for it but to jump into the cart, tell Magnin, who had finished his sketch, to lock up my studio, and go bumping off to obey these commands. We drove to his lodgings in the Via del Governo Vecchio, and there I made a bundle of all that I could think of; the landlady hindering me by a thousand questions about when the Signore would return. He had paid for the rooms in advance, so she had no need to be anxious about her rent. When I told her where he was, she shook her head, and talked a great deal about the bad air out there, and said 'Poor Signorino!' in a melancholy way, as though he were already buried, and looked mournfully after us from the window when we drove away. She irritated me, and made me feel superstitious. At the corner of the Via del Tritone I jumped down and gave the man a franc out of pure sentimentality, and cried after him, 'Greet the Signore!' but he did not hear me, and jogged away stupidly whilst I was longing to be with him. Marcello was a cross to us sometimes, but we loved him always.

The eight days went by sooner than I had thought they would, and

Thursday came, bright and sunny, for my expedition. At one o'clock I descended into the Piazza di Spagna, and made a bargain with a man who had a well-fed horse, remembering how dearly Marcello's want of good sense had cost me a week ago, and we drove off at a good pace to the Vigna Marziali, as I was almost forgetting to say that it was called. My heart was beating, though I did not know why I should feel so much emotion. When we reached the iron gate the *guardiano* answered my ring directly, and I had no sooner set foot in the long flower-walk than I saw Marcello hastening to meet me.

'I knew you would come,' he said, drawing my arm within his, and so we walked towards the little grey house, which had a sort of portico and several balconies, and a sun-dial on its front. There were grated windows down to the ground floor, and the place, to my relief, looked safe and habitable. He told me that the man did not sleep there, but in a little hut down towards the Campagna, and that he, Marcello, locked himself in safely every night, which I was also relieved to know.

'What do you get to eat?' said I.

'Oh, I have goat's flesh, and dried beans and polenta, with pecorino cheese, and there is plenty of black bread and sour wine,' he answered smilingly. 'You see I am not starved.'

'Do not overwork yourself, *mon vieux*,' I said; 'you are worth more than your opera will ever be.'

'Do I look overworked?' he said, turning his face to me in the broad, outdoor light. He seemed a little offended at my saying that about his opera, and I was foolish to do it.

I examined his face critically, and he looked at me half defiantly. 'No, not yet,' I answered rather unwillingly, for I could not say that he did; but there was a restless, inward look in his eyes, and an almost imperceptible shadow lay around them. It seemed to me as though the full temples had grown slightly hollow, and a sort of faint mist lay over his beauty, making it seem strange and far off. We were standing before the door, and he pushed it open, the *guardiano* following us with slow, loud-resounding steps.

'Here is my Paradise,' said Marcello, and we entered the house, which was like all the others of its kind. A hall, with stucco bas-reliefs, and a stairway adorned with antique fragments, gave access to the upper rooms. Marcello ran up the steps lightly, and I heard him lock a door somewhere above and draw out the key, then he came and met me on the landing.

'This,' he said, 'is my workroom,' and he threw open a low door. The key was in the lock, so this room could not be the one I heard him close. 'Tell me I shall not write like an angel here!' he cried. I was so dazzled by the flood of bright sunshine after the dusk of the passage, that I blinked like an owl at first, and then I saw a large room, quite bare except for a rough table and chair, the chair covered with manuscript music.

'You are looking for the furniture,' he said, laughing; 'it is outside. Look here!' and he drew me to a rickety door of worm-eaten wood and coarse greenish glass, and flung it open on to a rusty iron balcony. He was right; the furniture was outside: that is to say, a divine view met my eyes. The Sabine Mountains, the Alban Hills, and broad Campagna, with its mediaeval towers and ruined aqueducts, and the open plain to the sea. All this glowing and yet calm in the sunlight. No wonder he could write there! The balcony ran round the corner of the house, and to the right I looked down upon an alley of ilexes, ending in a grove of tall laurel trees—very old, apparently. There were bits of sculpture and some ancient sarcophagi standing gleaming against them, and even from so high I could hear a little stream of water pouring from an antique mask into a long, rough trough. I saw the brown *guardiano* digging at his cabbages and onions, and I laughed to think that I could fancy him a murderer! He had a little bag of relics, which dangled to and fro over his sun-burned breast, and he looked very innocent when he sat down upon an old column to eat a piece of black bread with an onion which he had just pulled out of the ground, slicing it with a knife not at all like a dagger. But I kept my thoughts to myself, for Marcello would have laughed at them. We were standing together, looking down at the man as he drank from his hands at the running fountain, and Marcello now leaned down over the balcony, and called out a long 'Ohé!' The lazy *guardiano* looked up, nodded, and then got up slowly from the stone where he had been half-kneeling to reach the jet of water.

'We are going to dine,' Marcello explained. 'I have been waiting for you.' Presently he heard the man's heavy tread upon the stairs, and he entered bearing a strange meal in a basket.

There came to light pecorino cheese made from ewe's milk, black bread of the consistency of a stone, a great bowl of salad apparently composed of weeds, and a sausage which filled the room with a strong smell of garlic. Then he disappeared and came back with a dish full of ragged-looking goat's flesh cooked together with a mass of smoking polenta, and I am not sure that there was not oil in it.

'I told you I lived well, and now you see!' said Marcello. It was a terrible meal, but I had to eat it, and was glad to have some rough, sour wine to help me, which tasted of earth and roots. When we had finished I said, 'And your opera! How are you getting on?'

'Not a word about that!' he cried. 'You see how I have written!' and he turned over a heap of manuscript; 'but do not talk to me about it. I will not lose my ideas in words.' This was not like Marcello, who loved to discuss his work, and I looked at him astonished.

'Come,' he said, 'we will go down into the garden, and you shall tell me about the comrades. What are they doing? Has Magnin found a model for his Clytemnestra?'

I humoured him, as I always did, and we sat upon a stone bench behind the house, looking towards the laurel grove, talking of the pictures and the students. I wanted to walk down the ilex alley, but he stopped me.

'If you are afraid of the damp, don't go down there,' he said, 'the place is like a vault. Let us stay here and be thankful for this heavenly view.'

'Well, let us stay here,' I answered, resigned as ever. He lit a cigar and offered me one in silence. If he did not care to talk, I could be still too. From time to time he made some indifferent observation, and I answered it in the same tone. It almost seemed to me as though we, the old heart-comrades, had become strangers who had not known each other a week, or as though we had been so long apart that we had grown away from each other. There was something about him which escaped me. Yes, the days of solitude had indeed put years and a sort of shyness, or rather ceremony, between us! It did not seem natural to me now to clap him on the back, and make the old, harmless jokes at him. He must have felt the constraint too, for we were like children who had looked forward to a game, and did not know now what to play at.

At six o'clock I left him. It was not like parting with Marcello. I felt rather as though I should find my old friend in Rome that evening, and here only left a shadowy likeness of him. He accompanied me to the gate, and pressed my hand, and for a moment the true Marcello looked out of his eyes; but we called out no last word to each other as I drove away. I had only said, 'Let me know when you want me'; and he said, 'Merci!' and all the way back to Rome I felt a chill upon me, his hand had been so cold, and I thought and thought what could be the matter with him.

That evening I spoke out my anxiety to Pierre Magnin, who shook his head and declared that malaria fever must be taking hold of him, and that people often begin to show it by being a little odd.

'He must not stay there! We must get him away as soon as possible,' I cried.

'We both know Marcello, and that nothing can make him stir against his will,' said Pierre. 'Let him alone, and he will get tired of his whim. It will not kill him to have a touch of malaria, and some evening he will turn up amongst us as merry as ever.'

But he did not. I worked hard at my picture and finished it, but for a few touches, and he had not yet appeared. Perhaps it was the extreme application, perhaps the sitting out in that damp place, for I insist upon tracing it to something more material than emotion. Well, whatever it was, I fell ill; more ill than I had even been in my life. It was almost twilight when it overtook me, and I remember it distinctly, though I forget what happened afterwards, or, rather, I never knew, for I was found by Magnin quite unconscious, and he has told me that I remained so for some time, and then became delirious, and talked of nothing but Marcello. I have told you that it was very nearly twilight; but just at the moment when the sun is gone the colours show in their true value. Artists know this, and I was putting last touches here and there to my picture and especially to my head of Mucius Scaevola, or rather, Marcello.

The rest of the picture came out well enough; but that head, which should have been the principal one, seemed faded and sunk in. The face appeared to grow paler and paler, and to recede from me; a strange veil spread over it, and the eyes seemed to close. I am not easily frightened, and I know what tricks some peculiar methods of colour will play by certain lights, for the moment I spoke of had gone, and the twilight greyness had set in; so I stepped back to look at it. Just then the lips, which had become almost white, opened a little, and sighed! An illusion, of course. I must have been very ill and quite delirious already, for to my imagination it was a real sigh, or, rather, a sort of exhausted gasp. Then it was that I fainted, I suppose, and when I came to myself I was in my bed, with Magnin and Monsieur Sutton standing by me, and a Soeur de Charité moving softly about among medicine bottles, and speaking in whispers. I stretched out my hands, and they were thin and yellow, with long, pale nails; and I heard Magnin's voice, which sounded very far away, say, 'Dieu Merci!' And now Monsieur Sutton will tell you what I did not know until long afterwards.

II

Robert Sutton's Account of What Happened at the Vigna Marziali

I am attached to Detaille, and was very glad to be of use to him, but I never fully shared his admiration for Marcello Souvestre, though I appreciated his good points. He was certainly very promising—I must say that. But he was an odd, flighty sort of fellow, not of the kind which we English care to take the trouble to understand. It is my business to write stories, but not having need of such characters I have never particularly studied them. As I say, I was glad to be of use to Detaille, who is a thorough good fellow, and I willingly gave up my work to go and sit by his bedside. Magnin knew that I was a friend of his, and very properly came to me when he found that Detaille's illness was a serious one and likely to last for a long time. I found him perfectly delirious, and raving about Marcello.

'Tell me what the *motif* is! I know it is a *Marche Funèbre*!' And here he would sing a peculiar melody, which, as I have a knack at music, I noted down, it being like nothing I had heard before. The Sister of Charity looked at me with severe eyes; but how could she know that all is grist for our mill, and that observation becomes with us a mechanical habit? Poor Detaille kept repeating this curious melody over and over, and then would stop and seem to be looking at his picture, crying that it was fading away.

'Marcello! Marcello! You are fading too! Let me come to you!' He was as weak as a baby, and could not have moved from his bed unless in the strength of delirium.

'I cannot come!' he went on; 'they have tied me down.' And here he made as though he were trying to gnaw through a rope at his wrists, and then burst into tears. 'Will no one go for me and bring me a word from you? Ah! if I could know that you are alive!'

Magnin looked at me. I knew what he was thinking. He would not leave his comrade, but I must go. I don't mind acknowledging that I did not undertake this unwillingly. To sit by Detaille's bedside and listen to his ravings enervated me, and what Magnin wanted struck me as troublesome but not uninteresting to one of my craft, so I agreed to go. I had heard all about Marcello's strange seclusion from Magnin and Detaille himself, who lamented over it openly in his simple way at supper at the Academy, where I was a frequent guest.

I knew that it would be useless to ring at the gate of the Vigna Marziali. Not only should I not be admitted, but I should arouse Marcello's anger and suspicion, for I did not for a moment believe that he was not alive, though I thought it very possible that he was becoming a little crazy, as his countrymen are so easily put off their balance. Now, odd people are oddest late in the day and at evening time. Their nerves lose the power of resistance then, and the real man gets the better of them. So I determined to try to discover something at night, reflecting also that I should be safer from detection then. I knew his liking for wandering about when he ought to be in his bed, and I did not doubt that I should get a glimpse of him, and that was really all I needed.

My first step was to take a long walk out of the Porta San Giovanni, and this I did in the early morning, tramping along steadily until I came to an iron gate on the right of the road, with 'Vigna Marziali' over it; and then I walked straight on, never stopping until I had reached a little bushy lane running down towards the Campagna to the right. It was pebbly, and quite shut in by luxuriant ivy and elder bushes, and it bore deep traces of the last heavy rains. These had evidently been effaced by no footprints, so I concluded that it was little used. Down this path I made my way cautiously, looking behind and before me, from a habit contracted in my lonely wanderings in the Abruzzi. I had a capital revolver with me—an old friend—and I feared no man; but I began to feel a dramatic interest in my undertaking, and determined that it should not be crossed by any disagreeable surprises. The lane led me further down the plain that I had reckoned upon, for the bushy edge shut out the view; and when I had got to the bottom and faced round, the Vigna Marziali was lying quite far to my left. I saw at a glance that behind the grey casino an alley of ilexes ended in a laurel grove; then there were plantations of kitchen stuff, with a sort of thatched cabin in their midst, probably that of a gardener. I looked about for a kennel, but saw none, so there was no watchdog. At the end of this primitive kitchen garden was a broad patch of grass, bounded by a fence, which I could take at a spring. Now, I knew my way, but I could not resist tracing it out a little further. It was well that I did so, for I found just within the fence a sunken stream, rather full at the time, in consequence of the rains, too deep to wade and too broad to jump. It struck me that it would be easy enough to take a board from the fence and lay it over for a bridge. I measured the breadth with my eye, and decided the board would span it; then I went back as I had come, and returned to find Detaille still raving.

As he could understand nothing it seemed to me rather a fool's errand to go off in search of comfort for him; but a conscious moment might come, and moreover, I began to be interested in my undertaking; and so I agreed with Magnin that I should go and take some food and rest and return to the Vigna that night. I told my landlady that I was going into the country and should return the next day, and I went to Nazarri's and laid in a stock of sandwiches and filled my flask with something they called sherry, for, though I was no great wine-drinker, I feared the night chill.

It was about seven o'clock when I started, and I retraced my morning's steps exactly. As I reached the lane, it occurred to me that it was still too light for me to pass unobserved over the stream, and I made a place for myself under the hedge and lay down, quite screened by the thick curtain of tangled overhanging ivy.

I must have been out of training, and tired by the morning's walk, for I fell asleep. When I awoke it was night; the stars were shining, a dank mist made its way down my throat, and I felt stiff and cold. I took a pull at my flask, finding it nasty stuff, but it warmed me. Then I rang my repeater, which struck a quarter to eleven, got up and shook myself free of the leaves and brambles, and went on down the lane. When I got to the fence I sat down and thought the thing over. What did I expect to discover? What *was* there to discover? Nothing! Nothing but that Marcello was alive; and that was no discovery at all for I felt sure of it. I was a fool, and had let myself be allured by the mere stage nonsense and mystery of the business, and a mouse would creep out of this mountain of precautions! Well, at least, I could turn it to account by describing my own absurd behaviour in some story yet to be written, and, as it was not enough for a chapter, I would add to it by further experience. 'Come along!' I said to myself. 'You're an ass, but it may prove instructive.' I raised the top board from the fence noiselessly. There was a little stile there, and the boards were easily moved. I laid down my bridge with some difficulty, and stepped carefully across, and made my way to the laurel grove as quickly and noiselessly as possible.

There all was thick darkness, and my eyes only grew slowly accustomed to it. After all there was not much to see; some stone seats in a semi-circle, and some fragments of columns set upright with antique busts upon them. Then a little to the right a sort of arch, with apparently some steps descending into the ground, probably the entrance to some discovered branch of a catacomb. In the midst of the enclosure, not a very large one, stood a stone table, deeply fixed in the earth. No one was there; of that I felt certain, and I sat down, having now got used to the gloom, and fell to eat my sandwiches, for I was desperately hungry.

Now that I had come so far, was nothing to take place to repay me for my trouble? It suddenly struck me that it was absurd to expect Marcello to come out to meet me and perform any mad antics he might be meditating there before my eyes for my especial satisfaction. Why had I supposed that something would take place in the grove I do not know, except that this seemed a fit place for it. I would go and watch the house, and if I saw a light anywhere I might be sure he was within. Any fool might have though of that, but a novelist lays the scene of his drama and expects his charcters to slide about in the grooves like puppets. It is only when mine surprise me that I feel they are alive. When I reached the end of the ilex alley I saw the house before me. There were more cabbages and onions after I had left the trees, and I saw that in this open space I could easily be perceived by any one standing on the balcony above. As I drew back again under the ilexes, a window above, not the one on the balcony, was suddenly lighted up; but the light did not remain long, and presently a gleam shone through the glass oval over the door below.

I had just time to spring behind the thickest trunk near me when the door opened. I took advantage of its creaking to creep up the slanting tree like a cat, and lie out upon a projecting branch.

As I expected, Marcello came out. He was very pale, and moved mechanically like a sleepwalker. I was shocked to see how hollow his face had become as he held the candle still lighted in his hand, and it cast deep shadows on his sunken cheeks and fixed eyes, which burned wildly and seemed to see nothing. His lips were quite white, and so drawn that I could see his gleaming teeth. Then the candle fell from his hand, and he came slowly and with a curiously regular step on into the darkness of the ilexes, I watching him from above. But I scarcely think he would have noticed me had I been standing in his path. When he had passed I let myself down and followed him. I had taken off my shoes, and my tread was absolutely noiseless; moreover, I felt sure he would not turn around.

On he went with the same mechanical step until he reached the grove. There I knelt behind an old sarcophagus at the entrance, and waited. What would he do? He stood perfectly still, not looking about him, but as though the clockwork within him had suddenly stopped. I felt that he was becoming psychologically interesting, after all. Suddenly he threw up his arms as men do when they are mortally wounded on the battle-field, and I expected to see him fall at full length. Instead of this he made a step forward.

I looked in the same direction, and saw a woman, who must have concealed herself there while I was waiting before the house, come from out of the gloom, and as she slowly approached and laid her head upon his shoulder, the outstretched arms clasped themselves closely around her, so that her face was hidden upon his neck.

So this was the whole matter, and I had been sent off on a wild-goose chase to spy out a common love affair! His opera and his seclusion for the sake of work, his tyrannical refusal to see Detaille unless he sent for him—all this was but a mask to a vulgar intrigue which, for reasons best known to himself, could not be indulged in in the city. I was thoroughly angry! If Marcello passed his time mooning about in that damp hole all night, no wonder that he looked so wretchedly ill, and seemed half mad! I knew very well that Marcello was no saint. Why should he be? But I had not taken him for a fool! He had had plenty of romantic episodes, and as he was discreet without being uselessly mysterious, no one had ever unduly pryed into them, nor should we have done so now. I said to myself that that mixture of French and Italian blood was at the bottom of it; French flimsiness and light-headedness and Italian love of cunning! I looked back upon all the details of my mysterious expedition. I suppose at the root of my anger lay a certain dramatic disappointment at not finding him lying murdered, and I despised myself for all the trouble I had taken to this ridiculous end: just to see him holding a woman in his arms. I could not see her face, and her figure was enveloped from head to foot in something long and dark; but I could make out that she was tall and slender, and that a pair of white hands gleamed from her drapery. As I was looking intently, for all my indignation, the couple moved on, and still clinging to one another descended the steps. So even the solitude of the lonely laurel grove could not satisfy Marcello's insane love of secrecy! I kept still awhile; then I stole to where they had disappeared, and listened; but all was silent, and I cautiously struck a match and peered down. I could see the steps for a short distance below me, and then the darkness seemed to rise and swallow them. It must be a catacomb as I had imagined, or an old Roman bath, perhaps, which Marcello had made comfortable enough, no doubt, and as likely as not they were having a nice little cold supper there. My empty stomach told me that I could have forgiven him even then could I have shared it;

I was in truth frightfully hungry as well as angry, and sat down on one of the stone benches to finish my sandwiches.

The thought of waiting to see this love-sick pair return to upper earth never for a moment occurred to me. I had found out the whole thing, and a great humbug it was! Now I wanted to get back to Rome before my temper had cooled, and to tell Magnin on what a fool's errand he had sent me. If he liked to quarrel with me, all the better!

All the way home I composed cutting French speeches, but they suddenly cooled and petrified like a gust of lava from a volcano when I discovered that the gate was closed. I had never thought of getting a pass, and Magnin ought to have warned me. Another grievance against the fellow! I enjoyed my resentment, and it kept me warm as I patrolled up and down. There are houses, and even small eating-shops outside the gate, but no light was visible, and I did not care to attract attention by pounding at the doors in the middle of the night; so I crept behind a bit of wall. I was getting used to hiding by this time, and made myself as comfortable as I could with my ulster, took another pull at my flask, and waited. At last the gate was opened and I slipped through, trying not to look as though I had been out all night like a bandit. The guard looked at me narrowly, evidently wondering at my lack of luggage. Had I had a knapsack I might have been taken for some innocently mad English tourist indulging in the mistaken pleasure of trudging in from Frascati or Albano; but a man in an ulster, with his hands in his pockets, sauntering in at the gate of the city at break of day as though returning from a stroll, naturally puzzled the officials, who looked at me and shrugged their shoulders.

Luckily I found an early cab in the Piazza of the Lateran, for I was dead-beat, and was soon at my lodgings in the Via della Croce, where my landlady let me in very speedily. Then at last I had the comfort of throwing off my clothes, all damp with the night dew, and turning in. My wrath had cooled to a certain point, and I did not fear to lower its temperature too greatly by yielding to an overwhelming desire for sleep. An hour or two could make no great difference to Magnin—let him fancy me still hanging about the Vigna Marziali! Sleep I must have, no matter what he thought.

I slept long, and was awakened at last by my landlady, Sora Nanna, standing over me, and saying, 'There is a Signore who wants you.'

'It is I, Magnin!' said a voice behind her. 'I could not wait for you to come!' He looked haggard with anxiety and watching.

'Detaille is raving still,' he went on 'only worse than before. Speak, for Heaven's sake! Why don't you tell me something?' And he shook me by the arm as though he thought I was still asleep.

'Have you nothing to say? You must have seen something! Did you see Marcello?'

'Oh! yes, I saw him.'

'Well?'

'Well, he was very comfortable—quite alive. He had a woman's arms around him.'

I heard my door violently slammed to, a ferocious 'Sacré gamin!' and then steps springing down the stairs. I felt perfectly happy at having made such an impression, and turned and resumed my broken sleep with almost a kindly feeling towards Magnin, who was at that moment probably tearing up the Spanish Scalinata two steps at a time, and making himself horribly hot. It could not help Detaille, poor fellow! He could not understand my news. When I had slept long enough I got up, refreshed myself with a bath and something to eat, and went off to see Detaille. It was not his fault that I had been made a fool of, so I felt sorry for him.

I found him raving just as I had left him the day before, only worse, as Magnin said. He persisted in continually crying, 'Marcello, take care! no one can save you!' in hoarse, weak tones, but with the regularity of a knell, keeping up a peculiar movement with his feet, as though he were weary with a long road, but must press forward to his goal. Then he would stop and break into childish sobs.

'My feet are so sore,' he murmured piteously, 'and I am so tired! But I will come! They are following me, but I am strong!' Then a violent struggle with his invisible pursuers, in which he would break off into that singing of his, alternating with the warning cry. The singing voice was quite another from the speaking one. He went on and on repeating the singular air which he had himself called A Funeral March, and which had become intensely disagreeable to me. If it was one indeed, it surely was intended for no Christian burial. As he sang, the tears kept trickling down his cheeks, and Magnin sat wiping them away as tenderly as a woman. Between his song he would clasp his hands, feebly enough, for he was very weak when the delirium did not make him violent, and cry in heart-rending tones, 'Marcello, I shall never see you again! Why did you leave us?' At last, when he stopped for a moment, Magnin left his side, beckoning the Sister to take it, and drew me into the other room, closing the door behind him.

'Now tell me exactly how you saw Marcello,' said he; so I related my whole absurd experience—forgetting, however, my personal irritation, for he looked too wretched and worn for anybody to be angry with him. He made me repeat several times my description of Marcello's face and manner as he had come out of the house. That seemed to make more impression upon him than the love-business.

'Sick people have strange intuitions,' he said gravely; 'and I persist in thinking that Marcello is very ill and in danger. Tenez!' And here he broke off, went to the door, and called 'Ma Sœur!' under his breath. She understood, and after having drawn the bedclothes straight, and once more dried the trickling tears, she came noiselessly to where we stood, the wet handkerchief still in her hand. She was a singularly tall and strong-looking woman, with piercing black eyes and a self-controlled manner. Strange to say, she bore the adopted name of Claudius, instead of a more feminine one.

'*Ma Sœur*,' said Magnin, 'at what o'clock was it that he sprang out of bed and we had to hold him for so long?'

'Half-past eleven and a few minutes,' she answered promptly. Then he turned to me.

'At what time did Marcello come out into the garden?'

'Well, it might have been half-past eleven,' I answered unwillingly. 'I should say that three-quarters of an hour might possibly have passed since I rang my repeater. Mind you, I won't swear it!' I hate to have people try to prove mysterious coincidences, and this was just what they were attempting.

'Are you sure of the hour, *ma sœur*?' I asked, a little tartly.

She looked at me calmly with her great, black eyes, and said:

'I heard the Trinità de' Monti strike the half-hour just before it happened.'

'Be so good as to tell Monsieur Sutton exactly what took place,' said Magnin.

'One moment, Monsieur,' and she went swiftly and softly to Detaille, raised him on her strong arm, and held a glass to his lips, from which he drank mechanically. Then she same and stood where she could watch him through the open door.

'He hears nothing,' she said, as she hung the handkerchief to dry over a chair; and then she went on. 'It was half-past eleven, and my patient had been very uneasy—that is to say, more so even than before. It might have been four or five minutes after the clock had finished striking that he became suddenly quite still, and then began to tremble all over, so that the bed shook with him.' She spoke admirable English, as many of the Sisters do, so I need not translate, but will give her own words.

'He went on trembling until I thought he was going to have a fit, and told Monsieur Magnin to be ready to go for the doctor, when just then the trembling stopped, he became perfectly stiff, his hair stood up upon his head, and his eyes seemed coming out of their sockets, though he could see nothing, for I passed the candle before them. All at once he sprang out of his bed and rushed to the door. I did not know he was so strong. Before he got there I had him in my arms, for he has become very light, and I carried him back to bed again, though he was struggling, like a child. Monsieur Magnin came in from the next room just as he was trying to get up again, and we held him down until it was past, but he screamed Monsieur Souvestre's name for a long time after that. Afterwards he was very cold and exhausted, of course, and I gave him some beef-tea, though it was not the hour for it.'

'I think you had better tell the Sister all about it,' said Magnin turning to me. 'It is the best that the nurse should know everything.'

'Very well,' said I; 'though I do not think it's much in her line.' She answered me herself: 'Everything which concerns our patients is our business. Nothing shocks me.' Thereupon she sat down and thrust her hands into her long sleeves, prepared to listen. I repeated the whole affair as I had done to Magnin. She never took her brilliant eyes from off my face, and listened as coolly as though she had been a doctor hearing an account of a difficult case, though to me it seemed almost sacrilege to be describing the behaviour of a love-stricken youth to a Sister of Charity.

'What do you say to that, *ma sœur?*' asked Magnin, when I had done.

'I say nothing, monsieur. It is sufficient that I know it;' and she withdrew her hands from her sleeves, took up the handkerchief, which was dry by this time, and returned quietly to her place at the bedside.

'I wonder if I have shocked her, after all?' I said to Magnin.

'Oh, no,' he answered. 'They see many things, and a *sœur* is as abstract as a confessor; they do not allow themselves any personal feelings. I have seen Sœur Claudius listen perfectly unmoved to the most abominable ravings, only crossing herself beneath her cape at the most hideous blasphemies. It was late summer when poor Justin Revol died. You were not here.' Magnin put his hand to his forehead.

'You are looking ill yourself,' I said. 'Go and try to sleep, and I will stay.'

'Very well,' he answered; 'but I cannot rest unless you promise to remember everything he says, that I may hear it when I wake;' and he threw himself down on the hard sofa like a sack, and was asleep in a moment; and I, who had felt so angry with him but a few hours ago, put a cushion under his head and made him comfortable.

I sat down in the next room and listened to Detaille's monotonous ravings, while Sœur Claudius read in her book of prayers. It was getting dusk, and several of the academicians stole in and stood over the sick man and shook their heads. They looked around for Magnin, but I pointed to the other room with my finger on my lips, and they nodded and went away on tiptoe.

It required no effort of memory to repeat Detaille's words to Magnin when he woke, for they were always the same. We had another Sister that night, and as Sœur Claudius was not to return till the next day at midday, I offered to share the watch with Magnin, who was getting very nervous and exhausted, and who seemed to think that some such attack might be expected as had occurred the night before. The new sister was a gentle, delicate-looking little woman, with tears in her soft brown eyes as she bent over the sick man, and crossed herself from time to time, grasping the crucifix which hung from the beads at her waist. Nevertheless she was calm and useful, and as punctual as Sœur

Claudius herself in giving the medicines.

The doctor had come in the evening, and prescribed a change in these. He would not say what he thought of his patient, but only declared that it was necessary to wait for a crisis. Magnin sent for some supper, and we sat over it together in the silence, neither of us hungry. He kept looking at his watch.

'If the same thing happens tonight, he will die!' said he, and laid his head on his arms.

'He will die in a most foolish cause, then,' I said angrily, for I thought he was going to cry, as those Frenchmen have a way of doing, and I wanted to irritate him by way of a tonic; so I went on—

'It would be dying for a *vaurien* who is making an ass of himself in a ridiculous business which will be over in a week! Souvestre may get as much fever as he likes! Only don't ask me to come and nurse him.'

'It is not the fever,' said he slowly, 'it is a horrible nameless dread that I have; I suppose it is listening to Detaille that makes me nervous. Hark!' he added, 'it strikes eleven. We must watch!'

'If you really expect another attack you had better warn the Sister,' I said; so he told her in a few words what might happen.

'Very well, monsieur,' she answered, and sat down quietly near the bed, Magnin at the pillow and I near him. No sound was to be heard but Detaille's ceaseless lament.

And now, before I tell you more, I must stop to entreat you to believe me. It will be almost impossible for you to do so, I know, for I have laughed myself at such tales, and no assurances would have made me credit them. But I, Robert Sutton, swear that this thing happened. More I cannot do. It is the truth.

We had been watching Detaille intently. He was lying with closed eyes, and had been very restless. Suddenly he became quite still, and then began to tremble, exactly as Sœur Claudius had described. It was a curious, uniform trembling, apparently in every fibre, and his iron bedstead shook as though strong hands were at its head and foot. Then came the absolute rigidity she had also described, and I do not exaggerate when I say that not only did his short-cropped hair seem to stand erect, but that it literally did so. A lamp cast the shadow of his profile against the wall to the left of his bed, and as I looked at the immovable outline which seemed painted on the wall, I saw the hair slowly rise until the line where it joined the forehead was quite a different one—abrupt instead of a smooth sweep. His eyes opened wide and were frightfully fixed, then as frightfully strained, but they certainly did not see us.

We waited breathlessly for what might follow. The little Sister was standing close to him, her lips pressed together and a little pale, but very calm. 'Do not be frightened, *ma sœur*,' whispered Magnin; and she answered in a business-like tone, 'No, monsieur,' and drew still nearer to her patient, and took his hands, which were stiff as those of a corpse, between her own to warm them. I laid mine upon his heart; it was beating so imperceptibly that I almost thought it had stopped, and as I leaned my face to his lips I could feel no breath issue from them. It seemed as thought the rigour would last for ever.

Suddenly, without any transition, he hurled himself with enormous force, and literally at one bound, almost into the middle of the room, scattering us aside like leaves in the wind. I was upon him in a moment, grappling with him with all my strength, to prevent him from reaching the door. Magnin had been thrown backwards against the table, and I heard the medicine bottles crash with his fall. He had flung back his hand to save himself, and rushed to help me with blood dripping from a cut in his wrist. The little Sister sprang to us. Detaille had thrown her violently back upon her knees, and now, with a nurse's instinct, she tried to throw a shawl over his bare breast. We four must have made a strange group!

Four? *We were five!* Marcello Souvestre stood before us, just within the door! We all saw him, for he was there. His bloodless face was turned towards us unmoved; his hands hung by his side as white as his face; only his eyes had life in them; they were fixed on Detaille.

'Thank God you have come at last!' I cried. 'Don't stand there like a fool! Help us, can't you?' But he never moved. I was furiously angry, and, leaving my hold, sprang upon him to drag him forwards. My outstretched hands struck hard against the door, and I felt a thing like a spider's web envelop me. It seemed to draw itself over my mouth and eyes, and to blind and choke me, and then to flutter and tear and float from me.

Marcello was gone!

Detaille had slipped from Magnin's hold, and lay in a heap upon the floor, as though his limbs were broken. The Sister was trembling violently as she knelt over him and tried to raise his head. We gazed at one another, stooped and lifted him in our arms, and carried him back to his bed, while Sœur Marie quietly collected the broken phials.

'You saw it, *ma sœur?*' I heard Magnin whisper hoarsely.

'Yes, monsieur!' she only answered, in a trembling voice, holding on to her crucifix. Then she said in a professional tone—

'Will monsieur let me bind up his wrist?' And though her fingers trembled and his hand was shaking, the bandage was an irreproachable one.

Magnin went into the next room, and I heard him throw himself heavily into a chair. Detaille seemed to be sleeping. His breath came regularly; his eyes were closed with a look of peace about the lids, his hands lying in a natural way upon the quilt. He had not moved since we laid him there. I went softly to where Magnin was sitting in the dark. He did not move, but only said: 'Marcello is dead!'

'He is either dead or dying,' I answered, 'and we must go to him.'

'Yes,' Magnin whispered, 'we must go to him, but we shall not reach him.'

'We will go as soon as it is light,' I said, and then we were still again.

When the morning came at last he went and found a comrade to take his place, and only said to Sœur Marie, 'It is not necessary to speak of this night;' and at her quiet, 'You are right, monsieur,' we felt we could trust her. Detaille was still sleeping. Was this the crisis the doctor had expected? Perhaps; but surely not in such fearful form. I insisted upon my companion having some breakfast before we started, and I breakfasted myself, but I cannot say I tasted what passed between my lips.

We engaged a closed carriage, for we did not know what we might bring home with us, though neither of us spoke out his thoughts. It was early morning still when we reached the Vigna Marziali, and we had not exchanged a word all the way. I rang at the bell, while the coachman looked on curiously. It was answered promptly by the *guardiano*, of whom Detaille has already told you.

'Where is the Signore?' I asked through the gate.

'*Chi lo sa?*' he answered, 'He is here, of course; he has not left the Vigna. Shall I call him?'

'*Call him?*' I knew that no mortal voice could reach Marcello now, but I tried to fancy he was still alive.

'No,' I said. 'Let us in. We want to surprise him; he will be pleased.'

The man hesitated, but he finally opened the gate, and we entered, leaving the carriage to wait outside. We went straight to the house; the door at the back was wide open. There had been a gale in the night, and it had torn some leaves and bits of twigs from the trees and blown them into the entrance hall. They lay scattered across the threshold, and were evidence that the door had remained open ever since they had fallen. The *guardiano* left us, probably to escape Marcello's anger at having let us in, and we went up the stairs unhindered, Magnin foremost, for he knew the house better than I, from Detaille's description. He had told him about the corner room with the balcony, and we pretended that Marcello might be there, absorbed betimes in his work, but we did not call him.

He was not there. His papers were strewn over the table as though he had been writing, but the inkstand was dry and full of dust; he could not have used it for days. We went silently into the other chambers. Perhaps he was still asleep? But, no! We found his bed untouched, so he could not have lain in it that night. The rooms were all unlocked but one, and this closed door made our hearts beat. Marcello could scarcely be there, however, for there was no key in the lock; I saw the daylight shining through the key-hole. We called his name, but there came no answer. We knocked loudly; still no sign from within; so I put my shoulder to the door, which was old and cracked in several places, and succeeded in bursting it open.

Nothing was there but a sculptor's modelling-stand, with something upon it covered with a white cloth, and the modelling-tools on the floor. At the sight of the cloth, still damp, we drew a deep breath. It could have hung there for many hours, certainly not for twenty-four. We did not raise it. 'He would be vexed,' said Magnin, and I nodded, for it is accounted almost a crime in the artist's world to unveil a sculptor's work behind his back. We expressed no surprise at the fact of his modelling: a ban seemed to lie upon our tongues. The cloth hung tightly to the object beneath it, and showed us the outline of a woman's head and rounded-bust, and so veiled we left her. There was a little winding stair leading out of the passage, and we climbed it, to find ourselves in a sort of belvedere, commanding a superb view. It was a small, open terrace, on the roof of the house, and we saw at a glance that no one was there.

We had now been all over the casino, which was small and simply built, being evidentally intended only for short summer use. As we stood leaning over the balustrade we could look down into the garden. No one was there but the *guardiano*, lying amongst his cabbages with his arms behind his head, half asleep. The laurel grove had been in my mind from the beginning, only it had seemed more natural to go to the house first. Now we descended the stairs silently and directed our steps thither.

As we approached it, the *guardiano* came towards us lazily.

'Have you seen the Signore?' he asked, and his stupidly placid face showed me that he, at least, had no hand in his disappearance.

'No, not yet,' I answered, 'but we shall come across him somewhere, no doubt. Perhaps he has gone to take a walk, and we will wait for him. What is this?' I went on, trying to seem careless. We were standing now by the little arch of which you know.

'This?' said he; 'I have never been down there, but they say it is something old. Do the Signori want to see it? I will fetch a lantern.'

I nodded, and he went off to his cabin. I had a couple of candles in my pocket, for I had intended to explore the place, should we not find Marcello. It was there that he had disappeared that night, and my thoughts had been busy with it; but I kept my candles concealed, reflecting that they would give our search an air of premeditation which would excite curiosity.

'When did you see the Signore last?' I asked, when he had returned with the lantern.

'I brought him his supper yesterday evening.'

'At what o'clock?'

'It was the Ave Maria, Signore,' he replied. 'He always sups then.'

It would be useless to put any more questions. He was evidently utterly unobserving, and would lie to please us.

'Let me go first,' said Magnin, taking the lantern. We set our feet upon the steps; a cold air seemed to fill our lungs and yet to choke us, and a thick darkness lay beneath. The steps, as I could see by the light of my candle, were modern, as well as the vaulting above them. A tablet was let into the wall, and in spite of my excitement I paused to read it, perhaps because I was glad to delay whatever awaited us below. It ran thus:

'Questo antico sepolcro Romano scoprì il Conte Marziali nell' anno 1853, e piamente conservò.' In plain English:

'Count Marziali discovered this ancient Roman sepulchre in the year 1853, and piously preserved it.'

I read it more quickly than it has taken time to write here, and hurried after Magnin, whose footsteps sounded faintly below me. As I hastened, a draught of cold air extinguished my candle, and I was trying to make my way down by feeling along the wall, which was horribly dark and clammy, when my heart stood still at a cry from far beneath me—a cry of horror!

'Where are you?' I shouted; but Magnin was calling my name, and could not hear me. 'I am here. I am in the dark!'

I was making haste as fast as I could, but there were several turnings.

'I have found him!' came up from below.

'Alive?' I shouted. No answer.

One last short flight brought me face to face with the gleam of the lantern. It came from a low doorway, and within stood Magnin, peering into the darkness. I knew by his face, as he held the light high above him, that our fears were realized.

Yes; Marcello was there. He was lying stretched upon the floor, staring at the ceiling, dead, and already stiff, as I could see at a glance. We stood over him, saying not a word, then I knelt down and felt him, for mere form's sake, and said, as though I had not known it before, 'He has been dead for some hours.'

'Since yesterday evening,' said Magnin, in a horror-stricken voice, yet with a certain satisfaction in it, as though to say, 'You see, I was right.'

Marcello was lying with his head slightly thrown back, no contortions in his handsome features; rather the look of a person who has quietly died of exhaustion—who has slipped unconsciously from life to death. His collar was thrown open and a part of his breast, of a ghastly white, was visible. Just over the heart was a small spot.

'Give me the lantern,' I whispered, as I stooped over it. It was a very little spot, of a faint purplish-brown, and must have changed colour within the night.

I examined it intently, and should say that the blood had been sucked to the surface, and then a small prick or incision made. The slight subcutaneous effusion led me to this conclusion. One tiny drop of coagulated blood closed the almost imperceptible wound. I probed it with the end of one of Magnin's matches. It was scarcely more than skin deep, so it could not be the stab of a stiletto, however slender, or the track of a bullet. Still, it was strange, and with one impulse we turned to see if no one were concealed there, or if there were no second exit. It would be madness to suppose that the murderer, if there was one, would remain by his victim. Had Marcello been making love to a pretty *contadina*, and was this some jealous lover's vengeance? But it was not a stab. Had one drop of poison in the little wound done this deadly work?

We peered about the place, and I saw that Magnin's eyes were blinded by tears and his face as pale as that upturned one on the floor, whose lids I had vainly tried to close. The chamber was low, and beautifully ornamented with stucco bas-reliefs, in the manner of the well-known one not far from there upon the same road. Winged genii, griffins, and arabesques, modelled with marvellous lightness, covered the walls and ceiling. There was no other door than the one we had entered by. In the centre stood a marble sarcophagus, with the usual subjects sculptured upon it, on the one side Hercules conducting a veiled figure, on the other a dance of nymphs and fauns. A space in the middle contained the following inscription, deeply cut in the stone, and still partially filled with red pigment:

D. M.
VESPERTILIAE·THC·AIMA-
TOΠΩΤΙΔOC · Q · FLAVIVS ·
VIX·IPSE·SOSPES·MON·
POSVIT

'What is this?' whispered Magnin. It was only a pickaxe and a long crowbar, such as the country people use in hewing out their blocks of 'tufa', and his foot had struck against them. Who could have brought them here? They must belong to the *guardiano* above, but he said that he had never come here, and I believed him, knowing the Italian horror of darkness and lonely places; but what had Marcello wanted with them? It did not occur to us that archaeological curiosity could have led him to attempt to open the sarcophagus, the lid of which had evidently never been raised, thus justifying the expression, 'piously preserved'.

As I rose from examining the tools my eyes fell upon the line of mortar where the cover joined to the stone below, and I noticed that some of it had been removed, perhaps with the pickaxe which lay at my feet. I tried it with my nails and found that it was very crumbly. Without a word I took the tool in my hand, Magnin instinctively following my movements with the lantern. What impelled us I do not know. I had myself no thought, only an irresistible desire to see what was within. I saw that much of the mortar had been broken away, and lay in small fragments upon the ground, which I had not noticed before. It did not take long to complete the work. I snatched the lantern from Magnin's hand and set it upon the ground, where it shone full upon Marcello's dead face, and by its light I found a little break between the two masses of stone and managed to insert the end of my crowbar, driving it in with a blow of the pickaxe. The stone chipped and then cracked a little. Magnin was shivering.

'What are you going to do?' he said, looking around at where Marcello lay.

'Help me!' I cried, and we two bore with all our might upon the crowbar. I am a strong man, and I felt a sort of blind fury as the stone refused to yield. What if the bar should snap? With another blow I drove it in still further, then using it as a lever, we weighed upon it with our outstretched arms until every muscle was at its highest tension. The stone moved a little, and almost fainting we stopped to rest.

From the ceiling hung the rusty remnant of an iron chain which must once have held a lamp. To this, by scrambling upon the sarcophagus, I contrived to make fast the lantern.

'Now!' said I, and we heaved again at the lid. It rose, and we alternately heaved and pushed until it lost its balance and fell with a thundering crash upon the other side; such a crash that the walls seemed to shake, and I was for a moment utterly deafened, while little pieces of stucco rained upon us from the ceiling. When we had paused to recover from the shock we leaned over the sarcophagus and looked in.

The light shone full upon it, and we saw—how is it possible to tell? We saw lying there, amidst folds of mouldering rags, the body of a woman, perfect as in life, with faintly rosy face, soft crimson lips, and a breast of living pearl, which seemed to heave as though stirred by some delicious dream. The rotten stuff swathed about her was in ghastly contrast to this lovely form, fresh as the morning! Her hands lay stretched at her side, the pink palms were turned a little outwards, her eyes were closed as peacefully as those of a sleeping child, and her long hair, which shone red-gold in the dim light from above, was wound around her head in numberless finely plaited tresses, beneath which little locks escaped in rings upon her brow. I could have sworn that the blue veins on that divinely perfect bosom held living blood!

We were absolutely paralyzed, and Magnin leaned gasping over the edge as pale as death, paler by far than this living, almost smiling face to which his eyes were glued. I do not doubt that I was as pale as he at this inexplicable vision. As I looked the red lips seemed to grow redder. They *were* redder! The little pearly teeth showed between them. I had not seen them before, and now a clear ruby drop trickled down to her rounded chin and from there slipped sideways and fell upon her neck. Horror-struck I gazed upon the living corpse, till my eyes could not bear the sight any longer. As I looked away my glance fell once more upon the inscription, but now I could see—*and read*—it all. 'To Vespertilia'—that was in Latin, and even the Latin name of the woman suggested a thing of evil flitting in the dusk. But the full horror of the nature of that thing had been veiled to Roman eyes under the Greek της αἱματοπωτίδος, 'The blood-drinker, the vampire woman.' And Flavius—her lover—*vix ipse sospes*, 'himself hardly saved' from that deadly embrace, had buried her here, and set a seal upon her sepulchre, trusting to the weight of stone and the strength of clinging mortar to imprison for ever the beautiful monster he had loved.

'Infamous murderess!' I cried, 'you have killed Marcello!' and a sudden, vengeful calm came over me.

'Give me the pickaxe,' I said to Magnin; I can hear myself saying it still. He picked it up and handed it to me as in a dream; he seemed little better than an idiot, and the beads of sweat were shining on his forehead. I took my knife, and from the long wooden handle of the pickaxe I cut a fine, sharp stake. Then I clambered, scarcely feeling any repugnance, over the side of the sarcophagus, my feet amongst the folds of Vespertilia's decaying winding-sheet, which crushed like ashes beneath my boot.

I looked for one moment at that white breast, but only to choose the loveliest spot, where the network of azure veins shimmered like veiled turquoises, and then with one blow I drove the pointed stake deep down through the breathing snow and stamped it in with my heel.

An awful shriek, so ringing and horrible that I thought my ears must have burst; but even then I felt neither fear nor horror. There are times when these cannot touch us. I stopped and gazed once again at the face, now undergoing a fearful change—fearful and final!

'Foul vampire!' I said quietly in my concentrated rage. 'You will do no more harm now!' And then, without looking back upon her cursed face, I clambered out of the horrible tomb.

We raised Marcello, and slowly carried him up the steep stairs—a difficult task, for the way was narrow and he was so stiff. I noticed that the steps were ancient up to the end of the second flight; above, the modern passage was somewhat broader. When we reached the top, the *guardiano* was lying upon one of the stone benches; he did not mean us to cheat him out of his fee. I gave him a couple of francs.

'You see that we have found the signore,' I tried to say in a natural voice. 'He is very weak, and we will carry him to the carriage.' I had thrown my handkerchief over Marcello's face, but the man knew as well as I did that he was dead. Those stiff feet told their own story, but Italians are timid of being involved in such affairs. They have a childish dread of the police, and he only answered, 'Poor signorino! He is very ill; it is better to take him to Rome,' and kept cautiously clear of us as we went up to the ilex alley with our icy burden, and he did not go to the gate with us, not liking to be observed by the coachman who was dozing on his box. With difficulty we got Marcello's corpse into the carriage, the driver turning to look at us suspiciously. I explained we had found our friend very ill, and at the same time slipped a gold piece into his hand, telling him to drive to the Via del Governo Vecchio. He pocketed the money, and whipped his horses into a trot, while we sat supporting the stiff body, which swayed like a broken doll at every pebble in the road. When we reached the Via del Governo Vecchio at last, no one saw us carry him into the house. There was no step before the door, and we drew up so close to it that it was possible to screen our burden from sight. When we had brought him into his room and laid him upon his bed, we noticed that his eyes were closed; from the movement of the carriage, perhaps, though that was scarcely possible. The landlady behaved very much as I had expected her to do, for, as I told you, I know the Italians. She pretended, too, that the signore was very ill, and made a pretence of offering to fetch a doctor, and when I thought it best to tell her that he was dead, declared that it must have happened that very moment, for she had seen him look at us and close his eyes again. She had always told him that he ate too little and that he would be ill. Yes, it was weakness and that bad air out there which had killed him; and then he worked too hard. When she had successfully established this fiction, which we were glad enough to agree to, for neither did we wish for the publicity of an inquest, she ran out and fetched a gossip to come and keep her company.

So died Marcello Souvestre, and so died Vespertilia the blood-drinker at last.

There is not much more to tell. Marcello lay calm and beautiful upon his bed, and the students came and stood silently looking at him, then knelt down for a moment to say a prayer, crossed themselves, and left him for ever.

We hastened to the Villa Medici, where Detaille was sleeping, and Sister Claudius watching him with a satisfied look on her strong face. She rose noiselessly at our entrance, and came to us at the threshold.

'He will recover,' said she, softly. She was right. When he awoke and opened his eyes he knew us directly, and Magnin breathed a devout 'Thank God!'

'Have I been ill, Magnin?' he asked, very feebly.

'You have had a little fever,' answered Magnin, promptly; 'but it is over now. Here is Monsieur Sutton come to see you.'

'Has Marcello been here?' was the next question. Magnin looked at him very steadily.

'No,' he only said, letting his face tell the rest.

'Is he dead, then?' Magnin only bowed his head. 'Poor friend!' Detaille murmured to himself, then closed his heavy eyes and slept again.

A few days after Marcello's funeral we went to the fatal Vigna Marziali to bring back the objects which had belonged to him. As I laid the manuscript score of the opera carefully together, my eye fell upon a passage which struck me as the identical one which Detaille had so constantly sung in his delirium, and which I noted down. Strange to say, when I reminded him of it later, it was perfectly new to him, and he declared that Marcello had not let him examine his manuscript. As for the veiled bust in the other room, we left it undisturbed, and to crumble away unseen.

KEN'S MYSTERY

Julian Hawthorne

Julian Hawthorne (1846–1934) was a busy writer and editor for sixty years, with a penchant for the weird and the fantastic, like his more celebrated father—Nathaniel Hawthorne—before him. One of his best short stories in this vein is the little-known Irish vampire tale 'Ken's Mystery', which appeared in his collection *David Poindexter's Disappearance* (1888). Julian Hawthorne was acquainted with Bram Stoker, and was a frequent guest at the Lyceum during his visits to London. This tale may have given Stoker some ideas and inspiration, nine years before the publication of *Dracula*. Stories about vampires in Ireland are particularly rare.

ONE cool October evening—it was the last day of the month, and unusually cool for the time of year—I made up my mind to go and spend an hour or two with my friend Keningale. Keningale was an artist (as well as a musical amateur and poet), and had a very delightful studio built onto his house, in which he was wont to sit of an evening. The studio had a cavernous fire-place, designed in imitation of the old-fashioned fire-places of Elizabethan manor-houses, and in it, when the temperature out-doors warranted, he would build up a cheerful fire of dry logs. It would suit me particularly well, I thought, to go and have a quiet pipe and chat in front of that fire with my friend.

I had not had such a chat for a very long time—not, in fact, since Keningale (or Ken, as his friends called him) had returned from his visit to Europe the year before. He went abroad, as he affirmed at the time, 'for purposes of study', whereat we all smiled, for Ken, so far as we knew him, was more likely to do anything else than to study. He was a young fellow of buoyant temperament, lively and social in his habits, of a brilliant and versatile mind, and possessing an income of twelve or fifteen thousand dollars a year; he could sing, play, scribble, and paint very cleverly, and some of his heads and figure-pieces were really well done, considering that he never had any regular training in art; but he was not a worker. Personally he was fine-looking, of good height and figure, active, healthy, and with a remarkably fine brow, and clear, full-gazing eye. Nobody was surprised at his going to Europe, nobody expected him to do anything there except amuse himself, and few anticipated that he would be soon again seen in New York. He was one of the sort that find Europe agrees with them. Off he went, therefore; and in the course of a few months the rumour reached us that he was engaged to a handsome and wealthy New York girl whom he had met in London. This was nearly all we did hear of him until, not very long afterward, he turned up again on Fifth Avenue, to every one's astonishment; made no satisfactory answer to those who wanted to know how he happened to tire so soon of the Old World; while, as to the reported engagement, he cut short all allusion to that in so peremptory a manner as to show that it was not a permissible topic of conversation with him. It was surmised that the lady had jilted him; but on the other hand, she herself returned home not a great while after, and, though she had plenty of opportunities, she has never married to this day.

Be the rights of that matter what they may, it was soon remarked that Ken was no longer the careless and merry fellow he used to be; on the contrary, he appeared grave, moody, averse from general society, and habitually taciturn and undemonstrative even in the company of his most intimate friends. Evidently something had happened to him, or he had done something. What? Had he committed a murder? or joined the Nihilists? or was his unsuccessful love affair at the bottom of it? Some declared that the cloud was only temporary, and would soon pass away. Nevertheless, up to the period of which I am writing, it had not passed away, but had rather gathered additional gloom, and threatened to become permanent.

Meanwhile I had met him twice or thrice at the club, at the opera, or in the street, but had as yet had no opportunity of regularly renewing my acquaintance with him. We had been on a footing of more than common intimacy in the old days, and I was not disposed to think that he would refuse to renew the former relations now. But what I had heard and myself seen of his changed condition imparted a stimulating tinge of suspense or curiosity to the pleasure with which I looked forward to the prospects of this evening. His house stood at a distance of two or three miles beyond the general range of habitations in New York at this time, and as I walked briskly along in the clear twilight air I had leisure to go over in my mind all that I had known of Ken and had divined of his character. After all, had there not always been something in his nature—deep down, and held in abeyance by the activity of his animal spirits—but something strange and separate, and capable of developing under suitable conditions into—into what? As I asked myself this question I arrived at his door; and it was with a feeling of relief that I felt the next moment the cordial grasp of his hand, and his voice bidding me welcome in a tone that indicated unaffected gratification at my presence. He drew me at once into the studio, relieved me of my hat and cane, and then put his hand on my shoulder.

'I am glad to see you,' he repeated, with singular earnestness—'glad to see you and to feel you; and tonight of all nights in the year.'

'Why tonight especially?'

'Oh, never mind. It's just as well, too, you didn't let me know beforehand you were coming; the unreadiness is all, to paraphrase the poet. Now, with you to help me, I can drink a glass of whisky and water and take a bit draw of the pipe. This would have been a grim night for me if I'd been left to myself.'

'In such a lap of luxury as this, too!' said I, looking round at the glowing fire-place, the low, luxurious chairs, and all the rich and sumptuous fittings of the room. 'I should have thought a condemned murderer might make himself comfortable here.'

'Perhaps; but that's not exactly my category at present. But have you forgotten what night this is? This is November-eve, when, as tradition asserts, the dead arise and walk about, and fairies, goblins, and spiritual beings of all kinds have more freedom and power than on any other day of the year. One can see you've never been in Ireland.'

'I wasn't aware till now that you had been there, either.'

'Yes, I have been in Ireland. Yes—' He paused, sighed, and fell into a reverie, from which, however, he soon roused himself by an effort, and went to a cabinet in a corner of the room for the liquor and tobacco. While he was thus employed I sauntered about the studio, taking note of the various beauties, grotesquenesses, and curiosities that it contained. Many things were there to repay study and arouse admiration; for Ken was a good collector, having excellent taste as well as means to back it. But, upon the whole, nothing interested me more than some studies of a female head, roughly done in oils, and, judging from the sequestered positions in which I found them, not intended by the artist for exhibition or criticism. There were three or four of these studies, all of the same face, but in different poses and costumes. In one the head was enveloped in a dark hood, overshadowing and partly concealing the features; in another she seemed to be peering duskily through a latticed casement, lit by a faint moonlight; a third showed her splendidly attired in evening costume, and jewels in her hair and ears, and sparkling on her snowy bosom. The expressions were as various as the poses; now it was demure penetration, now a subtle inviting glance, now burning passion, and again a look of elfish and elusive mockery. In whatever phase, the countenance possessed a singular and poignant fascination, not of beauty merely, though that was very striking, but of character and quality likewise.

'Did you find this model abroad?' I inquired at length. 'She has evidently inspired you, and I don't wonder at it.'

Ken, who had been mixing the punch, and had not noticed my movements, now looked up, and said: 'I didn't mean those to be seen. They don't satisfy me, and I am going to destroy them; but I couldn't rest till I'd made some attempts to reproduce— What was it you asked? Abroad? Yes—or no. They were all painted here within the last six weeks.'

'Whether they satisfy you or not, they are by far the best things of yours I have ever seen.'

'Well, let them alone, and tell me what you think of this beverage. To my thinking, it goes to the right spot. It owes its existence to your coming here. I can't drink alone, and those portraits are not company, though, for aught I know, she might have come out of the canvas tonight and sat down in that chair.' Then, seeing my inquiring look, he added, with a hasty laugh, 'It's November-eve, you know, when anything may happen, provided it's strange enough. Well, here's to ourselves.'

We each swallowed a deep draught of the smoking and aromatic liquor, and set down our glasses with approval. The punch was excellent. Ken now opened a box of cigars, and we seated ourselves before the fire-place.

'All we need now,' I remarked, after a short silence, 'is a little music. By-the-by, Ken, have you still got the banjo I gave you before you went abroad?'

He paused so long before replying that I supposed he had not heard my question. 'I have got it,' he said, at length, 'but it will never make any more music.'

'Got broken, eh? Can't it be mended? It was a fine instrument.'

'It's not broken, but it's past mending. You shall see for yourself.'

He arose as he spoke, and going to another part of the studio, opened a black oak coffer, and took out of it a long object wrapped up in a piece of faded yellow silk. He handed it to me, and when I had unwrapped it, there appeared a thing that might once have been a banjo, but had little resemblance to one now. It bore every sign of extreme age. The wood of the handle was honey-combed with the gnawings of worms, and dusty with dry-rot. The parchment head was green with mould, and hung in shrivelled tatters. The hoop, which was of solid silver, was so blackened and tarnished that it looked like dilapidated iron. The strings were gone, and most of the tuning-screws had dropped out of their decayed sockets. Altogether it had the appearance of having been made before the Flood, and been forgotten in the forecastle of Noah's Ark ever since.

'It is a curious relic, certainly,' I said. 'Where did you come across it? I had no idea that the banjo was invented so long ago as this. It certainly can't be less than two hundred years old, and may be much older than that.'

Ken smiled gloomily. 'You are quite right,' he said; 'it is at least two hundred years old, and yet it is the very same banjo that you gave me a year ago.'

'Hardly,' I returned, smiling in my turn, 'since that was made to my order with a view to presenting it to you.'

'I know that; but the two hundred years have passed since then. Yes; it is absurd and impossible, I know, but nothing is truer. That banjo, which was made last year, existed in the sixteenth century, and has been rotting ever since. Stay. Give it to me a moment, and I'll convince you. You recollect that your name and mine, with the date, were engraved on the silver hoop?'

'Yes; and there was a private mark of my own there, also.'

'Very well,' said Ken, who had been rubbing a place on the hoop with a corner of the yellow silk wrapper; 'look at that.'

I took the decrepit instrument from him, and examined the spot which he had rubbed. It was incredible, sure enough; but there were the names and the date precisely as I had caused them to be engraved; and there, moreover, was my own private mark, which I had idly made with an old etching point not more than eighteen months before. After convincing myself that there was no mistake, I laid the banjo across my knees, and stared at my friend in bewilderment. He sat smoking with a kind of grim composure, his eyes fixed upon the blazing logs.

'I'm mystified, I confess,' said I. 'Come; what is the joke? What method have you discovered of producing the decay of centuries on this unfortunate banjo in a few months? And why did you do it? I have heard of an elixir to counteract the effects of time, but your recipe seems to work the other way—to make time rush forward at two hundred times his usual rate, in one place, while he jogs on at his usual gait elsewhere. Unfold your mystery, magician. Seriously, Ken, how on earth did the thing happen?'

'I know no more about it than you do,' was his reply. 'Either you and I and all the rest of the living world are insane, or else there has been wrought a miracle as strange as any in tradition. How can I explain it? It is a common saying—a common experience, if you will—that we may, on certain trying or tremendous occasions, live years in one moment. But that's a mental experience, not a physical one, and one that applies, at all events, only to human beings, not to senseless things of wood and metal. You imagine the thing is some trick or jugglery. If it be, I don't know the secret of it. There's no chemical appliance that I ever heard of that will get a piece of solid wood into that condition in a few months, or a few years. And it wasn't done in a few years, or a few months either. A year ago today at this very hour that banjo was as sound as when it left the maker's hands, and twenty-four hours afterward—I'm telling you the simple truth—it was as you see it now.'

The gravity and earnestness with which Ken made this astounding statement were evidently not assumed. He believed every word that he uttered. I knew not what to think. Of course my friend might be insane, though he betrayed none of the ordinary symptoms of mania; but, however that might be, there was the banjo, a witness whose silent testimony there was no gainsaying. The more I meditated on the matter the more inconceivable did it appear. Two hundred years— twenty-four hours; these were the terms of the proposed equation. Ken and the banjo both affirmed that the equation had been made; all worldly knowledge and experience affirmed it to be impossible. What was the explanation? What is time? What is life? I felt myself beginning to doubt the reality of all things. And so this was the mystery which my friend had been brooding over since his return from abroad. No wonder it had changed him. More to be wondered at was it that it had not changed him more.

'Can you tell me the whole story?' I demanded at length.

Ken quaffed another draught from his glass of whisky and water and rubbed his hand through his thick brown beard. 'I have never spoken to any one of it heretofore,' he said, 'and I had never meant to speak of it. But I'll try and give you some idea of what it was. You know me better than any one else; you'll understand the thing as far as it can ever be understood, and perhaps I may be relieved of some of the oppression it has caused me. For it is rather a ghastly memory to grapple with alone, I can tell you.'

Hereupon, without further preface, Ken related the following tale. He was, I may observe in passing, a naturally fine narrator. There were deep, lingering tones in his voice, and he could strikingly enhance the comic or pathetic effect of a sentence by dwelling here and there upon some syllable. His features were equally susceptible of humorous and of solemn expressions, and his eyes were in form and hue wonderfully adapted to showing great varieties of emotion. Their mournful aspect was extremely earnest and affecting; and when Ken was giving utterance to some mysterious passage of the tale they had a doubtful, melancholy, exploring look which appealed irresistibly to the imagination. But the interest of his story was too pressing to allow of noticing these incidental embellishments at the time, though they doubtless had their influence upon me all the same.

'I left New York on an Inman Line steamer, you remember,' began Ken, 'and landed at Havre. I went the usual round of sight-seeing on the Continent, and got round to London in July, at the height of the season. I had good introductions, and met any number of agreeable and famous people. Among others was a young lady, a countrywoman of my own—you know whom I mean—who interested me very much, and before her family left London she and I were engaged. We parted there for the time, because she had the Continental trip still to make, while I wanted to take the opportunity to visit the north of England and Ireland. I landed at Dublin about the 1st of October, and, zigzagging about the country, I found myself in County Cork about two weeks later.

'There is in that region some of the most lovely scenery that human eyes ever rested on, and it seems to be less known to tourists than many places of infinitely less picturesque value. A lonely region too: during my rambles I met not a single stranger like myself, and few enough natives. It seems incredible that so beautiful a country should be so deserted. After walking a dozen Irish miles you come across a group of two or three one-roomed cottages, and, like as not, one or more of those will have the roof off and the walls in ruins. The few peasants whom one sees, however, are affable and hospitable, especially when they hear you are from that terrestrial heaven whither most of their friends and relatives have gone before them. They seem simple and primitive enough at first sight, and yet they are as strange and incomprehensible a race as any in the world. They are as superstitious, as credulous of marvels, fairies, magicians, and omens, as the men whom St Patrick preached to, and at the same time they are shrewd, sceptical, sensible, and bottomless liars. Upon the whole, I met with no nation on my travels whose company I enjoyed so much, or who inspired me with so much kindliness, curiosity, and repugnance.

'At length I got to a place on the sea-coast, which I will not further specify than to say that it is not many miles from Ballymacheen, on the south shore. I have seen Venice and Naples, I have driven along the Cornice Road, I have spent a month at our own Mount Desert, and I say that all of them together are not so beautiful as this glowing, deep-hued, soft-gleaming, silvery-lighted, ancient harbour and town, with the tall hills crowding round it and the black cliffs and headlands planting their iron feet in the blue, transparent sea. It is a very old place, and has had a history which it has outlived ages since. It may once have had two or three thousand inhabitants; it has scarce five or six hundred today. Half the houses are in ruins or have disappeared; many of the remainder are standing empty. All the people are poor, most of them abjectly so; they saunter about with bare feet and uncovered heads, the women in quaint black or dark-blue cloaks, the men in such anomalous attire as only an Irishman knows how to get together, the children half naked. The only comfortable-looking people are the monks and the priests, and the soldiers in the fort. For there is a fort there, constructed on the huge ruins of one which may have done duty in the reign of Edward the Black Prince, or earlier, in whose mossy embrasures are mounted a couple of cannon, which occasionally sent a practice-shot or two at the cliff on the other side of the harbour. The garrison consists of a dozen men and three or four officers and non-commissioned officers. I suppose they are relieved occasionally, but those I saw seemed to have become component parts of their surroundings.

'I put up at a wonderful little old inn, the only one in the place, and took my meals in a dining-saloon fifteen feet by nine, with a portrait of George I (a print varnished to preserve it) hanging over the mantel-piece. On the second evening after dinner a young gentleman came in—the dining-saloon being public property of course—and ordered some bread and cheese and a bottle of Dublin stout. We presently fell into talk; he turned out to be an officer from the fort, Lieutenant O'Connor, and a fine young specimen of the Irish soldier he was. After telling me all he knew about the town, the surrounding country, his friends, and himself, he intimated a readiness to sympathize with whatever tale I might choose to pour into his ear; and I had pleasure in trying to rival his own outspokenness. We became excellent friends; we had up a half-pint of Kinahan's whisky, and the lieutenant expressed himself in terms of high praise of my countrymen, my country, and my own particular cigars. When it became time for him to depart I accompanied him—for there was a splendid moon abroad—and bade him farewell at the fort entrance, having promised to come over the next day and make the acquaintance of the other fellows. 'And mind your eye, now, going back, my dear boy,' he called out, as I turned my face homeward. 'Faith, 'tis a spooky place, that graveyard, and you'll as likely meet the black woman there as anywhere else!'

'The graveyard was a forlorn and barren spot on the hill-side, just the hither side of the fort: thirty or forty rough head-stones, few of which retained any semblance of the perpendicular, while many were so shattered and decayed as to seem nothing more than irregular natural projections from the ground. Who the black woman might be I knew not, and did not stay to inquire. I had never been subject to ghostly apprehensions, and as a matter of fact, though the path I had to follow was in places very bad going, not to mention a haphazard scramble over a ruined bridge that covered a deep-lying brook, I reached my inn without any adventure whatever.

'The next day I kept my appointment at the fort, and found no reason to regret it; and my friendly sentiments were abundantly reciprocated, thanks more especially, perhaps, to the success of my banjo, which I carried with me, and which was as novel as it was popular with those who listened to it. The chief personages in the social circle besides my friend the lieutenant were Major Molloy, who was in command, a racy and juicy old campaigner, with a face like a sunset, and the surgeon, Dr Dudeen, a long, dry, humorous genius, with a wealth of anecdotical and traditional lore at his command that I have never seen surpassed. We had a jolly time of it, and it was the precursor of many more like it. The remains of October slipped away rapidly, and I was obliged to remember that I was a traveller in Europe, and not a resident in Ireland. The major, the surgeon, and the lieutenant all

protested cordially against my proposed departure, but, as there was no
help for it, they arranged a farewell dinner to take place in the fort on
All-halloween.

'I wish you could have been at that dinner with me! It was the essence
of Irish good-fellowship. Dr Dudeen was in great force; the major was
better than the best of Lever's novels; the lieutenant was overflowing
with hearty good-humour, merry chaff, and sentimental rhapsodies
anent this or the other pretty girl of the neighbourhood. For my part I
made the banjo ring as it had never rung before, and the others joined in
the chorus with a mellow strength of lungs such as you don't often hear
outside of Ireland. Among the stories that Dr Dudeen regaled us with
was one about the Kern of Querin and his wife, Ethelind Fionguala—
which being interpreted signifies "the white-shouldered". The lady, it
appears, was originally betrothed to one O'Connor (here the lieutenant
smacked his lips), but was stolen away on the wedding night by a party
of vampires, who, it would seem, were at that period a prominent
feature among the troubles of Ireland. But as they were bearing her
along—she being unconscious—to that supper where she was not to eat
but to be eaten, the young Kern of Querin, who happened to be out
duck-shooting, met the party, and emptied his gun at it. The vampires
fled, and the Kern carried the fair lady, still in a state of insensibility, to
his house. "And by the same token, Mr Keningale," observed the
doctor, knocking the ashes out of his pipe, "ye're after passing that
very house on your way here. The one with the dark archway
underneath it, and the big mullioned window at the corner, ye
recollect, hanging over the street as I might say—"

'"Go 'long wid the house, Dr Dudeen, dear," interrupted the
lieutenant; "sure can't you see we're all dying to know what happened
to sweet Miss Fionguala, God be good to her, when I was after getting
her safe upstairs—"

'"Faith, then, I can tell ye that myself, Mr O'Connor," exclaimed
the major, imparting a rotary motion to the remnants of whisky in his
tumbler. "'Tis a question to be solved on general principles, as Colonel
O'Halloran said that time he was asked what he'd do if he'd been the
Dook o' Wellington, and the Prussions hadn't come up in the nick o'
time at Waterloo. "Faith," says the colonel, "I'll tell ye—"

'"Arrah, then, major, why would ye be interruptin' the doctor, and
Mr Keningale there lettin' his glass stay empty till he hears— The Lord
save us! the bottle's empty!"

'In the excitement consequent upon this discovery, the thread of the
doctor's story was lost; and before it could be recovered the evening
had advanced so far that I felt obliged to withdraw. It took some time
to make my proposition heard and comprehended; and a still longer
time to put it in execution; so that it was fully midnight before I found
myself standing in the cool pure air outside the fort, with the farewells

of my boon companions ringing in my ears.

'Considering that it had been rather a wet evening indoors, I was in a remarkably good state of preservation, and I therefore ascribed it rather to the roughness of the road than to the smoothness of the liquor, when, after advancing a few rods, I stumbled and fell. As I picked myself up I fancied I had heard a laugh, and supposed that the lieutenant, who had accompanied me to the gate, was making merry over my mishap; but on looking round I saw that the gate was closed and no one was visible. The laugh, moreover, had seemed to be close at hand, and to be even pitched in a key that was rather feminine than masculine. Of course I must have been deceived; nobody was near me: my imagination had played me a trick, or else there was more truth than poetry in the tradition that Halloween is the carnival-time of disembodied spirits. It did not occur to me at the time that a stumble is held by the superstitious Irish to be an evil omen, and had I remembered it it would only have been to laugh at it. At all events, I was physically none the worse for my fall, and I resumed my way immediately.

'But the path was singularly difficult to find, or rather the path I was following did not seem to be the right one. I did not recognize it; I could have sworn (except I knew the contrary) that I had never seen it before. The moon had risen, though her light was as yet obscured by clouds, but neither my immediate suroundings nor the general aspect of the region appeared familiar. Dark, silent hill-sides mounted up on either hand, and the road, for the most part, plunged downward, as if to conduct me into the bowels of the earth. The place was alive with strange echoes, so that at times I seemed to be walking through the midst of muttering voices and mysterious whispers, and a wild, faint sound of laughter seemed ever and anon to reverberate among the passes of the hills. Currents of colder air sighing up through narrow defiles and dark crevices touched my face as with airy fingers. A certain feeling of anxiety and insecurity began to take possession of me, though there was no definable cause for it, unless that I might be belated in getting home. With the perverse instinct of those who are lost I hastened my steps, but was impelled now and then to glance back over my shoulder, with a sensation of being pursued. But no living creature was in sight. The moon, however, had now risen higher, and the clouds that were drifting slowly across the sky flung into the naked valley dusky shadows, which occasionally assumed shapes that looked like the vague semblance of gigantic human forms.

'How long I had been hurrying onward I know not, when, with a kind of suddenness, I found myself approaching a graveyard. It was situated on the spur of a hill, and there was no fence around it, nor anything to protect it from the incursions of passers-by. There was something in the general appearance of this spot that made me half fancy I had seen it before; and I should have taken it to be the same that I had often noticed on my way to the fort, but that the latter was only a few hundred yards distant therefrom, whereas I must have traversed several miles at least. As I drew near, moreover, I observed that the head-stones did not appear so ancient and decayed as those of the other. But what chiefly attracted my attention was the figure that was leaning or half sitting upon one of the largest of the upright slabs near the road. It was a female figure draped in black, and a closer inspection—for I was soon within a few yards of her—showed that she wore the calla, or long hooded cloak, the most common as well as the most ancient garment of Irish women, and doubtless of Spanish origin.

'I was a trifle startled by this apparition, so unexpected as it was, and so strange did it seem that any human creature should be at that hour of the night in so desolate and sinister a place. Involuntarily I paused as I came opposite her, and gazed at her intently. But the moonlight fell behind her, and the deep hood of her cloak so completely shadowed her face that I was unable to discern anything but the sparkle of a pair of eyes, which appeared to be returning my gaze with much vivacity.

'"You seem to be at home here," I said, at length. "Can you tell me where I am?"

'Hereupon the mysterious personage broke into a light laugh, which, though in itself musical and agreeable, was of a timbre and intonation that caused my heart to beat rather faster than my late pedestrian exertions warranted; for it was the identical laugh (or so my imagination persuaded me) that had echoed in my ears as I arose from my tumble an hour or two ago. For the rest, it was the laugh of a young woman, and presumably of a pretty one; and yet it had a wild, airy, mocking quality, that seemed hardly human at all, or not, at any rate, characteristic of a being of affections and limitations like unto ours. But this impression of mine was fostered, no doubt, by the unusual and uncanny circumstances of the occasion.

'"Sure, sir," said she, "you're at the grave of Ethelind Fionguala."

'As she spoke she rose to her feet, and pointed to the inscription on the stone. I bent forward, and was able, without much difficulty, to decipher the name, and a date which indicated that the occupant of the grave must have entered the disembodied state between two and three centuries ago.

'"And who are you?" was my next question.

'"I'm called Elsie," she replied. "But where would your honour be going November-eve?"

'I mentioned my destination, and asked her whether she could direct me thither.

'"Indeed, then, 'tis there I'm going myself," Elsie replied; "and if your honour'll follow me, and play me a tune on the pretty instrument, 'tisn't long we'll be on the road."

'She pointed to the banjo which I carried wrapped up under my arm. How she knew that it was a musical instrument I could not imagine; possibly, I thought, she may have seen me playing on it as I strolled about the environs of the town. Be that as it may, I offered no opposition to the bargain, and further intimated that I would reward her more substantially on our arrival. At that she laughed again, and made a peculiar gesture with her hand above her head. I uncovered my banjo, swept my fingers across the strings, and struck into a fantastic dance-measure, to the music of which we proceeded along the path, Elsie slightly in advance, her feet keeping time to the airy measure. In fact, she trod so lightly, with an elastic, undulating movement, that with a little more it seemed as if she might float onward like a spirit. The extreme whiteness of her feet attracted my eye, and I was surprised to find that instead of being bare, as I had supposed, these were incased in white satin slippers quaintly embroidered with gold thread.

'"Elsie," said I, lengthening my steps so as to come up with her, "where do you live, and what do you do for a living?"

'"Sure, I live by myself," she answered; "and if you'd be after knowing how, you must come and see for yourself."

'"Are you in the habit of walking over the hills at night in shoes like that?"

'"And why would I not?" she asked, in her turn. "And where did your honour get the pretty gold ring on your finger?"

'The ring, which was of no great intrinsic value, had struck my eye in an old curiosity-shop in Cork. It wan an antique of very old-fashioned design, and might have belonged (as the vendor assured me was the case) to one of the early kings or queens of Ireland.

'"Do you like it?" said I.

'"Will your honour be after making a present of it to Elsie?" she returned, with an insinuating tone and turn of the head.

'"Maybe I will, Elsie, on one condition. I am an artist; I make pictures of people. If you will promise to come to my studio and let me paint your portrait, I'll give you the ring, and some money besides."

'"And will you give me the ring now?" said Elsie.

'"Yes, if you'll promise."

'"And will you play the music to me?" she continued.

'"As much as you like."

'"But maybe I'll not be handsome enough for ye,' said she, with a glance of her eyes beneath the dark hood.

'"I'll take the risk of that," I answered, laughing, "though, all the same, I don't mind taking a peep beforehand to remember you by." So saying, I put forth a hand to draw back the concealing hood. But Elsie eluded me, I scarce know how, and laughed a third time, with the same airy, mocking cadence.

'"Give me the ring first, and then you shall see me," she said, coaxingly.

'"Stretch out your hand, then," returned I, removing the ring from my finger. "When we are better acquainted, Elsie, you won't be so suspicious."

'She held out a slender, delicate hand, on the forefinger of which I slipped the ring. As I did so, the folds of her cloak fell a little apart, affording me a glimpse of a white shoulder and of a dress that seemed in that deceptive semi-darkness to be wrought of rich and costly material; and I caught, to, or so I fancied, the frosty sparkle of precious stones.

'"Arrah, mind where ye tread!" said Elsie, in a sudden, sharp tone.

'I looked round, and became aware for the first time that we were standing near the middle of a ruined bridge which spanned a rapid stream that flowed at a considerable depth below. The parapet of the bridge on one side was broken down, and I must have been, in fact, in imminent danger of stepping over into empty air. I made my way cautiously across the decaying structure; but, when I turned to assist Elsie, she was nowhere to be seen.

'What had become of the girl? I called, but no answer came. I gazed about on every side, but no trace of her was visible. Unless she had plunged into the narrow abyss at my feet, there was no place where she could have concealed herself—none at least that I could discover. She had vanished, nevertheless; and since her disappearance must have been premeditated, I finally came to the conclusion that it was useless to attempt to find her. She would present herself again in her own good time, or not at all. She had given me the slip very cleverly, and I must make the best of it. The adventure was perhaps worth the ring.

'On resuming my way, I was not a little relieved to find that I once more knew where I was. The bridge that I had just crossed was none other than the one I mentioned some time back; I was within a mile of the town, and my way lay clear before me. The moon, moreover, had now quite dispersed the clouds, and shone down with exquisite brilliance. Whatever her other failings, Elsie had been a trustworthy guide; she had brought me out of the depth of elf-land into the material world again. It had been a singular adventure, certainly; and I mused over it with a sense of mysterious pleasure as I sauntered along, humming snatches of airs, and accompanying myself on the strings. Hark! what light step was that behind me? It sounded like Elsie's; but no, Elsie was not there. The same impression or hallucination, however, recurred several times before I reached the outskirts of the town—the tread of an airy foot behind or beside my own. The fancy did not make me nervous; on the contrary, I was pleased with the notion of being thus haunted, and gave myself up to a romantic and genial vein of reverie.

'After passing one or two roofless and moss-grown cottages, I entered the narrow and rambling street which leads through the town. This street a short distance down widens a little, as if to afford the wayfarer space to observe a remarkable old house that stands on the northern side. The house was built of stone, and in a noble style of architecture; it reminded me somewhat of certain palaces of the old Italian nobility that I had seen on the Continent, and it may very probably have been built by one of the Italian or Spanish immigrants of the sixteenth or seventeenth century. The moulding of the projecting windows and arched doorway was richly carved, and upon the front of the building was an escutcheon wrought in high relief, though I could not make out the purport of the device. The moonlight falling upon this picturesque pile enhanced all its beauties, and at the same time made it seem like a vision that might dissolve away when the light ceased to shine. I must often have seen the house before, and yet I retained no definite recollection of it; I had never until now examined it with my eyes open, so to speak. Leaning against the wall on the opposite side of the street, I contemplated it for a long while at my leisure. The window at the corner was really a very fine and massive affair. It projected over the pavement below, throwing a heavy shadow aslant; the frames of the diamond-paned lattices were heavily mullioned. How often in past ages had that lattice been pushed open by some fair hand, revealing to a lover waiting beneath in the moonlight the charming countenance of his high-born mistress! Those were brave days. They had passed away long since. The great house had stood empty for who could tell how many years; only bats and vermin were its inhabitants. Where now were those who had built it? and who were they? Probably the very name of them was forgotten.

'As I continued to stare upward, however, a conjecture presented itself to my mind which rapidly ripened into a conviction. Was not this the house that Dr Dudeen had described that very evening as having been formerly the abode of the Kern of Querin and his mysterious bride? There was the projecting window, the arched doorway. Yes, beyond a doubt this was the very house. I emitted a low exclamation of renewed interest and pleasure, and my speculations took a still more imaginative, but also a more definite turn.

'What had been the fate of that lovely lady after the Kern had brought her home insensible in his arms? Did she recover, and were they married and made happy ever after; or had the sequel been a tragic one? I remembered to have read that the victims of vampires generally became vampires themselves. Then my thoughts went back to that grave on the hill-side. Surely that was unconsecrated ground. Why had they buried her there? Ethelind of the white shoulder! Ah! why had not I lived in those days; or why might not some magic cause them to live again for me? Then would I seek this street at midnight, and standing here beneath her window, I would lightly touch the strings of my bandore until the casement opened cautiously and she looked down. A sweet vision indeed! And what prevented my realizing it? Only a matter of a couple of centuries or so. And was time, then, at which poets and philosophers sneer, so rigid and real a matter that a little faith and imagination might not overcome it? At all events, I had my banjo, the bandore's legitimate and lineal descendant, and the memory of Fionguala should have the love-ditty.

'Hereupon, having retuned the instrument, I launched forth into an old Spanish love-song, which I had met with in some mouldy library during my travels, and had set to music of my own. I sang low, for the deserted street re-echoed the lightest sound, and what I sang must reach only my lady's ears. The words were warm with the fire of the ancient Spanish chivalry, and I threw into their expression all the passion of the lovers of romance. Surely Fionguala, the white-shouldered, would hear, and awaken from her sleep of centuries, and come to the latticed casement and look down! Hist! see yonder! What light—what shadow is that that seems to flit from room to room within the abandoned house, and now approaches the mullioned window? Are my eyes dazzled by the play of the moonlight, or does the casement move—does it open! Nay, this is no delusion; there is no error of the senses here. There is simply a woman, young, beautiful, and richly attired, bending forward from the window, and silently beckoning me to approach.

'Too much amazed to be conscious of amazement, I advanced until I stood directly beneath the casement, and the lady's face, as she stooped toward me, was not more than twice a man's height from my own. She smiled and kissed her finger-tips; something white fluttered in her hand, then fell through the air to the ground at my feet. The next moment she had withdrawn, and I heard the lattice close.

'I picked up what she had let fall; it was a delicate lace handkerchief, tied to the handle of an elaborately wrought bronze key. It was evidently the key of the house, and invited me to enter. I loosened it from the handkerchief, which bore a faint, delicious perfume, like the aroma of flowers in an ancient garden, and turned to the arched doorway. I felt no misgiving, and scarcely any sense of strangeness. All was as I had wished it to be, and as it should be; the mediæval age was alive once more, and as for myself, I almost felt the velvet cloak hanging from my shoulder and the long rapier dangling at my belt. Standing in front of the door I thrust the key into the lock, turned it, and felt the bolt yield. The next instant the door was opened, aparently from within; I stepped across the threshold, the door closed again, and I was alone in the house, and in darkness.

'Not alone, however! As I extended my hand to grope my way it was met by another hand, soft, slender, and cold, which insinuated itself gently into mine and drew me forward. Forward I went, nothing loath; the darkness was impenetrable, but I could hear the light rustle of a dress close to me, and the same delicious perfume that had emanated from the handkerchief enriched the air that I breathed, while the little hand that clasped and was clasped by my own alternately tightened and half relaxed the hold of its soft cold fingers. In this manner, and treading lightly, we traversed what I presumed to be a long, irregular passageway, and ascended a staircase. Then another corridor, until finally we paused, a door opened, emitting a flood of soft light, into which we entered, still hand in hand. The darkness and the doubt were at an end.

'The room was of imposing dimensions, and was furnished and decorated in a style of antique splendour. The walls were draped with mellow hues of tapestry; clusters of candles burned in polished silver sconces, and were reflected and multiplied in tall mirrors placed in the four corners of the room. The heavy beams of the dark oaken ceiling crossed each other in squares, and were laboriously carved; the curtains and the drapery of the chairs were of heavy-figured damask. At one end of the room was a broad ottoman, and in front of it a table, on which was set forth, in massive silver dishes, a sumptuous repast, with wines in crystal beakers. At the side was a vast and deep fire-place, with space enough on the broad hearth to burn whole trunks of trees. No fire, however, was there, but only a great heap of dead embers; and the room, for all its magnificence, was cold—cold as a tomb, or as my lady's hand—and it sent a subtle chill creeping to my heart.

'But my lady! how fair she was! I gave but a passing glance at the room; my eyes and my thoughts were all for her. She was dressed in white, like a bride; diamonds sparkled in her dark hair and on her snowy bosom; her lovely face and slender lips were pale, and all the paler for the dusky glow of her eyes. She gazed at me with a strange, elusive smile; and yet there was, in her aspect and bearing, something familiar in the midst of strangeness, like the burden of a song heard long ago and recalled among other conditions and surroundings. It seemed to me that something in me recognized her and knew her, had known her always. She was the woman of whom I had dreamed, whom I had beheld in visions, whose voice and face had haunted me from boyhood up. Whether we had ever met before, as human beings meet, I knew not; perhaps I had been blindly seeking her all over the world, and she had been awaiting me in this splendid room, sitting by those dead embers until all the warmth had gone out of her blood, only to be restored by the heat with which my love might supply her.

'"I thought you had forgotten me," she said, nodding as if in answer to my thought. "The night was so late—our one night of the year! How my heart rejoiced when I heard your dear voice singing the song I know so well! Kiss me—my lips are cold!"

'Cold indeed they were—cold as the lips of death. But the warmth of my own seemed to revive them. They were now tinged with a faint colour, and in her cheeks also appeared a delicate shade of pink. She drew fuller breath, as one who recovers from a long lethargy. Was it my life that was feeding her? I was ready to give her all. She drew me to the table and pointed to the viands and the wine.

'"Eat and drink," she said. "You have travelled far, and you need food."

'"Will you eat and drink with me?" said I, pouring out the wine.

'"You are the only nourishment I want," was her answer. "This wine is thin and cold. Give me wine as red as your blood and as warm, and I will drain a goblet to the dregs."

'At these words, I know not why, a slight shiver passed through me. She seemed to gain vitality and strength at every instant, but the chill of the great room struck into me more and more.

'She broke into a fantastic flow of spirits, clapping her hands, and dancing about me like a child. Who was she? And was I myself, or was she mocking me when she implied that we had belonged to each other of old? At length she stood still before me, crossing her hands over her breast. I saw upon the forefinger of her right hand the gleam of an antique ring.

'"Where did you get that ring?" I demanded.

'She shook her head and laughed. "Have you been faithful?" she asked. "It is my ring; it is the ring that unites us; it is the ring you gave me when you loved me first. It is the ring of the Kern—the fairy ring, and I am your Ethelind—Ethelind Fionguala."

'"So be it," I said, casting aside all doubt and fear, and yielding myself wholly to the spell of her inscrutable eyes and wooing lips. "You are mine, and I am yours, and let us be happy while the hours last."

'"You are mine, and I am yours," she repeated, nodding her head with an elfish smile. "Come and sit beside me, and sing that sweet song again that you sang to me so long ago. Ah, now I shall live a hundred years."

'We seated ourselves on the ottoman, and while she nestled luxuriously among the cushions, I took my banjo and sang to her. The song and the music resounded through the lofty room, and came back in throbbing echoes. And before me as I sang I saw the face and form of Ethelind Fionguala, in her jewelled bridal dress, gazing at me with burning eyes. She was pale no longer, but ruddy and warm, and life was like a flame within her. It was I who had become cold and bloodless, yet with the last life that was in me I would have sung to her of love that can never die. But at length my eyes grew dim, the room seemed to darken, the form of Ethelind alternately brightened and waxed indistinct, like the last flickerings of a fire; I swayed toward her, and felt myself lapsing into unconsciousness, with my head resting on her white shoulder.'

Here Keningale paused a few moments in his story, flung a fresh log upon the fire, and then continued:

'I awoke, I know not how long afterward. I was in a vast, empty room in a ruined building. Rotten shreds of drapery depended from the walls, and heavy festoons of spiders' webs gray with dust covered the windows, which were destitute of glass or sash; they had been boarded up with rough planks which had themselves become rotten with age, and admitted through their holes and crevices pallid rays of light and chilly draughts of air. A bat, disturbed by these rays or by my own movement, detached himself from his hold on a remnant of mouldy tapestry near me, and after circling dizzily around my head, wheeled the flickering noiselessness of his flight into a darker corner. As I arose unsteadily from the heap of miscellaneous rubbish on which I had been lying, something which had been resting across my knees fell to the floor with a rattle. I picked it up, and found it to be my banjo—as you see it now.

'Well, that is all I have to tell. My health was seriously impaired; all the blood seemed to have been drawn out of my veins; I was pale and haggard, and the chill—Ah, that chill,' murmured Keningale, drawing nearer to the fire, and spreading out his hands to catch the warmth—'I shall never get over it; I shall carry it to my grave.'

THE PARASITE

Sir Arthur Conan Doyle

Conan Doyle (1859–1930) was a regular visitor to the Lyceum and a good friend of both Henry Irving and Bram Stoker, who presented Doyle's first play, *A Story of Waterloo*, to great critical acclaim at Bristol in September 1894. 'To my own mind *Waterloo* as an acting play is perfect, and Irving's playing in it was the high-water mark of histrionic art,' declared Stoker later. In the same year as *Waterloo*'s premiere, Doyle's classic novella of psychic vampirism, *The Parasite*, was published as the first volume in Constable's Acme Library series. The second and companion volume was Bram Stoker's *The Watter's Mou'*. Both volumes are adorned with attractive decorations by Laurence Housman. (A revealing interview with Conan Doyle by Bram Stoker appeared in the *Daily Chronicle* in February 1908.)

I

MARCH 24. The spring is fairly with us now. Outside my laboratory window the great chestnut-tree is all covered with the big, glutinous, gummy buds, some of which have already begun to break into little green shuttlecocks. As you walk down the lanes you are conscious of the rich, silent forces of nature working all around you. The wet earth smells fruitful and luscious. Green shoots are peeping out everywhere. The twigs are stiff with their sap; and the moist, heavy English air is laden with a faintly resinous perfume. Buds in the hedges, lambs beneath them—everywhere the work of reproduction going forward!

I can see it without, and I can feel it within. We also have our spring when the little arterioles dilate, the lymph flows in a brisker stream, the glands work harder, winnowing and straining. Every year nature readjusts the whole machine. I can feel the ferment in my blood at this very moment, and as the cool sunshine pours through my window I could dance about in it like a gnat. So I should, only that Charles Sadler would rush upstairs to know what was the matter. Besides, I must remember that I am Professor Gilroy. An old professor may afford to be natural, but when fortune has given one of the first chairs in the university to a man of four-and-thirty he must try and act the part consistently.

What a fellow Wilson is! If I could only throw the same enthusiasm into physiology that he does into psychology, I should become a Claude Bernard at the least. His whole life and soul and energy work to one end. He drops to sleep collating his results of the past day, and he wakes to plan his researches for the coming one. And yet, outside the narrow circle who follow his proceedings, he gets so little credit for it. Physiology is a recognized science. If I add even a brick to the edifice, every one sees and applauds it. But Wilson is trying to dig the foundations for a science of the future. His work is underground and does not show. Yet he goes on uncomplainingly, corresponding with a hundred semi-maniacs in the hope of finding one reliable witness, sifting a hundred lies on the chance of gaining one little speck of truth, collating old books, devouring new ones, experimenting, lecturing, trying to light up in others the fiery interest which is consuming him. I am filled with wonder and admiration when I think of him, and yet, when he asks me to associate myself with his researches, I am compelled to tell him that, in their present state, they offer little attraction to a man who is devoted to exact science. If he could show me something positive and objective, I might then be tempted to approach the question from its physiological side. So long as half his subjects are tainted with charlatanry and the other half with hysteria we physiologists must content ourselves with the body and leave the mind to our descendants.

No doubt I am a materialist. Agatha says that I am a rank one. I tell her that is an excellent reason for shortening our engagement, since I am in such urgent need of her spirituality. And yet I may claim to be a curious example of the effect of education upon temperament, for by nature I am, unless I deceive myself, a highly psychic man. I was a nervous, sensitive boy, a dreamer, a somnambulist, full of impressions and intuitions. My black hair, my dark eyes, my thin, olive face, my tapering fingers, are all characteristic of my real temperament, and cause experts like Wilson to claim me as their own. But my brain is soaked with exact knowledge. I have trained myself to deal only with fact and with proof. Surmise and fancy have no place in my scheme of thought. Show me what I can see with my microscope, cut with my scalpel, weigh in my balance, and I will devote a lifetime to its investigation. But when you ask me to study feelings, impressions, suggestions, you ask me to do what is distasteful and even demoralizing. A departure from pure reason affects me like an evil smell or a musical discord.

Which is very sufficient reason why I am a little loath to go to Professor Wilson's tonight. Still I feel that I could hardly get out of the invitation without positive rudeness, and, now that Mrs Marden and

Agatha are going, of course I would not if I could. But I had rather meet them anywhere else. I know that Wilson would draw me into this nebulous semi-science of his if he could. In his enthusiasm he is perfectly impervious to hints or remonstrances. Nothing short of a positive quarrel will make him realize my aversion to the whole business. I have no doubt that he has some new mesmerist or clairvoyant or medium or trickster of some sort whom he is going to exhibit to us, for even his entertainments bear upon his hobby. Well, it will be a treat for Agatha, at any rate. She is interested in it, as woman usually is in whatever is vague and mystical and indefinite.

10.50 p.m. This diary-keeping of mine is, I fancy, the outcome of that scientific habit of mind about which I wrote this morning. I like to register impressions while they are fresh. Once a day at least I endeavour to define my own mental position. It is a useful piece of self-analysis, and has, I fancy, a steadying effect upon the character. Frankly, I must confess that my own needs what stiffening I can give it. I fear that, after all, much of my neurotic temperament survives, and that I am far from that cool, calm precision which characterizes Murdoch or Pratt-Haldane. Otherwise, why should the tomfoolery which I have witnessed this evening have set my nerves thrilling so that even now I am all unstrung? My only comfort is that neither Wilson nor Miss Penelosa nor even Agatha could have possibly known my weakness.

And what in the world was there to excite me? Nothing, or so little that it will seem ludicrous when I set it down.

The Mardens got to Wilson's before me. In fact, I was one of the last to arrive and found the room crowded. I had hardly time to say a word to Mrs Marden and to Agatha, who was looking charming in white and pink, with glittering wheat-ears in her hair, when Wilson came twitching at my sleeve.

'You want something positive, Gilroy,' said he, drawing me apart into a corner. 'My dear fellow, I have a phenomenon—a phenomenon!'

I should have been more impressed had I not heard the same before. His sanguine spirit turns every fire-fly into a star.

'No possible question about the *bona fides* this time,' said he, in answer, perhaps, to some little gleam of amusement in my eyes. 'My wife has known her for many years. They both come from Trinidad, you know. Miss Penelosa has only been in England a month of two, and knows no one outside the university circle, but I assure you that the things she has told us suffice in themselves to establish clairvoyance upon an absolutely scientific basis. There is nothing like her, amateur or professional. Come and be introduced!'

I like none of these mystery-mongers, but the amateur least of all. With the paid performer you may pounce upon him and expose him the instant that you have seen through his trick. He is there to deceive you, and you are there to find him out. But what are you to do with the friend of your host's wife? Are you to turn on a light suddenly and expose her slapping a surreptitious banjo? Or are you to hurl cochineal over her evening frock when she steals round with her phosphorus bottle and her supernatural platitude? There would be a scene, and you would be looked upon as a brute. So you have your choice of being that or a dupe. I was in no very good humour as I followed Wilson to the lady.

Any one less like my idea of a West Indian could not be imagined. She was a small, frail creature, well over forty, I should say, with a pale, peaky face, and hair of a very light shade of chestnut. Her presence was insignificant and her manner retiring. In any group of ten women she would have been the last whom one would have picked out. Her eyes were perhaps her most remarkable, and also, I am compelled to say, her least pleasant, feature. They were grey in colour,—grey with a shade of green,—and their expression struck me as being decidedly furtive. I wonder if furtive is the word, or should I have said fierce? On second thoughts, feline would have expressed it better. A crutch leaning against the wall told me what was painfully evident when she rose: that one of her legs was crippled.

So I was introduced to Miss Penelosa, and it did not escape me that as my name was mentioned she glanced across at Agatha. Wilson had evidently been talking. And presently, no doubt, thought I, she will inform me by occult means that I am engaged to a young lady with wheat-ears in her hair. I wondered how much more Wilson had been telling her about me.

'Professor Gilroy is a terrible sceptic,' said he; 'I hope, Miss Penelosa, that you will be able to convert him.'

She looked keenly up at me.

'Professor Gilroy is quite right to be sceptical if he has not seen anything convincing,' said she. 'I should have thought,' she added, 'that you would yourself have been an excellent subject.'

'For what, may I ask?' said I.

'Well, for mesmerism, for example.'

'My experience has been that mesmerists go for their subjects to those who are mentally unsound. All their results are vitiated, as it seems to me, by the fact that they are dealing with abnormal organisms.'

'Which of these ladies would you say possessed a normal organism?' she asked. 'I should like you to select the one who seems to you to have the best balanced mind. Should we say the girl in pink and white?— Miss Agatha Marden, I think the name is?'

'Yes, I should attach weight to any results from her.'

'I have never tried how far she is impressionable. Of course some people respond much more rapidly than others. May I ask how far your scepticism extends? I suppose that you admit the mesmeric sleep and the power of suggestion.'

'I admit nothing, Miss Penelosa.'

'Dear me, I thought science had got further than that. Of course I know nothing about the scientific side of it. I only know what I can do. You see the girl in red, for example, over near the Japanese jar. I shall will that she come across to us.'

She bent forward as she spoke and dropped her fan upon the floor. The girl whisked round and came straight toward us, with an enquiring look upon her face, as if some one had called her.

'What do you think of that, Gilroy?' cried Wilson, in a kind of ecstacy.

I did not dare to tell him what I thought of it. To me it was the most barefaced, shameless piece of imposture that I had ever witnessed. The collusion and the signal had really been too obvious.

'Professor Gilroy is not satisfied,' said she, glancing up at me with her strange little eyes. 'My poor fan is to get the credit of that experiment. Well, we must try something else. Miss Marden, would you have any objection to my putting you off?'

'Oh, I should love it!' cried Agatha.

By this time all the company had gathered round us in a circle, the shirt-fronted men, and the white-throated women, some awed, some critical, as though it were something between a religious ceremony and a conjurer's entertainment. A red velvet armchair had been pushed into the centre, and Agatha lay back in it, a little flushed and trembling slightly from excitement. I could see it from the vibration of the wheat-ears. Miss Penelosa rose from her seat and stood over her, leaning upon her crutch.

And there was a change in the woman. She no longer seemed small or insignificant. Twenty years were gone from her age. Her eyes were shining, a tinge of colour had come into her sallow cheeks, her whole figure had expanded. So I have seen a dull-eyed, listless lad change in an instant into briskness and life when given a task of which he felt himself master. She looked down at Agatha with an expression which I resented from the bottom of my soul—the expression with which a Roman empress might have looked at her kneeling slave. Then with a quick, commanding gesture she tossed up her arms and swept them slowly down in front of her.

I was watching Agatha narrowly. During three passes she seemed to be simply amused. At the fourth I observed a slight glazing of her eyes, accompanied by some dilation of her pupils. At the sixth there was a momentary rigor. At the seventh her lids began to droop. At the tenth her eyes were closed, and her breathing was slower and fuller than usual. I tried as I watched to preserve my scientific calm, but a foolish, causeless agitation convulsed me. I trust that I hid it, but I felt as a child feels in the dark. I could not have believed that I was still open to such weakness.

'She is in the trance,' said Miss Penelosa.

'She is sleeping!' I cried.

'Wake her, then!'

I pulled her by the arm and shouted in her ear. She might have been dead for all the impression that I could make. Her body was there on the velvet chair. Her organs were acting—her heart, her lungs. But her soul! It had slipped from beyond our ken. Whither had it gone? What power had dispossessed it? I was puzzled and disconcerted.

'So much for the mesmeric sleep,' said Miss Penelosa. 'As regards suggestion, whatever I may suggest Miss Marden will infallibly do, whether it be now or after she has awakened from her trance. Do you demand proof of it?'

'Certainly,' said I.

'You shall have it.' I saw a smile pass over her face, as though an amusing thought had struck her. She stooped and whispered earnestly into her subject's ear. Agatha, who had been so deaf to me, nodded her head as she listened.

'Awake!' cried Miss Penelosa, with a sharp tap of her crutch upon the floor. The eyes opened, the glazing cleared slowly away, and the soul looked out once more after its strange eclipse.

We went away early. Agatha was none the worse for her strange excursion, but I was nervous and unstrung, unable to listen to or answer the stream of comments which Wilson was pouring out for my benefit. As I bade her goodnight Miss Penelosa slipped a piece of paper into my hand.

'Pray forgive me,' said she, 'if I take means to overcome your scepticism. Open this note at ten o'clock tomorrow morning. It is a little private test.'

I can't imagine what she means, but there is the note, and it shall be opened as she directs. My head is aching, and I have written enough for tonight. Tomorrow I dare say that what seems so inexplicable will take quite another complexion. I shall not surrender my convictions without a struggle.

March 25. I am amazed, confounded. It is clear that I must reconsider my opinion upon this matter. But first let me place on record what has occurred.

I had finished breakfast, and was looking over some diagrams with which my lecture is to be illustrated, when my housekeeper entered to tell me that Agatha was in my study and wished to see me immediately. I glanced at the clock and saw with surprise that it was only half-past nine.

When I entered the room, she was standing on the hearth-rug facing me. Something in her pose chilled me and checked the words which were rising to my lips. Her veil was half down, but I could see that she was pale and that her expression was constrained.

'Austin,' she said, 'I have come to tell you that our engagement is at an end.'

I staggered. I believe that I literally did stagger. I know that I found myself leaning against the bookcase for support.

'But—but—' I stammered. 'This is very sudden, Agatha.'

'Yes, Austin, I have come here to tell you that our engagement is at an end.'

'But surely,' I cried, 'you will give me some reason! This is unlike you, Agatha. Tell me how I have been unfortunate enough to offend you.'

'It is all over, Austin.'

But why? You must be under some delusion, Agatha. Perhaps you have been told some falsehood about me. Or you may have misunderstood something that I have said to you. Only let me know what it is, and a word may set it all right.'

'We must consider it all at an end.'

'But you left me last night without a hint at any disagreement. What could have occurred in the interval to change you so? It must have been something that happened last night. You have been thinking it over and you have disapproved of my conduct. Was it the mesmerism? Did you blame me for letting that woman exercise her power over you? You know that at the least sign I should have interfered.'

'It is useless, Austin. All is over.'

Her voice was cold and measured; her manner strangely formal and hard. It seemed to me that she was absolutely resolved not to be drawn into any argument or explanation. As for me, I was shaking with agitation, and I turned my face aside, so ashamed was I that she should see my want of control.

'You must know what this means to me!' I cried. 'It is the blasting of all my hopes and the ruin of my life! You surely will not inflict such a punishment upon me unheard. You will let me know what is the matter. Consider how impossible it would be for me, under any circumstances, to treat you so. For God's sake, Agatha, let me know what I have done!'

She walked past me without a word and opened the door.

'It is quite useless, Austin,' said she. 'You must consider our engagement at an end.' An instant later she was gone, and, before I could recover myself sufficiently to follow her, I heard the hall door close behind her.

I rushed into my room to change my coat, with the idea of hurrying round to Mrs Marden's to learn from her what the cause of my misfortune might be. So shaken was I that I could hardly lace my boots. Never shall I forget those horrible ten minutes. I had just pulled on my overcoat when the clock upon the mantel-piece struck ten.

Ten! I associated the idea with Miss Penelosa's note. It was lying before me on the table, and I tore it open. It was scribbled in pencil in a peculiarly angular handwriting.

My dear Professor Gilroy [it said]: Pray excuse the personal nature of the test which I am giving you. Professor Wilson happened to mention the relations between you and my subject of this evening, and it struck me that nothing could be more convincing to you than if I were to suggest to Miss Marden that she should call upon you at half-past nine tomorrow morning and suspend your engagement for half an hour or so. Science is so exacting that it is difficult to give a satisfying test, but I am convinced that this at least will be an action which she would be most unlikely to do of her own free will. Forget anything that she may have said, as she has really nothing whatever to do with it, and will certainly not recollect anything about it. I write this note to shorten your anxiety, and to beg you to forgive me for the momentary unhappiness which my suggestion must have caused you.

Yours faithfully,
Helen Penelosa

Really, when I had read the note, I was too relieved to be angry. It was a liberty. Certainly it was a very great liberty indeed on the part of a lady whom I had only met once. But, after all, I had challenged her by my scepticism. It may have been, as she said, a little difficult to devise a test which would satisfy me.

And she had done that. There could be no question at all upon the point. For me hypnotic suggestion was finally established. It took its place from now onward as one of the facts of life. That Agatha, who of all women of my acquaintance has the best balanced mind, had been reduced to a condition of automatism appeared to be certain. A person at a distance had worked her as an engineer on the shore might guide a Brennan torpedo. A second soul had stepped in, as it were, had pushed her own aside, and had seized her nervous mechanism, saying: 'I will work this for half an hour.' And Agatha must have been unconscious as she came and as she returned. Could she make her way in safety through the streets in such a state? I put on my hat and hurried round to see if all was well with her.

Yes. She was at home. I was shown into the drawing-room and found her sitting with a book upon her lap.

'You are an early visitor, Austin,' said she, smiling.

'And you have been an even earlier one,' I answered.

She looked puzzled. 'What do you mean?' she asked.

'You have not been out today?'

'No, certainly not.'

'Agatha,' said I seriously, 'would you mind telling me exactly what you have done this morning?'

She laughed at my earnestness.

'You've got on your professional look, Austin. See what becomes of being engaged to a man of science. However, I will tell you, though I can't imagine what you want to know for. I got up at eight. I breakfasted at half-past. I came into this room at ten minutes past nine and began to read the 'Memoirs of Mme de Remusat.' In a few minutes I did the French lady the bad compliment of dropping to sleep over her pages, and I did you, sir, the very flattering one of dreaming about you. It is only a few minutes since I woke up.'

'And found yourself where you had been before?'

'Why, where else should I find myself?'

'Would you mind telling me, Agatha, what it was that you dreamed about me? It really is not mere curiosity on my part.'

'I merely had a vague impression that you came into it. I cannot recall anything definite.'

'If you have not been out today, Agatha, how is it that your shoes are dusty?'

A pained look came over her face.

'Really, Austin, I do not know what is the matter with you this morning. One would almost think that you doubted my word. If my boots are dusty, it must be, of course, that I have put on a pair which the maid has not cleaned.'

It was perfectly evident that she knew nothing whatever about the matter, and I reflected that, after all, perhaps it was better that I should not enlighten her. It might frighten her, and could serve no good purpose that I could see. I said no more about it, therefore, and left shortly afterward to give my lecture.

But I am immensely impressed. My horizon of scientific possibilities has suddenly been enormously extended. I no longer wonder at Wilson's demonic energy and enthusiasm. Who would not work hard who had a vast virgin field ready to his hand? Why, I have known the novel shape of a nucleolus, or a trifling peculiarity of striped muscular fibre seen under a 300 diameter lens, fill me with exultation. How petty do such researches seem when compared with this one which strikes at the very roots of life and the nature of the soul! I had always looked upon spirit as a product of matter. The brain, I thought, secreted the mind, as the liver does the bile. But how can this be when I see mind working from a distance and playing upon matter as a musician might upon a violin? The body does not give rise to the soul, then, but is rather the rough instrument by which the spirit manifests itself. The windmill does not give rise to the wind, but only indicates it. It was opposed to my whole habit of thought, and yet it was undeniably possible and worthy of investigation.

And why should I not investigate it? I see that under yesterday's date I said: 'If I could see something positive and objective, I might be tempted to approach it from the physiological aspect.' Well, I have got my test. I shall be as good as my word. The investigation would, I am sure, be of immense interest. Some of my colleagues might look askance at it, for science is full of unreasoning prejudices, but if Wilson has the courage of his convictions, I can afford to have it also. I shall go to him tomorrow morning—to him and to Miss Penelosa. If she can show us so much, it is probable that she can show us more.

II

March 26. Wilson was, as I had anticipated, very exultant over my conversion, and Miss Penelosa was also demurely pleased at the result of her experiment. Strange what a silent, colourless creature she is save only when she exercises her power! Even talking about it gives her colour and life. She seems to take a singular interest in me. I cannot help observing how her eyes follow me about the room.

We had the most interesting conversation about her own powers. It is just as well to put her views on record, though they cannot, of course, claim any scientific weight.

'You are on the very fringe of the subject,' said she, when I had expressed wonder at the remarkable instance of suggestion which she had shown me. 'I had no direct influence upon Miss Marden when she came round to you. I was not even thinking of her that morning. What I did was to set her mind as I might set the alarm of a clock so that at the hour named it would go off of its own accord. If six months instead of twelve hours had been suggested, it would have been the same.'

'And if the suggestion had been to assassinate me?'

'She would most inevitably have done so.'

'But this is a terrible power!' I cried.

'It is, as you say, a terrible power,' she answered gravely, 'and the more you know of it the more terrible will it seem to you.'

'May I ask,' said I, 'what you meant when you said that this matter of suggestion is only at the fringe of it? What do you consider the essential?'

'I had rather not tell you.'

I was surprised at the decision of her answer.

'You understand,' said I, 'that it is not out of curiosity I ask, but in the hope that I may find some scientific explanation for the facts with which you furnish me.'

'Frankly, Professor Gilroy,' said she, 'I am not at all interested in science, nor do I care whether it can or cannot classify these powers.'

'But I was hoping—'

'Ah, that is quite another thing. If you make it a personal matter,' said she, with the pleasantest of smiles, 'I shall be only too happy to tell you anything you wish to know. Let me see; what was it you asked me? Oh, about the further powers. Professor Wilson won't believe in them, but they are quite true all the same. For example, it is possible for an operator to gain complete command over his subject—presuming that the latter is a good one. Without any previous suggestion he may make him do whatever he likes.'

'Without the subject's knowledge?'

'That depends. If the force were strongly exerted, he would know no more about it than Miss Marden did when she came round and frightened you so. Or, if the influence was less powerful, he might be conscious of what he was doing, but be quite unable to prevent himself from doing it.'

'Would he have lost his own will power, then?'

'It would be over-ridden by another stronger one.'

'Have you ever exercised this power yourself?'

'Several times.'

'Is your own will so strong, then?'

'Well, it does not entirely depend upon that. Many have strong wills which are not detachable from themselves. The thing is to have the gift of projecting it into another person and superseding his own. I find that the power varies with my own strength and health.'

'Practically, you send your soul into another person's body.'

'Well, you might put it that way.'

'And what does your own body do?'

'It merely feels lethargic.'

'Well, but is there no danger to your own health?' I asked.

'There might be a little. You have to be careful never to let your own consciousness absolutely go; otherwise, you might experience some difficulty in finding your way back again. You must always preserve the connection, as it were. I am afraid I express myself very badly, Professor Gilroy, but of course I don't know how to put these things in a scientific way. I am just giving you my own experiences and my own explanations.'

Well, I read this over now at my leisure, and I marvel at myself! Is this Austin Gilroy, the man who has won his way to the front by his hard reasoning power and by his devotion to fact? Here I am gravely retailing the gossip of a woman who tells me how her soul may be projected from her body, and how, while she lies in a lethargy, she can control the actions of people at a distance. Do I accept it? Certainly not. She must prove and re-prove before I yield a point. But if I am still a sceptic, I have at least ceased to be a scoffer. We are to have a sitting this evening, and she is to try if she can produce any mesmeric effect upon me. If she can, it will make an excellent starting point for our investigation. No one can accuse *me*, at any rate, of complicity. If she cannot, we must try and find some subject who will be like Caesar's wife. Wilson is perfectly impervious.

10 p.m. I believe that I am on the threshold of an epoch-making investigation. To have the power of examining these phenomena from

inside—to have an organism which will respond, and at the same time a brain which will appreciate and criticize—that is surely a unique advantage. I am quite sure that Wilson would give five years of his life to be as susceptible as I have proved myself to be.

There was no one present except Wilson and his wife. I was seated with my head leaning back, and Miss Penelosa, standing in front and a little to the left, used the same long, sweeping strokes as with Agatha. At each of them a warm current of air seemed to strike me, and to suffuse a thrill and glow all through me from head to foot. My eyes were fixed upon Miss Penelosa's face, but as I gazed the features seemed to blur and to fade away. I was conscious only of her own eyes looking down at me, grey, deep, inscrutable. Larger they grew and larger, until they changed suddenly into two mountain lakes toward which I seemed to be falling with horrible rapidity. I shuddered, and as I did so some deeper stratum of thought told me that the shudder represented the rigor which I had observed in Agatha. An instant later I struck the surface of the lakes, now jointed into one and down I went beneath the water with a fullness in my head and a buzzing in my ears. Down I went, down, down, and then with a swoop up again until I could see the light streaming brightly through the green water. I was almost at the surface when the word 'Awake!' rang through my head, and, with a start, I found myself back in the armchair, with Miss Penelosa leaning on her crutch, and Wilson, his notebook in his hand, peeping over her shoulder. No heaviness or weariness was left behind. On the contrary, though it is only an hour or so since the experiment, I feel so wakeful that I am more inclined for my study than my bedroom. I see quite a vista of interesting experiments extending before us, and am all impatience to begin upon them.

March 27. A blank day, as Miss Penelosa goes with Wilson and his wife to the Suttons'. Have begun Binet and Ferré's 'Animal Magnetism.' What strange, deep waters these are! Results, results, results—and the cause an absolute mystery. It is stimulating to the imagination, but I must be on my guard against that. Let us have no inferences nor deductions, and nothing but solid facts. I *know* that the mesmeric trance is true; I *know* that mesmeric suggestion is true; I *know* that I am myself sensitive to this force. That is my present position. I have a large new notebook which shall be devoted entirely to scientific detail.

Long talk with Agatha and Mrs Marden in the evening about our marriage. We think that the summer vac. (the beginning of it) would be the best time for the wedding. Why should we delay? I grudge even those few months. Still, as Mrs Marden says, there are a good many things to be arranged.

March 28. Mesmerized again by Miss Penelosa. Experience much the same as before, save that insensibility came on more quickly. See Notebook A for temperature of room, barometric pressure, pulse, and respiration as taken by Professor Wilson.

March 29. Mesmerized again. Details in Notebook A.

March 30. Sunday, and a blank day. I grudge any interruption of our experiments. At present they merely embrace the physical signs which go with slight, with complete, and with extreme insensibility. Afterwards we hope to pass on to the phenomena of suggestion and of lucidity. Professors have demonstrated these things upon women at Nancy and at the Salpetriere. It will be more convincing when a woman demonstrates it upon a professor, with a second professor as a witness. And that I should be the subject—I, the sceptic, the materialist! At least, I have shown that my devotion to science is greater than to my own personal consistency. The eating of our own words is the greatest sacrifice which truth ever requires of us.

My neighbour, Charles Sadler, the handsome young demonstrator of anatomy, came in this evening to return a volume of Virchow's 'Archives' which I had lent him. I call him young, but, as a matter of fact, he is a year older than I am.

' I understand, Gilroy,' said he, 'that you are being experimented upon by Miss Penelosa.

'Well,' he went on, when I had acknowledged it, 'if I were you, I should not let it go any further. You will think me very impertinent, no doubt, but, none the less, I feel it to be my duty to advise you to have no more to do with her.'

Of course I asked him why.

'I am so placed that I cannot enter into particulars as freely as I could wish,' said he. 'Miss Penelosa is the friend of my friend, and my position is a delicate one. I can only say this: that I have myself been the subject of some of the woman's experiments, and that they have left a most unpleasant impression upon my mind.'

He could hardly expect me to be satisfied with that, and I tried hard to get something more definite out of him, but without success. Is it conceivable that he could be jealous at my having superseded him? Or is he one of those men of science who feel personally injured when facts run counter to their preconceived opinions? He cannot seriously suppose that because he has some vague grievance I am, therefore, to abandon a series of experiments which promise to be so fruitful of results. He appeared to be annoyed at the light way in which I treated his shadowy warnings, and we parted with some little coldness on both sides.

March 31. Mesmerized by Miss P.

April 1. Mesmerized by Miss P. (Notebook A.)

April 2. Mesmerized by Miss P. (Sphygmographic chart taken by Professor Wilson.)

April 3. It is possible that this course of mesmerism may be a little trying to the general constitution. Agatha says that I am thinner and darker under the eyes. I am conscious of a nervous irritability which I had not observed in myself before. The least noise, for example, makes me start, and the stupidity of a student causes me exasperation instead of amusement. Agatha wishes me to stop, but I tell her that every course of study is trying, and that one can never attain a result without paying some price for it. When she sees the sensation which my forthcoming paper on 'The Relation between Mind and Matter' may make, she will understand that it is worth a little nervous wear and tear. I should not be surprised if I got my F.R.S. over it.

Mesmerized again in the evening. The effect is produced more rapidly now, and the subjective visions are less marked. I keep full notes of each sitting. Wilson is leaving for town for a week or ten days, but we shall not interrupt the experiments, which depend for their value as much upon my sensations as on his observations.

April 4. I must be carefully on my guard. A complication has crept into our experiments which I had not reckoned upon. In my eagerness for scientific facts I have been foolishly blind to the human relations between Miss Penelosa and myself. I can write here what I would not breathe to a living soul. The unhappy woman appears to have formed an attachment for me.

I should not say such a thing, even in the privacy of my own intimate journal, if it had not come to such a pass that it is impossible to ignore it. For some time—that is, for the last week—there have been signs which I have brushed aside and refused to think of. Her brightness when I come, her dejection when I go, her eagerness that I should come often, the expression of her eyes, the tone of her voice—I tried to think that they meant nothing, and were, perhaps, only her ardent West Indian manner. But last night, as I awoke from the mesmeric sleep, I put out my hand, unconsciously, involuntarily, and clasped hers. When I came fully to myself, we were sitting with them locked, she looking up at me with an expectant smile. And the horrible thing was that I felt impelled to say what she expected me to say. What a false wretch I should have been! How I should have loathed myself today had I yielded to the temptation of that moment! But, thank God, I was strong enough to spring up and hurry from the room. I was rude, I fear, but I could not, no, I *could* not, trust myself another moment. I, a gentleman, a man of honour, engaged to one of the sweetest girls in England—and yet in a moment of reasonless passion I nearly professed love for this woman whom I hardly know. She is far older than myself and a cripple. It is monstrous, odious; and yet the impulse was so strong that, had I stayed another minute in her presence, I should have committed myself. What was it? I have to teach others the workings of our organism, and what do I know of it myself? Was it the sudden upcropping of some lower stratum in my nature—a brutal primitive instinct suddenly asserting itself? I could almost believe the tales of obsession by evil spirits, so overmastering was the feeling.

Well, the incident places me in a most unfortunate position. On the one hand, I am very loath to abandon a series of experiments which have already gone so far, and which promise such brilliant results. On the other, if this unhappy woman has conceived a passion for me—But surely even now I must have made some hideous mistake. She, with her age and her deformity! It is impossible. And then she knew about Agatha. She understood how I was placed. She only smiled out of amusement, perhaps, when in my dazed state I seized her hand. It was my half-mesmerized brain which gave it a meaning, and sprang with such bestial swiftness to meet it. I wish I could persuade myself that it was indeed so. On the whole, perhaps, my wisest plan would be to postpone our other experiments until Wilson's return. I have written a note to Miss Penelosa, therefore, making no allusion to last night, but saying that a press of work would cause me to interrupt our sittings for a few days. She has answered, formally enough, to say that if I should change my mind I should find her at home at the usual hour.

10 p.m. Well, well, what a thing of straw I am! I am coming to know myself better of late, and the more I know the lower I fall in my own estimation. Surely I was not always so weak as this. At four o'clock I should have smiled had anyone told me that I should go to Miss Penelosa's tonight, and yet, at eight, I was at Wilson's door as usual. I don't know how it occurred. The influence of habit, I suppose. Perhaps there is a mesmeric craze as there is an opium craze, and I am a victim to it. I only know that as I worked in my study I became more and more uneasy. I fidgeted. I worried. I could not concentrate my mind upon the papers in front of me. And then, at last, almost before I knew what I was doing, I seized my hat and hurried round to keep my usual appointment.

We had an interesting evening. Mrs Wilson was present during most of the time, which prevented the embarrassment which one at least of us must have felt. Miss Penclosa's manner was quite the same as usual, and she expressed no surprise at my having come in spite of my note. There was nothing in her bearing to show that yesterday's incident had made any impression upon her, and so I am inclined to hope that I overrated it.

April 6 (evening). No, no, no, I did not overrate it. I can no longer attempt to conceal from myself that this woman has conceived a passion for me. It is monstrous, but it is true. Again, tonight, I awoke from the mesmeric trance to find my hand in hers, and to suffer that odious feeling which urges me to throw away my honour, my career, everything, for the sake of this creature who, as I can plainly see when I am away from her influence, possesses no single charm upon earth. But when I am near her, I do not feel this. She rouses something in me, something evil, something I had rather not think of. She paralyzes my better nature, too, at the moment when she stimulates my worse. Decidedly it is not good for me to be near her.

Last night was worse than before. Instead of flying I actually sat for some time with my hand in hers talking over the most intimate subjects with her. We spoke of Agatha, among other things. What could I have been dreaming of? Miss Penelosa said that she was conventional, and I agreed with her. She spoke once or twice in a disparaging way of her, and I did not protest. What a creature I have been!

Weak as I have proved myself to be, I am still strong enough to bring this sort of thing to an end. It shall not happen again. I have sense enough to fly when I cannot fight. From this Sunday night onward I shall never sit with Miss Penelosa again. Never! Let the experiments go, let the research come to an end; anything is better than facing this monstrous temptation which drags me so low. I have said nothing to Miss Penelosa, but I shall simply stay away. She can tell the reason without any words of mine.

April 7. Have stayed away, as I said. It is a pity to ruin such an interesting investigation, but it would be a greater pity still to ruin my life, and I *know* that I cannot trust myself with that woman.

11 p.m. God help me! What is the matter with me? Am I going mad? Let me try and be calm and reason with myself. First of all I shall set down exactly what occurred.

It was nearly eight when I wrote the lines with which this day begins. Feeling strangely restless and uneasy, I left my rooms and walked round to spend the evening with Agatha and her mother. They both remarked that I was pale and haggard. About nine Professor Pratt-Haldane came in, and we played a game of whist. I tried hard to concentrate my attention upon the cards, but the feeling of restlessness grew and grew until I found it impossible to struggle against it. I simply *could* not sit still at the table. At last, in the very middle of a hand, I threw my cards down and, with some sort of incoherent apology about having an appointment, I rushed from the room. As if in a dream I have a vague recollection of tearing through the hall, snatching my hat from the stand, and slamming the door behind me. As if in a dream, too, I have the impression of the double line of gas-lamps, and my bespattered boots tell me that I must have run down the middle of the road. It was all misty and strange and unnatural. I came to Wilson's house; I saw Mrs Wilson and I saw Miss Penelosa. I hardly recall what we talked about, but I do remember that Miss P. shook the head of her crutch at me in a playful way, and accused me of being late and of losing interest in our experiments. There was no mesmerism, but I stayed some time and have only just returned.

My brain is quite clear again now, and I can think over what has occurred. It is absurd to suppose that it is merely weakness and force of habit. I tried to explain it in that way the other night, but it will no longer suffice. It is something much deeper and more terrible than that. Why, when I was at the Mardens' whist-table, I was dragged away as if the noose of a rope had been cast round me. I can no longer disguise it from myself. The woman has her grip upon me. I am in her clutch. But I must keep my head and reason it out and see what is best to be done.

But what a blind fool I have been! In my enthusiasm over my research I have walked straight into the pit, although it lay gaping before me. Did she not herself warn me? Did she not tell me, as I can read in my own journal, that when she has acquired power over a subject she can make him do her will? And she has acquired that power over me. I am for the moment at the beck and call of this creature with the crutch. I must come when she wills it. I must do as she wills. Worst of all, I must feel as she wills. I loathe her and fear her, yet, while I am under the spell, she can doubtless make me love her.

There is some consolation in the thought, then, that those odious impulses for which I have blamed myself do not really come from me at all. They are all transferred from her, little as I could have guessed it at the time. I feel cleaner and lighter for the thought.

April 8. Yes, now, in broad daylight, writing coolly and with time for reflection, I am compelled to confirm everything which I wrote in my journal last night. I am in a horrible position, but, above all, I must not lose my head. I must pit my intellect against her powers. After all, I am no silly puppet, to dance at the end of a string. I have energy, brains, courage. For all her devil's tricks I may beat her yet. May! I *must*, or what is to become of me?

Let me try to reason it out! This woman, by her own explanation, can dominate my nervous organism. She can project herself into my body and take command of it. She has a parasite soul; yes, she is a parasite, a monstrous parasite. She creeps into my frame as the hermit crab does into the whelk's shell. I am powerless. What can I do? I am dealing with forces of which I know nothing. And I can tell no one of my trouble. They would set me down as a madman. Certainly, if it got noised abroad, the university would say that they had no need of a devil-ridden professor. And Agatha! No, no, I must face it alone.

III

I read over my notes of what the woman said when she spoke about her powers. There is one point which fills me with dismay. She implies that when the influence is slight the subject knows what he is doing, but cannot control himself, whereas when it is strongly exerted he is absolutely unconscious. Now, I have always known what I did, though less so last night than on the previous occasions. That seems to mean that she has never yet exerted her full powers upon me. Was ever a man so placed before?

Yes, perhaps there was, and very near me, too. Charles Sadler must know something of this! His vague words of warning take a meaning now. Oh, if I had only listened to him then, before I helped by these repeated sittings to forge the links of the chain which binds me! But I will see him today. I will apologize to him for having treated his warning so lightly. I will see if he can advise me.

4 p.m. No, he cannot. I have talked with him, and he showed such surprise at the first words in which I tried to express my unspeakable secret that I went no further. As far as I can gather (by hints and inferences rather than by any statement), his own experience was limited to some words or looks such as I have myself endured. His abandonment of Miss Penelosa is in itself a sign that he was never really in her toils. Oh, if he only knew his escape! He has to thank his phlegmatic Saxon temperament for it. I am dark and Celtic, and this hag's clutch is deep in my nerves. Shall I ever get it out? Shall I ever be the same man that I was just one short fortnight ago?

Let me consider what I had better do. I cannot leave the university in the middle of the term. If I were free, my course would be obvious. I should start at once and travel in Persia. But would she allow me to start? And could her influence not reach me in Persia, and bring me back to within touch of her crutch? I can only find out the limits of this hellish power by my own bitter experience. I will fight and fight and fight—and what can I do more?

I know very well that about eight o'clock tonight that craving for her society, that irresistible restlessness, will come upon me. How shall I overcome it? What shall I do? I must make it impossible for me to leave the room. I shall lock the door and throw the key out of the window. But, then, what am I to do in the morning? Never mind about the morning. I must at all costs break this chain which holds me.

April 9. Victory! I have done splendidly! At seven o'clock last night I took a hasty dinner, and then locked myself up in my bedroom and dropped the key into the garden. I chose a cheery novel, and lay in bed for three hours trying to read it, but really in a horrible state of trepidation, expecting every instant that I should become conscious of the impulse. Nothing of the sort occurred, however, and I awoke this morning with the feeling that a black nightmare had been lifted off me. Perhaps the creature realized what I had done, and understood that it was useless to try to influence me. At any rate, I have beaten her once, and if I can do it once, I can do it again.

It was most awkward about the key in the morning. Luckily, there was an under-gardener below, and I asked him to throw it up. No doubt he thought I had just dropped it. I will have doors and windows screwed up and six stout men to hold me down in my bed before I will surrender myself to be hag-ridden in this way.

I had a note from Mrs Marden this afternoon asking me to go round and see her. I intended to do so in any case, but had not expected to find bad news waiting for me. It seems that the Armstrongs, from whom Agatha has expectations, are due home from Adelaide in the *Aurora*, and that they have written to Mrs Marden and her to meet them in town. They will probably be away for a month or six weeks, and, as the *Aurora* is due on Wednesday, they must go at once—tomorrow, if they are ready in time. My consolation is that when we meet again there will be no more parting between Agatha and me.

'I want you to do one thing, Agatha,' said I, when we were alone together. 'If you should happen to meet Miss Penelosa, either in town or here, you must promise me never again to allow her to mesmerize you.'

Agatha opened her eyes.

'Why, it was only the other day that you were saying how interesting it all was, and how determined you were to finish your experiments.'

'I know, but I have changed my mind since then.'

'And you won't have it any more?'

'No.'

'I am so glad, Austin. You can't think how pale and worn you have been lately. It was really our principal objection to going to London now that we did not wish to leave you when you were so pulled down. And your manner has been so strange occasionally—especially that night when you left poor Professor Pratt-Haldane to play dummy. I am convinced that these experiments are very bad for your nerves.'

'I think so, too, dear.'

'And for Miss Penelosa's nerves as well. You have heard that she is ill?'

'No.'

'Mrs Wilson told us so last night. She described it as a nervous fever. Professor Wilson is coming back this week, and of course Mrs Wilson is very anxious that Miss Penelosa should be well again then, for he has quite a programme of experiments which he is anxious to carry out.'

I was glad to have Agatha's promise, for it was enough that this woman should have one of us in her clutch. On the other hand, I was disturbed to hear about Miss Penelosa's illness. It rather discounts the victory which I appeared to win last night. I remember that she said that loss of health interfered with her power. That may be why I was able to hold my own so easily. Well, well, I must take the same precautions tonight and see what comes of it. I am childishly frightened when I think of her.

April 10. All went well last night. I was amused at the gardener's face when I had again to hail him this morning and to ask him to throw up my key. I shall get a name among the servants if this sort of thing goes on. But the great point is that I stayed in my room without the slightest inclination to leave it. I do believe that I am shaking myself clear of this incredible bond—or is it only that the woman's power is in abeyance until she recovers her strength? I can but pray for the best.

The Mardens left this morning, and the brightness seems to have gone out of the spring sunshine. And yet it is very beautiful also as it gleams on the green chestnuts opposite my windows, and gives a touch of gaiety to the heavy, lichen-mottled walls of the old colleges. How sweet and gentle and soothing is Nature! Who would think that there lurked in her also such vile forces, such odious possibilities! For of course I understand that this dreadful thing which has sprung out at me is neither supernatural nor even preternatural. No, it is a natural force which this woman can use and society is ignorant of. The mere fact that it ebbs with her strength shows how entirely it is subject to physical laws. If I had time, I might probe it to the bottom and lay my hands upon its antidote. But you cannot tame the tiger when you are beneath his claws. You can but try to writhe away from him. Ah, when I look in the glass and see my own dark eyes and clear-cut Spanish face, I long for a vitriol splash or a bout of the smallpox. One or the other might have saved me from this calamity.

I am inclined to think that I may have trouble tonight. There are two things which make me fear so. One is that I met Mrs Wilson in the street, and she tells me that Miss Penelosa is better, though still weak. I find myself wishing in my heart that the illness had been her last. The other is that Professor Wilson comes back in a day or two, and his presence would act as a constraint upon her. I should not fear our interviews if a third person were present. For both these reasons I have a presentiment of trouble tonight, and I shall take the same precautions as before.

April 10. No, thank God, all went well last night. I really could not face the gardener again. I locked my door and thrust the key underneath it, so that I had to ask the maid to let me out in the morning. But the precaution was really not needed, for I never had any inclination to go out at all. Three evenings in succession at home! I am surely near the end of my troubles, for Wilson will be home again either today or tomorrow. Shall I tell him of what I have gone through or not? I am convinced that I should not have the slightest sympathy from him. He would look upon me as an interesting case, and read a paper about me at the next meeting of the Psychical Society, in which he would gravely discuss the possibility of my being a deliberate liar, and weigh it against the chances of my being in an early stage of lunacy. No, I shall get no comfort out of Wilson.

I am feeling wonderfully fit and well. I don't think I ever lectured with greater spirit. Oh, if I could only get this shadow off my life, how happy I should be! Young, fairly wealthy, in the front rank of my profession, engaged to a beautiful and charming girl—have I not everything which a man could ask for? Only one thing to trouble me, but what a thing it is!

Midnight. I shall go mad. Yes, that will be the end of it. I shall go mad. I am not far from it now. My head throbs as I rest it on my hot hand. I am quivering all over like a scared horse. Oh, what a night I have had! And yet I have some cause to be satisfied also.

At the risk of becoming the laughing-stock of my own servant, I again slipped my key under the door, imprisoning myself for the night. Then, finding it too early to go to bed, I lay down with my clothes on and began to read one of Dumas's novels. Suddenly I was gripped— gripped and dragged from the couch. It is only thus that I can describe the overpowering nature of the force which pounced upon me. I clawed at the coverlet. I clung to the wood-work. I believe that I screamed out in my frenzy. It was all useless, hopeless, I *must* go. There was no way out of it. It was only at the outset that I resisted. The force soon became too overmastering for that. I thank goodness that there were no watchers there to interfere with me. I could not have answered for myself if there had been. And, besides the determination to get out, there came to me also, the keenest and coolest judgment in choosing my means. I lit a candle and endeavoured, kneeling in front of the door, to pull the key through with the feather-end of a quill pen. It was just too short and pushed it further away: Then with quiet persistence I got a paper-knife out of one of the drawers, and with that I managed to draw the key back. I opened the door, stepped into my study, took a photograph of myself from the bureau, wrote something across it, placed it in the inside pocket of my coat, and then started off for Wilson's.

It was all wonderfully clear, and yet disassociated from the rest of my life, as the incidents of even the most vivid dream might be. A peculiar double consciousness possessed me. There was the predominant alien will, which was bent upon drawing me to the side of its owner, and there was the feebler protesting personality, which I recognized as being myself, tugging feebly at the overmastering impulse as a led terrier might at its chain. I can remember recognizing these two conflicting forces, but I recall nothing of my walk, nor of how I was admitted to the house.

Very vivid, however, is my recollection of how I met Miss Penelosa. She was reclining on the sofa in the little boudoir in which our experiments had usually been carried out. Her head was rested on her hand, and a tiger-skin rug had been partly drawn over her. She looked up expectantly as I entered, and, as the lamp-light fell upon her face, I could see that she was very pale and thin, with dark hollows under her eyes. She smiled at me, and pointed to a stool beside her. It was with her left hand that she pointed, and I, running eagerly forward, seized it—I loathe myself as I think of it—and pressed it passionately to my lips. Then, seating myself upon the stool, and still retaining her hand, I gave her the photograph which I had brought with me, and talked and talked and talked—of my love for her, of my grief over her illness, of my joy at her recovery, of the misery it was to be absent a single evening from her side. She lay quietly looking down at me with imperious eyes and her provocative smile. Once I remember that she passed her hand over my hair as one caresses a dog; and it gave me pleasure—the caress. I thrilled under it. I was her slave, body and soul, and for the moment I rejoiced in my slavery.

And then came the blessed change. Never tell me that there is not a Providence! I was on the brink of perdition. My feet were on the edge. Was it a coincidence that at that very instant help should come? No, no, no; there is a Providence, and its hand has drawn me back. There is something in the universe stronger than this devil woman with her tricks. Ah, what a balm to my heart it is to think so!

As I looked up at her I was conscious of a change in her. Her face, which had been pale before, was now ghastly. Her eyes were dull, and the lids dropped heavily over them. Above all, the look of serene confidence had gone from her features. Her mouth had weakened. Her forehead had puckered. She was frightened and undecided. And as I watched the change my own spirit fluttered and struggled, trying hard to tear itself from the grip which held it—a grip which, from moment to moment, grew less secure.

'Austin,' she whispered, 'I have tried to do too much. I was not strong enough. I have not recovered yet from my illness. But I could not live longer without seeing you. You won't leave me, Austin? This is only a passing weakness. If you will only give me five minutes, I shall be myself again. Give me the small decanter from the table in the window.'

But I had regained my soul. With her waning strength the influence had cleared away from me and left me free. And I was aggressive—bitterly, fiercely aggressive. For once at least I could make this woman understand what my real feelings toward her were. My soul was filled with a hatred as bestial as the love against which it was a reaction. It was the savage, murderous passion of the revolted serf. I could have taken the crutch from her side and beaten her face in with it. She threw her hands up, as if to avoid a blow, and cowered away from me into the corner of the settee.

'The brandy!' she gasped. 'The brandy!'

I took the decanter and poured it over the roots of a palm in the window. Then I snatched the photograph from her hand and tore it into a hundred pieces.

'You vile woman,' I said, 'if I did my duty to society, you would never leave this room alive!'

'I love you, Austin; I love you!' she wailed.

'Yes,' I cried, 'and Charles Sadler before. And how many others before that?'

'Charles Sadler!' she gasped. 'He has spoken to you? So, Charles Sadler, Charles Sadler!' Her voice came through her white lips like a snake's hiss.

'Yes, I know you, and others shall know you, too. You shameless creature! You knew how I stood. And yet you used your vile power to bring me to your side. You may, perhaps, do so again, but at least you will remember that you have heard me say that I love Miss Marden from the bottom of my soul, and that I loathe you, abhor you! The very sight of you and the sound of your voice fill me with horror and disgust. The thought of you is repulsive. That is how I feel toward you, and if it pleases you by your tricks to draw me again to your side as you have done tonight, you will at least, I should think, have little satisfaction in trying to make a lover out of a man who has told you his real opinion of you. You may put what words you will into my mouth, but you cannot help remembering—'

I stopped, for the woman's head had fallen back, and she had fainted. She could not bear to hear what I had to say to her! What a glow of satisfaction it gives me to think that, come what may, in the future she can never misunderstand my true feelings toward her. But what will occur in the future? What will she do next? I dare not think of it. Oh, if only I could hope that she will leave me alone! But when I think of what I said to her—Never mind; I have been stronger than she for once.

April 11. I hardly slept last night, and found myself in the morning so unstrung and feverish that I was compelled to ask Pratt-Haldane to do my lecture for me. It is the first that I have ever missed. I rose at midday, but my head is aching, my hands quivering, and my nerves in a pitiable state.

Who should come round this evening but Wilson. He has just come back from London, where he has lectured, read papers, convened meetings, exposed a medium, conducted a series of experiments on thought transference, entertained Professor Richet of Paris, spent hours gazing into a crystal, and obtained some evidence as to the passage of matter through matter. All this he poured into my ears in a single gust.

'But you!' he cried at last. 'You are not looking well. And Miss Penelosa is quite prostrated today. How about the experiments?'

'I have abandoned them.'

'Tut, tut! Why?'

'The subject seems to me a dangerous one.'

Out came his big brown notebook.

'This is of great interest,' said he. 'What are your grounds for saying that it is a dangerous one? Please give your facts in chronological order, with approximate dates and names of reliable witnesses with their permanent addresses.'

'First of all,' I asked, 'would you tell me whether you have collected any cases where the mesmerist has gained a command over the subject and has used it for evil purposes?'

'Dozens!' he cried exultantly. 'Crime by suggestion—'

'I don't mean suggestion. I mean where a sudden impulse comes from a person at a distance—an uncontrollable impulse.'

'Obsession!' he shrieked, in an ecstasy of delight. 'It is the rarest condition. We have eight cases, five well attested. You don't mean to say—' His exultation made him hardly articulate.

'No, I don't,' said I. 'Good-evening! You will excuse me, but I am not very well tonight.' And so at last I got rid of him, still brandishing his pencil and his notebook. My troubles may be bad to bear, but at least it is better to hug them to myself than to have myself exhibited by Wilson, like a freak at a fair. He has lost sight of human beings. Everything to him is a case and a phenomenon. I will die before I speak to him again upon the matter.

April 12. Yesterday was a blessed day of quiet, and I enjoyed an uneventful night. Wilson's presence is a great consolation. What can the woman do now? Surely, when she has heard me say what I have said, she will conceive the same disgust for me which I have for her. She could not, no, she *could* not, desire to have a lover who had insulted her so. No, I believe I am free from her love—but how about her hate? Might she not use these powers of hers for revenge? Tut! why should I frighten myself over shadows? She will forget about me, and I shall forget about her, and all will be well.

April 13. My nerves have quite recovered their tone. I really believe that I have conquered the creature. But I must confess to living in some suspense. She is well again, for I hear that she was driving with Mrs Wilson in the High Street in the afternoon.

April 14. I do wish I could get away from the place altogether. I shall fly to Agatha's side the very day that the term closes. I suppose it is pitiably weak of me, but this woman gets upon my nerves most terribly. I have seen her again, and I have spoken with her.

It was just after lunch, and I was smoking a cigarette in my study, when I heard the step of my servant Murray in the passage. I was languidly conscious that a second step was audible behind, and had hardly troubled myself to speculate who it might be, when suddenly a slight noise brought me out of my chair with my skin creeping with apprehension. I had never particularly observed before what sort of sound the tapping of a crutch was, but my quivering nerves told me that I heard it now in the sharp wooden clack which alternated with the muffled thud of the foot-fall. Another instant and my servant had shown her in.

I did not attempt the usual conventions of society, nor did she. I simply stood with the smouldering cigarette in my hand, and gazed at her. She in turn looked silently at me, and at her look I remembered how in these very pages I had tried to define the expression of her eyes, whether they were furtive or fierce. Today they were fierce—coldly and inexorably so.

'Well,' said she, at last, 'are you still of the same mind as when I saw you last?'

'I have always been of the same mind.'

'Let us understand each other, Professor Gilroy,' said she slowly. 'I am not a very safe person to trifle with, as you should realize by now. It was you who asked me to enter into a series of experiments with you, it was you who won my affections, it was you who professed your love for me, it was you who brought me your own photograph with words of affection upon it, and, finally, it was you who on the very same evening thought it fit to insult me most outrageously, addressing me as no man has ever dared to speak to me yet. Tell me that those words came from you in a moment of passion and I am prepared to forget and forgive them. You did not mean what you said, Austin? You do not really hate me?'

I might have pitied this deformed woman—such a longing for love broke suddenly through the menace of her eyes. But then I thought of what I had gone through, and my heart set like flint.

'If ever you heard me speak of love,' said I, 'you know very well that it was your own voice which spoke, and not mine. The only words of truth which I have ever been able to say to you are those which you heard when last we met.'

'I know. Someone has set you against me. It was he!' She tapped with her crutch upon the floor. 'Well, you know very well that I could bring you this minute crouching like a spaniel to my feet. You will not find me again in my hour of weakness, when you can insult me with impunity. Have a care what you are doing, Professor Gilroy. You stand in a terrible position. You have not yet realized the hold which I have upon you.'

I shrugged my shoulders and turned away.

'Well,' said she, after a pause, 'if you despise my love, I must see what can be done with fear. You smile, but the day will come when you will come screaming to me for pardon. Yes, you will grovel on the ground before me, proud as you are, and you will curse the day that ever you turned me from your best friend into your most bitter enemy. Have a care, Professor Gilroy!' I saw a white hand shaking in the air, and a face which was scarcely human, so convulsed was it with passion. An instant later she was gone, and I heard the quick hobble and tap receding down the passage.

But she has left a weight upon my heart. Vague presentiments of coming misfortune lie heavy upon me. I try in vain to persuade myself that these are only words of empty anger. I can remember those relentless eyes too clearly to think so. What shall I do—ah, what shall I do? I am no longer master of my own soul. At any moment this loathsome parasite may creep into me, and then—? I must tell someone my hideous secret—I must tell it or go mad. If I had someone to sympathize and advise! Wilson is out of the question. Charles Sadler would understand me only so far as his own experience carries him. Pratt-Haldane! He is a well-balanced man, a man of great common sense and resource. I will go to him. I will tell him everything. God grant that he may be able to advise me!

IV

6.45 p.m. No, it is useless. There is no human help for me; I must fight this out single-handed. Two courses lie before me. I might become this woman's lover. Or I must endure such persecutions as she can inflict upon me. Even if none come, I shall live in a well of apprehension. But she may torture me, she may drive me mad, she may kill me: I will never, never, never give in. What can she inflict which would be worse that the loss of Agatha, and the knowledge that I am a perjured liar, and have forfeited the name of gentleman?

Pratt-Haldane was most amiable, and listened with all politeness to my story. But when I looked at his heavy-set features, his slow eyes, and the ponderous study furniture which surrounded him, I could hardly tell him what I had come to say. It was all so substantial, so material. And, besides, what would I myself have said a short month ago if one of my colleagues had come to me with a story of demonic possession? Perhaps I should have been less patient than he was. As it was, he took notes of my statement, asked me how much tea I drank, how many hours I slept, whether I had been overworking much, had I had sudden pains in the head, evil dreams, singing in the ears, flashing before the eyes—all questions which pointed to his belief that brain congestion was at the bottom of my trouble. Finally he dismissed me with a great many platitudes about open-air exercise, and avoidance of nervous excitement. His prescription, which was for chloral and bromide, I rolled up and threw into the gutter.

No, I can look for no help from any human being. If I consult any more, they may put their heads together and I may find myself in an asylum. I can but grip my courage with both hands, and pray that an honest man may not be abandoned.

April 15. It is the sweetest spring within the memory of man. So green, so mild, so beautiful! Ah, what a contrast between nature without and my own soul so torn with doubt and terror! It has been an uneventful day, but I know that I am on the edge of an abyss. I know it, and yet I go on with the routine of my life. The one bright spot is that Agatha is happy and well and out of all danger. If this creature had a hand on each of us, what might she not do?

April 16. The woman is ingenious in her torments. She knows how fond I am of my work, and how highly my lectures are thought of. So it is from that point that she now attacks me. It will end, I can see, in my losing my professorship, but I will fight to the finish. She shall not drive me out of it without a struggle.

I was not conscious of any change during my lecture this morning save that for a minute or two I had a dizziness and swimminess which rapidly passed away. On the contrary, I congratulated myself upon having made my subject (the functions of the red corpuscles) both interesting and clear. I was surprised, therefore, when a student came into my laboratory immediately after the lecture, and complained of being puzzled by the discrepancy between my statements and those in the textbooks. He showed me his notebook, in which I was reported as having in one portion of the lecture championed the most outrageous and unscientific heresies. Of course I denied it, and declared that he had misunderstood me, but on comparing his notes with those of his companions, it became clear that he was right, and that I really had made some most preposterous statements. Of course I shall explain it away as being the result of a moment of aberration, but I feel only too sure that it will be the first of a series. It is but a month now to the end of the session, and I pray that I may be able to hold out until then.

April 26. Ten days have elapsed since I have had the heart to make any entry in my journal. Why should I record my own humiliation and degradation? I had vowed never to open it again. And yet the force of habit is strong, and here I find myself taking up once more the record of my own dreadful experiences—in much the same spirit in which a suicide has been known to take notes of the effects of the poison which killed him.

Well, the crash which I had foreseen has come—and that no further back than yesterday. The university authorities have taken my lectureship away from me. It has been done in the most delicate way, purporting to be a temporary measure to relieve me from the effects of overwork, and to give me the opportunity of recovering my health. None the less, it has been done, and I am no longer Professor Gilroy. The laboratory is still in my charge, but I have little doubt that that also will soon go.

The fact is that my lectures had become the laughing-stock of the university. My class was crowded with students who came to see and hear what the eccentric professor would do or say next. I cannot go into the detail of my humiliation. Oh, that devilish woman! There is no depth of buffoonery and imbecility to which she has not forced me. I would begin my lecture clearly and well, but always with the sense of a coming eclipse. Then as I felt the influence I would struggle against it, striving with clenched hands and beads of sweat upon my brow to get the better of it, while the students, hearing my incoherent words and watching my contortions, would roar with laughter at the antics of their professor. And then, when she had once fairly mastered me, out would come the most outrageous things—silly jokes, sentiments as though I were proposing a toast, snatches of ballads, personal abuse even against some member of my class. And then in a moment my brain would clear again, and my lecture would proceed decorously to the end. No wonder that my conduct has been the talk of the colleges. No wonder that the University Senate has been compelled to take official notice of such a scandal. Oh, that devilish woman!

And the most dreadful part of it all is my own loneliness. Here I sit in a commonplace English bow-window, looking out upon a commonplace English street with its garish buses and its lounging policeman, and behind me there hangs a shadow which is out of all keeping with the age and place. In the home of knowledge I am weighed down and tortured by a power of which science knows nothing. No magistrate would listen to me. No paper would discuss my case. No doctor would believe my symptoms. My own most intimate friends would only look upon it as a sign of brain derangement. I am out of all touch with my kind. Oh, that devilish woman! Let her have a care! She may push me too far. When the law cannot help a man, he may make a law for himself.

She met me in the High Street yesterday evening and spoke to me. It was as well for her, perhaps, that it was not between the hedges of a lonely country road. She asked me with her cold smile whether I had been chastened yet. I did not deign to answer her. 'We must try another turn of the screw,' said she. Have a care, my lady, have a care! I had her at my mercy once. Perhaps another chance may come.

April 28. The suspension of my lectureship has had the effect also of taking away her means of annoying me, and so I have enjoyed two blessed days of peace. After all, there is no reason to despair. Sympathy pours in to me from all sides, and everyone agrees that it is my devotion to science and the arduous nature of my researches which have shaken my nervous system. I have had the kindest message from the council advising me to travel abroad, and expressing the confident hope that I may be able to resume all my duties by the beginning of the summer term. Nothing could be more flattering than their allusions to my career and to my services to the university. It is only in misfortune that one can test one's own popularity. This creature may weary of tormenting me, and then all may yet be well. May God grant it!

April 29. Our sleepy little town has had a small sensation. The only knowledge of crime which we ever have is when a rowdy undergraduate breaks a few lamps or comes to blows with a policeman. Last night, however, there was an attempt made to break into the branch of the Bank of England, and we are all in a flutter in consequence.

Parkinson, the manager, is an intimate friend of mine, and I found him very much excited when I walked round there after breakfast. Had the thieves broken into the counting-house, they would still have had the safes to reckon with, so that the defence was considerably stronger that the attack. Indeed, the latter does not appear to have ever been very formidable. Two of the lower windows have marks as if a chisel or some such instrument had been pushed under them to force them open. The police should have a good clue, for the woodwork had been done with green paint only the day before, and from the smears it is evident that some of it has found its way on to the criminal's hands or clothes.

4.30 p.m. Ah, that accursed woman! That thrice accursed woman! Never mind! She shall not beat me! No, she shall not! But, oh, the she-devil! She has taken my professorship. Now she would take my honour. Is there nothing I can do against her, nothing save—Ah, but, hard pushed as I am, I cannot bring myself to think of that!

It was about an hour ago that I went into my bedroom, and was brushing my hair before the glass, when suddenly my eyes lit upon something which left me so sick and cold that I sat down upon the edge of the bed and began to cry. It is many a long year since I shed tears, but all my nerve was gone, and I could but sob and sob in impotent grief and anger. There was my house jacket, the coat I usually wear after dinner, hanging on its peg by the wardrobe, with the right sleeve thickly crusted from wrist to elbow with daubs of green paint.

So this was what she meant by another turn of the screw! She had made a public imbecile of me. Now she would brand me as a criminal. This time she has failed. But how about the next? I dare not think of it—and of Agatha and my poor old mother! I wish that I were dead!

Yes, this is the other turn of the screw. And this is also what she meant, no doubt, when she said that I had not realized yet the power she has over me. I look back at my account of my conversation with her, and I see how she declares that with a slight exertion of her will her subject would be conscious, and with a stronger one unconscious. Last night I was unconscious. I could have sworn that I slept soundly in my bed without so much as a dream. And yet those stains tell me that I dressed, made my way out, attempted to open the bank windows, and returned. Was I observed? Is it possible that someone saw me do it and followed me home? Ah, what a hell my life has become! I have no peace, no rest. But my patience is nearing its end.

10 p.m. I have cleaned my coat with turpentine. I do not think that anyone could have seen me. It was with my screwdriver that I made the marks. I found it all crusted with paint, and I have cleaned it. My head aches as if it would burst, and I have taken five grains of antipyrine. If it were not for Agatha, I should have taken fifty and had an end of it.

May 3. Three quiet days. This hell-fiend is like a cat with a mouse. She lets me loose only to pounce upon me again. I am never so frightened as when everything is still. My physical state is deplorable—perpetual hiccough and ptosis of the left eyelid.

I have heard from the Mardens that they will be back the day after tomorrow. I do not know whether I am glad or sorry. They were safe in London. Once here they may be drawn into the miserable network in which I am myself struggling. And I must tell them of it. I cannot marry Agatha so long as I know that I am not responsible for my own actions. Yes, I must tell them, even if it brings everything to an end between us.

Tonight is the university ball, and I must go. God knows I never felt less in the humour for festivity, but I must not have it said that I am unfit to appear in public. If I am seen there, and have speech with some of the elders of the university it will go a long way toward showing them that it would be unjust to take my chair away from me.

11.30 p.m. I have been to the ball. Charles Sadler and I went together, but I have come away before him. I shall wait up for him, however, for, indeed, I fear to go to sleep these nights. He is a cheery, practical fellow, and a chat with him will steady my nerves. On the whole, the evening was a great success. I talked to everyone who has influence, and I think that I made them realize that my chair is not vacant quite yet. The creature was at the ball—unable to dance, of course, but sitting with Mrs Wilson. Again and again her eyes rested upon me. They were almost the last things I saw before I left the room. Once, as I sat sideways to her, I watched her, and saw that her gaze was following someone else. It was Sadler, who was dancing at the time with the second Miss Thurston. To judge by her expression, it is well for him that he is not in her grip as I am. He does not know the escape he has had. I think I hear his step in the street now, and I will go down and let him in. If he will—

May 4. Why did I break off in this way last night? I never went downstairs after all—at least, I have no recollection of doing so. But, on the other hand, I cannot remember going to bed. One of my hands is greatly swollen this morning, and yet I have no remembrance of injuring it yesterday. Otherwise, I am feeling all the better for last night's festivity. But I cannot understand how it is that I did not meet Charles Sadler when I so fully intended to do so. Is it possible—My God, it is only too probable! Has she been leading me some devil's dance again? I will go down to Sadler and ask him.

Midday. The thing has come to a crisis. My life is not worth living. But, if I am to die, then she shall come also. I will not leave her behind, to drive some other man mad as she has me. No, I have come to the limit of my endurance. She has made me as desperate and dangerous a man as walks the earth. God knows I have never had the heart to hurt a fly, and yet, if I had my hands now upon that woman, she should never leave this room alive. I shall see her this very day, and she shall learn what she has to expect of me.

I went to Sadler and found him, to my surprise, in bed. As I entered he sat up and turned a face toward me which sickened me as I looked at it.

'Why, Sadler, what has happened?' I cried, but my heart turned cold as I said it.

'Gilroy,' he answered, mumbling with his swollen lips, 'I have for some weeks been under the impression that you are a madman. Now I know it, and that you are a dangerous one as well. If it were not that I am unwilling to make a scandal in the college, you would now be in the hands of the police.'

'Do you mean—' I cried.

'I mean that as I opened the door last night you rushed out upon me, struck me with both your fists in the face, knocked me down, kicked me furiously in the side, and left me lying almost unconscious in the street. Look at your own hand bearing witness against you.'

Yes, there it was, puffed up, with sponge-like knuckles, as after some terrific blow. What could I do? Though he put me down as a madman, I must tell him all. I sat by his bed and went over all my troubles from the beginning. I poured them out with quivering hands and burning words which might have carried conviction to the most sceptical. 'She hates you and she hates me!' I cried. 'She revenged herself last night on both of us at once. She saw me leave the ball, and she must have seen you also. She knew how long it would take you to reach home. Then she had but to use her wicked will. Ah, your bruised face is a small thing beside my bruised soul!'

He was struck by my story. That was evident. 'Yes, yes, she watched me out of the room,' he muttered. 'She is capable of it. But is it possible that she has really reduced you to this? What do you intend to do?'

'To stop it!' I cried. 'I am perfectly desperate; I shall give her fair warning today, and the next time will be the last.'

'Do nothing rash,' said he.

'Rash!' I cried. 'The only rash thing is that I should postpone it another hour.' With that I rushed to my room, and here I am on the eve of what may be the great crisis of my life. I shall start at once. I have gained one thing today, for I have made one man, at least, realize the truth of this monstrous experience of mine. And, if the worst should happen, this diary remains as a proof of the goad that has driven me.

Evening. When I came to Wilson's, I was shown up, and found that he was sitting with Miss Penelosa. For half an hour I had to endure his fussy talk about his recent research into the exact nature of the spiritualistic rap, while the creature and I sat in silence looking across the room at each other. I read a sinister amusement in her eyes, and she must have seen hatred and menace in mine. I had almost despaired of having speech with her when he was called from the room, and we were left for a few moments together.

'Well, Professor Gilroy—or is it Mr Gilroy?' said she, with that bitter smile of hers. 'How is your friend Mr Charles Sadler after the ball?'

'You fiend!' I cried. 'You have come to the end of your tricks now. I will have no more of them. Listen to what I say.' I strode across and shook her roughly by the shoulder. 'As sure as there is a God in heaven, I swear that if you try another of your devilries upon me, I will have your life for it. Come what may, I will have your life. I have come to the end of what a man can endure.'

'Accounts are not quite settled between us,' said she, with a passion that equalled my own. 'I can love, and I can hate. You had your choice. You chose to spurn the first; now you must test the other. It will take a little more to break your spirit, I see, but broken it shall be. Miss Marden comes back tomorrow as I understand.'

'What has that to do with you?' I cried. 'It is a pollution that you should dare even to think of her. If I thought that you would harm her—'

She was frightened, I could see, though she tried to brazen it out. She read the black thought in my mind, and cowered away from me.

'She is fortunate in having such a champion,' said she. 'He actually dares to threaten a lonely woman. I must really congratulate Miss Marden upon her protector.'

The words were bitter, but the voice and manner were more acid still.

'There is no use talking,' said I. 'I only came here to tell you—and to tell you most solemnly—that your next outrage upon me will be your last.' With that, as I heard Wilson's step upon the stair, I walked from the room. Ay, she may look venomous and deadly, but, for all that, she is beginning to see now that she has as much to fear from me as I can have from her. Murder! It has an ugly sound. But you don't talk of murdering a snake or of murdering a tiger. Let her have a care now.

May 5. I met Agatha and her mother at the station at eleven o'clock. She is looking so bright, so happy, so beautiful. And she was so overjoyed to see me. What have I done to deserve such love? I went back home with them, and we lunched together. All the troubles seem in a moment to have been shredded back from my life. She tells me that I am looking pale and worried and ill. The dear child puts it down to my loneliness and the perfunctory attention of a housekeeper. I pray that she may never know the truth! May the shadow, if shadow there must be, lie ever black across my life and leave hers in the sunshine. I have just come back from them, feeling a new man. With her by my side I think that I could show a bold face to anything which life might send.

5 p.m. Now, let me try to be accurate. Let me try to say exactly how it occurred. It is fresh in my mind, and I can set it down correctly, though it is not likely that the time will ever come when I shall forget the doings of today.

I had returned from the Mardens' after lunch, and was cutting some microscopic sections in my freezing microtome, when in an instant I lost consciousness in the sudden hateful fashion which has become only too familiar to me of late.

When my senses came back to me I was sitting in a small chamber, very different from the one in which I had been working. It was cosy and bright, with chintz-covered settees, coloured hangings, and a thousand pretty little trifles upon the wall. A small ornamental clock ticked in front of me, and the hands pointed to half-past three. It was all quite familiar to me, and yet I stared about for a moment in a half-dazed way until my eyes fell upon a cabinet photograph of myself upon the top of the piano. On the other side stood one of Mrs Marden. Then, of course, I remembered where I was. It was Agatha's boudoir.

But how came I there, and what did I want? A horrible sinking came to my heart. Had I been sent there on some devilish errand? Had that errand already been done? Surely it must; otherwise, why should I be allowed to come back to consciousness? Oh, the agony of that moment! What had I done? I sprang to my feet in my despair, and as I did so a small glass bottle fell from my knees onto the carpet.

It was unbroken, and I picked it up. Outside was written 'Sulphuric Acid. Fort'. When I drew the round glass stopper, a thick fume rose slowly up, and a pungent, choking smell pervaded the room. I recognized it as one which I kept for chemical testing in my chambers. But why had I brought a bottle of vitriol into Agatha's chamber? Was it not this thick, reeking liquid with which jealous women had been known to mar the beauty of their rivals? My heart stood still as I held the bottle to the light. Thank God, it was full! No mischief had been done as yet. But had Agatha come in a minute sooner, was it not certain that the hellish parasite within me would have dashed the stuff into her—Ah, it will not bear to be thought of! But it must have been for that. Why else should I have brought it? At the thought of what I might have done my worn nerves broke down, and I sat shivering and twitching, the pitiable wreck of a man.

It was the sound of Agatha's voice and the rustle of her dress which restored me. I looked up, and saw her blue eyes, so full of tenderness and pity, gazing down at me.

'We must take you away to the country, Austin,' she said. 'You want rest and quiet. You look wretchedly ill.'

'Oh, it is nothing!' said I, trying to smile. 'It was only a momentary weakness. I am all right again now.'

'I am so sorry to keep you waiting. Poor boy, you must have been here quite half an hour! The vicar was in the drawing-room, and, as I knew that you did not care for him, I thought it better that Jane should show you up here. I thought the man would never go!'

'Thank God he stayed! Thank God he stayed!' I cried hysterically.

'Why, what is the matter with you, Austin?' she asked, holding my arm as I staggered up from the chair. 'Why are you glad that the vicar stayed? And what is this little bottle in your hand?'

'Nothing,' I cried, thrusting it into my pocket. 'But I must go. I have something important to do.'

'How stern you look, Austin! I have never seen your face like that. You are angry?'

'Yes, I am angry.'

'But not with me?'

'No, no, my darling! You would not understand.'

'But you have not told me why you came.'

'I came to ask you whether you would always love me—no matter what I did, or what shadow might fall on my name. Would you believe in me and trust me however black appearances might be against me?'

'You know that I would, Austin.'

'Yes, I know that you would. What I do I shall do for you. I am driven to it. There is no other way out, my darling!' I kissed her and rushed from the room.

The time for indecision was at an end. As long as the creature threatened my own prospects and my honour there might be a question as to what I should do. But now, when Agatha—my innocent Agatha—was endangered, my duty lay before me like a turnpike road. I had no weapon, but I never paused for that. What weapon should I need, when I felt every muscle quivering with the strength of a frenzied man? I ran through the streets, so set upon what I had to do that I was only dimly conscious also that Professor Wilson met me, running with equal precipitance in the opposite direction. Breathless but resolute I reached the house and rang the bell. A white-cheeked maid opened the door, and turned whiter yet when she saw the face that look in at her.

'Show me up at once to Miss Penelosa,' I demanded.

'Sir,' she gasped, 'Miss Penelosa died this afternoon at half-past three!'

GOOD LADY DUCAYNE

Mary E. Braddon

Mary Elizabeth Braddon (1835–1915) is now recognized as the liveliest and most productive of all the nineteenth-century sensation novelists. After the tremendous success of *Lady Audley's Secret* (in 1862) came *Aurora Floyd*, *Eleanor's Victory*, *Sir Jasper's Tenant*, and nearly seventy other popular novels. She was a close friend of Bram and Florence Stoker for many years. When she wrote to Stoker on 23 June 1897 congratulating him on *Dracula*, she added: 'We will talk of it more anon! when I have soberly read and meditated thereupon. I have done my humdrum little story of transfusion, in the Good Lady Ducayne—but your "bloofer lady". . . .!' Miss Braddon's 'Good Lady Ducayne' appeared in the *Strand Magazine* for February 1896, finely illustrated by Gordon Browne, son of 'Phiz'. It was not reprinted in any of her subsequent books.

I

BELLA ROLLESTON had made up her mind that her only chance of earning her bread and helping her mother to an occasional crust was by going out into the great unknown world as companion to a lady. She was willing to go to any lady rich enough to pay her a salary and so eccentric as to wish for a hired companion. Five shillings told off reluctantly from one of those sovereigns which were so rare with the mother and daughter, and which melted away so quickly, five solid shillings, had been handed to a smartly-dressed lady in an office in Harbeck Street, W., in the hope that this very Superior Person would find a situation and a salary for Miss Rolleston.

The Superior Person glanced at the two half-crowns as they lay on the table where Bella's hand had placed them, to make sure they were neither of them florins, before she wrote a description of Bella's qualifications and requirements in a formidable-looking ledger.

'Age?' she asked curtly.

'Eighteen, last July.'

'Any accomplishments?'

'No; I am not at all accomplished. If I were I should want to be a governess—a companion seems the lowest stage.'

'We have some highly accomplished ladies on our books as companions, or chaperon companions.'

'Oh, I know!' babbled Bella, loquacious in her youthful candour. 'But that is quite a different thing. Mother hasn't been able to afford a piano since I was twelve years old, so I'm afraid I've forgotten how to play. And I have had to help mother with her needlework, so there hasn't been much time to study.'

'Please don't waste time upon explaining what you can't do, but kindly tell me anything you can do,' said the Superior Person, crushingly, with her pen poised between delicate fingers waiting to write. 'Can you read aloud for two or three hours at a stretch? Are you active and handy, an early riser, a good walker, sweet tempered, and obliging?'

'I can say yes to all those questions except about the sweetness. I think I have a pretty good temper, and I should be anxious to oblige anybody who paid for my services. I should want them to feel that I was really earning my salary.'

'The kind of ladies who come to me would not care for a talkative companion,' said the Person, severely, having finished writing in her book. 'My connection lies chiefly among the aristocracy, and in that class considerable deference is expected.'

'Oh, of course,' said Bella; 'but it's quite different when I'm talking to you. I want to tell you all about myself once and for ever.'

'I am glad it is to be only once!' said the Person, with the edges of her lips.

The Person was of uncertain age, tightly laced in a black silk gown. She had a powdery complexion and a handsome clump of somebody else's hair on the top of her head. It may be that Bella's girlish freshness and vivacity had an irritating effect upon nerves weakened by an eight hours day in that over-heated second floor in Harbeck Street. To Bella the official apartment, with its Brussels carpet, velvet curtains and velvet chairs, and French clock, ticking loud on the marble chimney-piece, suggested the luxury of a palace, as compared with another second floor in Walworth where Mrs Rolleston and her daughter had managed to exist for the last six years.

'Do you think you have anything on your books that would suit me?' faltered Bella, after a pause.

'Oh, dear, no; I have nothing in view at present,' answered the Person, who had swept Bella's half-crowns into a drawer, absent-mindedly, with the tips of her fingers. 'You see, you are so very unformed—so much too young to be companion to a lady of position. It is a pity you have not enough education for a nursery governess; that would be more in your line.'

'And do you think it will be very long before you can get me a situation?' asked Bella, doubtfully.

'I really cannot say. Have you any particular reason for being so impatient—not a love affair, I hope?'

'A love affair!' cried Bella, with flaming cheeks. 'What utter nonsense. I want a situation because mother is poor, and I hate being a burden to her. I want a salary that I can share with her.'

'There won't be much margin for sharing in the salary you are likely to get at your age—and with your—very—unformed manners,' said the Person, who found Bella's peony cheeks, bright eyes, and unbridled vivacity more and more oppressive.

'Not a love affair, I hope?'

'Perhaps if you'd be kind enough to give me back the fee I could take it to an agency where the connection isn't quite so aristocratic,' said Bella, who—as she told her mother in her recital of the interview—was determined not to be sat upon.

'You will find no agency that can do more for you than mine,' replied the Person, whose harpy fingers never relinquished coin. 'You will have to wait for your opportunity. Yours is an exceptional case: but I will bear you in mind, and if anything suitable offers I will write to you. I cannot say more than that.'

The half-contemptuous bend of the stately head, weighted with borrowed hair, indicated the end of the interview. Bella went back to Walworth—tramped sturdily every inch of the way in the September afternoon—and 'took off' the Superior Person for the amusement of her mother and the landlady, who lingered in the shabby litle sitting-room after bringing in the tea-tray, to applaud Miss Rolleston's 'taking off'.

'Dear, dear, what a mimic she is!' said the landlady. 'You ought to have let her go on the stage, mum. She might have made her fortune as a hactress.'

II

Bella waited and hoped, and listened for the postman's knocks which brought such store of letters for the parlours and the first floor, and so few for that humble second floor, where mother and daughter sat sewing with hand and with wheel and treadle, for the greater part of the day. Mrs Rolleston was a lady by birth and education; but it had been her bad fortune to marry a scoundrel; for the last half-dozen years she had been that worst of widows, a wife whose husband had deserted her. Happily, she was courageous, industrious, and a clever needle-woman; and she had been able just to earn a living for herself and her only child, by making mantles and cloaks for a West-end house. It was not a luxurious living. Cheap lodgings in a shabby street off the Walworth Road, scanty dinners, homely food, well-worn raiment, had been the portion of mother and daughter; but they loved each other so dearly, and Nature had made them both so light-hearted, that they had contrived somehow to be happy.

But now this idea of going out into the world as companion to some fine lady had rooted itself into Bella's mind, and although she idolized her mother, and although the parting of mother and daughter must needs tear two loving hearts into shreds, the girl longed for enterprise and change and excitement, as the pages of old longed to be knights, and to start for the Holy Land to break a lance with the infidel.

She grew tired of racing downstairs every time the postman knock-ed, only to be told 'nothing for you, miss,' by the smudgy-faced drudge who picked up the letters from the passage floor. 'Nothing for you, miss,' grinned the lodging-house drudge, till at last Bella took heart of grace and walked up to Harbeck Street, and asked the Superior Person how it was that no situation had been found for her.

'You are too young,' said the Person, 'and you want a salary.'

'Of course I do,' answered Bella; 'don't other people want salaries?'

'Young ladies of your age generally want a comfortable home.'

'I don't,' snapped Bella; 'I want to help mother.'

'You can call again this day week,' said the Person; 'or, if I hear of anything in the meantime, I will write to you.'

No letter came from the Person, and in exactly a week Bella put on her neatest hat, the one that had been seldomest caught in the rain, and trudged off to Harbeck Street.

It was a dull October afternoon, and there was a greyness in the air which might turn to fog before night. The Walworth Road shops gleamed brightly through that grey atmosphere, and though to a young lady reared in Mayfair or Belgravia such shop-windows would have been unworthy of a glance, they were a snare and temptation for Bella. There were so many things that she longed for, and would never be able to buy.

Harbeck Street is apt to be empty at this dead season of the year, a long, long street, an endless perspective of eminently respectable houses. The Person's office was at the further end, and Bella looked down that long, grey vista almost despairingly, more tired than usual with the trudge from Walworth. As she looked, a carriage passed her, an old-fashioned, yellow chariot, on cee springs, drawn by a pair of high grey horses, with the stateliest of coachmen driving them, and a tall footman sitting by his side.

'It looks like the fairy god-mother's coach,' thought Bella. 'I shouldn't wonder if it began by being a pumpkin.'

It was a surprise when she reached the Person's door to find the yellow chariot standing before it, and the tall footman waiting near the doorstep. She was almost afraid to go in and meet the owner of that splendid carriage. She had caught only a glimpse of its occupant as the chariot rolled by, a plumed bonnet, a patch of ermine.

The Person's smart page ushered her upstairs and knocked at the official door. 'Miss Rolleston,' he announced, apologetically, while Bella waited outside.

'Show her in,' said the Person, quickly; and then Bella heard her murmuring something in a low voice to her client.

Bella went in fresh, blooming, a living image of youth and hope, and before she looked at the Person her gaze was riveted by the owner of the chariot.

Never had she seen anyone as old as the old lady sitting by the Person's fire: a little old figure, wrapped from chin to feet in an ermine mantle; a withered, old face under a plumed bonnet—a face so wasted by age that it seemed only a pair of eyes and a peaked chin. The nose was peaked, too, but between the sharply pointed chin and the great, shining eyes, the small, aquiline nose was hardly visible.

'This is Miss Rolleston, Lady Ducayne.'

Claw-like fingers, flashing with jewels, lifted a double eyeglass to Lady Ducayne's shining black eyes, and through the glasses Bella saw those unnaturally bright eyes magnified to a gigantic size, and glaring at her awfully.

'Miss Torpinter has told me all about you,' said the old voice that belonged to the eyes. 'Have you good health? Are you strong and active, able to eat well, sleep well, walk well, able to enjoy all that there is good in life?'

'Lady Ducayne'

'I have never known what it is to be ill, or idle,' answered Bella.

'Then I think you will do for me.'

'Of course, in the event of references being perfectly satisfactory,' put in the Person.

'I don't want references. The young woman looks frank and innocent. I'll take her on trust.'

'So like you, dear Lady Ducayne,' murmured Miss Torpinter.

'I want a strong young woman whose health will give me no trouble.'

'You have been so unfortunate in that respect,' cooed the Person, whose voice and manner were subdued to a melting sweetness by the old woman's presence.

'Yes, I've been rather unlucky,' grunted Lady Ducayne.

'But I am sure Miss Rolleston will not disappoint you, though certainly after your unpleasant experience with Miss Tomson, who looked the picture of health—and Miss Blandy, who said she had never seen a doctor since she was vaccinated——'

'Lies, no doubt,' muttered Lady Ducayne, and then turning to Bella, she asked, curtly, 'You don't mind spending the winter in Italy, I suppose?'

In Italy! The very word was magical. Bella's fair young face flushed crimson.

'It has been the dream of my life to see Italy,' she gasped.

From Walworth to Italy! How far, how impossible such a journey had seemed to that romantic dreamer.

'Well, your dream will be realized. Get yourself ready to leave Charing Cross by the train deluxe this day week at eleven. Be sure you are at the station a quarter before the hour. My people will look after you and your luggage.'

Lady Ducayne rose from her chair, assisted by her crutch-stick, and Miss Torpinter escorted her to the door.

'And with regard to salary?' questioned the Person on the way.

'Salary, oh, the same as usual—and if the young woman wants a quarter's pay in advance you can write to me for a cheque,' Lady Ducayne answered, carelessly.

Miss Torpinter went all the way downstairs with her client, and waited to see her seated in the yellow chariot. When she came upstairs again she was slightly out of breath, and she had resumed that superior manner which Bella had found so crushing.

'You may think yourself uncommonly lucky, Miss Rolleston,' she said. 'I have dozens of young ladies on my books whom I might have recommended for this situation—but I remembered having told you to call this afternoon—and I thought I would give you a chance. Old Lady Ducayne is one of the best people on my books. She gives her companion a hundred a year, and pays all travelling expenses. You will live in the lap of luxury.'

'A hundred a year! How too lovely! Shall I have to dress very grandly? Does Lady Ducayne keep much company?'

'At her age! No, she lives in seclusion—in her own apartments—her French maid, her footman, her medical attendant, her courier.'

'Why did those other companions leave her?' asked Bella.

'Their health broke down!'

'Poor things, and so they had to leave?'

'Yes, they had to leave. I suppose you would like a quarter's salary in advance?'

'Oh, yes, please. I shall have things to buy.'

'Very well, I will write for Lady Ducayne's cheque, and I will send you the balance—after deducting my commission for the year.'

'To be sure, I had forgotten the commission.'

'You don't suppose I keep this office for pleasure.'

'Of course not,' murmured Bella, remembering the five shillings entrance fee; but nobody could expect a hundred a year and a winter in Italy for five shillings.

III

'From Miss Rolleston, at Cap Ferrino, to Mrs Rolleston, in Beresford Street, Walworth.

'How I wish you could see this place, dearest; the blue sky, the olive woods, the orange and lemon orchards between the cliffs and the sea—sheltering in the hollow of the great hills—and with summer waves dancing up to the narrow ridge of pebbles and weeds which is the Italian idea of a beach! Oh, how I wish you could see it all, mother dear, and bask in this sunshine, that makes it so difficult to believe the date at the head of this paper. November! The air is like an English June—the sun is so hot that I can't walk a few yards without an umbrella. And to think of you at Walworth while I am here! I could cry at the thought that perhaps you will never see this lovely coast, this wonderful sea, these summer flowers that bloom in winter. There is a hedge of pink geraniums under my window, mother—a thick, rank hedge, as if the flowers grew wild—and there are Dijon roses climbing over arches and palisades all along the terrace—a rose garden full of bloom in November! Just picture it all! You could never imagine the luxury of this hotel. It is nearly new, and has been built and decorated regardless of expense. Our rooms are upholstered in pale blue satin, which shows up Lady Ducayne's parchment complexion; but as she sits all day in a corner of the balcony basking in the sun, except when she is in her carriage, and all the evening in her armchair close to the fire, and never sees anyone but her own people, her complexion matters very little.

'She has the handsomest suite of rooms in the hotel. My bedroom is inside hers, the sweetest room—all blue satin and white lace—white enamelled furniture, looking-glasses on every wall, till I know my pert little profile as I never knew it before. The room was really meant for Lady Ducayne's dressing-room, but she ordered one of the blue satin couches to be arranged as a bed for me—the prettiest little bed, which I can wheel near the window on sunny mornings, as it is on castors and easily moved about. I feel as if Lady Ducayne were a funny old grandmother, who had suddenly appeared in my life, very, very rich, and very, very kind.

'She is not at all exacting. I read aloud to her a good deal, and she dozes and nods while I read. Sometimes I hear her moaning in her sleep—as if she had troublesome dreams. When she is tired of my reading she orders Francine, her maid, to read a French novel to her, and I hear her chuckle and groan now and then, as if she were more

'In the olive woods'

interested in those books than in Dickens or Scott. My French is not good enough to follow Francine, who reads very quickly. I have a great deal of liberty, for Lady Ducayne often tells me to run away and amuse myself; I roam about the hills for hours. Everything is so lovely. I lose myself in olive woods, always climbing up and up towards the pine woods above—and above the pines there are the snow mountains that just show their white peaks above the dark hills. Oh, you poor dear, how can I ever make you understand what this place is like—you, whose poor, tired eyes have only the opposite side of Beresford Street? Sometimes I go no farther than the terrace in front of the hotel, which is a favourite lounging-place with everybody. The gardens lie below, and the tennis courts where I sometimes play with a very nice girl, the only person in the hotel with whom I have made friends. She is a year older than I, and has come to Cap Ferrino with her brother, a doctor—or a medical student, who is going to be a doctor. He passed his M.B. exam at Edinburgh just before they left home, Lotta told me. He came to Italy entirely on his sister's account. She had a troublesome chest attack last summer and was ordered to winter abroad. They are orphans, quite alone in the world, and so fond of each other. It is very nice for me to have such a friend as Lotta. She is so thoroughly respectable. I can't help using that word, for some of the girls in this hotel go on in a way that I know you would shudder at. Lotta was brought up by an aunt, deep down in the country, and knows hardly anything about life. Her brother won't allow her to read a novel, French or English, that he has not read and approved.

'"He treats me like a child," she told me, "but I don't mind, for it's nice to know somebody loves me, and cares about what I do, and even about my thoughts."

'Perhaps this is what makes some girls so eager to marry—the want of someone strong and brave and honest and true to care for them and order them about. I want no one, mother darling, for I have you, and you are all the world to me. No husband could ever come between us two. If I ever were to marry he would have only the second place in my heart. But I don't suppose I ever shall marry, or even know what it is like to have an offer of marriage. No young man can afford to marry a penniless girl nowadays. Life is too expensive.

'Mr Stafford, Lotta's brother, is very clever, and very kind. He thinks it is rather hard for me to have to live with such an old woman as Lady Ducayne, but then he does not know how poor we are—you and I—and what a wonderful life this seems to me in this lovely place. I feel a selfish wretch for enjoying all my luxuries, while you, who want them so much more than I, have none of them—hardly know what they are like—do you, dearest?——for my scamp of a father began to go to the dogs soon after you were married, and since then life has been all trouble and care and struggle for you.'

This letter was written when Bella had been less than a month at Cap Ferrino, before the novelty had worn off the landscape, and before the pleasure of luxurious surroundings had begun to cloy. She wrote to her mother every week, such long letters as girls who have lived in closest companionship with a mother alone can write; letters that are like a diary of heart and mind. She wrote gaily always; but when the new year began Mrs Rolleston thought she detected a note of melancholy under all those lively details about the place and the people.

'My poor girl is getting homesick,' she thought. 'Her heart is in Beresford Street.'

It might be that she missed her new friend and companion, Lotta Stafford, who had gone with her brother for a little tour to Genoa and Spezzia, and as far as Pisa. They were to return before February; but in the meantime Bella might naturally feel very solitary among all those strangers, whose manners and doings she described so well.

The mother's instinct had been true. Bella was not so happy as she had been in that first flush of wonder and delight which followed the change from Walworth to the Riviera. Somehow, she knew not how, lassitude had crept upon her. She no longer loved to climb the hills, no longer flourished her orange stick in sheer gladness of heart as her light feet skipped over the rough ground and the coarse grass on the mountain side. The odour of rosemary and thyme, the fresh breath of the sea, no longer filled her with rapture. She thought of Beresford Street and her mother's face with a sick longing. They were so far—so far away! And then she thought of Lady Ducayne, sitting by the heaped-up olive logs in the over-heated salon—thought of that wizened-nut-cracker profile, and those gleaming eyes, with an invincible horror.

Visitors at the hotel had told her that the air of Cap Ferrino was relaxing—better suited to age than to youth, to sickness than to health. No doubt it was so. She was not so well as she had been at Walworth; but she told herself that she was suffering only from the pain of separation from the dear companion of her girlhood, the mother who had been nurse, sister, friend, flatterer, all things in this world to her. She had shed many tears over that parting, had spent many a melancholy hour on the marble terrace with yearning eyes looking westward, and with her heart's desire a thousand miles away.

She was sitting in her favourite spot, an angle at the eastern end of the terrace, a quiet little nook sheltered by orange trees, when she heard a couple of Riviera habitués talking in the garden below. They were sitting on a bench against the terrace wall.

She had no idea of listening to their talk, till the sound of Lady Ducayne's name attracted her, and then she listened without any thought of wrong-doing. They were talking no secrets—just casually discussing an hotel acquaintance.

They were two elderly people whom Bella only knew by sight. An English clergyman who had wintered abroad for half his lifetime; a stout, comfortable, well-to-do spinster, whose chronic bronchitis obliged her to migrate annually.

'I have met her about Italy for the last ten years,' said the lady; 'but have never found out her real age.'

'With yearning eyes looking westward'

'I put her down at a hundred—not a year less,' replied the parson.
'Her reminiscences all go back to the Regency. She was evidently then
in her zenith; and I have heard her say things that showed she was in
Parisian society when the First Empire was at its best—before Josephine
was divorced.'

'She doesn't talk much now.'

'No; there's not much life left in her. She is wise in keeping herself
secluded. I only wonder that wicked old quack, her Italian doctor,
didn't finish her off years ago.'

'I should think it must be the other way, and that he keeps her alive.'

'My dear Miss Manders, do you think foreign quackery ever kept
anybody alive?'

'Well, there she is—and she never goes anywhere without him. He
certainly has an unpleasant countenance.'

'Unpleasant,' echoed the parson, 'I don't believe the foul fiend
himself can beat him in ugliness. I pity that poor young woman who
has to live between old Lady Ducayne and Dr Parravicini.'

'But the old lady is very good to her companions.'

'No doubt. She is very free with her cash; the servants call her good Lady Ducayne. She is a withered old female Crœsus, and knows she'll never be able to get through her money, and doesn't relish the idea of other people enjoying it when she's in her coffin. People who live to be as old as she is become slavishly attached to life. I daresay she's generous to those poor girls—but she can't make them happy. They die in her service.'

'Don't say they, Mr Carton; I know that one poor girl died at Mentone last spring.'

'Yes, and another poor girl died in Rome three years ago. I was there at the time. Good Lady Ducayne left her there in an English family. The girl had every comfort. The old woman was very liberal to her—but she died. I tell you, Miss Manders, it is not good for any young woman to live with two such horrors as Lady Ducayne and Parravicini.'

They talked of other things—but Bella hardly heard them. She sat motionless, and a cold wind seemed to come down upon her from the mountains and to creep up to her from the sea, till she shivered as she sat there in the sunshine, in the shelter of the orange trees in the midst of all that beauty and brightness.

Yes, they were uncanny, certainly, the pair of them—she so like an aristocratic witch in her withered old age; he of no particular age, with a face that was more like a waxen mask than any human countenance Bella had ever seen. What did it matter? Old age is venerable, and worthy of all reverence; and Lady Ducayne had been very kind to her. Dr Parravicini was a harmless, inoffensive student, who seldom looked up from the book he was reading. He had his private sitting-room, where he made experiments in chemistry and natural science—perhaps in alchemy. What could it matter to Bella? He had always been polite to her, in his far-off way. She could not be more happily placed than she was—in this palatial hotel, with this rich old lady.

No doubt she missed the young English girl who had been so friendly, and it might be that she missed the girl's brother, for Mr Stafford had talked to her a good deal—had interested himself in the books she was reading, and her manner of amusing herself when she was not on duty.

'You must come to our little salon when you are "off," as the hospital nurses call it, and we can have some music. No doubt you play and sing?' upon which Bella had to own with a blush of shame that she had forgotten how to play the piano ages ago.

'Mother and I used to sing duets sometimes between the lights, without accompaniment,' she said, and the tears came into her eyes as she thought of the humble room, the half-hour's respite from work, the sewing-machine standing where a piano ought to have been, and her mother's plaintive voice, so sweet, so true, so dear.

Sometimes she found herself wondering whether she would ever see that beloved mother again. Strange forebodings came into her mind. She was angry with herself for giving way to melancholy thoughts.

One day she questioned Lady Ducayne's French maid about those two companions who had died within three years.

'They were poor, feeble creatures,' Francine told her. 'They looked fresh and bright enough when they came to Miladi; but they ate too much and they were lazy. They died of luxury and idleness. Miladi was too kind to them. They had nothing to do; and so they took to fancying things; fancying the air didn't suit them, that they couldn't sleep.'

'I sleep well enough, but I have had a strange dream several times since I have been in Italy.'

'Ah, you had better not begin to think about dreams, or you will be like those other girls. They were dreamers—and they dreamt themselves into the cemetery.'

The dream troubled her a little, not because it was a ghastly or frightening dream, but on account of sensations which she had never felt before in sleep—a whirring of wheels that went round in her brain, a great noise like a whirlwind, but rhythmical like the ticking of a gigantic clock: and then in the midst of this uproar as of winds and waves she seemed to sink into a gulf of unconsciousness, out of sleep into far deeper sleep—total extinction. And then, after that blank interval, there had come the sound of voices, and then again the whirr of wheels, louder and louder—and again the blank—and then she knew no more till morning, when she awoke, feeling languid and oppressed.

She told Dr Parravicini of her dream one day, on the only occasion when she wanted his professional advice. She had suffered rather severely from the mosquitoes before Christmas—and had been almost frightened at finding a wound upon her arm which she could only attribute to the venomous sting of one of these torturers. Parravicini put on his glasses, and scrutinized the angry mark on the round, white arm, as Bella stood before him and Lady Ducayne with her sleeve rolled up above her elbow.

'Yes, that's rather more than a joke,' he said, 'he has caught you on the top of a vein. What a vampire! But there's no harm done, signorina, nothing that a litle dressing of mine won't heal. You must always show me any bite of this nature. It might be dangerous if neglected. These creatures feed on poison and disseminate it.'

'And to think that such tiny creatures can bite like this,' said Bella; 'my arm looks as if it had been cut by a knife.'

'If I were to show you a mosquito's sting under my microscope you wouldn't be surprised at that,' replied Parravicini.

Bella had to put up with the mosquito bites, even when they came on the top of a vein, and produced that ugly wound. The wound recurred now and then at longish intervals, and Bella found Dr Parravicini's

'What a vampire!'

dressing a speedy cure. If he were the quack his enemies called him, he had at least a light hand and a delicate touch in performing this small operation.

'Bella Rolleston to Mrs Rolleston—April 14th.

'Ever Dearest,—Behold the cheque for my second quarter's salary—five and twenty pounds. There is no one to pinch off a whole tenner for a year's commission as there was last time, so it is all for you, mother, dear. I have plenty of pocket-money in hand from the cash I brought away with me, when you insisted on my keeping more than I wanted. It isn't possible to spend money here—except on occasional tips to servants, or sous to beggars and children—unless one had lots to spend, for everything one would like to buy—tortoise-shell, coral, lace—is so ridiculously dear that only a millionaire ought to look at it. Italy is a dream of beauty: but for shopping, give me Newington Causeway.

'You ask me so earnestly if I am quite well that I fear my letters must have been very dull lately. Yes, dear, I am well—but I am not quite so strong as I was when I used to trudge to the West-end to buy half a pound of tea—just for a constitutional walk—or to Dulwich to look at the pictures. Italy is relaxing; and I feel what the people here call "slack". But I fancy I can see your dear face looking worried as you read this. Indeed, and indeed, I am not ill. I am only a little tired of this lovely scene—as I suppose one might get tired of looking at one of Turner's pictures if it hung on a wall that was always opposite one. I think of you every hour in every day—think of you and our homely little room—our dear little shabby parlour, with the armchairs from the wreck of your old home, and Dick singing in his cage over the sewing-machine. Dear, shrill, maddening Dick, who, we flattered ourselves, was so passionately fond of us. Do tell me in your next that he is well.

'My friend Lotta and her brother never came back after all. They went from Pisa to Rome. Happy mortals! And they are to be on the Italian lakes in May; which lake was not decided when Lotta last wrote to me. She has been a charming correspondent, and has confided all her little flirtations to me. We are all to go to Bellaggio next week—by Genoa and Milan. Isn't that lovely? Lady Ducayne travels by the easiest stages—except when she is bottled up in the train de luxe. We shall stop two days at Genoa and one at Milan. What a bore I shall be to you with my talk about Italy when I come home.

'Love and love—and ever more love from your adoring, Bella.'

IV

Herbert Stafford and his sister had often talked of the pretty English girl with her fresh complexion, which made such a pleasant touch of rosy colour among all those sallow faces at the Grand Hotel. The young doctor thought of her with a compassionate tenderness—her utter loneliness in that great hotel where there were so many people, her bondage to that old, old woman, where everybody else was free to think of nothing but enjoying life. It was a hard fate; and the poor child was evidently devoted to her mother, and felt the pain of separation—'only two of them, and very poor, and all the world to each other,' he thought.

Lotta told him one morning that they were to meet again at Bellaggio. 'The old thing and her court are to be there before we are,' she said. 'I shall be charmed to have Bella again. She is so bright and gay—in spite of an occasional touch of homesickness. I never took to a girl on a short acquaintance as I did to her.'

'I like her best when she is homesick,' said Herbert; 'for then I am sure she has a heart.'

'What have you to do with hearts, except for dissection? Don't forget that Bella is an absolute pauper. She told me in confidence that her mother makes mantles for a West-end shop. You can hardly have a lower depth than that.'

'I shouldn't think any less of her if her mother made match-boxes.'

'Not in the abstract—of course not. Match-boxes are honest labour. But you couldn't marry a girl whose mother makes mantles.'

'We haven't come to the consideration of that question yet,' answered Herbert, who liked to provoke his sister.

In two years' hospital practice he had seen too much of the grim realities of life to retain any prejudices about rank. Cancer, phthisis, gangrene, leave a man with little respect for the outward differences which vary the husk of humanity. The kernel is always the same— fearfully and wonderfully made—a subject for pity and terror.

Mr Stafford and his sister arrived at Bellaggio in a fair May evening. The sun was going down as the steamer approached the pier; and all that glory of purple bloom which curtains every wall at this season of the year flushed and deepened in the glowing light. A group of ladies were standing on the pier watching the arrivals, and among them Herbert saw a pale face that startled him out of his wonted composure.

'There she is,' murmured Lotta, at his elbow, 'but how dreadfully changed. She looks a wreck.'

They were shaking hands with her a few minutes later, and a flush had lighted up her poor pinched face in the pleasure of meeting.

'I thought you might come this evening,' she said. 'We have been here a week.'

She did not add that she had been there every evening to watch the boat in, and a good many times during the day. The Grand Bretagne was close by, and it had been easy for her to creep to the pier when the boat bell rang. She felt a joy in meeting these people again; a sense of being with friends; a confidence which Lady Ducayne's goodness had never inspired in her.

'Oh, you poor darling, how awfully ill you must have been,' exclaimed Lotta, as the two girls embraced.

Bella tried to answer, but her voice was choked with tears.

'What has been the matter, dear? That horrid influenza, I suppose?'

'No, no, I have not been ill—I have only felt a little weaker than I used to be. I don't think the air of Cap Ferrino quite agreed with me.'

'It must have disagreed with you abominably. I never saw such a change in anyone. Do let Herbert doctor you. He is fully qualified, you know. He prescribed for ever so many influenza patients at the Londres. They were glad to get advice from an English doctor in a friendly way.'

'I am sure he must be very clever!' faltered Bella, 'but there is really nothing the matter. I am not ill, and if I were ill, Lady Ducayne's physician——'

'That dreadful man with the yellow face? I would as soon one of the Borgias prescribed for me. I hope you haven't been taking any of his medicines.'

'No, dear, I have taken nothing. I have never complained of being ill.'

This was said while they were all three walking to the hotel. The Staffords' rooms had been secured in advance, pretty ground-floor rooms, opening into the garden. Lady Ducayne's statelier apartments were on the floor above.

'I believe these rooms are just under ours,' said Bella.

'Then it will be all the easier for you to run down to us,' replied Lotta, which was not really the case, as the grand staircase was in the centre of the hotel.

'Oh, I shall find it easy enough,' said Bella. 'I'm afraid you'll have too much of my society. Lady Ducayne sleeps away half the day in this warm weather, so I have a good deal of idle time; and I get awfully moped thinking of mother and home.'

Her voice broke upon the last word. She could not have thought of that poor lodging which went by the name of home more tenderly had it been the most beautiful that art and wealth ever created. She moped and pined in this lovely garden, with the sunlit lake and the romantic hills spreading out their beauty before her. She was homesick and she had dreams: or, rather, an occasional recurrence of that one bad dream with all its strange sensations—it was more like a hallucination than dreaming—the whirring of wheels; the sinking into an abyss; the struggling back to consciousness. She had the dream shortly before she left Cap Ferrino, but not since she had come to Bellaggio, and she began to hope the air in this lake district suited her better, and that those strange sensations would never return.

Mr Stafford wrote a prescription and had it made up at the chemist's near the hotel. It was a powerful tonic, and after two bottles, and a row or two on the lake, and some rambling over the hills and in the meadows where the spring flowers made earth seem paradise, Bella's spirits and looks improved as if by magic.

'It is a wonderful tonic,' she said, but perhaps in her heart of hearts she knew that the doctor's kind voice and the friendly hand that helped her in and out of the boat, and the watchful care that went with her by land and lake, had something to do with her cure.

'I hope you don't forget that her mother makes mantles,' Lotta said, warningly.

'Or match-boxes: it is just the same thing, so far as I am concerned.'

'You mean that in no circumstances could you think of marrying her?'

'I mean that if ever I love a woman well enough to think of marrying her, riches or rank will count for nothing with me. But I fear—I fear your poor friend may not live to be any man's wife.'

'Do you think her so very ill?'

He sighed, and left the question unanswered.

One day, while they were gathering wild hyacinths in an upland meadow, Bella told Mr Stafford about her bad dream.

'It is curious only because it is hardly like a dream,' she said. 'I daresay you could find some common-sense reason for it. The position of my head on my pillow, or the atmosphere, or something.'

And then she described her sensations; how in the midst of sleep there came a sudden sense of suffocation; and then those whirring wheels, so loud, so terrible; and then a blank, and then a coming back to waking consciousness.

'Have you ever had chloroform given you—by a dentist, for instance?'

'Never—Dr Parravicini asked me that question one day.'

'Lately?'

'No, long ago, when we were in the train de luxe.'

'Has Dr Parravicini prescribed for you since you began to feel weak and ill?'

'Oh, he has given me a tonic from time to time, but I hate medicine, and took very little of the stuff. And then I am not ill, only weaker than I used to be. I was ridiculously strong and well when I lived at Walworth, and used to take long walks every day. Mother made me take those tramps to Dulwich or Norwood, for fear I should suffer from too much sewing-machine; sometimes—but very seldom—she went with me. She was generally toiling at home while I was enjoying fresh air and exercise. And she was very careful about our food—that, however plain it was, it should be always nourishing and ample. I owe it to her care that I grew up such a great, strong creature.'

'You don't look great or strong now, you poor dear,' said Lotta.

'I'm afraid Italy doesn't agree with me.'

'Perhaps it is not Italy, but being cooped up with Lady Ducayne that has made you ill.'

'But I am never cooped up. Lady Ducayne is absurdly kind, and lets me roam about or sit in the balcony all day if I like. I have read more novels since I have been with her than in all the rest of my life.'

'Then she is very different from the average old lady, who is usually a slave-driver,' said Stafford. 'I wonder why she carries a companion about with her if she has so little need of society.'

'Oh, I am only part of her state. She is inordinately rich—and the salary she gives me doesn't count. Apropos of Dr Parravicini, I know he is a clever doctor, for he cures my horrid mosquito bites.'

'A little ammonia would do that, in the early stage of the mischief. But there are no mosquitoes to trouble you now.'

'Oh, yes, there are; I had a bite just before we left Cap Ferrino.'

She pushed up her loose lawn sleeve, and exhibited a scar, which he scrutinized intently, with a surprised and puzzled look.

'This is no mosquito bite,' he said.

'Oh, yes it is—unless there are snakes or adders at Cap Ferrino.'

'It is not a bite at all. You are trifling with me. Miss Rolleston—you have allowed that wretched Italian quack to bleed you. They killed the greatest man in modern Europe that way, remember. How very foolish of you.'

'I was never bled in my life, Mr Stafford.'

'Nonsense! Let me look at your other arm. Are there any more mosquito bites?'

'Yes; Dr Parravicini says I have a bad skin for healing, and that the poison acts more virulently with me than with most people.'

Stafford examined both her arms in the broad sunlight, scars new and old.

'You have been very badly bitten, Miss Rolleston,' he said, 'and if ever I find the mosquito I shall make him smart. But, now tell me, my dear girl, on your word of honour, tell me as you would tell a friend who is sincerely anxious for your health and happiness—as you would tell your mother if she were here to question you—have you no knowledge of any cause for these scars except mosquito bites—no suspicion even?'

'No, indeed! No, upon my honour! I have never seen a mosquito biting my arm. One never does see the horrid little fiends. But I have heard them trumpeting under the curtains, and I know that I have often had one of the pestilent wretches buzzing about me.'

Later in the day Bella and her friends were sitting at tea in the garden, while Lady Ducayne took her afternoon drive with her doctor.

'How long do you mean to stop with Lady Ducayne, Miss Rolleston?' Herbert Stafford asked, after a thoughtful silence, breaking suddenly upon the trivial talk of the two girls.

'As long as she will go on paying me twenty-five pounds a quarter.'

'Even if you feel your health breaking down in her service?'

'It is not the service that has injured my health. You can see that I have really nothing to do—to read aloud for an hour or so once or twice a week; to write a letter once in a way to a London tradesman. I shall never have such an easy time with anybody else. And nobody else would give me a hundred a year.'

'Then you mean to go on till you break down; to die at your post?'

'Like the other two companions? No! If ever I feel seriously ill—really ill—I shall put myself in a train and go back to Walworth without stopping.'

'What about the other two companions?'

'They both died. It was very unlucky for Lady Ducayne. That's why she engaged me; she chose me because I was ruddy and robust. She must feel rather disgusted at my having grown white and weak. By-the-bye, when I told her about the good your tonic had done me, she said she would like to see you and have a litle talk with you about her own case.'

'And I should like to see Lady Ducayne. When did she say this?'

'The day before yesterday.'

'Will you ask her if she will see me this evening?'

'With pleasure! I wonder what you will think of her? She looks rather terrible to a stranger; but Dr Parravicini says she was once a famous beauty.'

It was nearly ten o'clock when Mr Stafford was summoned by message from Lady Ducayne, whose courier came to conduct him to her ladyship's salon. Bella was reading aloud when the visitor was admitted; and he noticed the languor in the low, sweet tones, the evident effort.

'Shut up the book,' said the querulous old voice. 'You are beginning to drawl like Miss Blandy.'

Stafford saw a small, bent figure crouching over the piled-up olive logs; a shrunken old figure in a gorgeous garment of black and crimson brocade, a skinny throat emerging from a mass of old Venetian lace, clasped with diamonds that flashed like fire-flies as the trembling old head turned towards him.

The eyes that looked at him out of the face were almost as bright as the diamonds—the only living feature in that narrow parchment mask. He had seen terrible faces in the hospital—faces on which disease had set dreadful marks—but he had never seen a face that impressed him so painfully as this withered countenance, with its indescribable horror of death outlived, a face that should have been hidden under a coffin-lid years and years ago.

The Italian physician was standing on the other side of the fireplace, smoking a cigarette, and looking down at the little old woman brooding over the hearth as if he were proud of her.

'Good evening, Mr Stafford; you can go to your room, Bella, and write your everlasting letter to your mother at Walworth,' said Lady Ducayne. 'I believe she writes a page about every wild flower she discovers in the woods and meadows. I don't know what else she can find to write about,' she added, as Bella quietly withdrew to the pretty little bedroom opening out of Lady Ducayne's spacious apartment. Here, as at Cap Ferrino, she slept in a room adjoining the old lady's.

'You are a medical man, I understand, Mr Stafford.'

'I am a qualified practitioner, but I have not begun to practise.'

'You have begun upon my companion, she tells me.'

'I have prescribed for her, certainly, and I am happy to find my prescription has done her good; but I look upon that improvement as temporary. Her case will require more drastic treatment.'

'Never mind her case. There is nothing the matter with the girl— absolutely nothing—except girlish nonsense; too much liberty and not enough work.'

'I understand that two of your ladyship's previous companions died of the same disease,' said Stafford, looking first at Lady Ducayne, who gave her tremulous old head an impatient jerk, and then at Parravicini, whose yellow complexion had paled a little under Stafford's scrutiny.

'Don't bother me about my companions, sir,' said Lady Ducayne. 'I sent for you to consult you about myself—not about a parcel of anæmic girls. You are young, and medicine is a progressive science, the newspapers tell me. Where have you studied?'

'In Edinburgh—and in Paris.'

'Two good schools. And you know all the new-fangled theories, the modern discoveries—that remind one of the mediæval witchcraft, of Albertus Magnus, and George Ripley; you have studied hypnotism— electricity?'

'And the transfusion of blood,' said Stafford, very slowly, looking at Parravicini.

'Have you made any discovery that teaches you to prolong human life—any elixir—any mode of treatment? I want my life prolonged, young man. That man there has been my physician for thirty years. He does all he can to keep me alive—after his lights. He studies all the new theories of all the scientists—but he is old; he gets older every day—his brain-power is going—he is bigoted—prejudiced—can't receive new ideas—can't grapple with new systems. He will let me die if I am not on my guard against him.'

'You are of an unbelievable ingratitude, Ecclenza,' said Parravicini.

'Oh, you needn't complain. I have paid you thousands to keep me alive. Every year of my life has swollen your hoards; you know there is nothing to come to you when I am gone. My whole fortune is left to endow a home for indigent women of quality who have reached their ninetieth year. Come, Mr Stafford, I am a rich woman. Give me a few years more in the sunshine, a few years more above ground, and I will give you the price of a fashionable London practice—I will set you up at the West-end.'

'How old are you, Lady Ducayne?'

'I was born the day Louis XVI was guillotined.'

'Then I think you have had your share of the sunshine and the

'His brain power is going.'

pleasures of the earth, and that you should spend your few remaining days in repenting your sins and trying to make atonement for the young lives that have been sacrificed to your love of life.'

'What do you mean by that, sir?'

'Oh, Lady Ducayne, need I put your wickedness and your physician's still greater wickedness in plain words? The poor girl who is now in your employment has been reduced from robust health to a condition of absolute danger by Dr Parravicini's experimental surgery; and I have no doubt those other two young women who broke down in your service were treated by him in the same manner. I could take upon myself to demonstrate—by most convincing evidence, to a jury of medical men—that Dr Parravicini has been bleeding Miss Rolleston, after putting her under chloroform, at intervals, ever since she has been in your service. The deterioration in the girl's health speaks for itself; the lancet marks upon the girl's arms are unmistakable; and her description of a series of sensations, which she calls a dream, points unmistakably to the administration of chloroform while she was sleeping. A practice so nefarious, so murderous, must, if exposed, result in a sentence only less severe than the punishment of murder.'

'I laugh,' said Parravicini, with an airy motion of his skinny fingers; 'I laugh at once at your theories and at your threats. I, Parravicini Leopold, have no fear that the law can question anything I have done.'

'Take the girl away, and let me hear no more of her,' cried Lady Ducayne, in the thin, old voice, which so poorly matched the energy and fire of the wicked old brain that guided its utterances. 'Let her go back to her mother—I want no more girls to die in my service. There are girls enough and to spare in the world, God knows.'

'If you ever engage another companion—or take another English girl into your service, Lady Ducayne, I will make all England ring with the story of your wickedness.'

'I want no more girls. I don't believe in his experiments. They have been full of danger for me as well as for the girl—an air bubble, and I should be gone. I'll have no more of his dangerous quackery. I'll find some new man—a better man than you, sir, a discoverer like Pasteur, or Virchow, a genius—to keep me alive. Take your girl away, young man. Marry her if you like. I'll write her a cheque for a thousand pounds, and let her go and live on beef and beer, and get strong and plump again. I'll have no more such experiments. Do you hear, Parravicini?' she screamed, vindictively, the yellow, wrinkled face distorted with fury, the eyes glaring at him.

The Staffords carried Bella Rolleston off to Varese next day, she very loth to leave Lady Ducayne, whose liberal salary afforded such help for the dear mother. Herbert Stafford insisted, however, treating Bella as coolly as if he had been the family physician, and she had been given over wholly to his care.

'Do you suppose your mother would let you stop here to die?' he asked. 'If Mrs Rolleston knew how ill you are, she would come post haste to fetch you.'

'I shall never be well again till I get back to Walworth,' answered Bella, who was low-spirited and inclined to tears this morning, a reaction after her good spirits of yesterday.

'We'll try a week or two at Varese first,' said Stafford. 'When you can walk half-way up Monte Generoso without palpitation of the heart, you shall go back to Walworth.'

'Poor mother, how glad she will be to see me, and how sorry that I've lost such a good place.'

This conversation took place on the boat when they were leaving Bellaggio. Lotta had gone to her friend's room at seven o'clock that morning, long before Lady Ducayne's withered eyelids had opened to the daylight, before even Francine, the French maid, was astir, and had helped to pack a Gladstone bag with essentials, and hustled Bella downstairs and out of doors before she could make any strenuous resistance.

'It's all right.' Lotta assured her. 'Herbert had a good talk with Lady Ducayne last night and it was settled for you to leave this morning. She doesn't like invalids, you see.'

'No,' sighed Bella, 'she doesn't like invalids. It was very unlucky that I should break down, just like Miss Tomson and Miss Blandy.'

'At any rate, you are not dead, like them,' answered Lotta, 'and my brother says you are not going to die.'

It seemed rather a dreadful thing to be dismissed in that off-hand way, without a word of farewell from her employer.

'I wonder what Miss Torpinter will say when I go to her for another situation,' Bella speculated, ruefully, while she and her friends were breakfasting on board the steamer.

'Perhaps you may never want another situation,' said Stafford.

'You mean that I may never be well enough to be useful to anybody?'

'A cheque for a thousand!'

'No, I don't mean anything of the kind.'

It was after dinner at Varese, when Bella had been induced to take a whole glass of Chianti, and quite sparkled after that unaccustomed stimulant, that Mr Stafford produced a letter from his pocket.

'I forgot to give you Lady Ducayne's letter of adieu!' he said.

'What, did she write to me? I am so glad—I hated to leave her in such a cool way; for after all she was very kind to me, and if I didn't like her it was only because she was too dreadfully old.'

She tore open the envelope. The letter was short and to the point:

'Goodbye, child. Go and marry your doctor. I enclose a farewell gift for your trousseau.—Adeline Ducayne.'

'A hundred pounds, a whole year's salary—no—why, it's for a—A cheque for a thousand!' cried Bella. 'What a generous old soul! She really is the dearest old thing.'

'She just missed being very dear to you, Bella,' said Stafford.

He had dropped into the use of her Christian name while they were on board the boat. It seemed natural now that she was to be in his charge till they all three went back to England.

'I shall take upon myself the privileges of an elder brother till we land at Dover,' he said; 'after that—well, it must be as you please.'

The question of their future relations must have been satisfactorily settled before they crossed the Channel, for Bella's next letter to her mother communicated three startling facts.

First, that the enclosed cheque for £1,000 was to be invested in debenture-stock in Mrs Rolleston's name, and was to be her very own, income and principal, for the rest of her life.

Next, that Bella was going home to Walworth immediately.

And last, that she was going to be married to Mr Herbert Stafford in the following autumn.

'And I am sure you will adore him, mother, as much as I do,' wrote Bella. 'It is all good Lady Ducayne's doing. I never could have married if I had not secured that little nest-egg for you. Herbert says we shall be able to add to it as the years go by, and that wherever we live there shall be always a room in our house for you. The word "mother-in-law" has no terrors for him.'

LET LOOSE

Mary Cholmondeley

Mary Cholmondeley (1859–1925) was a noted 'New Woman' novelist of the 1890s whose best-known novel *Red Pottage* (1899) created a sensation with its attack on middle-class hypocrisy. Her little-known tale 'Let Loose' originally appeared in an 1890s magazine and was reprinted in the American edition of *Moth and Rust* (1902), but curiously *not* the British edition. It has been favourably compared to F.G. Loring's classic vampire tale 'The Tomb of Sarah' (1900), which was written shortly after 'Let Loose' appeared. In 1902 Mary Cholmondeley felt obliged to defend herself in print against charges of plagiarism over the Loring story.

The dead abide with us! Though stark and cold
Earth seems to grip them, they are with us still.

SOME years ago I took up architecture, and made a tour through Holland, studying the buildings of that interesting country. I was not then aware that it is not enough to take up art. Art must take you up, too. I never doubted but that my passing enthusiasm for her would be returned. When I discovered that she was a stern mistress, who did not immediately respond to my attentions, I naturally transferred them to another shrine. There are other things in the world besides art. I am now a landscape gardener.

But at the time of which I write I was engaged in a violent flirtation with architecture. I had one companion on this expedition, who has since become one of the leading architects of the day. He was a thin, determined-looking man with a screwed-up face and heavy jaw, slow of speech, and absorbed in his work to a degree which I quickly found tiresome. He was possessed of a certain quiet power of overcoming obstacles which I have rarely seen equalled. He has since become my brother-in-law, so I ought to know; for my parents did not like him much and opposed the marriage, and my sister did not like him at all, and refused him over and over again; but, nevertheless, he eventually married her.

I have thought since that one of his reasons for choosing me as his travelling companion on this occasion was because he was getting up steam for what he subsequently termed 'an alliance with my family', but the idea never entered my head at the time. A more careless man as to dress I have rarely met, and yet, in all the heat of July in Holland, I noticed that he never appeared without a high, starched collar, which had not even fashion to commend it at that time.

I often chaffed him about his splended collars, and asked him why he wore them, but without eliciting any response. One evening, as we were walking back to our lodgings in Middleberg, I attacked him for about the thirtieth time on the subject.

'Why on earth do you wear them?' I said.

'You have, I believe, asked me that question many times,' he replied, in his slow, precise utterance; 'but always on occasions when I was occupied. I am now at leisure, and I will tell you.'

And he did.

I have put down what he said, as nearly in his own words as I can remember them.

Ten years ago, I was asked to read a paper on English Frescoes at the Institute of British Architects. I was determined to make the paper as good as I could, down to the slightest details, and I consulted many books on the subject, and studied every fresco I could find. My father, who had been an architect, had left me, at his death, all his papers and notebooks on the subject of architecture. I searched them diligently, and found in one of them a slight unfinished sketch of nearly fifty years ago that specially interested me. Underneath was noted, in his clear small hand—*Frescoed east wall of crypt. Parish Church. Wet Waste-on-the-Wolds, Yorkshire (via Pickering.)*

The sketch had such a fascination for me that I decided to go there and see the fresco for myself. I had only a very vague idea as to where Wet Waste-on-the-Wolds was, but I was ambitious for the success of my paper; it was hot in London, and I set off on my long journey not without a certain degree of pleasure, with my dog Brian, a large nondescript brindled creature, as my only companion.

I reached Pickering, in Yorkshire, in the course of the afternoon, and then began a series of experiments on local lines which ended, after several hours, in my finding myself deposited at a little out-of-the-world station within nine or ten miles of Wet Waste. As no conveyance of any kind was to be had, I shouldered my portmanteau, and set out on a long white road that stretched away into the distance over the bare, treeless wold. I must have walked for several hours, over a waste of moorland patched with heather, when a doctor passed me, and gave me a lift to within a mile of my destination. The mile was a long one, and it was quite dark by the time I saw the feeble glimmer of lights in front of me, and found that I had reached Wet Waste. I had considerable difficulty in getting anyone to take me in; but at last I persuaded the owner of the public-house to give me a bed, and quite tired out, I got into it as soon as possible, for fear he should change his mind, and fell asleep to the sound of a little stream below my window.

I was up early next morning, and inquired directly after breakfast the way to the clergyman's house, which I found was close at hand. At Wet Waste everything was close at hand. The whole village seemed composed of a straggling row of one-storied grey stone houses, the same colour as the stone walls that separated the few fields enclosed from the surrounding waste, and as the little bridges over the beck that ran down one side of the grey wide street. Everything was grey. The church, the low tower of which I could see at a little distance, seemed to have been built of the same stone; so was the parsonage when I came up to it, accompanied on my way be a mob of rough, uncouth children, who eyed me and Brian with half-defiant curiosity.

The clergyman was at home, and after a short delay I was admitted. Leaving Brian in charge of my drawing materials, I followed the servant into a low panelled room, in which, at a latticed window, a very old man was sitting. The morning light fell on his white head bent low over a litter of papers and books.

'Mr er—?' he said, looking up slowly, with one finger keeping his place in a book.

'Blake.'

'Blake,' he repeated after me, and was silent.

I told him that I was an architect; that I had come to study a fresco in the crypt of his church, and asked for the keys.

'The crypt,' he said, pushing up his spectacles and peering hard at me. 'The crypt has been closed for thirty years. Ever since—' and he stopped short.

'I should be much obliged for the keys,' I said again.

He shook his head.

'No,' he said. 'No one goes in there now.'

'It is a pity,' I remarked, 'for I have come a long way with that one object;' and I told him about the paper I had been asked to read, and the trouble I was taking with it.

He became interested. 'Ah!' he said, laying down his pen, and removing his finger from the page before him, 'I can understand that. I also was young once, and fired with ambition. The lines have fallen to me in somewhat lonely places, and for forty years I have held the cure of souls in this place, where, truly, I have seen but little of the world, though I myself may be not unknown in the paths of literature. Possibly you may have read a pamphlet, written by myself, on the Syrian version of the Three Authentic Epistles of Ignatius?'

'Sir,' I said, 'I am ashamed to confess that I have not time to read even the most celebrated books. My one object in life is my art. *Ars longa, vita brevis*, you know.'

'You are right, my son,' said the old man, evidently disappointed, but looking at me kindly. 'There are diversities of gifts, and if the Lord has entrusted you with a talent, look to it. Lay it not up in a napkin.'

I said I would not do so if he would lend me the keys of the crypt. He seemed startled by my recurrence to the subject and looked undecided.

'Why not?' he murmured to himself. 'The youth appears a good youth. And superstition! What is it but distrust in God!'

He got up slowly, and taking a large bunch of keys out of his pocket, opened with one of them an oak cupboard in the corner of the room.

'They should be here,' he muttered, peering in; 'but the dust of many years deceives the eye. See, my son, if among these parchments there be two keys; one of iron and very large, and the other steel, and of a long and thin appearance.'

I went eagerly to help him, and presently found in a back drawer two keys tied together, which he recognized at once.

'Those are they,' he said. 'The long one opens the first door at the bottom of the steps which go down against the outside wall of the church hard by the sword graven in the wall. The second opens (but it is hard of opening and of shutting) the iron door within the passage leading to the crypt itself. My son, is it necessary to your treatise that you should enter this crypt?'

I replied that it was absolutely necessary.

'Then take them,' he said, 'and in the evening you will bring them to me again.'

I said I might want to go several days running, and asked if he would not allow me to keep them till I had finished my work; but on that point he was firm.

'Likewise,' he added, 'be careful that you lock the first door at the foot of the steps before you unlock the second, and lock the second also while you are within. Furthermore, when you come out lock the iron inner door as well as the wooden one.'

I promised I would do so, and, after thanking him, hurried away, delighted at my success in obtaining the keys. Finding Brian and my sketching materials waiting for me in the porch, I eluded the vigilance of my escort of children by taking the narrow private path between the parsonage and the church which was close at hand, standing in a quadrangle of ancient yews.

The church itself was interesting, and I noticed that it must have arisen out of ruins of a previous building, judging from the number of fragments of stone caps and arches, bearing traces of very early carving, now built into the walls. There were incised crosses, too, in some places, and one especially caught my attention, being flanked by a large sword. It was in trying to get a nearer look at this that I stumbled, and, looking down, saw at my feet a flight of narrow stone steps green with moss and mildew. Evidently this was the entrance to the crypt. I at once descended the steps, taking care of my footing, for they were damp and slippery in the extreme. Brian accompanied me, as nothing would induce him to remain behind. By the time I had reached the bottom of the stairs, I found myself almost in darkness, and I had to strike a light before I could find the keyhole and the proper key to fit into it. The door, which was of wood, opened inwards fairly easily, although an accumulation of mould and rubbish on the ground outside showed it had not been used for many years. Having got through it, which was not altogether an easy matter, as nothing would induce it to open more than about eighteen inches, I carefully locked it behind me, although I should have preferred to leave it open, as there is to some minds an unpleasant feeling in being locked in anywhere, in case of sudden exit seeming advisable.

I kept my candle alight with some difficulty, and after groping my way down a low and of course exceedingly dank passage, came to another door. A toad was squatting against it, who looked as if he had been sitting there about a hundred years. As I lowered the candle to the floor, he gazed at the light with unblinking eyes, and then retreated slowly into a crevice in the wall, leaving against the door a small cavity in the dry mud which had gradually silted up round his person. I noticed that this door was of iron, and had a long bolt, which, however, was broken. Without delay, I fitted the second key into the lock, and pushing the door open after considerable difficulty, I felt the cold breath of the crypt upon my face. I must own I experienced a momentary regret at locking the second door again as soon as I was well inside, but I felt it my duty to do so. Then, leaving the key in the lock, I seized my candle and looked round. I was standing in a low vaulted chamber with groined roof, cut out of the solid rock. It was difficult to see where the crypt ended, as further light thrown on any point only showed other rough archways or openings, cut in the rock, which had probably served at one time for family vaults. A peculiarity of the Wet Waste crypt, which I had not noticed in other places of that description, was the tasteful arrangement of skulls and bones which were packed about four feet high on either side. The skulls were symmetrically built up to within a few inches of the top of the low archway on my left, and the shin bones were arranged in the same manner on my right. *But the fresco!* I looked round for it in vain. Perceiving at the further end of the crypt a very low and very massive archway, the entrance to which was not filled up with bones, I passed under it, and found myself in a second smaller chamber. Holding my candle above my head, the first object its light fell upon was—the fresco, and at a glance I saw that it was unique. Setting down some of my things with a trembling hand on a rough stone shelf hard by, which had evidently been a credence table, I examined the work more closely. It was a reredos over what had probably been the altar at the time the priests were proscribed. The fresco belonged to the earliest part of the fifteenth century, and was so perfectly preserved that I could almost trace the limts of each day's work in the plaster, as the artist had dashed it on and smoothed it out with his trowel. The subject was the Ascension, gloriously treated. I can hardly describe my elation as I stood and looked at it, and reflected that this magnificent specimen of English fresco painting would be made known to the world by myself. Recollecting myself at last, I opened my sketching bag, and, lighting all the candles I had brought with me, set to work.

Brian walked about near me, and though I was not otherwise than glad of his company in my rather lonely position, I wished several times I had left him behind. He seemed restless, and even the sight of so many bones appeared to exercise no soothing effect upon him. At last, however, after repeated commands, he lay down, watchful but motionless, on the stone floor.

I must have worked for several hours, and I was pausing to rest my eyes and hands, when I noticed for the first time the intense stillness that surrounded me. No sound from *me* reached the outer world. The church clock which had clanged out so loud and ponderously as I went down the steps, had not since sent the faintest whisper of its iron tongue down to me below. All was silent as the grave. This *was* the grave. Those who had come here had indeed gone down into silence. I repeated the words to myself, or rather they repeated themselves to me.

Gone down into silence.

I was awakened from my reverie by a faint sound. I sat still and listened. Bats occasionally frequent vaults and underground places.

The sound continued, a faint, stealthy, rather unpleasant sound. I do not know what kinds of sounds bats make, whether pleasant or otherwise. Suddenly there was a noise as of something falling, a momentary pause—and then—an almost imperceptible but distinct jangle as of a key.

I had left the key in the lock after I had turned it, and I now regretted having done so. I got up, took one of the candles, and went back into the larger crypt—for though I trust I am not so effeminate as to be rendered nervous by hearing a noise for which I cannot instantly account; still, on occasions of this kind, I must honestly say I should prefer that they did not occur. As I came towards the iron door, there was another distinct (I had almost said hurried) sound. The impression on my mind was one of great haste. When I reached the door, and held the candle near the lock to take out the key, I perceived that the other one, which hung by a short string to its fellow, was vibrating slightly. I should have preferred not to find it vibrating, as there seemed no occasion for such a course; but I put them both into my pocket, and turned to go back to my work. As I turned, I saw on the ground what had occasioned the louder noise I had heard, namely a skull which had evidently just slipped from its place on the top of one of the walls of bones, and had rolled almost to my feet. There, disclosing a few more inches of the top of an archway behind was the place from which it had been dislodged. I stooped to pick it up, but fearing to displace any more skulls by meddling with the pile, and not liking to gather up its scattered teeth, I let it lie, and went back to my work, in which I was soon so completely absorbed that I was only roused at last by my candles beginning to burn low and go out one after another.

Then, with a sigh of regret, for I had not nearly finished, I turned to go. Poor Brian, who had never quite reconciled himself to the place, was beside himself with delight. As I opened the iron door he pushed past me, and a moment later I heard him whining and scratching, and I had almost added, beating, against the wooden one. I locked the iron door, and hurried down the passage as quickly as I could, and almost before I had got the other one ajar there seemed to be a rush past me into the open air, and Brian was bounding up the steps and out of sight. As I stopped to take out the key, I felt quite deserted and left behind. When I came out once more into the sunlight, there was a vague sensation all about me in the air of exultant freedom.

It was already late in the afternoon, and after I had sauntered back to the parsonage to give up the keys, I persuaded the people of the public-house to let me join in the family meal, which was spread out in the kitchen. The inhabitants of Wet Waste were primitive people, with the frank, unabashed manner that flourishes still in lonely places, especially in the wilds of Yorkshire; but I had no idea that in these days of penny posts and cheap newspapers such entire ignorance of the outer world could have existed in any corner, however remote, of Great Britain.

When I took one of the neighbour's children on my knee—a pretty little girl with the palest aureole of flaxen hair I had ever seen—and began to draw pictures for her of the birds and beasts of other countries, I was instantly surrounded by a crowd of children, and even grown-up people, while others came to their doorways and looked on from a distance, calling to each other in the strident unknown tongue which I have since discovered goes by the name of 'Broad Yorkshire'.

The following morning, as I came out of my room, I perceived that something was amiss in the village. A buzz of voices reached me as I passed the bar, and in the next house I could hear through the open window a high-pitched wail of lamentation.

The woman who brought me my breakfast was in tears, and in answer to my questions, told me that the neighbour's child, the little girl whom I had taken on my knee the evening before, had died in the night.

I felt sorry for the general grief that the little creature's death seemed to arouse, and the uncontrolled wailing of the poor mother took my appetite away.

I hurried off early to my work, calling on my way for the keys, and with Brian for my companion descended once more into the crypt and drew and measured with an absorption that gave me no time that day to listen for sounds real or fancied. Brian, too, on this occasion seemed quite content, and slept peacefully beside me on the stone floor. When I had worked as long as I could, I put away my books with regret that even then I had not quite finished, as I had hoped to do. It would be necessary to come again for a short time on the morrow. When I returned the keys late that afternoon, the old clergyman met me at the door, and asked me to come in and have tea with him.

'And has the work prospered?' he asked, as we sat down in the long, low room, into which I had just been ushered, and where he seemed to live entirely.

I told him it had, and showed it to him.

'You have seen the original, of course?' I said.

'Once,' he replied, gazing fixedly at it. He evidently did not care to be communicative, so I turned the conversation to the age of the church.

'All here is old,' he said. 'When I was young, forty years ago, and came here because I had no means of mine own, and was much moved to marry at that time, I felt oppressed that all was so old; and that this place was so far removed from the world, for which I had at times longings grievous to be borne; but I had chosen my lot, and with it I was forced to be content. My son, marry not in youth, for love, which truly in that season is a mighty power, turns away the heart from study, and young children break the back of ambition. Neither marry in middle life, when a woman is seen to be but a woman and her talk a weariness, so you will not be burdened with a wife in your old age.'

I had my own views on the subject of marriage, for I am of opinion that a well-chosen companion of domestic tastes and docile and devoted temperament may be of material assistance to a professional man. But, my opinions once formulated, it is not of moment to me to discuss them with others, so I changed the subject, and asked if the neighbouring villages were as antiquated as Wet Waste.

'Yes, all about here is old,' he repeated. 'The paved road leading to Dyke Fens is an ancient pack road, made even in the time of the Romans. Dyke Fens, which is very near here, a matter of but four or five miles, is likewise old, and forgotten by the world. The Reformation never reached it. It stopped here. And at Dyke Fens they still have a priest and a bell, and bow down before the saints. It is a damnable heresy, and weekly I expound it as such to my people, showing them true doctrines; and I have heard that this same priest has so far yielded himself to the Evil One that he has preached against me as withholding gospel truths from my flock; but I take no heed of it, neither of his pamphlet touching the Clementine Homilies, in which he vainly contradicts that which I have plainly set forth and proven beyond doubt, concerning the word *Asaph*.'

The old man was fairly off on his favourite subject, and it was some time before I could get away. As it was, he followed me to the door, and I only escaped because the old clerk hobbled up at that moment, and claimed his attention.

The following morning I went for the keys for the third and last time. I had decided to leave early the next day. I was tired of Wet Waste, and a certain gloom seemed to my fancy to be gathering over the place. There was a sensation of trouble in the air, as if, although the day was bright and clear, a storm were coming.

This morning, to my astonishment, the keys were refused to me when I asked for them. I did not, however, take the refusal as final—I make it a rule never to take a refusal as final—and after a short delay I was shown into the room where, as usual, the clergyman was sitting, or rather, on this occasion, was walking up and down.

'My son,' he said with vehemence, 'I know wherefore you have come, but it is of no avail. I cannot lend the keys again.'

I replied that, on the contrary, I hoped he would give them to me at once.

'It is impossible,' he repeated. 'I did wrong, exceeding wrong. I will never part with them again.'

'Why not?'

He hesitated, and then said slowly:

'The old clerk, Abraham Kelly, died last night.' He paused, and then went on: 'The doctor has just been here to tell me of that which is a mystery to him. I do not wish the people of the place to know it, and only to me has he mentioned it, but he has discovered plainly on the throat of the old man, and also, but more faintly on the child's, marks as of strangulation. None but he has observed it, and he is at a loss how to account for it. I, alas! can account for it but in one way, but in one way!'

I did not see what all this had to do with the crypt, but to humour the old man, I asked what that way was.

'It is a long story, and, haply, to a stranger it may appear but foolishness, but I will even tell it; for I perceive that unless I furnish a reason for withholding the keys, you will not cease to entreat me for them.

'I told you at first when you inquired of me concerning the crypt, that it had been closed these thirty years, and so it was. Thirty years ago a certain Sir Roger Despard departed this life, even the Lord of the manor of Wet Waste and Dyke Fens, the last of his family, which is now, thank the Lord, extinct. He was a man of a vile life, neither fearing God nor regarding man, nor having compassion on innocence, and the Lord appeared to have given him over to the tormentors even in this world, for he suffered many things of his vices, more especially from drunkenness, in which seasons, and they were many, he was as one possessed by seven devils, being an abomination to his household and a root of bitterness to all, both high and low.

'And, at last, the cup of his iniquity being full to the brim, he came to die, and I went to exhort him on his death-bed; for I heard that terror had come upon him, and that evil imaginations encompassed him so thick on every side, that few of them that were with him could abide in his presence. But when I saw him I perceived that there was no place of repentance left for him, and he scoffed at me and my superstition, even as he lay dying, and swore there was no God and no angel, and all were damned even as he was. And the next day, towards evening, the pains of death came upon him, and he raved the more exceedingly, inasmuch as he said he was being strangled by the Evil One. Now on his table was his hunting knife, and with his last strength he crept and laid hold upon it, no man withstanding him, and swore a great oath that if he went down to burn in hell, he would leave one of his hands behind on earth, and that it would never rest until it had drawn blood from the throat of another and strangled him, even as he himself was being strangled. And he cut off his own right hand at the wrist, and no man dared go near him to stop him, and the blood went through the floor, even down to the ceiling of the room below, and thereupon he died.

'And they called me in the night, and told me of his oath, and I counselled that no man should speak of it, and I took the dead hand, which none had ventured to touch, and I laid it beside him in his coffin; for I thought it better he should take it with him, so that he might have it, if haply some day after much tribulation he should perchance be moved to stretch forth his hands towards God. But the story got spread about, and the people were affrighted, so, when he came to be buried in the place of his fathers, he being the last of his family, and the crypt likewise full, I had it closed, and kept the keys myself, and suffered no man to enter therein any more; for truly he was a man of an evil life, and the devil is not yet wholly overcome, nor cast chained into the lake of fire. So in time the story died out, for in thirty years much is forgotten. And when you came and asked me for the keys, I was at the first minded to withhold them; but I thought it was a vain superstition, and I perceived that you do but ask a second time for what is first refused; so I let you have them, seeing it was not an idle curiosity, but a desire to improve the talent committed to you, that led you to require them.'

The old man stopped, and I remained silent, wondering what would be the best way to get them just once more.

'Surely, sir,' I said at last, 'one so cultivated and deeply read as yourself cannot be biased by an idle superstition.'

'I trust not,' he replied, 'and yet—it is a strange thing that since the crypt was opened two people have died, and the mark is plain upon the throat of the old man and visible on the young child. No blood was drawn, but the second time the grip was stronger than the first. The third time, perhance——'

'Superstition such as that,' I said with authority, 'is an entire want of faith in God. You once said so yourself.'

I took a high moral tone which is often efficacious with conscientious, humble-minded people.

He agreed, and accused himself of not having faith as a grain of mustard seed; but even when I had got him so far as that, I had a severe struggle for the keys. It was only when I finally explained to him that if any malign influence *had* been let loose the first day, at any rate, it was out now for good or evil, and no further going or coming of mine could make any difference, that I finally gained my point. I was young, and he was old; and, being much shaken by what had occurred, he gave way at last, and I wrested the keys from him.

I will not deny that I went down the steps that day with a vague, indefinable repugnance, which was only accentuated by the closing of the two doors behind me. I remembered then, for the first time, the faint jangling of the key and other sounds which I had noticed the first day, and how one of the skulls had fallen. I went to the place where it still lay. I have already said these walls of skulls were built up so high as to be within a few inches of the top of the low archways that led into more distant portions of the vault. The displacement of the skull in question had left a small hole just large enough for me to put my hand through. I noticed for the first time, over the archway above it, a carved coat-of-arms, and the name, now almost obliterated, of Despard. This, no doubt, was the Despard vault. I could not resist moving a few more skulls and looking in, holding my candle as near the aperture as I could. The vault was full. Piled high, one upon another, were old coffins, and remnants of coffins, and strewn bones. I attribute my present determination to be cremated to the painful impression produced on me by this spectacle. The coffin nearest the archway alone was intact, save for a large crack across the lid. I could not get a ray from my candle to fall on the brass plates, but I felt no doubt this was the coffin of the wicked Sir Roger. I put back the skulls, including the one which had rolled down, and carefully finished my work. I was not there much more than an hour, but I was glad to get away.

If I could have left Wet Waste at once I should have done so, for I had a totally unreasonable longing to leave the place; but I found that only one train stopped during the day at the station from which I had come, and that it would not be possible to be in time for it that day.

Accordingly I submitted to the inevitable, and wandered about with Brian for the remainder of the afternoon and until late in the evening, sketching and smoking. The day was oppressively hot, and even after the sun had set across the burnt stretches of the wolds, it seemed to grow very little cooler. Not a breath stirred. In the evening, when I was tired of loitering in the lanes, I went up to my own room, and after contemplating afresh my finished study of the fresco, I suddenly set to work to write the part of my paper bearing upon it. As a rule, I write with difficulty, but that evening words came to me with winged speed, and with them a hovering impression that I must make haste, that I was much pressed for time. I wrote and wrote, until my candles guttered out and left me trying to finish by the moonlight, which, until I endeavoured to write by it, seemed as clear as day.

I had to put away my MS, and, feeling it was too early to go to bed, for the church clock was just counting out ten, I sat down by the open window and leaned out to try and catch a breath of air. It was a night of exceptional beauty; and as I looked out my nervous haste and hurry of mind were allayed. The moon, a perfect circle, was—if so poetic an expression be permissible—as it were, sailing across a calm sky. Every detail of the little village was as clearly illuminated by its beams as if it were broad day; so, also, was the adjacent church with its primeval yews, while even the wolds beyond were dimly indicated, as if through tracing paper.

I sat a long time leaning against the window-sill. The heat was still intense. I am not, as a rule, easily elated or readily cast down; but as I sat that night in the lonely village on the moors, with Brian's head against my knee, how, or why, I know not, a great depression gradually came upon me.

My mind went back to the crypt and the countless dead who had been laid there. The sight of the goal to which all human life, and strength, and beauty, travel in the end, had not affected me at the time, but now the very air about me seemed heavy with death.

What was the good, I asked myself, of working and toiling, and grinding down my heart and youth in the mill of long and strenuous effort, seeing that in the grave folly and talent, idleness and labour lie together, and are alike forgotten? Labour seemed to stretch before me till my heart ached to think of it, to stretch before me even to the end of life, and then came, as the recompense of my labour—the grave. Even if I succeeded, if, after wearing my life threadbare with toil, I succeeded, what remained to me in the end? The grave. A little sooner, while the hands and eyes were still strong to labour, or a little later, when all power and vision had been taken from them; sooner or later only—*the grave*.

I do not apologize for the excessively morbid tenor of these reflections, as I hold that they were caused by the lunar effects which I have endeavoured to transcribe. The moon in its various quarterings has always exerted a marked influence on what I may call the sub-dominant, namely, the poetic side of my nature.

I roused myself at last, when the moon came to look in upon me where I sat, and, leaving the window open, I pulled myself together and went to bed.

I fell asleep almost immediately, but I do not fancy I could have been alseep very long when I was wakened by Brian. He was growling in a low, muffled tone, as he sometimes did in his sleep, when his nose was buried in his rug. I called out to him to shut up; and as he did not do so, turned in bed to find my match box or something to throw at him. The moonlight was still in the room, and as I looked at him I saw him raise his head and evidently wake up. I admonished him, and was just on the point of falling asleep when he began to growl again in a low, savage manner that waked me most effectually. Presently he shook himself and got up, and began prowling about the room. I sat up in bed and called to him, but he paid no attention. Suddenly I saw him stop short in the moonlight; he showed his teeth, and crouched down, his eyes following something in the air. I looked at him in horror. Was he going mad? His eyes were glaring, and his head moved slightly as if he were following the rapid movements of an enemy. Then, with a furious snarl, he suddenly sprang from the ground, and rushed in great leaps across the room towards me, dashing himself against the furniture, his eyes rolling, snatching and tearing wildly in the air with his teeth. I saw he had gone mad. I leaped out of bed, and rushing at him, caught him by the throat. The moon had gone behind a cloud; but in the darkness I felt him turn upon me, felt him rise up, and his teeth close in my throat. I was being strangled. With all the strength of despair, I kept my grip of his neck and, dragging him across the room, tried to crush in his head against the iron rail of my bedstead. It was my only chance. I felt the blood running down my neck. I was suffocating. After one moment of frightful struggle, I beat his head against the bar and heard his skull give way. I felt him give one strong shudder, a groan, and then I fainted away.

When I came to myself I was lying on the floor, surrounded by the people of the house, my reddened hands still clutching Brian's throat. Someone was holding a candle towards me, and the draught from the window made it flare and waver. I looked at Brian. He was stone dead. The blood from his battered head was trickling slowly over my hands. His great jaw was fixed in something that—in the uncertain light—I could not see.

They turned the light a little.

'Oh, God!' I shrieked. 'There! Look! look!'

'He's off his head,' said someone, and I fainted again.

I was ill for about a fortnight without regaining consciousness, a waste of time of which even now I cannot think without poignant regret. When I did recover consciousness, I found I was being carefully nursed by the old clergyman and the people of the house. I have often heard the unkindness of the world in general inveighed against, but for my part I can honestly say that I have received many more kindnesses than I have time to repay. Country people especially are remarkably attentive to strangers in illness.

I could not rest until I had seen the doctor who attended me, and had received his assurance that I should be equal to reading my paper on the appointed day. This pressing anxiety removed, I told him of what I had seen before I fainted the second time. He listened attentively and then assured me, in a manner that was intended to be soothing, that I was suffering from an hallucination, due, no doubt, to the shock of my dog's sudden madness.

'Did you see the dog after it was dead?' I asked.

He said he did. The whole jaw was covered with blood and foam; the teeth certainly seemed convulsively fixed, but the case being evidently one of extraordinarily virulent hydrophobia, owing to the intense heat, he had had the body buried immediately.

My companion stopped speaking as we reached our lodgings, and went upstairs. Then lighting a candle, he slowly turned down his collar.

'You see I have the marks still,' he said, 'but I have no fear of dying of hydrophobia. I am told such peculiar scars could not have been made by the teeth of a dog. If you look closely you see the pressure of five fingers. That is the reason why I wear high collars.'

WILL

Vincent O'Sullivan

Vincent James O'Sullivan (1868–1940) was a ubiquitous figure in the literary circles of 1890s London, closely acquainted with Oscar Wilde, George Moore, Frank Harris, and Bram Stoker, though his two best friends were Ernest Dowson and Aubrey Beardsley. He produced many colourful, decadent short stories and vignettes in the elaborate, *fin de siècle* manner. Two pieces from his first collection, *A Book of Bargains* (1896), have appeared in several anthologies of ghost stories—'When I Was Dead' and 'The Business of Madame Jahn'—but most of the others have never been reprinted. 'Will' is taken from *The Green Window*, published by Leonard Smithers in 1899. Previously it had appeared under a different title, 'Le Scarabée Funèbre', in the Parisian magazine *Mercurie de France*. O'Sullivan spent his last years in France in dire poverty, surviving on charity and the occasional sale of articles to the *Dublin Magazine*. His last book was the illuminating *Aspects of Wilde* (1936).

I

HAVE the dead still power after they are laid in the earth? Do they rule us, by the power of the dead, from their awful thrones? Do their closed eyes become menacing beacons, and their paralyzed hands reach out to scourge our feet into the paths which they have marked out? Ah, surely when the dead are given to the dust, their power crumbles into the dust!

Often during the long summer afternoons, as they sat together in a deep window looking out at the Park of the Sombre Fountains, he thought of these things. For it was at the hour of sundown, when the gloomy house was splashed with crimson, that he most hated his wife. They had been together for some months now; and their days were always spent in the same manner—seated in the window of a great room with dark oak furniture, heavy tapestry, and rich purple hangings, in which a curious decaying scent of lavender ever lingered. For an hour at a time he would stare at her intensely as she sat before him—tall, and pale, and fragile, with her raven hair sweeping about her neck, and her languid hands turning over the leaves of an illuminated missal—and then he would look once more at the Park of the Sombre Fountains, where the river lay, like a silver dream, at the end. At sunset the river became for him turbulent and boding—a pool of blood; and the trees, clad in scarlet, brandished flaming swords. For long days they sat in that room, always silent, watching the shadows turn from steel to crimson, from crimson to grey, from grey to black. If by rare chance they wandered abroad, and moved beyond the gates of the Park of the Sombre Fountains, he might hear one passenger say to another, 'How beautiful she is!' And then his hatred of his wife increased a hundred-fold.

So he was poisoning her surely and lingeringly—with a poison more wily and subtle than that of Cæsar Borgia's ring—with a poison distilled in his eyes. He was drawing out her life as he gazed at her; draining her veins, grudging the beats of her heart. He felt no need of the slow poisons which wither the flesh, of the dread poisons which set fire to the brain; for his hate was a poison which he poured over her white body, till it would no longer have the strength to hold back the escaping soul. With exultation he watched her growing weaker and weaker as the summer glided by : not a day, not an hour passed that she did not pay toll to his eyes: and when in the autumn there came upon her two long faints which resembled catalepsy, he fortified his will to hate, for he felt that the end was at hand.

At length one evening, when the sky was grey in a winter sunset, she lay on a couch in the dark room, and he knew she was dying. The doctors had gone away with death on their lips, and they were left, for the moment, alone. Then she called him to her side from the deep window where he was seated looking out over the Park of the Sombre Fountains.

'You have your will,' she said. 'I am dying.'

'My will?' he murmured, waving his hands.

'Hush!' she moaned. 'Do you think I do not know? For days and months I have felt you drawing the life of my body into your life, that you might spill my soul on the ground. For days and months as I have sat with you, as I have walked by your side, you have seen me imploring pity. But you relented not, and you have your will; for I am going down to death. You have your will, and my body is dead; but my soul cannot die. No!' she cried, raising herself a little on the pillows: 'my soul shall not die, but live, and sway an all-touching sceptre lighted at the stars.'

'My wife!'

'You have thought to live without me, but you will never be without me. Through long nights when the moon is hid, through dreary days when the sun is dulled, I shall be at your side. In the deepest chaos illumined by lightning, on the loftiest mountain-top, do not seek to escape me. You are my bond-man: for this is the compact I have made with the Cardinals of Death.'

At the noon of night she died; and two days later they carried her to a burying-place set about a ruined abbey, and there they laid her in the grave. When he had seen her buried, he left the Park of the Sombre Fountains and travelled to distant lands. He penetrated the most unknown and difficult countries; he lived for months amid Arctic seas; he took part in tragic and barbarous scenes. He used himself to sights of cruelty and terror: to the anguish of women and children, to the agony and fear of men. And when he returned after years of adventure, he went to live in a house the windows of which overlooked the ruined abbey and the grave of his wife, even as the window where they had erewhile sat together overlooked the Park of the Sombre Fountains.

And here he spent dreaming days and sleepless nights—nights painted with monstrous and tumultuous pictures, and moved by waking dreams. Phantoms haggard and ghastly swept before him; ruined cities covered with a cold light edified themselves in his room; while in his ears resounded the trample of retreating and advancing armies, the clangour of squadrons, and noise of breaking war. He was haunted by women who prayed him to have mercy, stretching out beseeching hands—always women—and sometimes they were dead. And when the day came at last, and his tired eyes reverted to the lonely grave, he would soothe himself with some eastern drug, and let the hours slumber by as he fell into long reveries, murmuring at times to himself the rich, sonorous, lulling cadences of the poems in prose of Baudelaire, or dim meditative phrases, laden with the mysteries of the inner rooms of life and death, from the pages of Sir Thomas Browne.

On a night, which was the last of the moon, he heard a singular scraping noise at his window, and upon throwing open the casement he smelt the heavy odour which clings to vaults and catacombs where the dead are entombed. Then he saw that a beetle—a beetle, enormous and unreal—had crept up the wall of his house from the graveyard, and was now crawling across the floor of his room. With marvellous swiftness it climbed on a table placed near a couch on which he was used to lie, and as he approached, shuddering with loathing and disgust, he perceived to his horror that it had two red eyes like spots of blood. Sick with hatred of the thing as he was, those eyes fascinated him—held him like teeth. That night his other visions left him, but the beetle never let him go—nay! compelled him, as he sat weeping and helpless, to study its hideous conformation, to dwell upon its fangs, to ponder on its food. All through the night that was like a century—all through the pulsing hours—did he sit oppressed with horror gazing at that unutterable, slimy vermin. At the first streak of dawn it glided away, leaving in its trail the same smell of the charnel-house; but to him the day brought no rest, for his dreams were haunted by the abominable thing. All day in his ears a music sounded—a music thronged with passion and wailing of defeat, funereal and full of great alarums; all day he felt that he was engaged in a conflict with one in armour, while he himself was unharnessed and defenceless—all day, till the dark night came, when he observed the abhorred monster crawling slowly from the ruined abbey, and the calm, neglected Golgotha which lay there in his sight. Calm outwardly; but beneath perhaps—how disturbed, how swept by tempest! With trepidation, with a feeling of inexpiable guilt, he awaited the worm—the messenger of the dead. And this night and day were the type of nights and days to come. From the night of the new moon, indeed, till the night when it began to wane, the beetle remained in the grave; but so awful was the relief of those hours, the transition so poignant, that he could no nothing but shudder in a depression as of madness. And his circumstances were not merely those of physical horror and disgust: clouds of spiritual fear enveloped him: he felt that this abortion, this unspeakable visitor, was really an agent that claimed his life, and the flesh fell from his bones. So did he pass each day looking forward with anguish to the night; and then, at length, came the distorted night full of overwhelming anxiety and pain.

II

At dawn, when the dew was still heavy on the grass, he would go forth into the graveyard and stand before the iron gates of the vault in which his wife was laid. And as he stood there, repeating wild litanies of supplication, he would cast into the vault things of priceless value: skins of man-eating tigers and of leopards; skins of beasts that drank from the Ganges, and of beasts that wallowed in the mud of the Nile; gems that were the ornament of the Pharaohs; tusks of elephants, and corals that men had given their lives to obtain. Then holding up his arms, in a voice that raged against heaven he would cry: 'Take these, O avenging soul, and leave me in quiet! Are not these enough?'

And after some weeks he came to the vault again bringing with him a consecrated chalice studded with jewels which had been used by a priest at Mass, and a ciborium of the purest gold. These he filled with the rare wine of a lost vintage, and placing them within the vault he called in a voice of storm: 'Take these, O implacable soul, and spare thy bondman! Are not these enough?'

And last he brought with him the bracelets of the woman he loved, whose heart he had broken by parting with her to propitiate the dead. He brought a long strand of her hair, and a handkerchief damp with her tears. And the vault was filled with the misery of his heart-quaking whisper: 'O my wife, are not *these* enough?'

But it became plain to those who were about him that he had come to the end of his life. His hatred of death, his fear of its unyielding caress, gave him strength; and he seemed to be resisting with his thin hands some palpable assailant. Plainer and more deeply coloured than the visions of delirium, he saw the company which advanced to combat him: in the strongest light he contemplated the scenery which surrounds the portals of dissolution. And at the supreme moment, it was with a struggle far greater than that of the miser who is forcibly parted from his gold, with an anguish far more intense than that of the lover who is torn from his mistress, that he gave up his soul.

On a shrewd, grey evening in the autumn they carried him down to bury him in the vault by the side of his wife. This he had desired; for he thought that in no other vault however dark, would the darkness be quite still; in no other resting-place would he be allowed to repose. As they carried him they intoned a majestic threnody—a chaunt which had the deep tramp and surge of a triumphant march, which rode on the winds, and sobbed through the boughs of ancient trees. And having come to the vault they gave him to the grave, and knelt on the ground to pray for the ease of his spirit. *Requiem æternam dona ei, Domine!*

But as they prepared to leave the precincts of the ruined abbey, a dialogue began within the vault—a dialogue so wonderful, so terrible, in its nature, its cause, that as they hearkened they gazed at one another in the twilight with wry and pallid faces.

And first a woman's voice.

'You are come.'

'Yes, I am come,' said the voice of a man. 'I yield myself to you—the conqueror.'

'Long have I awaited you,' said the woman's voice. 'For years I have lain here while the rain soaked through the stones, and snow was heavy on my breast. For years while the sun danced over the earth, and the moon smiled her mellow smile upon gardens and pleasant things. I have lain here in the company of the worm, and I have leagued with the worm. You did nothing but what I willed; you were the toy of my dead hands. Ah, you stole my body from me, but I have stolen your soul from you!'

'And is there peace for me—now—at the last?'

The woman's voice became louder, and rang through the vault like a proclaiming trumpet. 'Peace is not mine! You and I are at last together in the city of one who queens it over a mighty empire. Now shall we tremble before the queen of Death.'

The watchers flung aside the gates of the vault and struck open two coffins. In a mouldy coffin they found the body of a woman having the countenance and warmth of one who has just died. But the body of the man was corrupt and most horrid, like a corpse that has lain for years in a place of graves.

THE STONE CHAMBER

H.B. Marriott Watson

Henry Brereton Marriott Watson (1863–1921) was an Australian writer, educated in New Zealand and resident in England since 1885. He wrote nearly fifty novels and short story collections from 1888 to 1919. His most famous horror tale, 'The Devil of the Marsh' (1893), has appeared in many anthologies. 'The Stone Chamber' (from *The Heart of Miranda*, 1899) is one of several vampire stories written by popular writers at the turn of the century, directly influenced by the success of *Dracula* (which had already passed through six impressions by that date). The stories in *The Heart of Miranda* were dedicated to Henry James.

IT was not until early summer that Warrington took possession of Marvyn Abbey. He had bought the property in the preceding autumn, but the place had so fallen into decay through the disorders of time that more than six months elapsed ere it was inhabitable. The delay, however, fell out conveniently for Warrington; for the Bosanquets spent the winter abroad, and nothing must suit but he must spend it with them. There was never a man who pursued his passion with such ardour. He was ever at Miss Bosanquet's skirts, and bade fair to make her as steadfast a husband as he was attached a lover. Thus it was not until after his return from that prolonged exile that he had the opportunity of inspecting the repairs discharged by his architect. He was nothing out of the common in character, but was full of kindly impulses and a fellow of impetuous blood. When he called upon me in my chambers he spoke with some excitement of his Abbey, as also of his approaching marriage; and finally, breaking into an exhibition of genuine affection, declared that we had been so long and so continuously intimate that I, and none other, must help him warm his house and marry his bride. It had indeed been always understood between us that I should serve him at the ceremony, but now it appeared that I must start my duties even earlier. The prospect of a summer holiday in Utterbourne pleased me. It was a charming village, set upon the slope of a wooded hill and within call of the sea. I had a slight knowledge of the district from a riding excursion taken through that part of Devonshire; and years before, and ere Warrington had come into his money, had viewed the Abbey ruins from a distance with the polite curiosity of a passing tourist.

I examined them now with new eyes as we drove up the avenue. The face which the ancient building presented to the valley was of magnificent design, but now much worn and battered. Part of it, the right wing, I judged to be long past the uses of a dwelling, for the walls had crumbled away, huge gaps opened in the foundations, and the roof was quite dismantled. Warrington had very wisely left this portion to its own sinister decay; it was the left wing which had been restored, and which we were to inhabit. The entrance, I will confess, was a little mean, for the large doorway had been bricked up and an ordinary modern door gave upon the spacious terrace and the winding gardens. But apart from this, the work of restoration had been undertaken with skill and piety, and the interior had retained its native dignity, while resuming an air of proper comfort. The old oak had been repaired congruous with the original designs, and the great rooms had been as little altered as was requisite to adapt them for daily use.

Warrington passed quickly from chamber to chamber in evident delight, directing my attention upon this and upon that, and eagerly requiring my congratulations and approval. My comments must have satisfied him, for the place attracted me vastly. The only criticism I ventured was to remark upon the size of the rooms and to question if they might dwarf the insignificant human figures they were to entertain.

He laughed. 'Not a bit,' said he. 'Roaring fires in winter in those fine old fireplaces; and as for summer, the more space the better. We shall be jolly.'

I followed him along the noble hall, and we stopped before a small door of very black oak.

'The bedrooms,' he explained, as he turned the key, 'are all upstairs, but mine is not ready yet. And besides, I am reserving it; I won't sleep in it till—you understand,' he concluded, with a smiling suggestion of embarrassment.

I understood very well. He threw the door open.

'I am going to use this in the meantime,' he continued. 'Queer little room, isn't it? It used to be a sort of library. How do you think it looks?'

We had entered as he spoke, and stood, distributing our glances in that vague and general way in which a room is surveyed. It was a chamber of much smaller proportions than the rest, and was dimly lighted by two long narrow windows sunk in the great walls. The bed and the modern fittings looked strangely out of keeping with its ancient privacy. The walls were rudely distempered with barbaric frescos, dating, I conjectured, from the fourteenth century; and the floor was of stone, worn into grooves and hollows with the feet of many generations. As I was taking in these facts, there came over me a sudden curiosity as to those dead Marvyns who had held the Abbey for so long. This silent chamber seemed to suggest questions of their history; it spoke eloquently of past ages and past deeds, fallen now into oblivion. Here, within these thick walls, no echo from the outer world might carry, no sound would ring within its solitary seclusion. Even the silence seemed to confer with one upon the ancient transactions of that extinct House.

Warrington stirred, and turned suddenly to me. 'I hope it's not damp,' said he, with a slight shiver. 'It looks rather solemn. I thought furniture would brighten it up.'

'I should think it would be very comfortable,' said I. 'You will never be disturbed by any sounds at any rate.'

'No,' he answered, hesitatingly; and then, quickly, on one of his impulses: 'Hang it, Heywood, there's too much silence here for me.' Then he laughed. 'Oh, I shall do very well for a month or two.' And with that appeared to return to his former placid cheerfulness.

The train of thought started in that sombre chamber served to entertain me several times that day. I questioned Warrington at dinner, which we took in one of the smaller rooms, commanding a lovely prospect of dale and sea. He shook his head. Archæological lore, as indeed anything else out of the borders of actual life, held very little interest for him.

'The Marvyns died out in 1714, I believe,' he said, indifferently; 'someone told me that—the man I bought it from, I think. They might just as well have kept the place up since; but I think it has been only occupied twice between then and now, and the last time was forty years ago. It would have rotted to pieces if I hadn't taken it. Perhaps Mrs Batty could tell you. She's lived in these parts almost all her life.'

To humour me, and affected, I doubt not, by a certain pride in his new possession, he put the query to his housekeeper upon her appearance subsequently; but it seemed that her knowledge was little fuller than his own, though she had gathered some vague traditions of the countryside. The Marvyns had not left a reputable name, if rumour spoke truly; theirs was a family to which black deeds had been credited. They were ill-starred also in their fortunes, and had become extinct suddenly; but for the rest, the events had fallen too many generations ago to be current now between the memories of the village.

Warrington, who was more eager to discuss the future than to recall the past, was vastly excited by his anticipations. St Pharamond, Sir William Bosanquet's house, lay across the valley, barely five miles away; and as the family had now returned, it was easy to forgive Warrington's elation.

'What do you think?' he said, late that evening; and clapping me upon the shoulder, 'You have seen Marion; here is the house. Am I not lucky? Damn it, Heywood, I'm not pious, but I am disposed to thank God! I'm not a bad fellow, but I'm no saint; it's fortunate that it's not only the virtuous that are rewarded. In fact, it's usually contrariwise. I owe this to—Lord, I don't know what I owe it to. Is it my money? Of course, Marion doesn't care a rap for that; but then, you see, I mightn't have known her without it. Of course, there's the house, too. I'm thankful I have money. At any rate, here's my new life. Just look about and take it in, old fellow. If you knew how a man may be ashamed of himself! But there, I've done. You know I'm decent at heart—you must count my life from today.' And with this outbreak he lifted the glass between fingers that trembled with the warmth of his emotions, and tossed off his wine.

He did himself but justice when he claimed to be a good fellow; and, in truth, I was myself somewhat moved by his obvious feeling. I remember that we shook hands very affectionately, and my sympathy was the prelude to a long and confidential talk, which lasted until quite a late hour.

At the foot of the staircase, where we parted, he detained me. 'This is the last of my wayward days,' he said, with a smile. 'Late hours—liquor—all go. You shall see. Goodnight. You know your room. I shall be up long before you.' And with that he vanished briskly into the darkness that hung about the lower parts of the passage.

I watched him go, and it struck me quite vaguely what a slight impression his candle made upon that channel of opaque gloom. It seemed merely as a thread of light that illumined nothing. Warrington himself was rapt into the prevalent blackness; but long afterwards, and even when his footsteps had died away upon the heavy carpet, the tiny beam was visible, advancing and flickering in the distance.

My window, which was modern, opened upon a little balcony, where, as the night was warm and I was indisposed for sleep, I spent half an hour enjoying the air. I was in a sentimental mood, and my thoughts turned upon the suggestions which Warrington's conversation had induced. It was not until I was in bed, and had blown out the light, that they settled upon the square, dark chamber in which my host was to pass the night. As I have said, I was wakeful, owing, no doubt, to the high pitch of the emotions which we had encouraged; but presently my fancies became inarticulate and incoherent, and then I was overtaken by profound sleep.

Warrington was up before me, as he had predicted, and met me in the breakfast-room.

'What a beggar you are to sleep!' he said, with a smile. 'I've hammered at your door for half an hour.'

I apologized for myself, alleging the rich country air in my defence, and mentioned that I had had some difficulty in getting to sleep.

'So had I,' he remarked, as we sat down to the table. 'We got very excited, I suppose. Just see what you have there, Heywood. Eggs? Oh, damn it, one can have too much of eggs!' He frowned, and lifted a third cover. 'Why in the name of common sense can't Mrs Batty give us more variety?' he asked, impatiently.

I deprecated his displeasure, suggesting that we should do very well; indeed, his discontent seemed to me quite unnecessary. But I supposed Warrington had been rather spoiled by many years of club life.

He settled himself without replying, and began to pick over his plate in a gingerly manner.

'There's one thing I will have here, Heywood,' he observed. 'I will have things well appointed. I'm not going to let life in the country mean an uncomfortable life. A man can't change the habits of a lifetime.'

In contrast with his exhilarated professions of the previous evening, this struck me with a sense of amusement at the moment; and the incongruity may have occurred to him, for he went on: 'Marion's not over strong, you know, and must have things *comme il faut*. She shan't decline upon a lower level. The worst of these rustics is that they have no imagination.' He held up a piece of bacon on his fork, and surveyed it with disgust. 'Now, look at that! Why the devil don't they take tips from civilized people like the French?'

It was so unlike him to exhibit this petulance that I put it down to a bad night, and without discovering the connection of my thoughts, asked him how he liked his bedroom.

'Oh, pretty well, pretty well,' he said, indifferently. 'It's not so cold as I thought. But I slept badly. I always do in a strange bed'; and pushing aside his plate, he lit a cigarette. 'When you've finished that garbage, Heywood, we'll have a stroll round the Abbey,' he said.

His good temper returned during our walk, and he indicated to me various improvements which he contemplated, with something of his old ardour. The left wing of the house, as I have said, was entire, but a little apart were the ruins of a chapel. Surrounded by a low moss-grown wall, it was full of picturesque charm; the roofless chancel was spread with ivy, but the aisles were intact. Grass grew between the stones and the floor, and many creepers had strayed through chinks in the wall into those sacred precincts. The solemn quietude of the ruin, maintained under the spell of death, awed me a little, but upon Warrington apparently it made no impression. He was only zealous that I should properly appreciate the distinction of such a property. I stooped and drew the weeds away from one of the slabs in the aisle, and was able to trace upon it the relics of lettering, well-nigh obliterated under the corrosion of time.

'There are tombs,' said I.

'Oh, yes,' he answered, with a certain relish. 'I understand the Marvyns used it as a mausoleum. They are all buried here. Some good brasses, I am told.'

The associations of the place engaged me; the aspect of the Abbey faced the past; it seemed to refuse communion with the present; and somehow the thought of those two decent humdrum lives which should be spent within its shelter savoured of the incongruous. The white-capped maids and the emblazoned butlers that should tread these halls offered a ridiculous appearance beside my fancies of the ancient building. For all that, I envied Warrington his home, and so I told him, with a humorous hint that I was fitter to appreciate its glories than himself.

He laughed. 'Oh, I don't know,' said he. 'I like the old-world look as much as you do. I have always had a notion of something venerable. It seems to serve you for ancestors.' And he was undoubtedly delighted with my enthusiasm.

But at lunch again he chopped round to his previous irritation, only now quite another matter provoked his anger. He had received a letter by the second post from Miss Bosanquet, which, if I may judge from his perplexity, must have been unusually confused. He read and re-read it, his brow lowering.

'What the deuce does she mean?' he asked, testily. 'She first makes an arrangement for us to ride over today, and now I can't make out whether we are to go to St Pharamond, or they are coming to us. Just look at it, will you, Heywood?'

I glanced through the note, but could offer no final solution, whereupon he broke out again:

'That's just like women—they never can say anything straightfor-wardly. Why, in the name of goodness, couldn't she leave things as they were? You see,' he observed, rather in answer, as I fancied, to my silence, 'we don't know what to do now; if we stay here they mayn't come, and if we go probably we shall cross them.' And he snapped his fingers in annoyance.

I was cheerful enough, perhaps because the responsibility was not mine, and ventured to suggest that we might ride over, and return if we missed them. But he dismissed the subject sharply by saying:

'No, I'll stay. I'm not going on a fool's errand,' and drew my attention to some point in the decoration of the room.

The Bosanquets did not arrive during the afternoon, and Warring-ton's ill-humour increased. His love-sick state pleaded in excuse of him, but he was certainly not a pleasant companion. He was sour and snappish, and one could introduce no statement to which he would not find a contradiction. So unamiable did he grow that at last I discovered a pretext to leave him, and rambled to the back of the Abbey into the precincts of the old chapel. The day was falling, and the summer sun flared through the western windows upon the bare aisle. The creepers rustled upon the gaping walls, and the tall grasses waved in shadows over the bodies of the forgotten dead. As I stood contemplating the effect, and meditating greatly upon the anterior fortunes of the Abbey, my attention fell upon a huge slab of marble, upon which the yellow light struck sharply. The faded lettering rose into greater definition before my eyes and I read slowly:

'*Here lyeth the body of Sir Rupert Marvyn.*'

Beyond a date, very difficult to decipher, there was nothing more; of eulogy, of style, of record, of pious considerations such as were usual to the period, not a word. I read the numerals variously as 1723 and 1745; but however they ran it was probable that the stone covered the resting-place of the last Marvyn. The history of this futile house interested me not a little, partly for Warrington's sake, and in part from a natural bent towards ancient records; and I made a mental note of the name and date.

When I returned Warrington's surliness had entirely vanished, and had given place to an effusion of boisterous spirits. He apologized jovially for his bad temper.

'It was the disappointment of not seeing Marion,' he said. 'You will understand that some day, old fellow. But, anyhow, we'll go over tomorrow'; and forthwith proceeded to enliven the dinner with an ostentation of good-fellowship I had seldom witnessed in him. I began to suspect that he had heard again from St Pharamond, though he chose to conceal the fact from me. The wine was admirable; though Warrington himself was no great judge, he had entrusted the selection to a good palate. We had a merry meal, drank a little more than was prudent, and smoked our cigars upon the terrace in the fresh air. Warrington was restless. He pushed his glass from him. 'I'll tell you what, old chap,' he broke out, 'I'll give you a game of billiards. I've got a decent table.'

I demurred. The air was too delicious, and I was in no humour for a sharp use of my wits. He laughed, though he seemed rather disappointed.

'It's almost sacrilege to play billiards in an Abbey,' I said, whimsically. 'What would the ghosts of the old Marvyns think?'

'Oh, hang the Marvyns!' he rejoined, crossly. 'You're always talking of them.'

He rose and entered the house, returning presently with a flagon of whisky and some glasses.

'Try this,' he said. 'We've had no liqueurs'; and pouring out some spirit he swallowed it raw.

I stared, for Warrington rarely took spirits, being more of a wine drinker; moreover, he must have taken nearly the quarter of a tumbler. But he did not notice my surprise, and, seating himself, lit another cigar.

'I don't mean to have things quiet here,' he observed, reflectively. 'I don't believe in your stagnant rustic life. What I intend to do is to keep the place warm—plenty of house parties, things going on all the year. I shall expect you down for the shooting, Ned. The coverts promise well this year.'

I assented willingly enough, and he rambled on again.

'I don't know that I shall use the Abbey so much. I think I'll live in town a good deal. It's brighter there. I don't know though. I like the place. Hang it, it's a rattling good shop, there's no mistake about it. Look here,' he broke off, abruptly, 'bring your glass in, and I'll show you something.'

I was little inclined to move, but he was so peremptory that I followed him with a sigh. We entered one of the smaller rooms which overlooked the terrace, and had been diverted into a comfortable library. He flung back the windows.

'There's air for you,' he cried. 'Now, sit down,' and walking to a cupboard produced a second flagon of whisky. 'Irish!' he ejaculated, clumping it on the table. 'Take your choice,' and turning again to the cupboard, presently sat down with his hands under the table. 'Now, then, Ned,' he said, with a short laugh. 'Fill up, and we'll have some fun,' with which he suddenly threw a pack of cards upon the board.

I opened my eyes, for I do not suppose Warrington had touched cards since his college days; but, interpreting my look in his own way, he cried:

'Oh, I'm not married yet. Warrington's his own man still. Poker? Eh?'

'Anything you like,' said I, with resignation.

A peculiar expression of delight gleamed in his eyes, and he shuffled the cards feverishly.

'Cut,' said he, and helped himself to more whisky.

It was shameful to be playing there with that beautiful night without, but there seemed no help for it. Warrington had a run of luck, though he played with little skill; and his excitement grew as he won.

'Let us make it ten shillings,' he suggested.

I shook my head. 'You forget I'm not a millionaire,' I replied.

'Bah!' he cried. 'I like a game worth the victory. Well, fire away.'

His eyes gloated upon the cards, and he fingered them with unctuous affection. The behaviour of the man amazed me. I began to win.

Warrington's face slowly assumed a dull, lowering expression; he played eagerly, avariciously; he disputed my points, and was querulous.

'Oh, we've had enough!' I cried in distaste.

'By Jove, you don't!' he exclaimed, jumping to his feet. 'You're the winner, Heywood, and I'll see you damned before I let you off my revenge!'

The words startled me no less than the fury which rang in his accents. I gazed at him in stupefaction. The whites of his eyes showed wildly, and a sullen, angry look determined his face. Suddenly I was arrested by the suspicion of something upon his neck.

'What's that?' I asked. 'You've cut yourself.'

He put his hand to his face. 'Nonsense,' he replied, in a surly fashion.

I looked closer, and then I saw my mistake. It was a round, faint red mark, the size of a florin, upon the column of his throat, and I set it down to the accidental pressure of some button.

'Come on!' he insisted, impatiently.

'Bah! Warrington,' I said, for I imagined that he had been over-excited by the whisky he had taken. 'It's only a matter of a few pounds. Why make a fuss? Tomorrow will serve.'

After a moment his eyes fell, and he gave an awkward laugh. 'Oh, well, that'll do,' said he. 'But I got so infernally excited.'

'Whisky,' said I, sententiously.

He glanced at the bottle. 'How many glasses have I had?' and he whistled. 'By Jove, Ned, this won't do! I must turn over a new leaf. Come on; let's look at the night.'

I was only too glad to get away from the table, and we were soon upon the terrace again. Warrington was silent, and his gaze went constantly across the valley, where the moon was rising, and in the direction in which, as he had indicated to me, St Pharamond lay. When he said goodnight he was still pre-occupied.

'I hope you will sleep better,' he said.

'And you, too,' I added.

He smiled. 'I don't suppose I shall wake the whole night through,' he said; and then, as I was turning to go, he caught me quickly by the arm.

'Ned,' he said, impulsively and very earnestly, 'don't let me make a fool of myself again. I know it's the excitement of everything. But I want to be as good as I can for her.'

I pressed his hand. 'All right, old fellow,' I said; and we parted.

I think I have never enjoyed sounder slumber than that night. The first thing I was aware of was the singing of thrushes outside my window. I rose and looked forth, and the sun was hanging high in the eastern sky, the grass and the young green of the trees were shining with dew. With an uncomfortable feeling that I was very late I hastily dressed and went downstairs. Warrington was waiting for me in the breakfast-room, as upon the previous morning, and when he turned from the window at my approach, the sight of his face startled me. It was drawn and haggard, and his eyes were shot with blood; it was a face broken and savage with dissipation. He made no answer to my questioning, but seated himself with a morose air.

'Now you have come,' he said, sullenly, 'we may as well begin. But it's not my fault if the coffee's cold.'

I examined him critically, and passed some comment upon his appearance.

'You don't look up to much,' I said. 'Another bad night?'

'No; I slept well enough,' he responded, ungraciously; and then, after a pause: 'I'll tell you what, Heywood. You shall give me my revenge after breakfast.'

'Nonsense,' I said, after a momentary silence. 'You're going over to St Pharamond.'

'Hang it!' was his retort, 'one can't be always bothering about women. You seem mightily indisposed to meet me again.'

'I certainly won't this morning,' I answered, rather sharply, for the man's manner grated upon me. 'This evening, if you like; and then the silly business shall end.'

He said something in an undertone of grumble, and the rest of the meal passed in silence. But I entertained an uneasy suspicion of him, and after all he was my friend, with whom I was under obligations not to quarrel; and so when we rose, I approached him.

'Look here, Warrington,' I said. 'What's the matter with you? Have you been drinking? Remember what you asked me last night.'

'Hold your damned row!' was all the answer he vouchsafed, as he whirled away from me, but with an embarrassed display of shame.

But I was not to be put off in that way, and I spoke somewhat more sharply.

'We're going to have this out, Warrington,' I said. 'If you are ill, let us understand that; but I'm not going to stay here with you in this cantankerous spirit.'

'I'm not ill,' he replied testily.

'Look at yourself,' I cried, and turned him about to the mirror over the mantelpiece.

He started a little, and a frown of perplexity gathered on his forehead.

'Good Lord! I'm not like that, Ned,' he said, in a different voice. 'I must have been drunk last night.' And with a sort of groan, he directed a piteous look at me.

'Come,' I was constrained to answer, 'pull yourself together. The ride will do you good. And no more whisky.'

'No, by Heaven, no!' he cried vehemently, and seemed to shiver; but then, suddenly taking my arm, he walked out of the room.

The morning lay still and golden. Warrington's eyes went forth across the valley.

'Come round to the stables, Ned,' he said, impulsively. 'You shall choose you own nag.'

I shook my head. 'I'll choose yours,' said I, 'but I am not going with you.' He looked surprised. 'No, ride by yourself. You don't want a companion on such an errand. I'll stay here, and pursue my investigations into the Marvyns.'

A scowl crossed his face, but only for an instant, and then he answered: 'All right, old chap; do as you like. Anyway, I'm off at once.' And presently, when his horse was brought, he was laughing merrily.

'You'll have a dull day, Ned; but it's your own fault, you duffer. You'll have to lunch by yourself, as I shan't be back till late.' And, gaily flourishing his whip, he trotted down the drive.

It was some relief to me to be rid of him, for, in truth, his moods had worn my nerves, and I had not looked for a holiday of this disquieting nature. When he returned, I had no doubt it would be with quite another face, and meanwhile I was excellent company for myself. After lunch I amused myself for half an hour with idle tricks upon the billiard-table, and, tiring of my pastime, fell upon the housekeeper as I returned along the corridor. She was a woman nearer to sixty than fifty, with a comfortable, portly figure, and an amiable expression. Her eyes invited me ever so respectfully to conversation, and stopping, I entered into talk. She inquired if I liked my room and how I slept.

''Tis a nice look-out you have, Sir,' said she. 'That was where old Lady Martin slept.'

It appeared that she had served as kitchen-maid to the previous tenants of the Abbey, nearly fifty years before.

'Oh, I know the old house in and out,' she asserted; 'and I arranged the rooms with Mr Warrington.'

We were standing opposite the low doorway which gave entrance to Warrington's bedroom, and my eyes unconsciously shot in that direction. Mrs Batty followed my glance.

'I didn't want him to have that,' she said; 'but he was set upon it. It's smallish for a bedroom, and in my opinion isn't fit for more than a lumber-room. That's what Sir William used it for.'

I pushed open the door and stepped over the threshold, and the housekeeper followed me.

'No,' she said, glancing round; 'and it's in my mind that it's damp, Sir.'

Again I had a curious feeling that the silence was speaking in my ear; the atmosphere was thick and heavy, and a musty smell, as of faded draperies, penetrated my nostrils. The whole room looked indescribably dingy, despite the new hangings. I went over to the narrow window and peered through the diamond panes. Outside, but seen dimly through that ancient and discoloured glass, the ruins of the chapel confronted me, bare and stark, in the yellow sunlight. I turned.

'There are no ghosts in the Abbey, I suppose, Mrs Batty?' I asked, whimsically.

But she took my inquiry very gravely. 'I have never heard tell of one, Sir,' she protested; 'and if there was such a thing I should have known it.'

As I was rejoining her a strange low whirring was audible, and looking up I saw in a corner of the high-arched roof a horrible face watching me out of black narrow eyes. I confess that I was very much startled at the apparition, but the next moment realized what it was. The creature hung with its ugly fleshy wings extended over a grotesque stone head that leered down upon me, its evil-looking snout projecting into the room; it lay perfectly still, returning me glance for glance, until moved by the repulsion of its presence I clapped my hands, and cried loudly; then, slowly flitting in a circle round the roof, it vanished with a flapping of wings into some darker corner of the rafters. Mrs Batty was astounded, and expressed surprise that it had managed to conceal itself for so long.

'Oh, bats live in holes,' I answered. 'Probably there is some small access through the masonry.' But the incident had sent an uncomfortable shiver through me all the same.

Later that day I began to recognize that, short of an abrupt return to town, my time was not likely to be spent very pleasantly. But it was the personal problem so far as it concerned Warrington himself that distressed me even more. He came back from St Pharamond in a morose and ugly temper, quite alien to his kindly nature. It seems that he had quarrelled bitterly with Miss Bosanquet, but upon what I could not determine, nor did I press him for an explanation. But the fumes of his anger were still rising when we met, and our dinner was a most depressing meal. He was in a degree of irritation which rendered it impossible to address him, and I soon withdrew into my thoughts. I saw, however, that he was drinking far too much, as, indeed, was plain subsequently when he invited me into the library. Once more he produced the hateful cards, and I was compelled to play, as he reminded me somewhat churlishly that I had promised him his revenge.

'Understand, Warrington,' I said, firmly, 'I play tonight, but never again, whatever the result. In fact, I am in half the mind to return to town tomorrow.'

He gave me a look as he set down, but said nothing, and the game began. He lost heavily from the first, and as nothing would content him but we must constantly raise the stakes, in a short time I had won several hundred pounds. He bore the reverses very ill, breaking out from time to time into some angry exclamation, now petulantly questioning my playing, and muttering oaths under his breath. But I was resolved that he should have no cause of complaint against me for this one night, and disregarding his insane fits of temper, I played steadily and silently. As the tally of my gains mounted he changed colour slowly, his face assuming a ghastly expression, and his eyes suspiciously denoting my actions. At length he rose, and throwing himself quickly across the table, seized my hand ferociously as I dealt a couple of cards.

'Damn you! I see your tricks,' he cried, in frenzied passion. 'Drop that hand, do you hear? Drop that hand, or by——'

But he got no further, for, rising myself, I wrenched my hand from his grasp, and turned upon him, in almost as great a passion as himself. But suddenly, and even as I opened my mouth to speak, I stopped short with a cry of horror. His face was livid to the lips, his eyes were cast with blood, and upon the dirty white of his flesh, right in the centre of his throat, the round red scar, flaming and ugly as a wound, stared upon me.

'Warrington!' I cried, 'what is this? What have you——' And I pointed in alarm to the spot.

'Mind your own business,' he said, with a sneer. 'It is well to try and draw off attention from your knavery. But that trick won't answer with me.'

Without another word I flung the IOU's upon the table, and turning on my heel, left the room. I was furious with him, and fully resolved to leave the Abbey in the morning. I made my way upstairs to my room, and then, seating myself upon the balcony, endeavoured to recover my self-possession.

The more I considered, the more unaccountable was Warrington's behaviour. He had always been a perfectly courteous man, with a great lump of kindness in his nature; whereas these last few days he had been nothing other than a savage. It seemed certain that he must be ill or going mad; and as I reflected upon this the conjecture struck me with a sense of pity. If it was that he was losing his senses, how horrible was the tragedy in face of the new and lovely prospects opening in his life. Stimulated by this growing conviction, I resolved to go down and see him, more particularly as I now recalled his pleading voice that I should help him, on the previous evening. Was it not possible that this pathetic appeal derived from the instinct of the insane to protect themselves?

I found him still in the library; his head had fallen upon the table, and the state of the whisky bottle by his arm showed only too clearly his condition. I shook him vigorously, and he opened his eyes.

'Warrington, you must go to bed,' I said.

He smiled, and greeted me quite affectionately. Obviously he was not so drunk as I had supposed.

'What is the time, Ned?' he asked.

I told him it was one o'clock, at which he rose briskly.

'Lord, I've been asleep,' he said. 'Help me, Ned. I don't think I'm sober. Where have you been?'

I assisted him to his room, and he undressed slowly, and with an effort. Somehow, as I stood watching him, I yielded to an unknown impulse and said, suddenly:

'Warrington, don't sleep here. Come and share my room.'

'My dear fellow,' he replied, with a foolish laugh, 'yours is not the only room in the house. I can use half-a-dozen if I like.'

'Well, use one of them,' I answered.

He shook his head. 'I'm going to sleep here,' he returned, obstinately.

I made no further effort to influence him, for, after all, now that the words were out, I had absolutely no reason to give him or myself for my proposition. And so I left him. When I had closed the door, and was turning to go along the passage, I heard very clearly, as it seemed to me, a plaintive cry, muffled and faint, but very disturbing, which sounded from the room. Instantly I opened the door again. Warrington was in bed, and the heavy sound of his breathing told me that he was asleep. It was impossible that he could have uttered the cry. A night-light was burning by his bedside, shedding a strong illumination over the immediate vicinity, and throwing antic shadows on the walls. As I turned to go, there was a whirring of wings, a brief flap behind me, and the room was plunged in darkness. The obscene creature that lived in the recesses of the roof must have knocked out the tiny light with its wings. Then Warrington's breathing ceased, and there was no sound at all. And then once more the silence seemed to gather round me slowly and heavily, and whisper to me. I had a vague sense of being prevailed upon, of being enticed and lured by something in the surrounding air; a sort of horror circumscribed me, and I broke from the invisible ring and rushed from the room. The door clanged behind me, and as I hastened along the hall, once more there seemed to ring in my ears the faint and melancholy cry.

I awoke, in the sombre twilight that precedes the dawn, from a sleep troubled and encumbered with evil dreams. The birds had not yet begun their day, and a vast silence brooded over the Abbey gardens. Looking out of my window, I caught sight of a dark figure stealing cautiously round the corner of the ruined chapel. The furtive gait, as well as the appearance of a man at that early hour, struck me with surprise; and hastily throwing on some clothes, I ran downstairs, and, opening the hall-door, went out. When I reached the porch which gave entrance to the aisle I stopped suddenly, for there before me, with his head to the ground, and peering among the tall grasses, was the object of my pursuit. Then I stepped quickly forward and laid a hand upon his shoulder. It was Warrington.

'What are you doing here?' I asked.

He turned and looked at me in bewilderment. His eyes wore a dazed expression, and he blinked in perplexity before he replied.

'It's you, is it?' he said weakly. 'I thought——' and then paused. 'What is it?' he asked.

'I followed you here,' I explained. 'I only saw your figure, and thought it might be some intruder.'

He avoided my eyes. 'I thought I heard a cry out here,' he answered.

'Warrington,' I said, with some earnestness, 'come back to bed.'

He made no answer, and slipping my arm in his, I led him away. On the doorstep he stopped, and lifted his face to me.

'Do you think it's possible——' he began, as if to inquire of me, and then again paused. With a slight shiver he proceeded to his room, while I followed him. He sat down upon his bed, and his eyes strayed to the barred window absently. The black shadow of the chapel was visible through the panes.

'Don't say anything about this,' he said, suddenly. 'Don't let Marion know.'

I laughed, but it was an awkward laugh.

'Why, that you were alarmed by a cry for help, and went in search like a gentleman?' I asked, jestingly.

'You heard it, then?' he said, eagerly.

I shook my head, for I was not going to encourage his fancies. 'You had better go to sleep,' I replied, 'and get rid of these nightmares.'

He sighed and lay back upon his pillow, dressed as he was. Ere I left him he had fallen into a profound slumber.

If I had expected a surly mood in him at breakfast I was much mistaken. There was not a trace of his nocturnal dissipations; he did not seem even to remember them, and he made no allusion whatever to our adventure in the dawn. He perused a letter carefully, and threw it over to me with a grin.

'Lor', what queer sheep women are!' he exclaimed, with rather a coarse laugh.

I glanced at the letter without thinking, but ere I had read half of it I put it aside. It was certainly not meant for my eyes, and I marvelled at Warrington's indelicacy in making public, as it were, that very private matter. The note was from Miss Bosanquet, and was clearly designed for his own heart, couched as it was in the terms of warm and fond affection. No man should see such letters save he for whom they are written.

'You see, they're coming over to dine,' he remarked, carelessly. 'Trust a girl to make it up if you let her alone long enough.'

I made no answer; but though Warrington's grossness irritated me, I reflected with satisfaction upon his return to good humour, which I attributed to the reconciliation.

When I moved out upon the terrace the maid had entered to remove the breakfast things. I was conscious of a slight exclamation behind me, and Warrington joined me presently, with a loud guffaw.

'That's a damned pretty girl!' he said, with unction. 'I'm glad Mrs Batty got her. I like to have good-looking servants.'

I suddenly interpreted the incident, and shrugged my shoulders.

'You're a perfect boor this morning, Warrington,' I exclaimed, irritably.

He only laughed. 'You're a dull dog of a saint, Heywood,' he retorted. 'Come along,' and dragged me out in no amiable spirit.

I had forgotten how perfect a host Warrington could be, but that evening he was displayed at his best. The Bosanquets arrived early. Sir William was an easy-going man, fond of books and of wine, and I now guessed at the taste which had decided Warrington's cellar. Miss Bosanquet was as charming as I remembered her to be; and if any objection might be taken to Warrington himself by my anxious eyes it was merely that he seemed a trifle excited, a fault which, in the circumstances, I was able to condone. Sir William hung about the table, sipping his wine. Warrington, who had been very abstemious, grew restless, and, finally apologizing in his graceful way, left me to keep the baronet company. I was the less disinclined to do so as I was anxious not to intrude upon the lovers, and Sir William was discussing the history of the Abbey. He had an old volume somewhere in his library which related to it, and, seeing that I was interested, invited me to look it up.

We sat long, and it was not until later that the horrible affair which I must narrate occurred. The evening was close and oppressive, owing to the thunder, which already rumbled far away in the south. When we rose we found that Warrington and Miss Bosanquet were in the garden, and thither we followed. As at first we did not find them, Sir William, who had noted the approaching storm with some uneasiness, left me to make arrangements for his return; and I strolled along the paths by myself, enjoying a cigarette. I had reached the shrubbery upon the further side of the chapel, when I heard the sound of voices—a man's rough and rasping, a woman's pleading and informed with fear. A sharp cry ensued, and without hesitation I plunged through the thicket in the direction of the speakers. The sight that met me appalled me for the moment. Darkness was falling, lit with ominous flashes; and the two figures stood out distinctly in the bushes, in an attitude of struggle. I could not mistake the voices now. I heard Warrington's, brusque with anger, and almost savage in its tones, crying, 'You shall!' and there followed a murmur from the girl, a little sob, and then a piercing cry. I sprang forward and seized Warrington by the arm; when, to my horror, I perceived that he had taken her wrist in both hands and was roughly twisting it, after the cruel habit of schoolboys. The malevolent cruelty of the action so astounded me that for an instant I remained motionless; I almost heard the bones in the frail wrist cracking; and then, in a second, I had seized Warrington's hands in a grip of iron, and flung him violently to the ground. The girl fell with him, and as I picked her up he rose too, and, clenching his fists, made as though to come at me, but instead turned and went sullenly, and with a ferocious look of hate upon his face, out of the thicket.

Miss Bosanquet came to very shortly, and though the agony of the pain must have been considerable to a delicate girl, I believe it was rather the incredible horror of the act under which she swooned. For my part I had nothing to say: not one word relative to the incident dared pass my lips. I inquired if she was better, and then, putting her arm in mine, led her gently towards the house. Her heart beat hard against me, and she breathed heavily, leaning on me for support. At the chapel I stopped, feeling suddenly that I dare not let her be seen in this condition, and bewildered greatly by the whole atrocious business.

'Come and rest in here,' I suggested, and we entered the chapel.

I set her on a slab of marble, and stood waiting by her side. I talked fluently about anything; for lack of a subject, upon the state of the chapel and the curious tomb I had discovered. Recovering a little, she joined presently in my remarks. It was plain that she was putting a severe restraint upon herself. I moved aside the grasses, and read aloud the inscription on Sir Rupert's grave-piece, and turning to the next, which was rankly overgrown, feigned to search further. As I was bending there, suddenly, and by what thread of thought I know not, I identified the spot with that upon which I had found Warrington stooping that morning. With a sweep of my hand I brushed back the weeds, uprooting some with my fingers, and kneeling in the twilight, pored over the monument. Suddenly a wild flare of light streamed down the sky, and a great crash of thunder followed. Miss Bosanquet started to her feet and I to mine. The heaven was lit up, as it were, with sunlight, and, as I turned, my eyes fell upon the now uncovered stone. Plainly the lettering flashed in my eyes:

'*Priscilla, Lady Marvyn.*'

Then the clouds opened, and the rain fell in spouts, shouting and dancing upon the ancient roof overhead.

We were under a very precarious shelter, and I was uneasy that Miss Bosanquet should run the risk of that flimsy, ravaged edifice; and so in a momentary lull I managed to get her to the house. I found Sir William in a restless state of nerves. He was a timorous man, and the thunder had upset him, more particularly as he and his daughter were now storm-bound for some time. There was no possibility of venturing into those rude elements for an hour or more. Warrington was not inside, and no one had seen him. In the light Miss Bosanquet's face frightened me; her eyes were large and scared, and her colour very dead white. Clearly she was very near a breakdown. I found Mrs Batty, and told her that the young lady had been severely shaken by the storm, suggesting that she had better lie down for a little. Returning with me, the housekeeper led off the unfortunate girl, and Sir William and I were left together. He paced the room impatiently, and constantly inquired if there were any signs of improvement in the weather. He also asked for

Warrington, irritably. The burden of the whole dreadful night seemed fallen upon me. Passing through the hall I met Mrs Batty again. Her usually placid features were disturbed and aghast.

'What is the matter?' I asked. 'Is Miss Bosanquet——'

'No, Sir; I think she's sleeping,' she replied. 'She's in—she is in Mr Warrington's room.'

I started. 'Are there no other rooms?' I asked, abruptly.

'There are none ready, Sir, except yours,' she answered, 'and I thought——'

'You should have taken her there,' I said, sharply. The woman looked at me and opened her mouth. 'Good heavens!' I said, irritably, 'what is the matter? Everyone is mad tonight.'

'Alice is gone, Sir,' she blurted forth.

Alice, I remembered, was the name of one of her maids.

'What do you mean?' I asked, for her air of panic betokened something graver than her words. The thunder broke over the house and drowned her voice.

'She can't be out in this storm—she must have taken refuge somewhere,' I said.

At that the strings of her tongue loosened, and she burst forth with her tale. It was an abominable narrative.

'Where is Mr Warrington?' I asked; but she shook her head.

There was a moment's silence between us, and we eyed each other aghast. 'She will be all right,' I said at last, as if dismissing the subject.

The housekeeper wrung her hands. 'I never would have thought it!' she repeated, dismally. 'I never would have thought it!'

'There is some mistake,' I said; but, somehow, I knew better. Indeed, I felt now that I had almost been prepared for it.

'She ran towards the village,' whispered Mrs Batty. 'God knows where she was going! The river lies that way.'

'Pooh!' I exclaimed. 'Don't talk nonsense. It is all a mistake. Come, have you any brandy?'

Brought back to the material round of her duties she bustled away with a sort of briskness, and returned with a flagon and glasses. I took a strong nip, and went back to Sir William. He was feverish, and declaimed against the weather unceasingly. I had to listen to the string of misfortunes which he recounted in the season's crops. It seemed all so futile, with his daughter involved in her horrid tragedy in a neighbouring room. He was better after some brandy, and grew more cheerful, but assiduously wondered about Warrington.

'Oh, he's been caught in the storm and taken refuge somewhere,' I explained, vainly. I wondered if the next day would ever dawn.

By degrees that thunder rolled slowly into the northern parts of the sky, and only fitful flashes seamed the heavens. It had lasted now more than two hours. Sir William declared his intention of starting, and asked for his daughter. I rang for Mrs Batty, and sent her to rouse Miss Bosanquet. Almost immediately there was a knock upon the door, and the housekeeper was in the doorway, with an agitated expression, demanding to see me. Sir William was looking out of the window, and fortunately did not see her.

'Please come to Miss Bosanquet, Sir,' she cried, very scared. 'Please come at once.'

In alarm I hastily ran down the corridor and entered Warrington's room. The girl was lying upon the bed, her hair flowing upon the pillow; her eyes, wide open and filled with terror, stared at the ceiling, and her hands clutched and twined in the coverlet as if in an agony of pain. A gasping sound issued from her, as though she were struggling for breath under suffocation. Her whole appearance was as of one in the murderous grasp of an assailant.

I bent over. 'Throw the light, quick,' I called to Mrs Batty; and as I put my hand on her shoulder to lift her, the creature that lived in the chamber rose suddenly from the shadow upon the further side of the bed, and sailed with a flapping noise up to the cornice. With an exclamation of horror I pulled the girl's head forward, and the candle-light glowed on her pallid face. Upon the soft flesh of the slender throat was a round red mark, the size of a florin.

At the sight I almost let her fall upon the pillow again; but, commanding my nerves, I put my arms round her, and, lifting her bodily from the bed, carried her from the room. Mrs Batty followed.

'What shall we do?' she asked, in a low voice.

'Take her away from this damned chamber!' I cried. 'Anywhere—the hall, the kitchen rather.'

I laid my burden upon a sofa in the dining-room, and despatching Mrs Batty for the brandy, gave Miss Bosanquet a draught. Slowly the horror faded from her eyes; they closed, and then she looked at me.

'What have you?—where am I?' she asked.

'You have been unwell,' I said. 'Pray don't disturb yourself yet.'

She shuddered, and closed her eyes again.

Very little more was said. Sir William pressed for his horses, and as the sky was clearing I made no attempt to detain him, more particularly as the sooner Miss Bosanquet left the Abbey the better for herself. In half an hour she recovered sufficiently to go, and I helped her into the carriage. She never referred to her seizure, but thanked me for my kindness. That was all. No one asked after Warrington—not even Sir William. He had forgotten everything, save his anxiety to get back. As the carriage turned from the steps I saw the mark upon the girl's throat, now grown fainter.

I waited up till late into the morning, but there was no sign of Warrington when I went to bed. Nor had he made his appearance when I descended to breakfast. A letter in his handwriting, however, and with the London postmark, awaited me. It was a pitiful scrawl, in the very penmanship of which one might trace the desperate emotions by which he was torn. He implored my forgiveness. *'Am I a devil?'* he asked. *'Am I mad? It was not I! It was not I!'* he repeated, underlining the sentence with impetuous dashes. *'You know,'* he wrote; *'and you know, therefore, that everything is at an end for me. I am going abroad today. I shall never see the Abbey again.'*

It was well that he had gone, as I hardly think that I could have faced him; and yet I was loth myself to leave the matter in this horrible tangle. I felt that it was enjoined upon me to meet the problems, and I endeavoured to do so as best I might. Mrs Batty gave me news of the girl Alice. It was bad enough, though not so bad as both of us had feared. I was able to make arrangements on the instant, which I hoped might bury that lamentable affair for the time. There remained Miss Bosanquet; but that difficulty seemed beyond me. I could see no avenue out of the tragedy. I heard nothing save that she was ill—an illness attributed upon all hands to the shock of exposure to the thunderstorm. Only I knew better, and a vague disinclination to fly from the responsibilities of the position kept me hanging on at Utterbourne.

It was in those days before my visit to St Pharamond that I turned my attention more particularly to the thing which had forced itself relentlessly upon me. I was never a superstitious man; the gossip of old wives interested me merely as a curious and unsympathetic observer. And yet I was vaguely discomfited by the transaction in the Abbey, and it was with some reluctance that I decided to make a further test of Warrington's bedroom. Mrs Batty received my determination to change my room easily enough, but with a protest as to the dampness of the Stone Chamber. It was plain that her suspicions had not marched with mine. On the second night after Warrington's departure I occupied the room for the first time.

I lay awake for a couple of hours, with a reading lamp by my bed, and a volume of travels in my hand, and then, feeling very tired, put out the light and went to sleep. Nothing distracted me that night; indeed, I slept more soundly and peaceably than before in that house. I rose, too, experiencing quite an exhilaration, and it was not until I was dressing before the glass that I remembered the circumstances of my mission; but then I was at once pulled up, startled swiftly out of my cheerful temper. Faintly visible upon my throat was the same round mark which I had already seen stamped upon Warrington and Miss Bosanquet. With that, all my former doubts returned in force, augmented and militant. My mind recurred to the bat, and tales of bloodsucking by those evil creatures revived in my memory. But when I had remembered that these were of foreign beasts, and that I was in England, I dismissed them lightly enough. Still, the impress of that mark remained, and alarmed me. It could not come by accident; to suppose so manifold a coincidence was absurd. The puzzle dwelt with me, unsolved, and the fingers of dread slowly crept over me.

Yet I slept again in the room. Having but myself for company, and being somewhat bored and dull, I fear I took more spirit than was my custom, and the result was that I again slept profoundly. I awoke about three in the morning, and was surprised to find the lamp still burning. I had forgotten it in my stupid state of somnolence. As I turned to put it out, the bat swept by me and circled for an instant above my head. So overpowered with torpor was I that I scarcely noticed it, and my head was no sooner at rest than I was once more unconscious. The red mark was stronger next morning, though, as on the previous day, it wore off with the fall of evening. But I merely observed the fact without any concern; indeed, now the matter of my investigation seemed to have drawn very remote. I was growing indifferent, I supposed, through familiarity. But the solitude was palling upon me, and I spent a very restless day. A sharp ride I took in the afternoon was the one agreeable experience of the day. I reflected that if this burden were to continue I must hasten up to town. I had no desire to tie myself to Warrington's apron, in his interest. So dreary was the evening, that after I had strolled round the grounds and into the chapel by moonlight, I returned to the library and endeavoured to pass the time with Warrington's cards. But it was poor fun with no antagonist to pit myself against; and I was throwing down the pack in disgust when one of the manservants entered with the whisky.

It was not until long afterwards that I fully realized the course of my action; but even at the time I was aware of a curious sub-feeling of shamefacedness. I am sure that the thing fell naturally, and that there was no awkwardness in my approaching him. Nor, after the first surprise, did he offer any objection. Later he was hardly expected to do so, seeing that he was winning very quickly. The reason of that I guessed afterwards, but during the play I was amazed to note at intervals how strangely my irritation was aroused. Finally, I swept the cards to the floor, and rose, the man, with a smile in which triumph blended with uneasiness, rose also.

'Damn you, get away!' I said, angrily.

True to his traditions to the close, he answered me with respect, and obeyed; and I sat staring at the table. With a sudden flush, the grotesque folly of the night's business came to me, and my eyes fell on the whisky bottle. It was nearly empty. Then I went to bed.

Voices cried all night in that chamber—soft, pleading voices. There was nothing to alarm in them; they seemed in a manner to coo me to sleep. But presently a sharper cry roused me from my semi-slumber; and getting up, I flung open the window. The wind rushed round the Abbey, sweeping with noises against the corners and gables. The black chapel lay still in the moonlight, and drew my eyes. But, resisting a strange, unaccountable impulse to go further, I went back to bed.

The events of the following day are better related without comment.

At breakfast I found a letter from Sir William Bosanquet, inviting me to come over to St Pharamond. I was at once conscious of an eager desire to do so: it seemed somehow as though I had been waiting for this. The visit assumed preposterous proportions, and I was impatient for the afternoon.

Sir William was polite, but not, as I thought, cordial. He never alluded to Warrington, from which I guessed that he had been informed of the breach, and I conjectured also that the invitation extended to me was rather an act of courtesy to a solitary stranger than due to a desire for my company. Nevertheless, when he presently suggested that I should stay to dinner, I accepted promptly. For, to say the truth, I had not yet seen Miss Bosanquet, and I experienced a strange curiosity to do so. When at last she made her appearance, I was struck, almost for the first time, by her beauty. She was certainly a handsome girl, though she had a delicate air of ill-health.

After dinner Sir William remembered by accident the book on the Abbey which he had promised to show me, and after a brief hunt in the library we found it. Shortly afterwards he was called away, and with an apology left me. With a curious eagerness I turned the pages of the volume and settled down to read.

It was published early in the century, and purported to relate the history of the Abbey and its owners. But it was one chapter which specially drew my interest—that which recounted the fate of the last Marvyn. The family had become extinct through a bloody tragedy; that fact held me. The bare narrative, long since passed from the memory of tradition, was here set forth in the baldest statements. The names of Sir Rupert Marvyn and Priscilla, Lady Marvyn, shook me strangely, but particularly the latter. Some links of connection with those gravestones lying in the Abbey chapel constrained me intimately. The history of that evil race was stained and discoloured with blood, and the end was in fitting harmony—a lurid holocaust of crime. There had been two brothers, but it was hard to choose between the foulness of their lives. If either, the younger, William, was the worse; so at least the narrative would have it. The details of his excesses had not survived, but it was abundantly plain that they were both notorious gamblers. The story of their deaths was wrapt in doubt, the theme of conjecture only, and probability; for none was by to observe save the three veritable actors—who were at once involved together in a bloody dissolution. Priscilla, the wife of Sir Rupert, was suspected of an intrigue with her brother-in-law. She would seem to have been tainted with the corruption of the family into which she had married. But according to a second rumour, chronicled by the author, there was some doubt if the woman were not the worst of the three. Nothing was known of her parentage; she had returned with the passionate Sir Rupert to the Abbey after one of his prolonged absences, and was accepted as his legal wife. This was the woman whose infamous beauty had brought a terrible sin between the brothers.

Upon the night which witnessed the extinction of this miserable family, the two brothers had been gambling together. It was known from the high voices that they had quarrelled, and it is supposed that, heated with wine and with the lust of play, the younger had thrown some taunt at Sir Rupert in respect to his wife. Whereupon—but this is all conjecture—the elder stabbed him to death. At least, it was understood that at this point the sounds of a struggle were heard, and a bitter cry. The report of the servants ran that upon this noise Lady Marvyn rushed into the room and locked the door behind her. Fright was busy with those servants, long used to the savage manners of the house. According to witnesses, no further sound was heard subsequently to Lady Marvyn's entrance; yet when the doors were at last broken open by the authorities, the three bodies were discovered upon the floor.

How Sir Rupert and his wife met their deaths there was no record. 'This tragedy', proceeded the scribe, 'took place in the Stone Chamber underneath the stairway.'

I had got so far when the entrance of Miss Bosanquet disturbed me. I remember rising in a dazed condition—the room swung about me. A conviction, hitherto resisted and stealthily entertained upon compulsion, now overpowered me.

'I thought my father was here,' explained Miss Bosanquet, with a quick glance round the room.

I explained the circumstances, and she hesitated in my neighbourhood with a slight air of embarrassment.

'I have not thanked you properly, Mr Heywood,' she said presently, in a low voice, scarcely articulate. 'You have been very considerate and kind. Let me thank you now.' And ended with a tiny spasmodic sob.

Somehow, an impulse overmastered my tongue. Fresh from the perusal of that chapter, queer possibilities crowded in my mind, odd considerations urged me.

'Miss Bosanquet,' said I, abruptly, 'let me speak of that a little. I will not touch on details.'

'Please,' she cried, with a shrinking notion as of one that would retreat in very alarm.

'Nay,' said I, eagerly; 'hear me. It is no wantonness that would press the memory upon you. You have been a witness to distressful acts; you have seen a man under the influence of temporary madness. Nay, even yourself, you have been a victim to the same unaccountable phenomena.'

'What do you mean?' she cried, tensely.

'I will say no more,' said I. 'I should incur your laughter. No, you would not laugh, but my dim suspicions would leave you still incredulous. But if this were so, and if these were the phenomena of a brief madness, surely you would make your memory a grave to bury the past.'

'I cannot do that,' said she, in low tones.

'What!' I asked. 'Would you turn from your lover, aye, even from a friend, because he was smitten with disease? Consider; if your dearest upon earth tossed in a fever upon his bed, and denied you in his ravings, using you despitefully, it would not be he that entreated you so. When he was quit of his madness and returned to his proper person, would you not forget—would you not rather recall his insanity with the pity of affection?'

'I do not understand you,' she whispered.

'You read your Bible,' said I. 'You have wondered at the evil spirits that possessed poor victims. Why should you decide that these things have ceased? We are too dogmatic in our modern world. Who can say under what malign influence a soul may pass, and out of its own custody?'

She looked at me earnestly, searching my eyes.

'You hint at strange things,' said she, very low.

But somehow, even as I met her eyes, the spirit of my mission failed me. My gaze, I felt, devoured her ruthlessly. The light shone on her pale and comely features; they burned me with an irresistible attraction. I put forth my hand and took hers gently. It was passive to my touch, as though in acknowledgment of my kindly offices. All the while I experienced a sense of fierce elation. In my blood ran, as it had been fire, a horrible incentive, and I knew that I was holding her hand very tightly. She herself seemed to grow conscious of this, for she made an effort to withdraw her fingers, at which, the passion rushing through my body, I clutched them closer, laughing aloud. I saw a wondering look dawn in her eyes, and her bosom thinly veiled, heaved with a tiny tremor. I was aware that I was drawing her steadily to me. Suddenly her bewildered eyes, dropping from my face, lit with a flare of terror, and, wrenching her hand away, she fell back with a cry, her gaze riveted upon my throat.

'That accursed mark! What is it? What is it?——' she cried, shivering from head to foot.

In an instant, the wild blood singing in my head, I sprang towards her. What would have followed I know not, but at that moment the door opened and Sir William returned. He regarded us with consternation; but Miss Bosanquet had fainted, and the next moment he was at her side. I stood near, watching her come to with a certain nameless fury, as of a beast cheated of its prey. Sir William turned to me, and in his most courteous manner begged me to excuse the untoward scene.

His daughter, he said, was not at all strong, and he ended by suggesting that I should leave them for a time.

Reluctantly I obeyed, but when I was out of the house, I took a sudden panic. The demoniac possession lifted, and in a craven state of trembling I saddled my horse, and rode for the Abbey as if my life depended upon my speed.

I arrived at about ten o'clock, and immediately gave orders to have my bed prepared in my old room. In my shaken condition the sinister influences of that stone chamber terrified me; and it was not until I had drunk deeply that I regained my composure.

But I was destined to get little sleep. I had steadily resolved to keep my thoughts off the matter until the morning, but the spell of the chamber was strong upon me. I awoke after midnight with an irresistible feeling drawing me to the room. I was conscious of the impulse, and combated it, but in the end succumbed; and throwing on my clothes, took a light and went downstairs. I flung wide the door of the room and peered in, listening, as though for some voice of welcome. It was as silent as a sepulchre; but directly I crossed the threshold voices seemed to surround and coax me. I stood wavering, with a curious fascination upon me. I knew I could not return to my own room, and I now had no desire to do so. As I stood, my candle flaring solemnly against the darkness, I noticed upon the floor in an alcove bare of carpet, a large black mark, which appeared to be a stain. Bending down, I examined it, passing my fingers over the stone. It moved to my touch. Setting the candle upon the floor, I put my fingertips to the edges, and pulled hard. As I did so the sounds that were ringing in my ears died instantaneously; the next moment the slab turned with a crash, and discovered a gaping hole of impenetrable blackness.

The patch of chasm thus opened to my eyes was near a yard square. The candle held to it shed a dim light upon a stone step a foot or two below, and it was clear to me that a stairway communicated with the depths. Whether it had been used as a cellar in times gone by I could not divine, but I was soon to determine this doubt; for, stirred by a strange eagerness, I slipped my legs through the hole, and let myself cautiously down with the light in my hand. There were a dozen steps to descend ere I reached the floor and what turned out to be a narrow passage. The vault ran forward straight as an arrow before my eyes, and slowly I moved on. Dank and chill was the air in those close confines, and the sound of my feet returned from those walls dull and sullen. But I kept on, and, with infinite care, must have penetrated quite a hundred yards along that musty corridor ere I came out upon an ampler chamber. Here the air was freer, and I could perceive with the aid of my light that the dimensions of the place were lofty. Above, a solitary ray of moonlight, sliding through a crack, informed me that I was not far

from the level of the earth. It fell upon a block of stone, which rose in
the middle of the vault, and which I now inspected with interest. As the
candle threw its flickering beams upon this I realized where I was. I
scarcely needed the rude lettering upon the coffins to acquaint me that
here was the family vault of the Marvyns. And now I began to perceive
upon all sides whereon my feeble light fell the crumbling relics of the
forgotten dead—coffins fallen into decay, bones and grinning skulls
resting in corners, disposed by the hand of chance and time. This
formidable array of the mortal remains of that poor family moved me
to a shudder. I turned from those ugly memorials once more to the
central altar where the two coffins rested in this sombre silence. The lid
had fallen from the one, disclosing to my sight the grisly skeleton of a
man, that mocked and leered at me. It seemed in a manner to my
fascinated eyes to challenge my mortality, inviting me too to the rude
and grotesque sleep of death. I knew, as by an instinct, that I was
standing by the bones of Sir Rupert Marvyn, the protagonist in that
terrible crime which had locked three souls in eternal ruin. The
consideration of this miserable spectacle held me motionless for some
moments, and then I moved a step closer and cast my light upon the
second coffin.

As I did so I was aware of a change within myself. The grave and
melancholy thoughts which I had entertained, the sober bent of my
solemn reflections, gave place instantly to a strange exultation, an
unholy sense of elation. My pulse swung feverishly, and, while my
eyes were riveted upon the tarnished silver of the plate, I stretched forth
a tremulously eager hand and touched the lid. It rattled gently under
my fingers. Disturbed by the noise, I hastily withdrew them; but
whether it was the impetus offered by my touch, or through some
horrible and nameless circumstance—God knows—slowly and softly a
gap opened between the lid and the body of the coffin! Before my
startled eyes the awful thing happened, and yet I was conscious of no
terror, merely of surprise and—it seems terrible to admit—of a feeling
of eager expectancy. The lid rose slowly on the one side, and as it lifted
the dark space between it and the coffin grew gently charged with light.
At that moment my feeble candle, which had been gradually diminishing, guttered and flickered. I seemed to catch a glimpse of
something, as it were, of white and shining raiment inside the coffin;
and then came a rush of wings and a whirring sound within the vault. I
gave a cry, and stepping back missed my foothold; the guttering candle
was jerked from my grasp, and I fell prone to the floor in darkness. The
next moment a sheet of flame flashed in the chamber and lit up the
grotesque skeletons about me; and at the same time a piercing cry rang
forth. Jumping to my feet, I gave a dazed glance at the conflagration.
The whole vault was in flames. Dazed and horror-struck, I rushed
blindly to the entrance; but as I did so the horrible cry pierced my ears

again, and I saw the bat swoop round and circle swiftly into the flames. Then, finding the exit, I dashed with all the speed of terror down the passage, groping my way along the walls, and striking myself a dozen times in my terrified flight.

Arrived in my room, I pushed over the stone and listened. Not a sound was audible. With a white face and a body torn and bleeding I rushed from the room, and locking the door behind me, made my way upstairs to my bedroom. Here I poured myself out a stiff glass of brandy.

It was six months later ere Warrington returned. In the meantime he had sold the Abbey. It was inevitable that he should do so; and yet the new owner, I believe, has found no drawback in his property, and the Stone Chamber is still used for a bedroom upon occasions, being considered very old-fashioned. But there are some facts against which no appeal is possible, and so it was in his case. In my relation of the tragedy I have made no attempt at explanation, hardly even to myself; and it appears now for the first time in print, of course with supposititious names.

THE VAMPIRE MAID

Hume Nisbet

Hume Nisbet (1849–1923) was another Australian emigré (originally born in Scotland) who enjoyed a vogue in late Victorian and Edwardian London. His most popular books were romantic adventures set in Australasia and the East Indies, usually illustrated by himself. The following two stories are taken from his Christmas annual entitled *Stories Weird and Wonderful* (1900). The fate of Dracula's 'other victims' during his sojourn in England was never recorded, but the 'Vampire Maid' could easily have been one of them!

❧

It was the exact kind of abode that I had been looking after for weeks, for I was in that condition of mind when absolute renunciation of society was a necessity. I had become diffident of myself, and wearied of my kind. A strange unrest was in my blood; a barren dearth in my brains. Familiar objects and faces had grown distasteful to me. I wanted to be alone.

This is the mood which comes upon every sensitive and artistic mind when the possessor has been overworked or living too long in one groove. It is Nature's hint for him to seek pastures new; the sign that a retreat has become needful.

If he does not yield, he breaks down and becomes whimsical and hypochondriacal, as well as hypercritical. It is always a bad sign when a man becomes over-critical and censorious about his own or other people's work, for it means that he is losing the vital portions of work, freshness and enthusiasm.

Before I arrived at the dismal stage of criticism I hastily packed up my knapsack, and taking the train to Westmorland I began my tramp in search of solitude, bracing air and romantic surroundings.

Many places I came upon during that early summer wandering that appeared to have almost the required conditions, yet some petty drawback prevented me from deciding. Sometimes it was the scenery that I did not take kindly to. At other places I took sudden antipathies to the landlady or landlord, and felt I would abhor them before a week was spent under their charge. Other places which might have suited me I could not have, as they did not want a lodger. Fate was driving me to this Cottage on the Moor, and no one can resist destiny.

One day I found myself on a wide and pathless moor near the sea. I had slept the night before at a small hamlet, but that was already eight miles in my rear, and since I had turned my back upon it I had not seen any signs of humanity; I was alone with a fair sky above me, a balmy ozone-filled wind blowing over the stony and heather-clad mounds, and nothing to disturb my meditations.

How far the moor stretched I had no knowledge; I only knew that by keeping in a straight line I would come to the ocean cliffs, then perhaps after a time arrive at some fishing village.

I had provisions in my knapsack, and being young did not fear a night under the stars. I was inhaling the delicious summer air and once more getting back the vigour and happiness I had lost; my city-dried brains were again becoming juicy.

Thus hour after hour slid past me, with the paces, until I had covered about fifteen miles since morning, when I saw before me in the distance a solitary stone-built cottage with roughly slated roof. 'I'll camp there if possible,' I said to myself as I quickened my steps towards it.

To one in search of a quiet, free life, nothing could have possibly been more suitable than this cottage. It stood on the edge of lofty cliffs, with its front door facing the moor and the back-yard wall overlooking the ocean. The sound of the dancing waves struck upon my ears like a lullaby as I drew near; how they would thunder when the autumn gales came on and the seabirds fled shrieking to the shelter of the sedges.

A small garden spread in front, surrounded by a dry-stone wall just high enough for one to lean lazily upon when inclined. This garden was a flame of colour, scarlet predominating, with those other soft shades that cultivated poppies take on in their blooming, for this was all that the garden grew.

As I approached, taking notice of this singular assortment of poppies, and the orderly cleanness of the windows, the front door opened and a woman appeared who impressed me at once favourably as she leisurely came along the pathway to the gate, and drew it back as if to welcome me.

She was of middle age, and when young must have been remarkably good-looking. She was tall and still shapely, with smooth clear skin, regular features and a calm expression that at once gave me a sensation of rest.

To my inquiries she said that she could give me both a sitting and bedroom, and invited me inside to see them. As I looked at her smooth black hair, and cool brown eyes, I felt that I would not be too particular about the accommodation. With such a landlady, I was sure to find what I was after here.

The rooms surpassed my expectation, dainty white curtains and bedding with the perfume of lavender about them, a sitting-room homely yet cosy without being crowded. With a sigh of infinite relief I flung down my knapsack and clinched the bargain.

She was a widow with one daughter, whom I did not see the first day, as she was unwell and confined to her own room, but on the next day she was somewhat better, and then we met.

The fare was simple, yet it suited me exactly for the time, delicious milk and butter with home-made scones, fresh eggs and bacon; after a hearty tea I went early to bed in a condition of perfect content with my quarters.

Yet happy and tired out as I was I had by no means a comfortable night. This I put down to the strange bed. I slept certainly, but my sleep was filled with dreams so that I woke late and unrefreshed; a good walk on the moor, however, restored me, and I returned with a fine appetite for breakfast.

Certain conditions of mind, with aggravating circumstances, are required before even a young man can fall in love at first sight, as Shakespeare has shown in his Romeo and Juliet. In the city, where many fair faces passed me every hour, I had remained like a stoic, yet no sooner did I enter the cottage after that morning walk than I succumbed instantly before the weird charms of my landlady's daughter, Ariadne Brunnell.

She was somewhat better this morning and able to meet me at breakfast, for we had our meals together while I was their lodger. Ariadne was not beautiful in the strictly classical sense, her complexion being too lividly white and her expression too set to be quite pleasant at first sight; yet, as her mother had informed me, she had been ill for some time, which accounted for that defect. Her features were not regular, her hair and eyes seemed too black with that strangely white skin, and her lips too red for any except the decadent harmonies of an Aubrey Beardsley.

Yet my fantastic dreams of the preceding night, with my morning walk, had prepared me to be enthralled by this modern poster-like invalid.

The loneliness of the moor, with the singing of the ocean, had gripped my heart with a wistful longing. The incongruity of those flaunting and evanescent poppy flowers, dashing their giddy tints in the face of that sober heath, touched me with a shiver as I approached the cottage, and lastly that weird embodiment of startling contrasts completed my subjugation.

She rose from her chair as her mother introduced her, and smiled while she held out her hand. I clasped that soft snowflake, and as I did so a faint thrill tingled over me and rested on my heart, stopping for the moment its beating.

This contact seemed also to have affected her as it did me; a clear flush, like a white flame, lighted up her face, so that it glowed as if an alabaster lamp had been lit; her black eyes became softer and more humid as our glances crossed, and her scarlet lips grew moist. She was a living woman now, while before she had seemed half a corpse.

She permitted her white slender hand to remain in mine longer than most people do at an introduction, and then she slowly withdrew it, still regarding me with steadfast eyes for a second or two afterwards.

Fathomless velvety eyes these were, yet before they were shifted from mine they apeared to have absorbed all my willpower and made me her abject slave. They looked like deep dark pools of clear water, yet they filled me with fire and deprived me of strength. I sank into my chair almost as languidly as I had risen from my bed that morning.

Yet I made a good breakfast, and although she hardly tasted anything, this strange girl rose much refreshed and with a slight glow of colour on her cheeks, which improved her so greatly that she appeared younger and almost beautiful.

I had come here seeking solitude, but since I had seen Ariadne it seemed as if I had come for her only. She was not very lively; indeed, thinking back, I cannot recall any spontaneous remark of hers; she answered my questions by monosyllables and left me to lead in words; yet she was insinuating and appeared to lead my thoughts in her direction and speak to me with her eyes. I cannot describe her minutely, I only know that from the first glance and touch she gave me I was bewitched and could think of nothing else.

It was a rapid, distracting, and devouring infatuation that possessed me; all day long I followed her about like a dog, every night I dreamed of that white glowing face, those steadfast black eyes, those moist scarlet lips, and each morning I rose more languid than I had been the day before. Sometimes I dreamt that she was kissing me with those red lips, while I shivered at the contact of her silky black tresses as they covered my throat; sometimes that we were floating in the air, her arms about me and her long hair enveloping us both like an inky cloud, while I lay supine and helpless.

She went with me after breakfast on that first day to the moor, and before we came back I had spoken my love and received her assent. I held her in my arms and had taken her kisses in answer to mine, nor did I think it strange that all this had happened so quickly. She was mine, or rather I was hers, without a pause. I told her it was fate that had sent me to her, for I had no doubts about my love, and she replied that I had restored her to life.

Acting upon Ariadne's advice, and also from a natural shyness, I did not inform her mother how quickly matters had progressed between us, yet although we both acted as circumspectly as possible, I had no doubt Mrs Brunnell could see how engrossed we were in each other.

Lovers are not unlike ostriches in their modes of concealment. I was not afraid of asking Mrs Brunnell for her daughter, for she already showed her partiality towards me, and had bestowed upon me some confidences regarding her own position in life, and I therefore knew that, so far as social position was concerned, there could be no real objection to our marriage. They lived in this lonely spot for the sake of their health, and kept no servant because they could not get any to take service so far away from other humanity. My coming had been opportune and welcome to both mother and daughter.

For the sake of decorum, however, I resolved to delay my confession for a week or two and trust to some favourable opportunity of doing it discreetly.

Meantime Ariadne and I passed our time in a thoroughly idle and lotus-eating style. Each night I retired to bed meditating starting work next day, each morning I rose languid from those disturbing dreams with no thought for anything outside my love. She grew stronger every day, while I appeared to be taking her place as the invalid, yet I was more frantically in love than ever, and only happy when with her. She was my lode-star, my only joy—my life.

We did not go great distances, for I liked best to lie on the dry heath and watch her glowing face and intense eyes while I listened to the surging of the distant waves. It was love made me lazy, I thought, for unless a man has all he longs for beside him, he is apt to copy the domestic cat·and bask in the sunshine.

I had been enchanted quickly. My disenchantment came as rapidly, although it was long before the poison left my blood.

One night, about a couple of weeks after my coming to the cottage, I had retured after a delicious moonlight walk with Ariadne. The night was warm and the moon at the full, therefore I left my bedroom window open to let in what little air there was.

I was more than usually fagged out, so that I had only strength enough to remove my boots and coat before I flung myself wearily on the coverlet and fell almost instantly asleep without tasting the nightcap draught that was constantly placed on the table, and which I had always drained thirstily.

I had a ghastly dream this night. I thought I saw a monster bat, with the face and tresses of Ariadne, fly into the open window and fasten its white teeth and scarlet lips on my arm. I tried to beat the horror away, but could not, for I seemed chained down and thralled also with drowsy delight as the beast sucked my blood with a gruesome rapture.

I looked out dreamily and saw a line of dead bodies of young men lying on the floor, each with a red mark on their arms, on the same part where the vampire was then sucking me, and I remembered having seen and wondered at such a mark on my own arm for the past fortnight. In a flash I understood the reason for my strange weakness, and at the same moment a sudden prick of pain roused me from my dreamy pleasure.

The vampire in her eagerness had bitten a little too deeply that night, unaware that I had not tasted the drugged draught. As I woke I saw her fully revealed by the midnight moon, with her black tresses flowing loosely, and with her red lips glued to my arm. With a shriek of horror I dashed her backwards, getting one last glimpse of her savage eyes, glowing white face and blood-stained red lips; then I rushed out to the night, moved on by my fear and hatred, nor did I pause in my mad flight until I had left miles between me and that accursed Cottage on the Moor.

THE OLD PORTRAIT

OLD-FASHIONED frames are a hobby of mine. I am always on the prowl amongst the framers and dealers in curiosities for something quaint and unique in picture frames. I don't care much for what is inside them, for being a painter it is my fancy to get the frames first and then paint a picture which I think suits their probable history and design. In this way I get some curious and I think also some original ideas.

One day in December, about a week before Christmas, I picked up a fine but delapidated specimen of wood-carving in a shop near Soho. The gilding had been worn nearly away, and three of the corners broken off; yet as there was one of the corners still left, I hoped to be able to repair the others from it. As for the canvas inside this frame, it was so smothered with dirt and time stains that I could only distinguish it had been a very badly painted likeness of some sort, of some commonplace person, daubed in by a poor pot-boiling painter to fill the secondhand frame which his patron may have picked up cheaply as I had done after him; but as the frame was alright I took the spoiled canvas along with it, thinking it might come in handy.

For the next few days my hands were full of work of one kind and another, so that it was only on Christmas Eve that I found myself at liberty to examine my purchase which had been lying with its face to the wall since I had brought it to my studio.

Having nothing to do on this night, and not in the mood to go out, I got my picture and frame from the corner, and laying them upon the table, with a sponge, basin of water, and some soap, I began to wash so that I might see them the better. They were in a terrible mess, and I think I used the best part of a packet of soap-powder and had to change the water about a dozen times before the pattern began to show up on the frame, and the portrait within it asserted its awful crudeness, vile drawing, and intense vulgarity. It was the bloated, piggish visage of a publican clearly, with a plentiful supply of jewellery displayed, as is usual with such masterpieces, where the features are not considered of so much importance as a strict fidelity in the depicting of such articles as watch-guard and seals, finger rings, and breast pins; these were all there, as natural and hard as reality.

The frame delighted me, and the picture satisfied me that I had not cheated the dealer with my price, and I was looking at the monstrosity as the gaslight beat full upon it, and wondering how the owner could be pleased with himself as thus depicted, when something about the background attracted my attention—a slight marking underneath the thin coating as if the portrait had been painted over some other subject.

It was not much certainly, yet enough to make me rush over to my cupboard, where I kept my spirits of wine and turpentine, with which, and a plentiful supply of rags, I began to demolish the publican ruthlessly in the vague hope that I might find something worth looking at underneath.

A slow process that was, as well as a delicate one, so that it was close upon midnight before the gold cable rings and vermilion visage disappeared and another picture loomed up before me; then giving it the final wash over, I wiped it dry, and set it in a good light on my easel, while I filled and lit my pipe, and then sat down to look at it.

What had I liberated from that vile prison of crude paint? For I did not require to set it up to know that this bungler of the brush had covered and defiled a work as far beyond his comprehension as the clouds are from the caterpillar.

The bust and head of a young woman of uncertain age, merged within a gloom of rich accessories painted as only a master hand can paint who is above asserting his knowledge, and who has learnt to cover his technique. It was as perfect and natural in its sombre yet quiet dignity as if it had come from the brush of Moroni.

A face and neck perfectly colourless in their pallid whiteness, with the shadows so artfully managed that they could not be seen, and for this quality would have delighted the strong-minded Queen Bess.

At first as I looked I saw in the centre of a vague darkness a dim patch of grey gloom that drifted into the shadow. Then the greyness appeared to grow lighter as I sat from it, and leaned back in my chair until the features stole out softly, and became clear and definite, while the figure stood out from the background as if tangible, although, having washed it, I knew that it had been smoothly painted.

An intent face, with delicate nose, well-shaped, although bloodless, lips, and eyes like dark caverns without a spark of light in them. The hair loosely about the head and oval cheeks, massive, silky-textured, jet black, and lustreless, which hid the upper portion of her brow, with the ears, and fell in straight indefinite waves over the left breast, leaving the right portion of the transparent neck exposed.

The dress and background were symphonies of ebony, yet full of subtle colouring and masterly feeling; a dress of rich brocaded velvet with a background that represented vast receding space, wondrously suggestive and awe-inspiring.

I noticed that the pallid lips were parted slightly, and showed a glimpse of the upper front teeth, which added to the intent expression of the face. A short upper lip, which, curled upward, with the underlip full and sensuous, or rather, if colour had been in it, would have been so.

It was an eerie looking face that I had resurrected on this midnight hour of Christmas Eve; in its passive pallidity it looked as if the blood had been drained from the body, and that I was gazing upon an open-eyed corpse.

The frame, also, I noticed for the first time, in its details appeared to have been designed with the intention of carrying out the idea of life in death; what had before looked like scroll-work of flowers and fruit were loathsome snake-like worms twined amongst charnel-house bones which they half covered in a decorative fashion; a hideous design in spite of its exquisite workmanship, that made me shudder and wish that I had left the cleaning to be done by daylight.

I am not at all of a nervous temperament, and would have laughed had anyone told me that I was afraid, and yet, as I sat here alone, with that portrait opposite to me in this solitary studio, away from all human contact; for none of the other studios were tenanted on this night, and the janitor had gone on his holiday; I wished that I had spent my evening in a more congenial manner, for in spite of a good fire in the stove and the brilliant gas, that intent face and those haunting eyes were exercising a strange influence upon me.

I heard the clocks from the different steeples chime out the last hour of the day, one after the other, like echoes taking up the refrain and dying away in the distance, and still I sat spellbound, looking at that weird picture, with my neglected pipe in my hand, and a strange lassitude creeping over me.

It was the eyes which fixed me now with the unfathomable depths and absorbing intensity. They gave out no light, but seemed to draw my soul into them, and with it my life and strength as I lay inert before them, until overpowered I lost consciousness and dreamt.

I thought that the frame was still on the easel with the canvas, but the woman had stepped from them and was approaching me with a floating motion, leaving behind her a vault filled with coffins, some of them shut down whilst others lay or stood upright and open, showing the grizzly contents in their decaying and stained cerements.

I could only see her head and shoulders with the sombre drapery of the upper portion and the inky wealth of hair hanging round.

She was with me now, that pallid face touching my face and those cold bloodless lips glued to mine with a close lingering kiss, while the soft black hair covered me like a cloud and thrilled me through and through with a delicious thrill that, whilst it made me grow faint, intoxicated me with delight.

As I breathed she seemed to absorb it quickly into herself, giving me back nothing, getting stronger as I was becoming weaker, while the warmth of my contact passed into her and made her palpitate with vitality.

And all at once the horror of approaching death seized upon me, and with a frantic effort I flung her from me and started up from my chair dazed for a moment and uncertain where I was, then consciousness returned and I looked round wildly.

The gas was still blazing brightly, while the fire burned ruddy in the stove. By the timepiece on the mantel I could see that it was half-past twelve.

The picture and frame were still on the easel, only as I looked at them the portrait had changed, a hectic flush was on the cheeks while the eyes glittered with life and the sensuous lips were red and ripe-looking with a drop of blood still upon the nether one. In a frenzy of horror I seized my scraping knife and slashed out the vampire picture, then tearing the mutilated fragments out I crammed them into my stove and watched them frizzle with savage delight.

I have that frame still, but I have not yet had courage to paint a suitable subject for it.

MARSYAS IN FLANDERS

Vernon Lee

'Vernon Lee' (pseudonym of Violet Paget, 1856–1935) wrote all her highly acclaimed weird fiction in a relatively short period from 1881 to 1911. 'Marsyas in Flanders' was written in 1900 but did not appear in a collection until 1927 (*For Maurice: Five Unlikely Tales*). Montague Summers once declared that 'even Le Fanu and M. R. James cannot be ranked above the genius of this lady.'

I

'YOU are right. This is not the original crucifix at all. Another one has been put instead. *Il y a eu substitution*,' and the little old Antiquary of Dunes nodded mysteriously, fixing his ghostseer's eyes upon mine.

He said it in a scarce audible whisper. For it happened to be the vigil of the Feast of the Crucifix, and the once famous church was full of semi-clerical persons decorating it for the morrow, and of old ladies in strange caps, clattering about with pails and brooms. The Antiquary had brought me there the very moment of my arrival, lest the crowd of faithful should prevent his showing me everything next morning.

The famous crucifix was exhibited behind rows and rows of unlit candles, and surrounded by strings of paper flowers and coloured muslin, and garlands of sweet resinous maritime pine; and two lighted chandeliers illumined it.

'There has been an exchange,' he repeated, looking round that no one might hear him. '*Il y a eu substitution*.'

For I had remarked, as anyone would have done, at the first glance, that the crucifix had every appearance of French work of the thirteenth century, boldly realistic, whereas the crucifix of the legend, which was a work of St Luke, which had hung for centuries in the Holy Sepulchre at Jerusalem and been miraculously cast ashore at Dunes in 1195, would surely have been a more or less Byzantine image, like its miraculous companion of Lucca.

'But why should there have been a substitution?' I inquired innocently.

'Hush, hush,' answered the Antiquary, frowning, 'not here—later, later—'

He took me all over the church, once so famous for pilgrimages; but from which, even like the sea which has left it in a salt marsh beneath the cliffs, the tide of devotion has receded for centuries. It is a very dignified little church, of charmingly restrained and shapely Gothic, built of a delicate pale stone, which the sea damp has picked out, in bases and capitals and carved foliation, with stains of a lovely bright green. The Antiquary showed me where the transept and belfry had been left unfinished when the miracles had diminished in the fourteenth century. And he took me up to the curious warder's chamber, a large room up some steps in the triforium; with a fireplace and stone seats for the men who guarded the precious crucifix day and night. There had even been beehives in the window, he told me, and he remembered seeing them still as a child.

'Was it usual, here in Flanders, to have a guardroom in churches containing important relics?' I asked, for I could not remember having seen anything similar before.

'By no means,' he answered, looking round to make sure we were alone, 'but it was necessary here. You have never heard in what the chief miracles of this church consisted?'

'No,' I whispered back, gradually infected by his mysteriousness, 'unless you allude to the legend that the figure of the Saviour broke all the crosses until the right one was cast up by the sea?'

He shook his head but did not answer, and descended the steep stairs into the nave, while I lingered a moment looking down into it from the warder's chamber. I have never had so curious an impression of a church. The chandeliers on either side of the crucifix swirled slowly round, making great pools of light which were broken by the shadows of the clustered columns, and among the pews of the nave moved the flicker of the sacristan's lamp. The place was full of the scent of resinous pine branches, evoking dunes and mountainsides; and from the busy groups below rose a subdued chatter of women's voices, and a splash of water and clatter of pattens. It vaguely suggested preparations for a witches' sabbath.

'What sort of miracles did they have in this church?' I asked, when we had passed into the dusky square, 'and what did you mean about their having exchanged the crucifix—about a *substitution?*'

It seemed quite dark outside. The church rose black, a vague lopsided mass of buttresses and high-pitched roofs, against the watery, moonlit sky; the big trees of the churchyard behind wavering about in the seawind; and the windows shone yellow, like flaming portals, in the darkness.

'Please remark the bold effect of the gargoyles,' said the Antiquary pointing upwards.

They jutted out, vague wild beasts, from the roof-line; and, what was positively frightening, you saw the moonlight, yellow and blue through the open jaws of some of them. A gust swept through the trees, making the weathercock clatter and groan.

'Why, those gargoyle wolves seem positively to howl,' I exclaimed.

The old Antiquary chuckled. 'Aha,' he answered, 'did I not tell you that this church has witnessed things like no other church in Christendom? And it still remembers them! There—have you ever known such a wild, savage church before?'

And as he spoke there suddenly mingled with the sough of the wind and the groans of the weather-vane, a shrill quavering sound as of pipers inside.

'The organist trying his vox humana for tomorrow,' remarked the Antiquary.

II

Next day I bought one of the printed histories of the miraculous crucifix which they were hawking all round the church; and next day also, my friend the Antiquary was good enough to tell me all that he knew of the matter. Between my two informants, the following may be said to be the true story.

In the autumn of 1195, after a night of frightful storm, a boat was found cast upon the shore of Dunes, which was at that time a fishing village at the mouth of the Nys, and exactly opposite a terrible sunken reef.

The boat was broken and upset; and close to it, on the sand and bent grass, lay a stone figure of the crucified Saviour, without its cross and, as seems probable, also without its arms, which had been made of separate blocks. A variety of persons immediately came forward to claim it; the little church of Dunes, on whose glebe it was found; the Barons of Cröy, who had the right of jetsam on that coast, and also the great Abbey of St Loup of Arras, as possessing the spiritual overlordship of the place. But a holy man who lived close by in the cliffs, had a vision which settled the dispute. St Luke in person appeared and told him that he was the original maker of the figure; that it had been one of three which had hung round the Holy Sepulchre of Jerusalem; that three knights, a Norman, a Tuscan, and a man of Arras, had with the permission of Heaven stolen them from the Infidels and placed them on unmanned boats; that one of the images had been cast upon the Norman coast near Salenelles; that the second had run aground not far from the city of Lucca, in Italy, and that this third was the one which had been embarked by the knight from Artois. As regarded its final resting place, the hermit, on the authority of St Luke, recommended that the statue should be left to decide the matter itself. Accordingly, the crucified figure was solemnly cast back into the sea. The very next day it was found once more in the same spot, among the sand and bent grass at the mouth of the Nys. It was therefore deposited in the little church of Dunes; and very soon indeed the flocks of pious persons who brought it offerings from all parts made it necessary and possible to rebuild the church thus sanctified by its presence.

The Holy Effigy of Dunes—*Sacra Dunarum Effigies* as it was called—did not work the ordinary sort of miracles. But its fame spread far and wide by the unexampled wonders which became the constant accompaniment of its existence. The Effigy, as above mentioned, had been discovered without the cross to which it had evidently been fastened, nor had any researches or any subsequent storms brought the missing blocks to light, despite the many prayers which were offered for the purpose. After some time therefore, and a deal of discussion, it was decided that a new cross should be provided for the effigy to hang upon. And certain skilful stonemasons of Arras were called to Dunes for this purpose. But behold! the very day after the cross had been solemnly erected in the church, an unheard of and terrifying fact was discovered. The Effigy, which had been hanging perfectly straight the previous evening, had shifted its position, and was bent violently to the right, as if in an effort to break loose.

This was attested not merely by hundreds of laymen, but by the priests of the place, who notified the fact in a document, existing in the episcopal archives of Arras until 1790, to the Abbot of St Loup their spiritual overlord.

This was the beginning of a series of mysterious occurrences which spread the fame of the marvellous crucifix all over Christendom. The Effigy did not remain in the position into which it had miraculously worked itself: it was found, at intervals of time, shifted in some other manner upon its cross, and always as if it had gone through violent contortions. And one day, about ten years after it had been cast up by the sea, the priests of the church and the burghers of Dunes discovered the Effigy hanging in its original outstretched, symmetrical attitude, but O wonder! with the cross, broken in three pieces, lying on the steps of its chapel.

Certain persons, who lived in the end of the town nearest the church, reported to have been roused in the middle of the night by what they had taken for a violent clap of thunder, but which was doubtless the crash of the cross falling down; or perhaps, who knows? the noise with which the terrible Effigy had broken loose and spurned the alien cross from it. For that was the secret: the Effigy, made by a saint and come to Dunes by miracle, had evidently found some trace of unholiness in the stone to which it had been fastened. Such was the ready explanation afforded by the Prior of the church, in answer to an angry summons of the Abbot of St Loup, who expressed his disapproval of such unusual miracles. Indeed, it was discovered that the piece of marble had not been cleaned from sinful human touch with the necessary rites before the figure was fastened on; a most grave, though excusable oversight. So a new cross was ordered, although it was noticed that much time was lost about it; and the consecration took place only some years later.

Meanwhile the Prior had built the warder's chamber, with the fireplace and recess, and obtained permission from the Pope himself that a clerk in orders should watch day and night, on the score that so wonderful a relic might be stolen. For the relic had by this time entirely cut out all similar crucifixes, and the village of Dunes, through the concourse of pilgrims, had rapidly grown into a town, the property of the now fabulously wealthy Priory of the Holy Cross.

The Abbots of St Loup, however, looked upon the matter with an unfavourable eye. Although nominally remaining their vassals, the Priors of Dunes had contrived to obtain gradually from the Pope privileges which rendered them virtually independent, and in particular, immunities which sent to the treasury of St Loup only a small proportion of the tribute money brought by the pilgrims. Abbot Walterius in particular, showed himself actively hostile. He accused the Prior of Dunes of having employed his warders to trump up stories of strange movements and sounds on the part of the still crossless Effigy, and of suggesting, to the ignorant, changes in its attitude which were more credulously believed in now that there was no longer the straight line of the cross by which to verify. So finally the new cross was made, and consecrated, and on Holy Cross Day of the year, the Effigy was fastened to it in the presence of an immense concourse of clergy and laity. The Effigy, it was now supposed, would be satisfied, and no unusual occurrences would increase or perhaps fatally compromise its reputation for sanctity.

These expectations were violently dispelled. In November, 1293, after a year of strange rumours concerning the Effigy, the figure was again discovered to have moved, and continued moving, or rather (judging from the position on the cross) writhing; and on Christmas Eve of the same year, the cross was a second time thrown down and dashed in pieces. The priest on duty was, at the same time, found, it was thought, dead, in his warder's chamber. Another cross was made and this time privately consecrated and put in place, and a hole in the roof made a pretext to close the church for a while, and to perform the rites of purification necessary after its pollution by workmen. Indeed, it was remarked that on this occasion the Prior of Dunes took as much trouble to diminish and if possible to hide away the miracles, as his predecessor had done his best to blazon the preceding ones abroad. The priest who had been on duty on the eventful Christmas Eve disappeared mysteriously, and it was thought by many persons that he had gone mad and was confined in the Prior's prison, for fear of the revelations he might make. For by this time, and not without some encouragement from the Abbots at Arras, extraordinary stories had begun to circulate about the goings-on in the church of Dunes. This church, be it remembered, stood a little above the town, isolated and surrounded by big trees. It was surrounded by the precincts of the Priory and, save on the water side, by high walls. Nevertheless, persons there were who affirmed that, the wind having been in that direction, they had heard strange noises come from the church of nights. During storms, particularly, sounds had been heard which were variously described as howls, groans, and the music of rustic dancing. A master mariner affirmed that one Halloween, as his boat approached the mouth of the Nys, he had seen the church of Dunes brilliantly lit up, its immense windows flaming. But he was suspected of being drunk and of having exaggerated the effect of the small light shining from the warder's chamber. The interest of the townsfolk of Dunes coincided with that of the Priory, since they prospered greatly by the pilgrimages, so these tales were promptly hushed up. Yet they undoubtedly reached the ear of the Abbot of St Loup. And at last there came an event which brought them all back to the surface.

For, on the Vigil of All Saints, 1299, the church was struck by lightning. The new warder was found dead in the middle of the nave, the cross broken in two; and oh, horror! the Effigy was missing. The indescribable fear which overcame everyone was merely increased by the discovery of the Effigy lying behind the high altar, in an attitude of frightful convulsion, and, it was whispered, blackened by lightning.

This was the end of the strange doings at Dunes.

An ecclesiastical council was held at Arras, and the church shut once more for nearly a year. It was opened this time and re-consecrated by the Abbot of St Loup, whom the Prior of Holy Cross served humbly at mass. A new chapel had been built, and in it the miraculous crucifix was displayed, dressed in more splendid brocade and gems than usual, and its head nearly hidden by one of the most gorgeous crowns ever seen before; a gift, it was said, of the Duke of Burgundy.

All this new splendour, and the presence of the great Abbot himself, was presently explained to the faithful, when the Prior came forward to announce that a last and greatest miracle had now taken place. The original cross, on which the figure had hung in the Church of the Holy Sepulchre, and for which the Effigy had spurned all others made by less holy hands, had been cast on the shore of Dunes, on the very spot where, a hundred years before, the figure of the Saviour had been discovered in the sands. 'This,' said the Prior, 'was the explanation of the terrible occurrences which had filled all hearts with anguish. The Holy Effigy was now satisfied, it would rest in peace and its miraculous powers would be engaged only in granting the prayers of the faithful.'

One half of the forecast came true: from that day forward the Effigy never shifted its position; but from that day forward also, no considerable miracle was ever registered; the devotion of Dunes diminished, other relics threw the Sacred Effigy into the shade; and the pilgrimages dwindling to mere local gatherings, the church was never brought to completion.

What had happened? No one ever knew, guessed, or perhaps even asked. But, when in 1790 the Archiepiscopal palace of Arras was sacked, a certain notary of the neighbourhood bought a large portion of the archives at the price of waste paper, either from historical curiosity, or expecting to obtain thereby facts which might gratify his aversion to the clergy. These documents lay unexamined for many years, till my friend the Antiquary bought them. Among them taken helter skelter from the Archbishop's palace, were sundry papers referring to the suppressed Abbey of St Loup of Arras, and among these latter, a series of notes concerning the affairs of the church of Dunes; they were, so far as their fragmentary nature explained, the minutes of an inquest made in 1309, and contained the deposition of sundry witnesses. To understand their meaning it is necessary to remember that this was the time when witch trials had begun, and when the proceedings against the Templars had set the fashion of inquests which could help the finances of the country while furthering the interests of religion.

What appears to have happened is that after the catastrophe of the Vigil of All Saints, October, 1299, the Prior, Urbain de Luc, found himself suddenly threatened with a charge of sacrilege and witchcraft, of obtaining miracles of the Effigy by devilish means, and of converting his church into a chapel of the Evil One.

Instead of appealing to high ecclesiastical tribunals, as the privileges obtained from the Holy See would have warranted, Prior Urbain guessed that this charge came originally from the wrathful Abbot of St Loup, and, dropping all his pretensions in order to save himself, he threw himself upon the mercy of the Abbot whom he had hitherto flouted. The Abbot appears to have been satisfied by his submission, and the matter to have dropped after a few legal preliminaries, of which the notes found among the archiepiscopal archives of Arras represented a portion. Some of these notes my friend the Antiquary kindly allowed me to translate from the Latin, and I give them here, leaving the reader to make what he can of them.

'Item. The Abbot expresses himself satisfied that His Reverence the Prior has had no personal knowledge of or dealings with the Evil One (Diabolus). Nevertheless, the gravity of the charge requires . . .'—here the page is torn.

'Hugues Jacquot, Simon le Couvreur, Pierre Denis, burghers of

Dunes, being interrogated, witness:

'That the noises from the Church of the Holy Cross always happened on nights of bad storms, and foreboded shipwrecks on the coast; and were very various, such as terrible rattling, groans, howls as of wolves, and occasional flute playing. A certain Jehan, who has twice been branded and flogged for lighting fires on the coast and otherwise causing ships to wreck at the mouth of the Nys, being promised immunity, after two or three slight pulls on the rack, witnesses as follows: That the band of wreckers to which he belongs always knew when a dangerous storm was brewing, on account of the noises which issued from the church of Dunes. Witness has often climbed the walls and prowled round in the churchyard, waiting to hear such noises. He was not unfamiliar with the howlings and roarings mentioned by the previous witnesses. He has heard tell by a countryman who passed in the night that the howling was such that the countryman thought himself pursued by a pack of wolves, although it is well known that no wolf has been seen in these parts for thirty years. But the witness himself is of the opinion that the most singular of all the noises, and the one which always accompanied or foretold the worst storms, was a noise of flutes and pipes (*quod vulgo dicuntur flustes et musettes*) so sweet that the King of France could not have sweeter at his Court. Being interrogated whether he had ever seen anything? the witness answers: 'That he has seen the church brightly lit up from the sands; but on approaching found all dark, save the light from the warder's chamber. That once, by moonlight, the piping and fluting and howling being uncommonly loud, he thought he had seen wolves, and a human figure on the roof, but that he ran away from fear, and cannot be sure.'

'Item. His Lordship the Abbot desires the Right Reverend Prior to answer truly, placing his hand on the Gospels, whether or not he had himself heard such noises.

'The Right Reverend Prior denies ever having heard anything similar. But, being threatened with further proceedings (the rack?) acknowledges that he had frequently been told of these noises by the Warder on duty.

'*Query:* Whether the Right Reverend Prior was ever told anything else by the Warder?

'*Answer:* Yes; but under the seal of confession. The last Warder, moreover, the one killed by lightning, had been a reprobate priest, having committed the greatest crimes and obliged to take asylum, whom the Prior had kept there on account of the difficulty of finding a man sufficiently courageous for the office.

'*Query:* Whether the Prior has ever questioned previous Warders?

'*Answer:* That the Warders were bound to reveal only in confession whatever they had heard; that the Prior's predecessors had kept the seal of confession inviolate, and that though unworthy, the Prior himself desired to do alike.

'*Query:* What had become of the Warder who had been found in a swoon after the occurrences of Halloween?

'*Answer:* That the Prior does not know. The Warder was crazy. The Prior believes he was secluded for that reason.'

A disagreeable surprise had been, apparently, arranged for Prior Urbain de Luc. For the next entry states that:

'Item. By order of His Magnificence the Lord Abbot, certain servants of the Lord Abbot aforesaid introduce Robert Baudouin, priest, once Warder in the Church of the Holy Cross, who has been kept ten years in prison by His Reverence the Prior, as being of unsound mind. Witness manifests great terror on finding himself in the presence of their Lordships, and particularly of His Reverence the Prior. And refuses to speak, hiding his face in his hands and uttering shrieks. Being comforted with kind words by those present, nay even most graciously by My Lord the Abbot himself, *etiam* threatened with the rack if he continue obdurate, this witness deposes as follows, not without much lamentation, shrieking and senseless jabber after the manner of mad men.

'*Query:* Can he remember what happened on the Vigil of All Saints, in the church of Dunes, before he swooned on the floor of the church?

'*Answer:* He cannot. It would be sin to speak of such things before great spiritual Lords. Moreover he is but an ignorant man, and also mad. Moreover his hunger is great.

'Being given white bread from the Lord Abbot's own table, witness is again cross-questioned.

'*Query:* What can he remember of the events of the Vigil of All Saints?

'*Answer:* Thinks he was not always mad. Thinks he has not always been in prison. Thinks he once went in a boat on sea, etc.

'*Query:* Does witness think he has ever been in the church of Dunes?

'*Answer:* Cannot remember. But is sure that he was not always in prison.

'*Query:* Has witness ever heard anything like that? (My Lord the Abbot having secretly ordered that a certain fool in his service, an excellent musician, should suddenly play the pipes behind the Arras.)

'At which sound witness began to tremble and sob and fall on his knees, and catch hold of the robe even of My Lord the Abbot, hiding his head therein.

'*Query:* Wherefore does he feel such terror, being in the fatherly presence of so clement a prince as the Lord Abbot?

'*Answer:* That witness cannot stand that piping any longer. That it freezes his blood. That he has told the Prior many times that he will not remain any longer in the warder's chamber. That he is afraid for his life. That he dare not make the sign of the Cross nor say his prayers for fear of the Great Wild Man. That the Great Wild Man took the Cross and broke it in two and played at quoits with it in the nave. That all the wolves trooped down from the roof howling, and danced on their hind legs while the Great Wild man played the pipes on the high altar. That witness had surrounded himself with a hedge of little crosses, made of broken rye straw, to keep off the Great Wild Man from the warder's chamber. Ah—ah—ah! He is piping again! The wolves are howling! He is raising the tempest.

'*Item:* That no further information can be extracted from witness, who falls on the floor like one possessed and has to be removed from the presence of His Lordship the Abbot and His Reverence the Prior.'

III

Here the minutes of the inquest break off. Did those great spiritual dignitaries ever get to learn more about the terrible doings in the church of Dunes? Did they ever guess at their cause?

'For there was a cause,' said the Antiquary, folding his spectacles after reading me these notes, 'or more strictly the cause still exists. And you will understand, though those learned priests of six centuries ago could not.'

And rising, he fetched a key from a shelf and preceded me into the yard of his house, situated on the Nys, a mile below Dunes.

Between the low steadings one saw the salt marsh, lilac with sea lavender, the Island of Birds, a great sandbank at the mouth of the Nys, where every kind of sea fowl gathers; and beyond, the angry white-crested sea under an angry orange afterglow. On the other side, inland, and appearing above the farm roofs, stood the church of Dunes, its pointed belfry and jagged outlines of gables and buttresses and gargoyles and wind-warped pines black against the easterly sky of ominous livid red.

'I told you,' said the Antiquary, stopping with the key in the lock of a big outhouse, 'that there had been a *substitution*; that the crucifix at present at Dunes is not the one miraculously cast up by the storm of 1195. I believe the present one may be identified as a life-size statue, for which a receipt exists in the archives of Arras, furnished to the Abbot of St Loup by Estienne Le Mas and Guillaume Pernel, stonemasons, in the year 1299, that is to say the year of the inquest and of the cessation of all supernatural occurrences at Dunes. As to the original effigy, you shall see it and understand everything.'

The Antiquary opened the door of a sloping, vaulted passage, lit a lantern and led the way. It was evidently the cellar of some mediæval building; and a scent of wine, of damp wood, and of fir branches from innumerable stacked up faggots, filled the darkness among thickset columns.

'Here,' said the Antiquary, raising his lantern, 'he was buried beneath this vault and they had run an iron stake through his middle, like a vampire, to prevent his rising.'

The Effigy was erect against the dark wall, surrounded by brushwood. It was more than life-size, nude, the arms broken off at the shoulders, the head, with stubbly beard and clotted hair, drawn up with an effort, the face contracted with agony; the muscles dragged as of one hanging crucified, the feet bound together with a rope. The figure was familiar to me in various galleries. I came forward to examine the ear: it was leaf-shaped.

'Ah, you have understood the whole mystery,' said the Antiquary.

'I have understood,' I answered, not knowing how far his thought really went, 'that this supposed statue of Christ is an antique satyr, a Marsyas awaiting his punishment.'

The Antiquary nodded. 'Exactly,' he said drily, 'that is the whole explanation. Only I think the Abbot and the Prior were not so wrong to drive the iron stake through him when they removed him from the church.'

AN UNSCIENTIFIC STORY

Louise J. Strong

As with its contemporaries *Harpers*, *Pearsons*, *Pall Mall* and other quality magazines of the turn of the century, the *Cosmopolitan* (published in New York) was a treasure trove of supernatural, weird and bizarre fiction. It carried short stories by most of the leading writers of the era, including Bram Stoker, whose forgotten adventure yarn 'The Red Stockade', decorated with illustrations of crocodiles and heads impaled on long posts, appeared in the September 1894 issue. A young artist named John Barrymore was one of the artists who showed great promise as a macabre illustrator (with 'The Canonic Curse' in 1902), years before he became a world-famous stage and screen idol. Louise Jackson Strong's 'An Unscientific Story' is a unique combination of the Dracula and Frankenstein themes, featuring a small army of vampiric monstrosities created in a laboratory. This story originally appeared in the February 1903 number of the *Cosmopolitan* illustrated by E. Hering.

<hr>

HE sat, tense and rigid with excitement, expectancy, incredulity. Was it possible, after so many years of study, effort and failure? Could it be that at last success rewarded him? He hardly dared to breathe lest he should miss something of the wonderful spectacle. How long he had sat thus he did not know; he had not stirred for hours—or was it days?—except to adjust the light by means of the button under his hand.

His laboratory, at the foot of his garden, was lighted day and night in the inner room (his private workshop) with electricity, and no one was admitted but by especial privilege.

Some things he had accomplished for the good of mankind, more he hoped to accomplish, but most of all he had been searching for, and striving to create, the life-germ. He had spent many of his years and much of his great wealth in unsuccessful experiments. He had met ridicule and unbelief with Stoical indifference, upheld by the conviction that he would finally prove the truth of his theories. Over and over again, defeat and disappointment had dashed aside his hopes; over and over again, he had rallied and gone on with dogged persistence.

And now! He could not realize it yet! He leaned back, and clasped his hands over his closed eyes. Perhaps he had imagined it—his over-strained nerves having deceived him. Was it an optical illusion? It had happened before. There had been times when he felt that he had torn aside the veil, and grasped the secret, only to find that a few abortive movements were all that existed of his creation. In sudden haste he turned to the glass again.

A—h! He drew a long breath that was almost a shriek. It was not illusion of sight, no delusion of his mind. The creature—it was plainly a living creature—had grown, and taken shape, even in those few moments. It lived! It breathed! It moved! And his the power that had given it life! His breath came in gasps, his heart beat in great throbs, and his blood surged through his veins.

But soon his scientific sense asserted itself, and he carefully and minutely studied the prodigy. Its growth was phenomenal; the rapidity of its expansion was past belief. It took form, developed limbs, made repeated attempts at locomotion, and finally drew itself out of the glass receptacle of cunningly compounded liquid in which it had been created.

At that the learned professor leaped to his feet in a transport of exultation. The impossible had been achieved! Life! Life, so long the mystery and despair of man, had come at his bidding. He alone of all humanity held the secret in the hollow of his hand. He plunged about the room in a blind ecstasy of triumph. Tears ran unknown and unheeded down his cheeks. He tossed his arms aloft wildly, as if challenging Omnipotence itself. At that moment, he felt a very god! He could create worlds, and people them! A burning desire seized him to rush out, and proclaim the deed from the housetops, to the utter confounding of brother scientists and the theologians.

He dropped, panting, into his chair, and strove to collect and quiet his mind. Not yet the time to make known the incredible fact. He must wait until full development proved that it was indeed a living crea-tion—with animal nature and desires.

It had lain, quivering, on the marble slab, breathing regularly and steadily, making aimless movements. The four limbs, that had seemed but swaying feelers, grew into long, thin arms and legs, with claw-like hands, and flat, six-toed feet. It lost its spherical shape; an uneven protuberance, in which was situated the breathing-orifice, expanded into a head with rudimentary features. He took his spatula, and turned it over. It responded to the touch with an effort to rise; the head wobbled weakly, and two slits opened in the dim face, from which looked out dull, fishy eyes. It grew! Each moment found it larger, more developed; yet he could no more see the growth than he could see the movement of the hour-hand of his watch.

'It is probably of the simian order,' he made memorandum. 'Ape-like. Grows a strange caricature of humanity.'

An aperture appeared in the oblong head, forming a lipless mouth below the lump of a nose; large ears stood out on either side.

The caricature-like resemblance to humanity increased as it grew older. It crawled a space, sat up, made many futile efforts and at last succeeded in standing. It took a few staggering steps. It made wheezy, puffing sounds in its motions, and drivelled idiotically. Finally it squatted down on its haunches, the knobby knees drawn up against the rotund paunch, the hands grasping the ankles.

'It grew!'

'The attitude of primitive man,' the Professor muttered.

For long it crouched thus, increasing in size, and beginning to display a crude intelligence; looking about with eyes that evidently saw—noted things: the arc of light, the glistening glass and brass, and most of all, himself.

It had as yet made no manifestation that indicated desire; but soon a fly, alighting near it, was snatched up and thrust into its mouth with incredible quickness and an eager, sucking noise. At this expression of animalism, the Professor's hand shook so violently that he could scarcely record the movement.

Nervousness only! He would not admit to himself a feeling of startled misgiving. He was worn out. For days he scarcely tasted food, and he had dozed only at long intervals. A half-hour's sleep would refresh him, and the creature could not change much in that time, for its bodily development seemed nearly completed. His head dropped on his arms, and he slumbered profoundly.

He was awakened by a sense of suffocation and a gnawing at his neck; he started up with a cry, pushing off a clammy mass that lay heavy on the upturned side of his face. Merciful heaven! It was the beast attacking him; its teeth, which he had not before discovered, seeking his throat!

It lay where he had thrown it, its long tongue licking the shapeless mouth, its eyes hot with an awakened bloodthirstiness. In a wave of repulsion, he struck it savagely.

He was appalled at what he had done; he seemed to have committed a crime in striking it.

He went to the anteroom, where fresh food was left for him daily, and selected different sorts, questioning whether any would or could satisfy a creature which had been brought into existence in such a marvellous manner.

It met him, with alert expectancy, and ate, with a ravenous gluttony that was loathsome, of all that he put before it.

Apparently it possessed all the animal senses; all had been tested but hearing. He spoke a few words in an ordinary tone; it lifted its face, with an expression of inquiry.

He paced the room in perplexed thought. Could it possess mental faculties beyond those of an ordinary animal? He had not hoped to produce anything but a lower form of life. Never had he imagined a creature of his creating, with consciousness of its existence; that was a responsibility for which he was not prepared.

Exhausted in body and mind, he locked the creature in the inner room, and threw himself on the couch in his study for a night's rest.

The creature was standing when he entered, next morning, and, stepping toward him, it correctly repeated every word he had spoken the night before, as if reciting a lesson, showing an eager expectancy of approval.

'Good heavens!' ejaculated the Professor, reeling against the door.

'Good heavens!' it echoed, its small orbs sparkling.

He sprang toward it as if to force back this evidence of intelligent reason; it fled, keeping the table between them; brought to bay, it dropped on its knees, and put up beseeching hands, mumbling a prayer—a prayer from its own inner consciousness!

Aghast, terrified, he gazed at it, tremblingly assuring himself that many animals made imitative sounds—parrots readily learned human speech.

The curious creature had shown no bodily growth for several days; it had perhaps reached maturity, and would soon show signs of decay. Already a lump had appeared on its breast, which it picked at uneasily; he must not much longer delay exhibiting it. Yet he hesitated to do so until he was more certain concerning it.

He tested its power with a multitude of words that it not only easily repeated but retained perfectly, muttering them over, forming and reforming a number of proper sentences with various definitions, which it seemed to submit, in comparison, to some inner or waking intelligence.

Once, after long muttering, it came to him, with timid perplexity, and put the astonishing question: 'What am I?' And when he answered not for amazement the poor creature wandered about, repeating the words. Like one rallying from long unconsciousness, it seemed seeking a dimly remembered clue to its identity.

Fear clutched him! Impossible! Oh, impossible that he had a human soul imprisoned in such hideous form! A soul that would, by and by, fully awake to the wrong he had done it! No! No! He spurned the thought as a wild fancy. But even so—he had done nothing unlawful. Man was free to use his intellect to the utmost. He had brought into existence a living creature, but he was not responsible farther than the body. To the Keeper of souls be the rest.

Possibly some long-disembodied spirit, grown wise in its freedom, animated the creature, and its full development would open a channel for such knowledge as the earth had never before known, and the world would ring with his name, and honour and fame be his! Again he exulted while making record of its mental unfoldment, which was as rapid as had been the development of its uncouth body, and with much the same distortion. It recognized him as its creator, did him reverence, and obeyed his commands.

The lump, which he had taken for a symptom of decay, assumed the appearance of a large scale, and dropped off. When he would have examined it more closely, the creature put a hand over it, looking up at him with a show of hostility and cunning, for the first time disregarding his command; and he would not enforce obedience.

He was confounded next morning to find that the scale had developed into a second creature! About it the first hovered with evident joy and pride, inviting his attention to it with the gushing babble of a child. He had not imagined it possessed the power of generation, but here was reproduction with an ease and rapidity beyond any creature of like size in existence.

The second one, fed and taught by the first, matured in body and mind more quickly; and they invented or discovered a speech of their own—a strange jargon (of which he could make nothing) by which they exchanged thoughts and conversed, and which he tried in vain to help them reduce to a written language, through which he might obtain the wisdom for which he hoped.

And reproduction went on; while he subjected them to many tests to determine their nature.

As they grew in age and numbers, they began to evince for him less reverence; and an animosity appeared, that burst out at times in a horrible flow of invectives—a mingling of their own strange speech and his.

When he did not comply with their desires, they wailed piteously— demanding: 'Why?' 'Why'—or hurled blasphemous defiance at him.

These things convinced him that they were a lower order of humanity, possessing souls; for no creature but man observed, with like or dislike, the bodily form in which its life was manifested. He was torn and racked with dread and a crushing sense of guilt and responsibility. It was as if he had started an avalanche that might overwhelm the world.

Already they had become a heavy burden to him. He was obliged to make nightly visits to the markets for food to satisfy their rapacity— food which he flung to them as to so many dogs, and which they pounced upon and fought over, with curses at each other's greed. Yet at a word of reproof from him, they banded solidly against him, each for all.

All complacency over his handiwork had vanished; never could he bring himself to exhibit to mortal eye these repulsive creatures. His only thought was the unanswerable question: what should he do with them? On this he brooded continually, reaching no conclusion because he could no more contemplate destroying creatures possessing human intelligence, however distorted and degraded, than he could have taken the life of a born idiot or one insane.

In his absorption he neglected to lock the door one day, and roused to find them swarming in his study. Besides the high skylight there was one large window, securely closed by a heavy inside shutter, above which was a long narrow opening admitting air. Some of them, clinging to shutter and casement, and uttering low, sharp cries, like wolves scenting their prey, had climbed to the opening, and were peering out with gloating eyes. They clawed and jibbered, with hot tongues lolling eagerly, the saliva dripping from their ugly mouths— hideous pictures of unsatiated animal appetite.

And what was it that so aroused their ghoulish lust? His little children playing on the lawn, their innocent voices rising like heavenly music in contrast to the hellish sounds within. A rippling laugh floated on the air, and the creatures' eagerness increased to a fury; with tooth and nail they strove to enlarge the opening, not heeding his horrified commands.

In a frenzy of rage, he snatched an iron rod, and swept them to the floor, driving them with blows and maledictions to their room. They fled before his wrath, but when he turned his back to lock the door, they flung themselves upon him, with desperate attempts to reach his throat.

After a sharp battle, he beat them off, and sent them huddling and whimpering to a corner. 'Monsters! Monsters!' he cried, pale with the discovery. 'Monsters, who would prey on human flesh! What a curse I have called forth! It is of the devil!'

'Devil; devil; yes, devil,' one muttered, a leering and malicious knowledge gleaming in its oblique eyes.

In that moment he saw his duty—all hesitation vanished, and he made up his mind—they must be destroyed effectually, and he could not survive the destruction.

By that occult sense or power they possessed, which was beyond anything he had ever found in man, they divined his decision almost as soon as it was formed, and prostrated themselves with cries of mercy. They hastened to lay at his feet propitiatory offerings of their belongings: cards, pencils, picture-books—all that he had provided for their amusement and instruction—entreating him for life, the life that he himself had given them.

Their prayers and offerings rejected, the creatures became his open enemies. Intent on escaping from their prison, his every entrance was a battle with their persistent efforts to gain control of the door, the only outlet to the room.

They were not easily injured. No maiming nor bruises resulted from his hasty blows with the rod. Would it be possible to destroy them? Their bodily substance resembled clammy putty in appearance, with the consistency of rubber. He had never conquered his repugnance sufficiently to handle one. He could not experiment upon them, but the chemicals he meant to employ with the most powerful explosives, he trusted, would make the work of annihilation swift and thorough.

His preparations were delayed and hindered by their never-ending attempts to overcome him. The moment he became absorbed in his work, they crawled and crept with malignant insistence to a fresh attack. Once, in a movement of defence, he pricked the body of one with a sharpened tool, and he was almost suffocated by the fumes that arose from the yellow, viscid fluid that oozed from the wound.

Escaping from the affrighted, indignant uproar that followed, he stood at his study-window to recover from the dizzy sickness. 'That alone would make them formidable enemies of mankind,' he muttered.

'The slaughter of a few would put to flight an army. Turned loose, they are sufficient now in numbers, with all their hellish characteristics, to lay waste this teeming city. Wretched, impotent creator that I am! Could I but turn back the dial of time a few short weeks how happily I could take my place beside the most ignorant toiler, and meddle no more with the prerogative of the Almighty!'

In a few hours, the wound had healed, no trace of injury remaining; but they had learned new reason to fear him, and skulked about glowering, commenting upon him with shameless, insulting epithets.

He found a note from his wife in his mail, informing him of the arrival in the city of a noted scientist whose coming had been largely of his arranging, months before. There was much dissatisfaction expressed at his absence, and demands were made that he attend the forthcoming banquet.

'Of course, you will go,' she wrote. 'And, dear, do come in early enough to give a little time to your family. We have hardly seen you for weeks and weeks; and though I have obeyed the law, I so long to see you that I have been tempted to transgress, and boldly make my way to you. Baby, who was just beginning to totter about when you saw him last, runs easily now on his sturdy little legs, and he can say "papa" quite plainly. Do come, dear; a few hours with us will rest you.'

Rest indeed! Heaven itself could seem no sweeter to the miserable man than this glimpse of his home. His dear wife, content to live the life Omnipotence had planned for her; his sweet children, daily and harmoniously unfolding new graces of mind and body like lovely flowers—not for him was it to see their perfected maturity, from which he had hoped so much. With a groan he dropped his head, and wept bitter tears—tears that meant the renunciation of his own forfeited life.

All was complete when the banquet-day arrived. He had but to press a small knob in the floor, and the mighty currents of electricity would flash around the room, setting in motion forces of such tremendous power and instantaneous action that the entire space would instantly be one flame, of an intensity that no conceivable matter could withstand.

He had taken extraordinary precautions to guard the works from the curiosity and cunning of the creatures, protecting the button that controlled the whole with a metallic cover, which was held closely to the floor by screws.

And now he looked upon the creatures, itemizing their hideousness, as if to prepare a paper descriptive of them for this gathering of scientific authorities. Pygmies, between three and four feet in height, immensely strong; long, thin, crooked limbs, in some of unequal length; squat, thick bodies; pointed heads, bald but for a tuft of hair at the crown; huge ears, that loosely flapped, dog-like; nose, little more than wide nostrils; mouth, a mere long slit, with protruding teeth; and eyes, ah! eyes that showed plainly far more than animal intelligence.

They were small, oblique, set closely together, of a beady black, their only lids being a whitish membrane that swept them at intervals—but they sparkled and glowed with passion, dimmed with tears, and widened with thought. Those eyes, more than a score of them, were fixed upon him now with entreaty, menace, fear, revolt, and, most of all, judgment burning in their depths. Even the smaller ones, of which there were many in various sizes, eyed him with resentment and hate, while scurrying, like frightened rats, from corner to corner as he moved about.

Let accident put him for a moment in their power, and the whole pack would be upon him, and tear him to shreds, as they would any human being. Yet so strange, so monstrous was this unprecedented creation, mingling of lowest animal ferocity and human mind and soul, that he had found it quite possible to teach them to read and write, and work mathematical problems, and they were perhaps capable of considerable education—but without one redeeming trait. Earth had no place for such.

Their taste for blood was appalling; of all the food he offered, they preferred raw meat, the more gory the better. He had provided a quantity to employ them while he was away, and left them snarling over it.

He tried to put all thought of them behind him as he locked the doors. For a few hours he would be free, rid of torment and anticipation. But a deep melancholy shadowed the happiness of his reunion with his family, and gloom sat with him at the banquet-table. He took no part in the festivities and discussions, and was so manifestly unfit to do so that none urged him. Only when the distinguished guest touched on the subject of the possibility—or impossibility, as he viewed it—of producing life chemically, did he rouse to interest.

'It can never be done,' asserted the guest, 'for the giving of the breath of life is the prerogative of the Omnipotent alone.'

'Ah, but Professor Levison believes otherwise, and hopes some day to astonish us by exhibiting a creature which he has created, but whether beast or human we will have to wait for time to reveal!' one said, with light sarcasm.

'And in the impossibility to determine beforehand what the creation shall be lies my objection to man's assuming the responsibility, even if he could by any means attain to it. For who could say what a calamity might not be brought upon humanity in the shape of some detestable monstrosity, whose evil propensities would be beyond control? Science has a large field for research; one need not step aside to intrude where success, if possible, might mean widespread disaster.'

The Professor shrank as from a blow, and the desire he had momentarily felt to exhibit his creation to the scoffers, and prove the reality of his assumption, died out in despair as he thought what an intolerable, devilish curse that creation was.

No, Nothing remained but silence and annihilation. He wondered, vaguely, as to the state of himself and his creatures in that place beyond the seething crucible of fire through which they would shortly pass together.

His wife was alarmed at his worn face and the dull apathy with which he spoke of the meeting, to which he had formerly looked with such eagerness.

'Dear,' she said, pleadingly, 'you are wearing yourself out; drop everything, and rest. What will all the experiments and discoveries in the world matter to us if we have not you? Come, take a vacation, and let us go on our long-planned visit.'

'I cannot now,' he said, so decisively that she felt it useless to insist.

'At any rate, you can give yourself a few hours' rest. Do not go back to the laboratory tonight.'

'Oh, but I must!' he exclaimed. Then, taking her in his arms, he added: 'My dearest, I cannot stay now, but I am planning to take a long rest soon.' This was for her comfort afterwards.

He gazed at his sleeping children with yearning tenderness, and took leave of her with a solemn finality of manner that increased her anxiety. 'It is as if he never expected to see us again,' she murmured, tearfully.

From his study he could hear the creatures leaping, laughing, wrangling, forgetful as children of the impending fate they so clearly realized in his presence. He pitied, but could not save, them.

And now the hour had come— all things waited the last act. But, like the condemned criminal taking leave of earth in a last lingering gaze, he longed for another farewell glimpse of the home he would enter no more.

Going to the anteroom he threw open the shutter, and leaned out. How quiet the night! With what divine precision all things ran their appointed course, held and guided by Omnipotence! He lifted his heart in a prayer for protection and blessing upon the silent house which contained his dear ones. How dear he had never known till this sad hour in——

What was it? Had the day of doom burst in all its terrible grandeur? The earth rocked with awful thunderings, the very heavens were blotted out with belching flame—then, suddenly, silence and darkness enveloped him.

He opened his eyes, and looked about with feeble efforts at thought. He was in his own bed, and surely that was his wife's dear face, bathed in happy tears, bending over him, asking: 'Dear husband, are you better? Do you know me?'

He nodded, smiling faintly; then memory returned, and a stream of questions rushed from his lips.

'Hush! Hush!' She stopped him with her soft hand. 'Be quiet. I will tell you all, for I know you will not rest otherwise. There was a fearful explosion at the laboratory, so fearful that it was heard across the city; the whole building seemed to burst out at once into flame, and—oh, my dearest!—we feared you were in it; but a kind providence must have sent you to the outer room, for you were blown through the hall-window, and you were rescued from the burning debris.' She paused to control her emotion.

'How long?' he asked.

'Three weeks, and you have been in a raging fever till two days ago.'

'Was all destroyed?' he breathed, anxiously.

'Yes dear; everything. Nothing was left but a few scraps of twisted metal. But we will not mind that when your precious life was spared. You can rebuild when you are entirely recovered.'

'I belong to you and the children now,' he murmured, in ambiguous answer, drawing her face down to his, feeling his stored life not his own.

It was clear to him what had happened. The creatures had loosened the screws of the cap covering the knob, and had themselves brought about their destruction. With a thankful sigh, he fell into a restful slumber.

A DEAD FINGER

Sabine Baring-Gould

Sabine Baring-Gould (1834–1924), squire-parson of Lew Trenchard, will always be associated with the great hymns he wrote, especially 'Onward, Christian Soldiers', but he was amazingly prolific in other branches of literature, including novels, biographies, religious and travel books, and studies of antiquities and folklore. His fascinating volume, *The Book of Were-Wolves: Being an Account of a Terrible Superstition* (1865), contained many allegedly true reports of both wolfmen and vampires, and remains one of the most important works on the subject. Bram Stoker used both this book and *Curious Myths of the Middle Ages* while researching East European folklore and legends prior to writing *Dracula*. 'A Dead Finger' is reprinted from Baring-Gould's collection of supernatural short stories, *A Book of Ghosts* (1904).

I

WHY the National Gallery should not attract so many visitors as, say, the British Museum, I cannot explain. The latter does not contain much that, one would suppose, appeals to the interest of the ordinary sightseer. What knows such of prehistoric flints and scratched bones? Of Assyrian sculpture? Of Egyptian hieroglyphics? The Greek and Roman statuary is cold and dead. The paintings in the National Gallery glow with colour, and are instinct with life. Yet, somehow, a few listless wanderers saunter yawning through the National Gallery, whereas swarms pour through the halls of the British Museum, and talk and pass remarks about the objects there exposed, of the date and meaning of which they have not the faintest conception.

I was thinking of this problem, and endeavouring to unravel it, one morning whilst sitting in the room for English masters at the great collection in Trafalgar Square. At the same time another thought forced itself upon me. I had been through the rooms devoted to foreign schools, and had then come into that given over to Reynolds, Morland, Gainsborough, Constable, and Hogarth. The morning had been for a while propitious, but towards noon a dense umber-tinted fog had come ◉

on, making it all but impossible to see the pictures, and quite impossible to do them justice. I was tired, and so seated myself on one of the chairs, and fell into the consideration first of all of—why the National Gallery is not as popular as it should be; and secondly, how it was that the British School had no beginnings, like those of Italy and the Netherlands. We can see the art of the painter from its first initiation in the Italian peninsula, and among the Flemings. It starts on its progress like a child, and we can trace every stage of its growth. Not so with English art. It springs to life in full and splendid maturity. Who were there before Reynolds and Gainsborough and Hogarth? The great names of those portrait and subject painters who have left their canvases upon the walls of our country houses were those of foreigners—Holbein, Kneller, Van Dyck, and Lely for portraits, and Monnoyer for flower and fruit pieces. Landscapes, figure subjects were all importations, none home-grown. How came that about? Was there no limner that was native? Was it that fashion trampled on home-grown pictorial beginnings as it flouted and spurned native music?

Here was food for contemplation. Dreaming in the brown fog, looking through it without seeing its beauties, at Hogarth's painting of Lavinia Fenton as Polly Peachum, without wondering how so indifferent a beauty could have captivated the Duke of Bolton and held him for thirty years, I was recalled to myself and my surroundings by the strange conduct of a lady who had seated herself on a chair near me, also discouraged by the fog, and awaiting its dispersion.

I had not noticed her particularly. At the present moment I do not remember particularly what she was like. So far as I can recollect she was middle-aged, and was quietly yet well dressed. It was not her face nor her dress that attracted my attention and disturbed the current of my thoughts; the effect I speak of was produced by her strange movements and behaviour.

She had been sitting listless, probably thinking of nothing at all, or nothing in particular, when, in turning her eyes round, and finding that she could see nothing of the paintings, she began to study me. This did concern me greatly. A cat may look at the king; but to be contemplated by a lady is a compliment sufficient to please any gentleman. It was not gratified vanity that troubled my thoughts, but the consciousness that my appearance produced—first of all a startled surprise, then undisguised alarm, and, finally, indescribable horror.

Now a man can sit quietly leaning on the head of his umbrella, and glow internally, warmed and illumined by the consciousness that he is being surveyed with admiration by a lovely woman, even when he is middle-aged and not fashionably dressed; but no man can maintain his composure when he discovers himself to be an object of aversion and terror.

What was it? I passed my hand over my chin and upper lip, thinking it not impossible that I might have forgotten to shave that morning, and in my confusion not considering that the fog would prevent the lady from discovering neglect in this particular, had it occurred, which it had not. I am a little careless, perhaps, about shaving when in the country; but when in town, never.

The next idea that occurred to me was—a smut. Had a London black, curdled in that dense pea-soup atmosphere, descended on my nose and blackened it? I hastily drew my silk handkerchief from my pocket, moistened it, and passed to my nose, and then each cheek. I then turned my eyes into the corners and looked at the lady, to see whether by this means I had got rid of what was objectionable in my personal appearance.

Then I saw that her eyes, dilated with horror, were riveted, not on my face, but on my leg.

My leg! What on earth could that harmless member have in it so terrifying? The morning had been dull; there had been rain in the night, and I admit that on leaving my hotel I had turned up the bottoms of my trousers. That is a proceeding not so uncommon, not so outrageous as to account for the stony stare of this woman's eyes.

If that were all I would turn my trousers down.

Then I saw her shrink from the chair on which she sat to one further removed from me, but still with her eyes fixed on my leg—about the level of my knee. She had let fall her umbrella, and was grasping the seat of her chair with both hands, as she backed from me.

I need hardly say that I was greatly disturbed in mind and feelings, and forgot all about the origin of the English schools of painters, and the question why the British Museum is more popular than the National Gallery.

Thinking that I might have been spattered by a hansom whilst crossing Oxford Street, I passed my hand down my side hastily, with a sense of annoyance, and all at once touched something, cold, clammy, that sent a thrill to my heart, and made me start and take a step forward. At the same moment, the lady, with a cry of horror, sprang to her feet, and with raised hands fled from the room, leaving her umbrella where it had fallen.

There were other visitors to the Picture Gallery besides ourselves, who had been passing through the saloon, and they turned at her cry, and looked in surprise after her.

The policeman stationed in the room came to me and asked what had happened. I was in such agitation that I hardly knew what to answer. I told him that I could explain what had occurred little better than himself. I had noticed that the lady had worn an odd expression, and had behaved in most extraordinary fashion, and that he had best take charge of her umbrella, and wait for her return to claim it.

This questioning by the official was vexing, as it prevented me from at once and on the spot investigating the cause of her alarm and mine—hers at something she must have seen on my leg, and mine at something I had distinctly felt creeping up my leg.

The numbing and sickening effect on me of the touch of the object I had not seen was not to be shaken off at once. Indeed, I felt as though my hand were contaminated, and that I could have no rest till I had thoroughly washed the hand, and, if possible, washed away the feeling that had been produced.

I looked on the floor, I examined my leg, but saw nothing. As I wore my overcoat, it was probable that in rising from my seat the skirt had fallen over my trousers and hidden the thing, whatever it was. I therefore hastily removed my overcoat and shook it, then I looked at my trousers. There was nothing whatever on my leg, and nothing fell from my overcoat when shaken.

Accordingly I reinvested myself, and hastily left the Gallery; then took my way as speedily as I could, without actually running, to Charing Cross Station and down the narrow way leading to the Metropolitan, where I went into Faulkner's bath and hairdressing establishment, and asked for hot water to thoroughly wash my hand and well soap it. I bathed my hand in water as hot as I could endure it, employed carbolic soap, and then, after having a good brush down, especially on my left side where my hand had encountered the object that had so affected me, I left. I had entertained the intention of going to the Princess's Theatre that evening, and of securing a ticket in the morning; but all thought of theatre-going was gone from me. I could not free my heart from the sense of nausea and cold that had been produced by the touch. I went into Gatti's to have lunch, and ordered something, I forget what, but, when served, I found that my appetite was gone. I could eat nothing; the food inspired me with disgust. I thrust it from me untasted, and, after drinking a couple of glasses of claret, left the restaurant, and returned to my hotel.

Feeling sick and faint, I threw my overcoat over the sofa-back, and cast myself on my bed.

I do not know that there was any particular reason for my doing so, but as I lay my eyes were on my great-coat.

The density of the fog had passed away, and there was light again, not of first quality, but sufficient for a Londoner to swear by, so that I could see everything in my room, though through a veil, darkly.

I do not think my mind was occupied in any way. About the only occasions on which, to my knowledge, my mind is actually passive or inert is when crossing the Channel in *The Foam* from Dover to Calais, when I am always, in every weather, abjectly seasick—and thoughtless. But as I now lay on my bed, uncomfortable, squeamish, without knowing why—I was in the same inactive mental condition. But not for long.

I saw something that startled me.

First, it appeared to me as if the lappet of my overcoat pocket were in movement, being raised. I did not pay much attention to this, as I supposed that the garment was sliding down on to the seat of the sofa, from the back, and that this displacement of gravity caused the movement I observed. But this I soon saw was not the case. That which moved the lappet was something in the pocket that was struggling to get out. I could see now that it was working its way up the inside, and that when it reached the opening it lost balance and fell down again. I could make this out by the projections and indentations in the cloth; these moved as the creature, or whatever it was, worked its way up the lining.

'A mouse,' I said, and forgot my seediness; I was interested. 'The little rascal! However did he contrive to seat himself in my pocket? and I have worn that overcoat all the morning!' But no—it was not a mouse. I saw something white poke its way out from under the lappet; and in another moment an object was revealed that, though revealed, I could not understand, nor could I distinguish what it was.

Now roused by curiosity, I raised myself on my elbow. In doing this I made some noise, the bed creaked. Instantly the something dropped on the floor, lay outstretched for a moment, to recover itself, and then began, with the motions of a maggot, to run along the floor.

There is a caterpillar called 'The Measurer', because, when it advances, it draws its tail up to where its head is and then throws forward its full length, and again draws up its extremity, forming at each time a loop, and with each step measuring its total length. The object I now saw on the floor was advancing precisely like the measuring caterpillar. It had the colour of a cheese-maggot, and in length was about three and a half inches. It was not, however, like a caterpillar, which is flexible throughout its entire length, but this was, as it seemed to me, jointed in two places, one joint being more conspicuous than the other. For some moments I was so completely paralysed by astonishment that I remained motionless, looking at the thing as it crawled along the carpet—a dull green carpet with darker green, almost black, flowers in it.

It had, as it seemed to me, a glossy head, distinctly marked; but, as the light was not brilliant, I could not make out very clearly, and, moreover, the rapid movements prevented close scrutiny.

Presently, with a shock still more startling than that produced by its apparition at the opening of the pocket of my great-coat, I became convinced that what I saw was a finger, a human forefinger, and that the glossy head was no other than the nail.

The finger did not seem to have been amputated. There was no sign of blood or laceration where the knuckle should be, but the extremity of the finger, or root rather, faded away to indistinctness, and I was unable to make out the root of the finger.

I could see no hand, no body behind this finger, nothing whatever except a finger that had little token of warm life in it, no coloration as though blood circulated in it; and this finger was in active motion creeping along the carpet towards a wardrobe that stood against the wall by the fireplace.

I sprang off the bed and pursued it.

Evidently the finger was alarmed, for it redoubled its pace, reached the wardrobe, and went under it. By the time I had arrived at the article of furniture it had disappeared. I lit a vesta match and held it beneath the wardrobe, that was raised above the carpet by about two inches, on turned feet, but I could see nothing more of the finger.

I got my umbrella and thrust it beneath, and raked forwards and backwards, right and left, and raked out flue, and nothing more solid.

II

I packed my portmanteau next day and returned to my home in the country. All desire for amusement in town was gone, and the faculty to transact business had departed as well.

A languor and qualms had come over me, and my head was in a maze. I was unable to fix my thoughts on anything. At times I was disposed to believe that my wits were deserting me, at others that I was on the verge of a severe illness. Anyhow, whether likely to go off my head or not, or take to my bed, home was the only place for me, and homeward I sped, accordingly. On reaching my country habitation, my servant, as usual, took my portmaneau to my bedroom, unstrapped it, but did not unpack it. I object to his throwing out the contents of my Gladstone bag; not that there is anything in it he may not see, but that he puts my things where I cannot find them again. My clothes—he is welcome to place them where he likes and where they belong, and this latter he knows better than I do; but, then, I carry about with me other things than a dress suit, and changes of linen and flannel. There are letters, papers, books—and the proper destinations of these are known only to myself. A servant has a singular and evil knack of putting away literary matter and odd volumes in such places that it takes the owner half a day to find them again. Although I was uncomfortable, and my head in a whirl, I opened and unpacked my own portmanteau. As I was thus engaged I saw something curled up in my collar-box, the lid of which had got broken in by a boot-heel impinging on it. I had pulled off the damaged cover to see if my collars had been spoiled, when something curled up inside suddenly rose on end and leapt, just like a cheese-jumper, out of the box, over the edge of the Gladstone bag, and scurried away across the floor in a manner already familiar to me.

I could not doubt for a moment what it was—here was the finger again. It had come with me from London to the country.

Whither it went in its run over the floor I do not know, I was too bewildered to observe.

Somewhat later, towards evening, I seated myself in my easy-chair, took up a book, and tried to read. I was tired with the journey, with the knocking about in town, and the discomfort and alarm produced by the apparition of the finger. I felt worn out. I was unable to give my attention to what I read, and before I was aware was asleep. Roused for an instant by the fall of the book from my hands, I speedily relapsed into unconsciousness. I am not sure that a doze in an armchair ever does good. It usually leaves me in a semi-stupid condition and with a headache. Five minutes in a horizontal position on my bed is worth thirty in a chair. That is my experience. In sleeping in a sedentary position the head is a difficulty; it drops forward or lolls on one side or the other, and has to be brought back into a position in which the line to the centre of gravity runs through the trunk, otherwise the head carries the body over in a sort of general capsize out of the chair on to the floor.

I slept, on the occasion of which I am speaking, pretty healthily, because deadly weary; but I was brought to waking, not by my head falling over the arm of the chair, and my trunk tumbling after it, but by a feeling of cold extending from my throat to my heart. When I awoke I was in a diagonal position, with my right ear resting on my right shoulder, and exposing the left side of my throat, and it was here—where the jugular vein throbs—that I felt the greatest intensity of cold. At once I shrugged my left shoulder, rubbing my neck with the collar of my coat in so doing. Immediately something fell off, upon the floor, and I again saw the finger.

My disgust—horror, were intensified when I perceived that it was dragging something after it, which might have been an old stocking, and which I took at first glance for something of the sort.

The evening sun shone in through my window, in a brilliant golden ray that lighted the object as it scrambled along. With this illumination I was able to distinguish what the object was. It is not easy to describe it, but I will make the attempt.

The finger I saw was solid and material; what it drew after it was neither, or was in a nebulous, protoplasmic condition. The finger was attached to a hand that was curdling into matter and in process of acquiring solidity; attached to the hand was an arm in a very filmy condition, and this arm belonged to a human body in a still more vaporous, immaterial condition. This was being dragged along the floor by the finger, just as a silkworm might pull after it the tangle of its web. I could see legs and arms, and head, and coat-tail tumbling about and interlacing and disentangling again in a promiscuous manner. There were no bone, no muscle, no substance in the figure; the members were attached to the trunk, which was spineless, but they had evidently no functions, and were wholly dependent on the finger which pulled them along in a jumble of parts as it advanced.

In such confusion did the whole vaporous matter seem, that I think—I cannot say for certain it was so, but the impression left on my mind was—that one of the eyeballs was looking out at a nostril, and the tongue lolling out of one of the ears.

It was, however, only for a moment that I saw this germ-body; I cannot call by another name that which had not more substance than smoke. I saw it only so long as it was being dragged athwart the ray of sunlight. The moment it was pulled jerkily out of the beam into the shadow beyond, I could see nothing of it, only the crawling finger.

I had not sufficient moral energy or physical force in me to rise, pursue, and stamp on the finger, and grind it with my heel into the floor. Both seemed drained out of me. What became of the finger, whither it went, how it managed to secrete itself, I do not know. I had lost the power to inquire. I sat in my chair, chilled, staring before me into space.

'Please, sir,' a voice said, 'there's Mr Square below, electrical engineer.'

'Eh?' I looked dreamily round.

My valet was at the door.

'Please, sir, the gentleman would be glad to be allowed to go over the house and see that all the electrical apparatus is in order.'

'Oh, indeed! Yes—show him up.'

III

I had recently placed the lighting of my house in the hands of an electrical engineer, a very intelligent man, Mr Square, for whom I had contracted a sincere friendship.

He had built a shed with a dynamo out of sight, and had entrusted the laying of the wires to subordinates, as he had been busy with other orders and could not personally watch every detail. But he was not the man to let anything pass unobserved, and he knew that electricity was not a force to be played with. Bad or careless workmen will often insufficiently protect the wires, or neglect the insertion of the lead which serves as a safety-valve in the event of the current being too strong. Houses may be set on fire, human beings fatally shocked, by the neglect of a bad or slovenly workman.

The apparatus for my mansion was but just completed, and Mr Square had come to inspect it and make sure that all was right.

He was an enthusiast in the matter of electricity, and saw for it a vast perspective, the limits of which could not be predicted.

'All forces', said he, 'are correlated. When you have force in one form, you may just turn it into this or that, as you like. In one form it is motive power, in another it is light, in another heat. Now we have electricity for illumination. We employ it, but not as freely as in the States, for propelling vehicles. Why should we have horses drawing our buses? We should use only electric trams. Why do we burn coal to warm our shins? There is electricity, which throws out no filthy smoke as does coal. Why should we let the tides waste their energies in the Thames? in other estuaries? There we have Nature supplying us—free, gratis, and for nothing—with all the force we want for propelling, for heating, for lighting. I will tell you something more, my dear sir,' said Mr Square. 'I have mentioned but three modes of force, and have instanced but a limited number of uses to which electricity may be turned. How is it with photography? Is not electric light becoming an artistic agent? I bet you', said he, 'before long it will become a therapeutic agent as well.'

'Oh, yes; I have heard of certain impostors with their life-belts.'

Mr Square did not relish this little dig I gave him. He winced, but returned to the charge. 'We don't know how to direct it aright, that is all,' said he. 'I haven't taken the matter up, but others will, I bet; and we shall have electricity used as freely as now we use powders and pills. I don't believe in doctors' stuffs myself. I hold that disease lays hold of a man because he lacks physical force to resist it. Now, is it not obvious that you are beginning at the wrong end when you attack the disease? What you want is to supply force, make up for the lack of physical power, and force is force wherever you find it—here motive, there illuminating, and so on. I don't see why a physician should not utilize the tide rushing out under London Bridge for restoring the feeble vigour of all who are languid and a prey to disorder in the Metropolis. It will come to that, I bet, and that is not all. Force is force, everywhere. Political, moral force, physical force, dynamic force, heat, light, tidal waves, and so on—all are one, all is one. In time we shall know how to galvanize into aptitude and moral energy all the limp and crooked consciences and wills that need taking in hand, and such there always will be in modern civilisation. I don't know how to do it. I don't know how it will be done, but in the future the priest as well as the doctor will turn electricity on as his principal, nay, his only agent. And he can get his force anywhere, out of the running stream, out of the wind, out of the tidal wave.

'I'll give you an instance,' continued Mr Square, chuckling and rubbing his hands, 'to show you the great possibilities in electricity, used in a crude fashion. In a certain great city away far west in the States, a go-ahead place, too, more so than New York, they had electric trams all up and down and along the roads to everywhere. The union men working for the company demanded that the non-unionists should be turned off. But the company didn't see it. Instead, it turned off the union men. It had up its sleeve a sufficiency of the others, and filled all places at once. Union men didn't like it, and passed word that at a given hour on a certain day every wire was to be cut. The company knew this by means of its spies, and turned on, ready for them, three times the power into all the wires. At the fixed moment, up the poles went the strikers to cut the cables, and down they came a dozen times quicker than they went up, I bet. Then there came wires to the hospitals from all quarters for stretchers to carry off the disabled men, some with broken legs, arms, ribs; two or three had their necks broken. I reckon the company was wonderfully merciful—it didn't put on sufficient force to make cinders of them then and there; possibly opinion might not have liked it. Stopped the strike, did that. Great moral effect—all done by electricity.'

In this manner Mr Square was wont to rattle on. He interested me, and I came to think that there might be something in what he said—that his suggestions were not mere nonsense. I was glad to see Mr Square enter my room, shown in by my man. I did not rise from my chair to shake his hand, for I had not sufficient energy to do so. In a languid tone I welcomed him and signed to him to take a seat. Mr Square looked at me with some surprise.

'Why, what's the matter?' he said. 'You seem unwell. Not got the 'flu, have you?'

'I beg your pardon?'

'The influenza. Every third person is crying out that he has it, and the sale of eucalyptus is enormous, not that eucalyptus is any good. Influenza microbes indeed! What care they for eucalyptus? You've gone down some steps of the ladder of life since I saw you last, squire. How do you account for that?'

I hesitated about mentioning the extraordinary circumstances that had occurred; but Square was a man who would not allow any beating about the bush. He was downright and straight, and in ten minutes had got the entire story out of me.

'Rather boisterous for your nerves that—a crawling finger,' said he. 'It's a queer story taken on end.'

Then he was silent, considering.

After a few minutes he rose, and said: 'I'll go and look at the fittings, and then I'll turn this little matter of yours over again, and see if I can't knock the bottom out of it, I'm kinder fond of these sort of things.'

Mr Square was not a Yankee, but he had lived for some time in America, and affected to speak like an American. He used expressions, terms of speech common in the States, but had none of the Transatlantic twang. He was a man absolutely without affectation in every other particular; this was his sole weakness, and it was harmless.

The man was so thorough in all he did that I did not expect his return immediately. He was certain to examine every portion of the dynamo engine, and all the connections and burners. This would necessarily engage him for some hours. As the day was nearly done, I knew he could not accomplish what he wanted that evening, and accordingly gave orders that a room should be prepared for him. Then, as my head was full of pain, and my skin was burning, I told my servant to apologize for my absence from dinner, and tell Mr Square that I was really forced to return to my bed by sickness, and that I believed I was about to be prostrated by an attack of influenza.

The valet—a worthy fellow, who has been with me for six years—was concerned at my appearance, and urged me to allow him to send for a doctor. I had no confidence in the local practitioner, and if I sent for another from the nearest town I should offend him, and a row would perhaps ensue, so I declined. If I were really in for an influenza attack, I knew about as much as any doctor how to deal with it. Quinine, quinine—that was all. I bade my man light a small lamp, lower it, so as to give sufficient illumination to enable me to find some lime-juice at my bed head, and my pocket-handkerchief, and to be able to read my watch. When he had done this, I bade him leave me.

I lay in bed, burning, racked with pain in my head, and with my eyeballs on fire.

Whether I fell asleep or went off my head for a while I cannot tell. I may have fainted. I have no recollection of anything after having gone to bed and taken a sip of lime-juice that tasted to me like soap—till I was roused by a sense of pain in my ribs—a slow, gnawing, torturing pain, waxing momentarily more intense. In half-consciousness I was partly dreaming and partly aware of actual suffering. The pain was real; but in my fancy I thought that a great maggot was working its way into my side between my ribs. I seemed to see it. It twisted itself half round, then reverted to its former position, and again twisted itself, moving like a ·bradawl, not like a gimlet, which latter forms a complete revolution.

This, obviously, must have been a dream, hallucination only, as I was lying on my back and my eyes were directed towards the bottom of the bed, and the coverlet and blankets and sheet intervened between my eyes and my side. But in fever one sees without eyes, and in every direction, and through all obstructions.

Roused thoroughly by an excruciating twinge, I tried to cry out, and succeeded in throwing myself over on my right side, that which was in pain. At once I felt the thing withdrawn that was awling—if I may use the word—in between my ribs.

And now I saw, standing beside the bed, a figure that had its arm under the bedclothes, and was slowly removing it. The hand was leisurely drawn from under the coverings and rested on the eiderdown coverlet, with the forefinger extended.

The figure was that of a man, in shabby clothes, with a sallow, mean face, a retreating forehead, with hair cut after the French fashion, and a moustache, dark. The jaws and chin were covered with a bristly growth, as if shaving had been neglected for a fortnight. The figure did not appear to be thoroughly solid, but to be of the consistency of curd, and the face was of the complexion of curd. As I looked at this object it withdrew, sliding backward in an odd sort of manner, and as though overweighted by the hand, which was the most substantial, indeed the only substantial portion of it. Though the figure retreated stooping, yet it was no longer huddled along by the finger, as if it had no material existence. If the same, it had acquired a consistency and a solidity which it did not possess before.

How it vanished I do not know, nor whither it went. The door opened, and Square came in.

'What!' he exclaimed with cheery voice; 'influenza is it?'

'I don't know—I think it's that finger again.'

IV

'Now, look here,' said Square, 'I'm not going to have that cuss at its pranks anymore. Tell me all about it.'

I was now so exhausted, so feeble, that I was not able to give a connected account of what had taken place, but Square put to me just a few pointed questions and elicited the main facts. He pieced them together in his own orderly mind, so as to form a connected whole. 'There is a feature in the case,' said he, 'that strikes me as remarkable and important. At first—a finger only, then a hand, then a nebulous figure attached to the hand, without backbone, without consistency. Lastly, a complete form, with consistency and with backbone, but the latter in a gelatinous condition, and the entire figure overweighted by the hand, just as hand and figure were previously overweighted by the finger. Simultaneously with this compacting and consolidating of the figure, came your degeneration and loss of vital force and, in a word, of health. What you lose, that object acquires, and what it acquires, it gains by contact with you. That's clear enough, is it not?'

'I dare say. I don't know. I can't think.'

'I suppose not; the faculty of thought is drained out of you. Very well, I must think for you, and I will. Force is force, and see if I can't deal with your visitant in such a way as will prove just as truly a moral dissuasive as that employed on the union men on strike in—never mind where it was. That's not to the point.'

'Will you kindly give me some lime-juice?' I entreated.

I sipped the acid draught, but without relief. I listened to Square, but without hope. I wanted to be left alone. I was weary of my pain, weary of everything, even of life. It was a matter of indifference to me whether I recovered or slipped out of existence.

'It will be here again shortly,' said the engineer. 'As the French say, *l'appetit vient en mangeant*. It has been at you thrice, it won't be content without another peck. And if it does get another, I guess it will pretty well about finish you.'

Mr Square rubbed his chin, and then put his hands into his trouser pockets. That also was a trick acquired in the States, an inelegant one. His hands, when not actively occupied, went into his pockets, inevitably they gravitated thither. Ladies did not like Square; they said he was not a gentleman. But it was not that he said or did anything 'off colour', only he spoke to them, looked at them, walked with them, always with his hands in his pockets. I have seen a lady turn her back on him deliberately because of this trick.

Standing now with his hands in his pockets, he studied my bed, and said contemptuously: 'Old-fashioned and bad, fourposter. Oughtn't to be allowed, I guess; unwholesome all the way round.'

I was not in a condition to dispute this. I like a fourposter with curtains at head and feet; not that I ever draw them, but it gives a sense of privacy that is wanting in one of your half-tester beds.

If there is a window at one's feet, one can lie in bed without the glare in one's eyes, and yet without darkening the room by drawing the blinds. There is much to be said for a fourposter, but this is not the place in which to say it.

Mr Square pulled his hands out of his pockets and began fiddling with the electric point near the head of my bed, attached a wire, swept it in a semicircle along the floor, and then thrust the knob at the end into my hand in the bed.

'Keep your eye open,' said he, 'and your hand shut and covered. If that finger comes again tickling your ribs, try it with the point. I'll manage the switch, from behind the curtain.'

Then he disappeared.

I was too indifferent in my misery to turn my head and observe where he was. I remained inert, with the knob in my hand, and my eyes closed, suffering and thinking of nothing but the shooting pains through my head and the aches in my loins and back and legs.

Some time probably elapsed before I felt the finger again at work at my ribs; it groped, but no longer bored. I now felt the entire hand, not a single finger, and the hand was substantial, cold, and clammy. I was aware, how, I know not, that if the finger-point reached the region of my heart, on the left side, the hand would, so to speak, sit down on it, with the cold palm over it, and that then immediately my heart would cease to beat, and it would be, as Square might express it, 'gone coon' with me.

In self-preservation I brought up the knob of the electric wire against the hand—against one of the fingers, I think—and at once was aware of a rapping, squealing noise. I turned my head languidly, and saw the form, now more substantial than before, capering in an ecstasy of pain, endeavouring fruitlessly to withdraw its arm from under the bed-clothes, and the hand from the electric point.

At the same moment Square stepped from behind the curtain, with a dry laugh, and said: 'I thought we should fix him. He has the coil about him, and can't escape. Now let us drop to particulars. But I shan't let you off till I know all about you.'

The last sentence was addressed, not to me, but to the apparition.

Thereupon he bade me take the point away from the hand of the figure—being—whatever it was, but to be ready with it at a moment's notice. He then proceeded to catechize my visitor, who moved restlessly within the circle of wire, but could not escape from it. It replied in a thin, squealing voice that sounded as if it came from a distance, and had a querulous tone in it. I do not pretend to give all that was said. I cannot recollect everything that passed. My memory was affected by my illness, as well as my body. Yet I prefer giving the scraps that I recollect to what Square told me he had heard.

'Yes—I was unsuccessful, always was. Nothing answered with me. The world was against me. Society was. I hate Society. I don't like work neither, never did. But I like agitating against what is established. I hate the Royal Family, the landed interest, the parsons, everything that is, except the people—that is, the unemployed. I always did. I couldn't get work as suited me. When I died they buried me in a cheap coffin, dirt cheap, and gave me a nasty grave, cheap, and a service rattled away cheap, and no monument. Didn't want none. Oh! there are lots of us. All discontented. Discontent! That's a passion, it is—it gets into the veins, it fills the brain, it occupies the heart; it's a sort of divine cancer that takes possession of the entire man, and makes him dissatisfied with everything, and hate everybody. But we must have our share of happiness at some time. We all crave for it in one way or other. Some think there's a future state of blessedness and so have hope, and look to attain to it, for hope is a cable and anchor that attaches to what is real, But when you have no hope of that sort, don't believe in any future state, you must look for happiness in life here. We didn't get it when we were alive, so we seek to procure it after we are dead. We can do it, if we can get out of our cheap and nasty coffins. But not till the greater part of us is mouldered away. If a finger or two remains, that can work its way up to the surface, those cheap deal coffins go to pieces quick enough. Then the only solid part of us left can pull the rest of us that has gone to nothing after it. Then we grope about after the living. The well-to-do if we can get at them—the honest working poor if we can't—we hate them too, because they are content and happy. If we reach any of these, and can touch them, then we can draw their vital force out of them into ourselves, and recuperate at their expense. That was about what I was going to do with you. Getting on famous.

Nearly solidified into a new man; and given another chance in life. But I've missed it this time. Just like my luck. Miss everything. Always have, except misery and disappointment. Get plenty of that.'

'What are you all?' asked Square. 'Anarchists out of employ?'

'Some of us go by that name, some by other designations, but we are all one, and own allegiance to but one monarch—Sovereign discontent. We are bred to have a distaste for manual work; and we grow up loafers, grumbling at everything and quarrelling with Society that is around us and the Providence that is above us.'

'And what do you call yourselves now?'

'Call ourselves? Nothing; we are the same, in another condition, that is all. Folk once called us Anarchists, Nihilists, Socialists, Levellers, now they call us the Influenza. The learned talk of microbes, and bacilli, and bacteria. Microbes, bacilli, and bacteria be blowed! We are the Influenza; we the social failures, the generally discontented, coming up out of our cheap and nasty graves in the form of physical disease. We are the Influenza.'

'There you are, I guess!' exclaimed Square triumphantly. 'Did I not say that all forces were correlated? If so, then all negations, deficiences of force are one in their several manifestations. Talk of Divine discontent as a force impelling to progress! Rubbish, it is a paralysis of energy. It turns all it absorbs to acid, to envy, spite, gall. It inspires nothing, but rots the whole moral system. Here you have it—moral, social, political discontent in another form, nay aspect—that is all. What Anarchism is in the body Politic, that Influenza is in the body Physical. Do you see that?'

'Ye-e-e-e-s,' I believe I answered, and dropped away into the land of dreams.

I recovered. What Square did with the Thing I know not, but believe that he reduced it again to its former negative and self-decomposing condition.

THE FEATHER PILLOW

Horacio Quiroga

Described as South America's nearest equivalent to Poe, Horacio Quiroga (1878–1937) was a superb storyteller whose own tragic life is reflected in his morbid psychological studies and Gothic horror tales. He spent many years in the jungles of northern Argentina, and his most popular stories were translated into English as *Jungle Tales*. 'The Feather Pillow', one of his most memorable weird tales, was originally published in 1907.

❦

ALICIA's entire honeymoon gave her hot and cold shivers. A blonde, angelic, and timid young girl, the childish fancies she had dreamed about being a bride had been chilled by her husband's rough character. She loved him very much, nonetheless, although sometimes she gave a light shudder when, as they returned home through the streets together at night, she cast a furtive glance at the impressive stature of her Jordan, who had been silent for an hour. He, for his part, loved her profoundly but never let it be seen.

For three months—they had been married in April—they lived in a special kind of bliss. Doubtless she would have wished less severity in the rigorous sky of love, more expansive and less cautious tenderness, but her husband's impassive manner always restrained her.

The house in which they lived influenced her chills and shuddering to no small degree. The whiteness of the silent patio—friezes, columns, and marble statues—produced the wintry impression of an enchanted palace. Inside the glacial brilliance of stucco, the completely bare walls, affirmed the sensation of unpleasant coldness. As one crossed from one room to another, the echo of his steps reverberated throughout the house, as if long abandonment had sensitized its resonance.

Alicia passed the autumn in this strange love nest. She had determined, however, to cast a veil over her former dreams and live like a sleeping beauty in the hostile house, trying not to think about anything until her husband arrived each evening.

It is not strange that she grew thin. She had a light attack of influenza that dragged on insidiously for days and days: after that Alicia's health never returned. Finally one afternoon she was able to go into the garden, supported on her husband's arm. She looked around listlessly. Suddenly Jordan, with deep tenderness, ran his hand very slowly over her head, and Alicia instantly burst into sobs, throwing her arms around his neck. For a long time she cried out all the fears she had kept silent, redoubling her weeping at Jordan's slightest caress. Then her sobs subsided, and she stood a long while, her face hidden in the hollow of his neck, not moving or speaking a word.

This was the last day Alicia was well enough to be up. On the following day she awakened feeling faint. Jordan's doctor examined her with minute attention, prescribing calm and absolute rest.

'I don't know,' he said to Jordan at the street door. 'She has a great weakness that I am unable to explain. And with no vomiting, nothing. . .if she wakes tomorrow as she did today, call me at once.'

When she awakened the following day, Alicia was worse. There was a consultation. It was agreed there was an anaemia of incredible progression, completely inexplicable. Alicia had no more fainting spells, but she was visibly moving toward death. The lights were lighted all day long in her bedroom, and there was complete silence. Hours went by without the slightest sound. Alicia dozed. Jordan virtually lived in the drawing room, which was also always lighted. With tireless persistence he paced ceaselessly from one end of the room to the other. The carpet swallowed his steps. At times he entered the bedroom and continued his silent pacing back and forth alongside the bed, stopping for an instant at each end to regard his wife.

Suddenly Alicia began to have hallucinations, vague images, at first seeming to float in the air, then descending to floor level. Her eyes excessively wide, she stared continuously at the carpet on either side of the head of her bed. One night she suddenly focused on one spot. Then she opened her mouth to scream, and pearls of sweat suddenly beaded her nose and lips.

'Jordan! Jordan!' she clamoured, rigid with fright, still staring at the carpet.

Jordan ran to the bedroom, and, when she saw him appear, Alicia screamed with terror.

'It's I, Alicia, it's I!'

Alicia looked at him confusedly; she looked at the carpet; she looked at him once again; and after a long moment of stupefied confrontation, she regained her senses. She smiled and took her husband's hand in hers, caressing it, trembling, for half an hour.

Among her most persistent hallucinations was that of an anthropoid poised on his fingertips on the carpet, staring at her.

The doctors returned, but to no avail. They saw before them a diminishing life, a life bleeding away day by day, hour by hour, absolutely without their knowing why. During their last consultation Alicia lay in a stupor while they took her pulse, passing her inert wrist from one to another. They observed her a long time in silence and then moved into the dining room.

'Phew. . .' The discouraged chief physician shrugged his shoulders. 'It is an inexplicable case. There is little we can do. . .'

'That's my last hope!' Jordan groaned. And he staggered blindly against the table.

Alicia's life was fading away in the subdelirium of anaemia, a delirium which grew worse through the evening hours but which let up somewhat after dawn. The illness never worsened during the daytime, but each morning she awakened pale as death, almost in a swoon. It seemed only at night that her life drained out of her in new waves of blood. Always when she awakened she had the sensation of lying collapsed in the bed with a million-pound weight on top of her. Following the third day of this relapse she never left her bed again. She could scarcely move her head. She did not want her bed to be touched, not even to have her bedcovers arranged. Her crepuscular terrors advanced now in the form of monsters that dragged themselves toward the bed and laboriously climbed upon the bedspread.

Then she lost consciousness. The final two days she raved ceaselessly in a weak voice. The lights funereally illuminated the bedroom and drawing room. In the deathly silence of the house the only sound was the monotonous delirium from the bedroom and the dull echoes of Jordan's eternal pacing.

Finally, Alicia died. The servant, when she came in afterward to strip the now empty bed, stared wonderingly for a moment at the pillow.

'Sir!' she called Jordan in a low voice. 'There are stains on the pillow that look like blood.'

Jordan approached rapidly and bent over the pillow. Truly, on the case, on both sides of the hollow left by Alicia's head, were two small dark spots.

'They look like punctures,' the servant murmured after a moment of motionless observation.

'Hold it up to the light,' Jordan told her.

The servant raised the pillow but immediately dropped it and stood staring at it, livid and trembling. Without knowing why, Jordan felt the hair rise on the back of his neck.

'What is it?' he murmured in a hoarse voice.

'It's very heavy,' the servant whispered, still trembling.

Jordan picked it up; it was extraordinarily heavy. He carried it out of the room, and on the dining room table he ripped open the case and the ticking with a slash. The top feathers floated away, and the servant, her mouth opened wide, gave a scream of horror and covered her face with her clenched fists: in the bottom of the pillowcase, among the feathers, slowly moving its hairy legs, was a monstrous animal, a living, viscous ball. It was so swollen one could scarcely make out its mouth.

Night after night, since Alicia had taken to her bed, this abomination had stealthily applied its mouth—its proboscis one might better say—to the girl's temples, sucking her blood. The puncture was scarcely perceptible. The daily plumping of the pillow had doubtlessly at first impeded its progress, but as soon as the girl could no longer move, the suction became vertiginous. In five days, in five nights, the monster had drained Alicia's life away.

These parasites of feathered creatures, diminutive in their habitual environment, reach enormous proportions under certain conditions. Human blood seems particularly favourable to them, and it is not rare to encounter them in feather pillows.

THE SINGULAR DEATH
OF MORTON

Algernon Blackwood

Algernon Blackwood (1869–1951) is undoubtedly in the first rank of horror writers. Always interested in the occult and nature mysticism, he was a member of the Hermetic Order of the Golden Dawn (which attracted several close acquaintances of Stoker, including Pamela Colman Smith and J.W. Brodie Innes, and writers such as Arthur Machen and A.E. Waite). One of Blackwood's most famous stories, 'The Transfer', has a vampiric theme; but none of his published collections contained his only traditional vampire tale, 'The Singular Death of Morton', which appears here in print for the first time since its original appearance over 75 years ago in *The Tramp* magazine (December 1910), illustrated by F. Gregory Brown.

❧

Dusk was melting into darkness as the two men slowly made their way through the dense forest of spruce and fir that clothed the flanks of the mountain. They were weary with the long climb, for neither was in his first youth, and the July day had been a hot one. Their little inn lay further in the valley among the orchards that separated the forest from the vineyards.

Neither of them talked much. The big man led the way, carrying the knapsack, and his companion, older, shorter, evidently the more fatigued of the two, followed with small footsteps. From time to time he stumbled among the loose rocks. An exceptionally observant mind would possibly have divined that his stumbling was not entirely due to fatigue, but to an absorption of spirit that made him careless how he walked.

'All right behind?' the big man would call from time to time, half glancing back.

'Eh? What?' the other would reply, startled out of a reverie.

'Pace too fast?'

'Not a bit. I'm coming.' And once he added: 'You might hurry on and see to supper, if you feel like it. I shan't be long behind you.'

But his big friend did not adopt the suggestion. He kept the same

distance between them. He called out the same question at intervals,
Once or twice *he* stopped and looked back too.

In this way they came at length to the skirts of the wood. A deep
hush covered all the valley; the limestone ridges they had climbed
gleamed down white and ghostly upon them from the fading sky.
Midway in its journeys, the evening wind dropped suddenly to watch
the beauty of the moonlight—to hold the branches still so that the light
might slip between and weave its silver pattern on the moss below.

And, as they stood a moment to take it in, a step sounded behind
them on the soft pine-needles, and the older man, still a little in the rear,
turned with a start as though he had been suddenly called by name.

'There's that girl—again!' he said, and his voice expressed a curious
mingling of pleasure, surprise and—apprehension.

Into a patch of moonlight passed the figure of a young girl, looked at
them as though about to stop yet thinking better of it, smiled softly,
and moved on out of sight into the surrounding darkness. The moon
just caught her eyes and teeth, so that they shone; the rest of her body
stood in shadow; the effect was striking—almost as though head and
shoulders hung alone in mid air, watching them with this shining
smile, then fading away.

'Come on, for heaven's sake,' the big man cried. There was
impatience in his manner, not unkindness. The other lingered a
moment, peering closely into the gloom where the girl had vanished.
His friend repeated his injunction, and a moment later the two had
emerged upon the high road with the village lights in sight beyond, and
the forest left behind them like a vast mantle that held the night within
its folds.

For some minutes neither of them spoke; then the big man waited for
his friend to draw up alongside.

'About all this valley of the Jura,' he said presently, 'there seems to
me something—rather weird.' He shifted the knapsack vigorously on
his back. It was a gesture of unconscious protest. 'Something uncanny,'
he added, as he set a good pace.

'But extraordinarily beautiful——'

'It attracts you more than it does me, I think,' was the short reply.

'The picturesque superstitions still survive here,' observed the older
man. 'They touch the imagination in spite of oneself.'

A pause followed during which the other tried to increase the pace.
The subject evidently made him impatient for some reason.

'Perhaps,' he said presently. 'Though I think myself it's due to the
curious loneliness of the place. I mean, we're in the middle of
tourist-Europe here, yet so utterly remote. It's such a neglected little
corner of the world. The contradiction bewilders. Then, being so near
the frontier, too, with the clock changing an hour a mile from the
village, makes one think of time as unreal and imaginary.' He laughed.

He produced several other reasons as well. His friend admitted their value, and agreed half-heartedly. He still turned occasionally to look back. The mountain ridge where they had climbed was clearly visible in the moonlight.

'Odd,' he said, 'but I don't see that farmhouse where we got the milk anywhere. It ought to be easily visible from here.'

'Hardly—in this light. It was a queer place rather, I thought,' he added. He did not deny the curiously suggestive atmosphere of the region, he merely wanted to find satisfactory explanations. 'A case in point, I mean. I didn't like it quite—that farmhouse—yet I'm hanged if I know why. It made me feel uncomfortable. That girl appeared so suddenly, although the place seemed deserted. And her silence was so odd. Why in the world couldn't she answer a single question? I'm glad I didn't take the milk. I spat it out. I'd like to know where she got it from, for there was no sign of a cow or a goat to be seen anywhere!'

'I swallowed mine—in spite of the taste,' said the other, half smiling at his companion's sudden volubility.

Very abruptly, then, the big man turned and faced his friend. Was it merely an effect of the moonlight, or had his skin really turned pale beneath the sunburn?

'I say, old man,' he said, his face grave and serious, 'What do you think she was? What made her seem like that, and why the devil do you think she followed us?'

'I think,' was the slow reply, 'it was *me* she was following.'

The words, and particularly the tone of conviction in which they were spoken, clearly were displeasing to the big man, who already regretted having spoken so frankly what was in his mind. With a companion so imaginative, so impressionable, so nervous, it had been foolish and unwise. He led the way home at a pace that made the other arrive five minutes in his rear, panting, limping and perspiring as if he had been running.

'I'm rather for going on into Switzerland tomorrow, or the next day,' he ventured that night in the darkness of their two-bedded room. 'I think we've had enough of this place. Eh? What do you think?'

But there was no answer from the bed across the room, for its occupant was sound asleep and snoring.

'Dead tired, I suppose!' he muttered to himself, and then turned over to follow his friend's example. But for a long time sleep refused him. Queer, unwelcome thoughts and feelings kept him awake—of a kind he rarely knew, and thoroughly disliked. It was rubbish, yet it made him uncomfortable, so that his nerves tingled. He tossed about in the bed. 'I'm overtired,' he persuaded himself, 'that's all.'

The strange feelings that kept him thus awake were not easy to analyse, perhaps, but their origin was beyond all question: they grouped themselves about the picture of that deserted, tumble-down châlet on the mountain ridge where they had stopped for refreshment a few hours before. It was a farmhouse, dilapidated and dirty, and the name stood in big black letters against a blue background on the wall above the door: 'La Chenille.' Yet not a living soul was to be seen anywhere about it; the doors were fastened, windows shuttered; chimneys smokeless; dirt, neglect and decay everywhere in evidence.

Then, suddenly, as they had turned to go, after much vain shouting and knocking at the door, a face appeared for an instant at a window, the shutter of which was half open. His friend saw it first, and called aloud. The face nodded in reply, and presently a young girl came round the corner of the house, apparently by a back door, and stood staring at them both from a little distance.

And from that very instant, so far as he could remember, these queer feelings had entered his heart—fear, distrust, misgiving. The thought of it now, as he lay in bed in the darkness, made his hair rise. There was something about that girl that struck cold into the soul. Yet she was a mere slip of a thing, very pretty, seductive even, with a certain serpent-like fascination about her eyes and movements; and although she only replied to their questions as to refreshment with a smile, uttering no single word, she managed to convey the impression that she was a managing little person who might make herself very disagreeable if she chose. In spite of her undeniable charm there was about her an atmosphere of something sinister. He himself did most of the questioning, but it was his older friend who had the benefit of her smile. Her eyes hardly ever left his face, and once she had slipped quite close to him and touched his arm.

The strange part of it now seemed to him that he could not remember in the least how she was dressed, or what was the colouring of her eyes and hair. It was almost as though he had *felt*, rather than seen, her presence.

The milk—she produced a jug and two wooden bowls after a brief disappearance round the corner of the house—was—well, it tasted so odd that he had been unable to swallow it, and had spat it out. His friend, on the other hand, savage with thirst, had drunk his bowl to the last drop too quickly to taste it even, and, while he drank, had kept his eyes fixed on those of the girl, who stood close in front of him.

And from that moment his friend had somehow changed. On the way down he said things that were unusual, talking chiefly about the 'Chenille', and the girl, and the delicious, delicate flavour of the milk, yet all phrased in such a way that it sounded singular, unfamiliar, unpleasant even. Now that he tried to recall the sentences the actual words evaded him; but the memory of the uneasiness and apprehension they caused him to feel remained. And night ever italicizes such memories!

Then, to cap it all, the girl had followed them. It was wholly foolish and absurd to feel the things he did feel; yet there the feelings were, and what was the good of arguing? That girl frightened him; the change in his friend was in some way or other a danger signal. More than this he could not tell. An explanation might come later, but for the present his chief desire was to get away from the place and to get his friend away, too.

And on this thought sleep overtook him—heavily.

The windows were wide open; outside was a garden with a rather high enclosing wall, and at the far end a gate that was kept locked because it led into private fields and so, by a back way, to the cemetery and the little church. When it was open the guests of the inn made use of it and got lost in the network of fields and vines, for there was no proper route that way to the road or the mountains. They usually ended up prematurely in the cemetery, and got back to the village by passing through the church, which was always open; or by knocking at the kitchen doors of the other houses and explaining their position. Hence the gate was locked now to save trouble.

After several hours of hot, unrefreshing sleep the big man turned in his bed and woke. He tried to stretch, but couldn't; then sat up panting with a sense of suffocation. And by the faint starlight of the summer night, he saw next that his friend was up and moving about the room. Remembering that sometimes he walked in his sleep, he called to him gently:

'Morton, old chap,' he said in a low voice, with a touch of authority in it, 'go back to bed! You've walked enough for one day!'

And the figure, obeying as sleep-walkers often will, passed across the room and disappeared among the shadows over his bed. The other plunged and burrowed himself into a comfortable position again for sleep, but the heat of the room, the shortness of the bed, and this tiresome interruption of his slumbers made it difficult to lose consciousness. He forced his eyes to keep shut, and his body to cease from fidgeting, but there was something nibbling at his mind like a spirit mouse that never permitted him to cross the frontier into actual oblivion. He slept with one eye open, as the saying is. Odours of hay and flowers and baked ground stole in through the open window; with them, too, came from time to time sounds—little sounds that disturbed him without being ever loud enough to claim definite attention.

Perhaps, after all, he did lose consciousness for a moment—when, suddenly, a thought came with a sharp rush into his mind and galvanized him once more into utter wakefulness. It amazed him that he had not grasped it before. It was this: the figure he had seen was *not the figure of his friend*.

Alarm gripped him at once before he could think or argue, and a cold perspiration broke out all over his body. He fumbled for matches, couldn't find them; then, remembering there was electric light, he scraped the wall with his fingers—and turned on the little white switch. In the sudden glare that filled the room he saw instantly that his friend's bed was no longer occupied. And his mind, then acting instinctively, without process of conscious reasoning, flew like a flash to their walk of the day—to the tumble-down 'Chenille,' the glass of milk, the odd behaviour of his friend, and—to the girl.

At the same second he noticed that the odour in the room which hitherto he had taken to be the composite odour of fields, flowers and night, was really something else: it was the odour of freshly turned earth. Immediately on the top of this discovery came another. Those slight sounds he had heard outside the window were not ordinary night-sounds, the murmur of wind and insects: they were footsteps moving softly, stealthily down the little paths of crushed granite.

He was dressed in wonderful short order, noticing as he did so that his friend's night-garments lay upon the bed, and that he, too, had therefore dressed; further—that the door had been unlocked and stood half an inch ajar. There was now no question that he *had* slept again: between the present and the moment when he had seen the figure there had been a considerable interval. A couple of minutes later he had made his way cautiously downstairs and was standing on the garden path in the moonlight. And as he stood there, his mind filled with the stories the proprietor had told a few days before of the superstitions that still lived in the popular imagination and haunted this little, remote pine-clad valley. The thought of that girl sickened him. The odour of newly-turned earth remained in his nostrils and made his gorge rise. Utterly and vigorously he rejected the monstrous fictions he had heard, yet for all that, could not prevent their touching his imagination as he stood there in the early hours of the morning, alone with night and silence. The spell was undeniable; only a mind without sensibility could have ignored it.

He searched the little garden from end to end. Empty! Opposite the high gate he stopped, peering through the iron bars, wet with dew to his hands. Far across the intervening fields he fancied something moved. A second later he was sure of it. Something down there to the right beyond the trees was astir. It was in the cemetery.

And this definite discovery sent a shudder of terror and disgust through him from head to foot. He framed the name of his friend with his lips, yet the sound did not come forth. Some deeper instinct warned him to hold it back. Instead, after incredible efforts, he climbed that iron gate and dropped down into the soaking grass upon the other side. Then, taking advantage of all the cover he could find, he ran, swiftly and stealthily, towards the cemetery. On the way, without quite knowing why he did so, he picked up a heavy stick; and a moment later he stood beside the low wall that separated the fields from the churchyard—stood and stared.

There, beside the tombstones, with their hideous metal wreaths and crowns of faded flowers, he made out the figure of his friend; he was stooping, crouched down upon the ground; behind him rose a couple of bushy yew trees, against the dark of which his form was easily visible. He was not alone; in front of him, bending close over him it seemed, was another figure—a slight, shadowy, slim figure.

This time the big man found his voice and called aloud:

'Morton, Morton!' he cried. 'What, in the name of heaven, are you doing? What's the matter——?'

And the instant his deep voice broke the stillness of the night with its clamour, the little figure, half hiding his friend, turned about and faced him. He saw a white face with shining eyes and teeth as the form rose; the moonlight painted it with its own strange pallor; it was weird, unreal, horrible; and across the mouth, downwards from the lips to the chin, ran a deep stain of crimson.

The next moment the figure slid with a queer, gliding motion towards the trees, and disappeared among the yews and tombstones in the direction of the church. The heavy stick, hurled whirling after it, fell harmlessly half way, knocking a metal cross from its perch upon an upright grave; and the man who had thrown it raced full speed towards the huddled up figure of his friend, hardly noticing the thin, wailing cry that rose trembling through the night air from the vanished form. Nor did he notice more particularly that several of the graves, newly made, showed signs of recent disturbance, and that the odour of turned earth he had noticed in the room grew stronger. All his attention was concentrated upon the figure at his feet.

'Morton, man, get up! Wake for God's sake! You've been walking in——'

Then the words died upon his lips. The unnatural attitude of his friend's shoulders, and the way the head dropped back to show the neck, struck him like a blow in the face. There was no sign of movement. He lifted the body up and carried it, all limp and unresisting, by ways he never remembered afterwards, back to the inn.

It was all a dreadful nightmare—a nightmare that carried over its ghastly horror into waking life. He knew that the proprietor and his wife moved busily to and fro about the bed, and that in due course the village doctor was upon the scene, and that he was giving a muddled and feverish description of all he knew, telling how his friend was a confirmed sleep-walker and all the rest. But he did not realize the truth until he saw the face of the doctor as he straightened up from the long examination.

'Will you wake him?' he heard himself asking, 'or let him sleep it out till morning?' And the doctor's expression, even before the reply came to confirm it, told him the truth. 'Ah, monsieur, your friend will not ever wake again, I fear! It is the heart, you see; *hélas*, it is sudden failure of the heart!'

The final scenes in the little tragedy which thus brought his holiday to so abrupt and terrible a close need no description, being in no way essential to this strange story. There were one or two curious details, however, that came to light afterwards. One was, that for some weeks before there had been signs of disturbance among newly-made graves in the cemetery, which the authorities had been trying to trace to the nightly wanderings of the village madman—in vain; and another, that the morning after the death a trail of blood had been found across the church floor, as though someone had passed through from the back entrance to the front. A special service was held that very week to cleanse the holy building from the evil of that stain; for the villagers, deep in their superstitions, declared that nothing human had left that trail; nothing could have made those marks but a vampire disturbed at midnight in its awful occupation among the dead.

Apart from such idle rumours, however, the bereaved carried with him to this day certain other remarkable details which cannot be so easily dismissed. For he had a brief conversation with the doctor, it appears, that impressed him profoundly. And the doctor, an intelligent man, prosaic as granite into the bargain, had questioned him rather closely as to the recent life and habits of his dead friend. The account of their climb to the 'Chenille' he heard with an amazement he could not conceal.

'But no such châlet exists,' he said. 'There is no "Chenille". A long time ago, fifty years or more, there was such a place, but it was destroyed by the authorities on account of the evil reputation of the people who lived there. They burnt it. Nothing remains today but a few bits of broken wall and foundation.'

'Evil reputation——?'

The doctor shrugged his shoulders 'Travellers, even peasants, disappeared,' he said. 'An old woman lived there with her daughter, and poisoned milk was supposed to be used. But the neighbourhood accused them of worse than ordinary murder——'

'In what way?'

'Said the girl was a vampire,' answered the doctor shortly.

And, after a moment's hesitation, he added, turning his face away as he spoke:

'It was a curious thing, though, that tiny hole in your friend's throat, small as a pin-prick, yet so deep. And the heart—did I tell you?—was almost completely drained of blood.'

AYLMER VANCE AND THE VAMPIRE

Alice and Claude Askew

Among the literary psychic detectives who investigated ghosts, vampires, elementals, and other occult manifestations during the twenty years preceding the First World War, the most celebrated were Algernon Blackwood's John Silence, William Hope Hodgson's John Carnacki, Hesketh Prichard's Flaxman Low, and of course Bram Stoker's great Professor Abraham Van Helsing. One of the least known is Aylmer Vance, who investigated a baffling series of cases in the pages of the *Weekly Tale-Teller* during the summer of 1914. He was the creation of the very popular husband and wife writers Alice and Claude Askew, best known for their novels *The Shulamite* and *The Etonian*. They were an amazingly hardworking and prolific couple, often seen in their leisure and social hours adding a quick two thousand words to a joint manuscript whenever a party flagged. Although they produced over a hundred volumes (in little more than twelve years), the Aylmer Vance stories were never collected in book form. The Askews died heroically when a hospital ship sank on 5 October 1917.

AYLMER VANCE had rooms in Dover Street, Piccadilly, and now that I had decided to follow in his footsteps and to accept him as my instructor in matters psychic, I found it convenient to lodge in the same house. Aylmer and I quickly became close friends, and he showed me how to develop that faculty of clairvoyance which I had possessed without being aware of it. And I may say at once that this particular faculty of mine proved of service on several important occasions.

At the same time I made myself useful to Vance in other ways, not the least of which was that of acting as recorder of his many strange adventures. For himself, he never cared much about publicity, and it was some time before I could persuade him, in the interests of science, to allow me to give any detailed account of his experiences to the world

The incidents which I will now narrate occurred very soon after we had taken up our residence together, and while I was still, so to speak, a novice.

It was about ten o'clock in the morning that a visitor was announced. He sent up a card which bore upon it the name of Paul Davenant.

The name was familiar to me, and I wondered if this could be the same Mr Davenant who was so well known for his polo playing and for his success as an amateur rider, especially over the hurdles? He was a young man of wealth and position, and I recollected that he had married, about a year ago, a girl who was reckoned the greatest beauty of the season. All the illustrated papers had given their portraits at the time, and I remember thinking what a remarkably handsome couple they made.

Mr Davenant was ushered in, and at first I was uncertain as to whether this could be the individual whom I had in mind, so wan and pale and ill did he appear. A finely-built, upstanding man at the time of his marriage, he had now acquired a languid droop of the shoulders and a shuffling gait, while his face, especially about the lips, was bloodless to an alarming degree.

And yet it was the same man, for behind all this I could recognize the shadow of the good looks that had once distinguished Paul Davenant.

He took the chair which Aylmer offered him—after the usual preliminary civilities had been exchanged—and then glanced doubtfully in my direction. 'I wish to consult you privately, Mr Vance,' he said. 'The matter is of considerable importance to myself, and, if I may say so, of a somewhat delicate nature.'

Of course I rose immediately to withdraw from the room, but Vance laid his hand upon my arm.

'If the matter is connected with research in my particular line, Mr Davenant,' he said, 'if there is any investigation you wish me to take up on your behalf, I shall be glad if you will include Mr Dexter in your confidence. Mr Dexter assists me in my work. But, of course—.'

'Oh, no,' interrupted the other, 'if that is the case, pray let Mr Dexter remain. I think,' he added, glancing at me with a friendly smile, 'that you are an Oxford man, are you not, Mr Dexter? It was before my time, but I have heard of your name in connection with the river. You rowed at Henley, unless I am very much mistaken.'

I admitted the fact, with a pleasurable sensation of pride. I was very keen upon rowing in those days, and a man's prowess at school and college always remain dear to his heart.

After this we quickly became on friendly terms, and Paul Davenant proceeded to take Aylmer and myself into his confidence.

He began by calling attention to his personal appearance. 'You would hardly recognize me for the same man I was a year ago,' he said. 'I've been losing flesh steadily for the last six months. I came up from Scotland about a week ago, to consult a London doctor. I've seen two—in fact, they've held a sort of consultation over me—but the result, I may say, is far from satisfactory. They don't seem to know what is really the matter with me.'

'Anaemia—heart,' suggested Vance. He was scrutinizing his visitor keenly, and yet without any particular appearance of doing so. 'I believe it not infrequently happens that you athletes overdo yourselves—put too much strain upon the heart—'

'My heart is quite sound,' responded Davenant. 'Physically it is in perfect condition. The trouble seems to be that it hasn't enough blood to pump into my veins. The doctors wanted to know if I had met with an accident involving a great loss of blood—but I haven't. I've had no accident at all, and as for anaemia, well, I don't seem to show the ordinary symptoms of it. The inexplicable thing is that I've lost blood without knowing it, and apparently this has been going on for some time, for I've been getting steadily worse. It was almost imperceptible at first—not a sudden collapse, you understand, but a gradual failure of health.'

'I wonder,' remarked Vance slowly, 'what induced you to consult me? For you know, of course, the direction in which I pursue my investigations. May I ask if you have reason to consider that your state of health is due to some cause which we may describe as super-physical?'

A slight colour came to Davenant's white cheeks.

'There are curious circumstances,' he said in a low and earnest tone of voice. 'I've been turning them over in my mind, trying to see light through them. I daresay it's all the sheerest folly—and I must tell you that I'm not in the least a superstitious sort of man. I don't mean to say that I'm absolutely incredulous, but I've never given thought to such things—I've led too active a life. But, as I have said, there are curious circumstances about my case, and that is why I decided upon consulting you.'

'Will you tell me everything without reserve?' said Vance. I could see that he was interested. He was sitting up in his chair, his feet supported on a stool, his elbows on his knees, his chin in his hands—a favourite attitude of his. 'Have you,' he suggested, slowly, 'any mark upon your body, anything that you might associate, however remotely, with your present weakness and ill-health?'

'It's a curious thing that you should ask me that question,' returned Davenant, 'because I have got a curious mark, a sort of scar, that I can't account for. But I showed it to the doctors, and they assured me that it could have nothing whatever to do with my condition. In any case, if it had, it was something altogether outside their experience. I think they imagined it to be nothing more than a birthmark, a sort of mole, for they asked me if I'd had it all my life. But that I can swear I haven't. I only noticed it for the first time about six months ago, when my health began to fail. But you can see for yourself.'

He loosened his collar and bared his throat. Vance rose and made a careful scrutiny of the suspicious mark. It was situated a very little to the left of the central line, just above the clavicle, and, as Vance pointed out, directly over the big vessels of the throat. My friend called to me so that I might examine it, too. Whatever the opinion of the doctors may have been, Aylmer was obviously deeply interested.

And yet there was very little to show. The skin was quite intact, and there was no sign of inflammation. There were two red marks, about an inch apart, each of which was inclined to be crescent in shape. They were more visible than they might otherwise have been owing to the peculiar whiteness of Davenant's skin.

'It can't be anything of importance,' said Davenant, with a slightly uneasy laugh. 'I'm inclined to think the marks are dying away.'

'Have you ever noticed them more inflamed than they are at present?' inquired Vance. 'If so, was it at any special time?'

Davenant reflected. 'Yes,' he replied slowly, 'there have been times, usually, I think perhaps invariably, when I wake up in the morning, that I've noticed them larger and more angry looking. And I've felt a slight sensation of pain—a tingling—oh, very slight, and I've never worried about it. Only now you suggest it to my mind, I believe that those same mornings I have felt particularly tired and done up—a sensation of lassitude absolutely unusual to me. And once, Mr Vance, I remember quite distinctly that there was a stain of blood close to the mark. I didn't think anything of it at the time, and just wiped it away '

'I see.' Aylmer Vance resumed his seat and invited his visitor to do the same. 'And now,' he resumed, 'you said, Mr Davenant, that there are certain peculiar circumstances you wish to acquaint me with. Will you do so?'

And so Davenant readjusted his collar and proceeded to tell his story. I will tell it as far as I can, without any reference to the occasional interruptions of Vance and myself.

Paul Davenant, as I have said, was a man of wealth and position, and so, in every sense of the word, he was a suitable husband for Miss Jessica MacThane, the young lady who eventually became his wife. Before coming to the incidents attending his loss of health, he had a great deal to recount about Miss MacThane and her family history.

She was of Scottish descent, and although she had certain characteristic features of her race, she was not really Scotch in appearance. Hers was the beauty of the far South rather than that of the Highlands from which she had her origin. Names are not always suited to their owners, and Miss MacThane's was peculiarly inappropriate. She had, in fact, been christened Jessica in a sort of pathetic effort to counteract her obvious departure from normal type. There was a reason for this which we were soon to learn.

Miss MacThane was especially remarkable for her wonderful red hair, hair such as one hardly ever sees outside of Italy—not the Celtic red—and it was so long that it reached to her feet, and it had an extraordinary gloss upon it so that it seemed almost to have individual life of its own. Then she had just the complexion that one would expect with such hair, the purest ivory white, and not in the least marred by freckles, as is so often the case with red-haired girls. Her beauty was derived from an ancestress who had been brought to Scotland from some foreign shore—no one knew exactly whence.

Davenant fell in love with her almost at once and he had every reason to believe, in spite of her many admirers, that his love was returned. At this time he knew very little about her personal history. He was aware only that she was very wealthy in her own right, an orphan, and the last representative of a race that had once been famous in the annals of history—or rather infamous, for the MacThanes had distinguished themselves more by cruelty and lust of blood than by deeds of chivalry. A clan of turbulent robbers in the past, they had helped to add many a blood-stained page to the history of their country.

Jessica had lived with her father, who owned a house in London, until his death when she was about fifteen years of age. Her mother had died in Scotland when Jessica was still a tiny child. Mr MacThane had been so affected by his wife's death that, with his little daughter, he had abandoned his Scotch estate altogether—or so it was believed—leaving it to the management of a bailiff—though, indeed, there was but little work for the bailiff to do, since there were practically no tenants left. Blackwick Castle had borne for many years a most unenviable reputation.

After the death of her father, Miss MacThane had gone to live with a certain Mrs Meredith, who was a connection of her mother's—on her father's side she had not a single relation left. Jessica was absolutely the last of a clan once so extensive that intermarriage had been a tradition of the family, but for which the last two hundred years had been gradually dwindling to extinction.

Mrs Meredith took Jessica into Society—which would never have been her privilege had Mr MacThane lived, for he was a moody, self-absorbed man, and prematurely old—one who seemed worn down by the weight of a great grief.

Well, I have said that Paul Davenant quickly fell in love with Jessica, and it was not long before he proposed for her hand. To his great surprise, for he had good reason to believe that she cared for him, he met with a refusal; nor would she give any explanation, though she burst into a flood of pitiful tears.

Bewildered and bitterly disappointed, he consulted Mrs Meredith, with whom he happened to be on friendly terms, and from her he learnt that Jessica had already had several proposals, all from quite desirable men, but that one after another had been rejected.

Paul consoled himself with the reflection that perhaps Jessica did not love them, whereas he was quite sure that she cared for himself. Under these circumstances he determined to try again.

He did so, and with better result. Jessica admitted her love, but at the same time she repeated that she would not marry him. Love and marriage were not for her. Then, to his utter amazement, she declared that she had been born under a curse—a curse which, sooner or later was bound to show itself in her, and which, moreover, must react cruelly, perhaps fatally, upon anyone with whom she linked her life. How could she allow a man she loved to take such a risk? Above all, since the evil was hereditary, there was one point upon which she had quite made up her mind: no child should ever call her mother—she must be the last of her race indeed.

Of course, Davenant was amazed and inclined to think that Jessica had got some absurd idea into her head which a little reasoning on his part would dispel. There was only one other possible explanation. Was it lunacy she was afraid of?

But Jessica shook her head, She did not know of any lunacy in her family. The ill was deeper, more subtle than that. And then she told him all that she knew.

The curse—she made us of that word for want of a better—was attached to the ancient race from which she had her origin. Her father had suffered from it, and his father and grandfather before him. All three had taken to themselves young wives who had died mysteriously, of some wasting disease, within a few years. Had they observed the ancient family tradition of intermarriage this might possibly not have happened, but in their case, since the family was so near extinction, this had not been possible.

For the curse—or whatever it was—did not kill those who bore the name of MacThane. It only rendered them a danger to others. It was as if they absorbed from the blood-soaked walls of their fatal castle a deadly taint which reacted terribly upon those with whom they were brought into contact, especially their nearest and dearest.

'Do you know what my father said we have it in us to become?' said Jessica with a shudder. 'He used the word vampires. Paul, think of it—vampires—preying upon the life blood of others.'

And then, when Davenant was inclined to laugh, she checked him. 'No,' she cried out, 'it is not impossible. Think. We are a decadent race. From the earliest times our history has been marked by bloodshed and cruelty. The walls of Blackwick Castle are impregnated with evil— every stone could tell its tale of violence, pain, lust, and murder. What can one expect of those who have spent their lifetime between its walls?'

'But you have not done so,' exclaimed Paul. 'You have been spared that, Jessica. You were taken away after your mother died, and you have no recollection of Blackwick Castle, none at all. And you need never set foot in it again.'

'I'm afraid the evil is in my blood,' she replied sadly, 'although I am unconscious of it now. And as for not returning to Blackwick—I'm not sure I can help myself. At least, that is what my father warned me of. He said there is something there, some compelling force, that will call me to it in spite of myself. But, oh, I don't know—I don't know, and that is what makes it so difficult. If I could only believe that all this is nothing but an idle superstition, I might be happy again, for I have it in me to enjoy life, and I'm young, very young, but my father told me these things when he was on his death-bed.' She added the last words in a low, awe-stricken tone.

Paul pressed her to tell him all that she knew, and eventually she revealed another fragment of family history which seemed to have some bearing upon the case. It dealt with her own astonishing likeness to that ancestress of a couple of hundred years ago, whose existence seemed to have presaged the gradual downfall of the clan of the MacThanes.

A certain Robert MacThane, departing from the traditions of his family, which demanded that he should not marry outside his clan, brought home a wife from foreign shores, a woman of wonderful beauty, who was possessed of glowing masses of red hair and a complexion of ivory whiteness—such as had more or less distinguished since then every female of the race born in the direct line.

It was not long before this woman came to be regarded in the neighbourhood as a witch. Queer stories were circulated abroad as to her doings, and the reputation of Blackwick Castle became worse than ever before.

And then one day she disappeared. Robert MacThane had been absent upon some business for twenty-four hours, and it was upon his return that he found her gone. The neighbourhood was searched, but without avail, and then Robert, who was a violent man and who had adored his foreign wife, called together certain of his tenants whom he suspected, rightly or wrongly, of foul play, and had them murdered in cold blood. Murder was easy in those days, yet such an outcry was raised that Robert had to take to flight, leaving his two children in the care of their nurse, and for a long while Blackwick Castle was without a master.

But its evil reputation persisted. It was said that Zaida, the witch, though dead, still made her presence felt. Many children of the tenantry and young people of the neighbourhood sickened and died—possibly of quite natural causes; but this did not prevent a mantle of terror settling upon the countryside, for it was said that Zaida had been seen—a pale woman clad in white—flitting about the cottages at night, and where she passed sickness and death were sure to supervene.

And from that time the fortune of the family gradually declined. Heir succeeded heir, but no sooner was he installed at Blackwick Castle than his nature, whatever it may previously have been, seemed to undergo a change. It was as if he absorbed into himself all the weight of evil that had stained his family name—as if he did, indeed, become a vampire, bringing blight upon any not directly connected with his own house.

And so, by degrees, Blackwick was deserted of its tenantry. The land around it was left uncultivated—the farms stood empty. This had persisted to the present day, for the superstitious peasantry still told their tales of the mysterious white woman who hovered about the neighbourhood, and whose appearance betokened death—and possibly worse than death.

And yet it seemed that the last representatives of the MacThanes could not desert their ancestral home. Riches they had, sufficient to live happily upon elsewhere, but, drawn by some power they could not contend against, they had preferred to spend their lives in the solitude of the now half-ruined castle, shunned by their neighbours, feared and execrated by the few tenants that still clung to their soil.

So it had been with Jessica's grandfather and great-grandfather. Each of them had married a young wife, and in each case their love story had been all too brief. The vampire spirit was still abroad, expressing itself—or so it seemed—through the living representatives of bygone generations of evil, and young blood had been demanded as the sacrifice.

And to them had succeeded Jessica's father. He had not profited by their example, but had followed directly in their footsteps. And the same fate had befallen the wife whom he passionately adored. She had died of pernicious anaemia—so the doctors said—but he had regarded himself as her murderer.

But, unlike his predecessors, he had torn himself away from Blackwick—and this for the sake of his child. Unknown to her, however, he had returned year after year, for there were times when the passionate longing for the gloomy, mysterious halls and corridors of the old castle, for the wild stretches of moorland, and the dark pinewoods, would come upon him too strongly to be resisted. And so he knew that for his daughter, as for himself, there was no escape, and he warned her, when the relief of death was at last granted to him, of what her fate must be.

This was the tale that Jessica told the man who wished to make her his wife, and he made light of it, as such a man would, regarding it all as foolish superstition, the delusion of a mind overwrought. And at last—perhaps it was not very difficult, for she loved him with all her heart and soul—he succeeded in inducing Jessica to think as he did, to banish morbid ideas, as he called them from her brain, and to consent to marry him at an early date.

'I'll take any risk you like,' he declared. 'I'll even go and live at

Blackwick if you should desire it. To think of you, my lovely Jessica, a vampire! Why, I never heard such nonsense in my life.'

'Father said I'm very like Zaida, the witch,' she protested, but he silenced her with a kiss.

And so they were married and spent their honeymoon abroad, and in the autumn Paul accepted an invitation to a house party in Scotland for the grouse shooting, a sport to which he was absolutely devoted, and Jessica agreed with him that there was no reason why he should forgo his pleasure.

Perhaps it was an unwise thing to do, to venture to Scotland, but by this time the young couple, more deeply in love with each other than ever, had got quite over their fears. Jessica was redolent with health and spirits, and more than once she declared that if they should be anywhere in the neighbourhood of Blackwick she would like to see the old castle out of curiosity, and just to show how absolutely she had got over the foolish terrors that used to assail her.

This seemed to Paul to be quite a wise plan, and so one day, since they were actually staying at no great distance, they motored over to Blackwick, and finding the bailiff, got him to show them over the castle.

It was a great castellated pile, grey with age, and in places falling into ruin. It stood on a steep hillside, with the rock of which it seemed to form part, and on one side of it there was a precipitous drop to a mountain stream a hundred feet below. The robber MacThanes of the old days could not have desired a better stronghold.

At the back, climbing up the mountainside were dark pinewoods, from which, here and there, rugged crags protruded, and these were fantastically shaped, some like gigantic and misshapen human forms, which stood up as if they mounted guard over the castle and the narrow gorge, by which alone it could be approached.

This gorge was always full of weird, uncanny sounds. It might have been a storehouse for the wind, which, even on calm days, rushed up and down as if seeking an escape, and it moaned among the pines and whistled in the crags and shouted derisive laughter as it was tossed from side to side of the rocky heights. It was like the plaint of lost souls—that is the expression Davenant made use of—the plaint of lost souls.

The road, little more than a track now, passed through this gorge, and then, after skirting a small but deep lake, which hardly knew the light of the sun so shut in was it by overhanging trees, climbed the hill to the castle.

And the castle! Davenant used but a few words to describe it, yet somehow I could see the gloomy edifice in my mind's eye, and something of the lurking horror that it contained communicated itself to my brain. Perhaps my clairvoyant sense assisted me, for when he spoke of them I seemed already acquainted with the great stone halls, the long corridors, gloomy and cold even on the brightest and warmest of days, the dark, oak-panelled rooms, and the broad central staircase up which one of the early MacThanes had once led a dozen men on horseback in pursuit of a stag which had taken refuge within the precincts of the castle. There was the keep, too, its walls so thick that the ravages of time had made no impression upon them, and beneath the keep were dungeons which could tell terrible tales of ancient wrong and lingering pain.

Well, Mr and Mrs Davenant visited as much as the bailiff could show them of this ill-omened edifice, and Paul, for his part, thought pleasantly of his own Derbyshire home, the fine Georgian mansion, replete with every modern comfort, where he proposed to settle with his wife. And so he received something of a shock when, as they drove away, she slipped her hand into his and whispered:

'Paul, you promised, didn't you, that you would refuse me nothing?'

She had been strangely silent till she spoke those words. Paul, slightly apprehensive, assured her that she only had to ask—but the speech did not come from his heart, for he guessed vaguely what she desired.

She wanted to go and live at the castle—oh, only for a little while, for she was sure she would soon tire of it. But the bailiff had told her that there were papers, documents, which she ought to examine, since the property was now hers—and, besides, she was interested in this home of her ancestors, and wanted to explore it more thoroughly. Oh, no, she wasn't in the least influenced by the old superstition—that wasn't the attraction—she had quite got over those silly ideas. Paul had cured her, and since he himself was so convinced that they were without foundation he ought not to mind granting her her whim.

This was a plausible argument, not easy to controvert. In the end Paul yielded, though it was not without a struggle. He suggested amendments. Let him at least have the place done up for her—that would take time; or let them postpone their visit till next year—in the summer—not move in just as the winter was upon them.

But Jessica did not want to delay longer than she could help, and she hated the idea of redecoration. Why, it would spoil the illusion of the old place, and, besides, it would be a waste of money since she only wished to remain there for a week or two. The Derbyshire house was not quite ready yet; they must allow time for the paper to dry on the walls.

And so, a week later, when their stay with their friends was concluded, they went to Blackwick, the bailiff having engaged a few raw servants and generally made things as comfortable for them as possible. Paul was worried and apprehensive, but he could not admit this to his wife after having so loudly proclaimed his theories on the subject of superstition.

They had been married three months at this time—nine had passed since then, and they had never left Blackwick for more than a few hours—till now Paul had come to London—alone.

'Over and over again,' he declared, 'my wife has begged me to go. With tears in her eyes, almost upon her knees, she has entreated me to leave her, but I have steadily refused unless she will accompany me. But that is the trouble, Mr Vance, she cannot; there is something, some mysterious horror, that holds her there as surely as if she were bound with fetters. It holds her more strongly even than it held her father—we found out that he used to spend six months at least of every year at Blackwick—months when he pretended that he was travelling abroad. You see the spell—or whatever the accursed thing may be—never really relaxed its grip of him.'

'Did you never attempt to take your wife away?' asked Vance.

'Yes, several times; but it was hopeless. She would become so ill as soon as we were beyond the limit of the estate that I invariably had to take her back. Once we got as far as Dorekirk—that is the nearest town, you know—and I thought I should be successful if only I could get through the night. But she escaped me; she climbed out of a window—she meant to go back on foot, at night, all those long miles. Then I have had doctors down; but it is I who wanted the doctors, not she. They have ordered me away, but I have refused to obey them till now.'

'Is your wife changed at all—physically?' interrupted Vance.

Davenant reflected. 'Changed,' he said, 'yes, but so subtly that I hardly know how to describe it. She is more beautiful than ever—and yet it isn't the same beauty, if you can understand me. I have spoken of her white complexion, well, one is more than ever conscious of it now, because her lips have become so red—they are almost like a splash of blood upon her face. And the upper one has a peculiar curve that I don't think it had before, and when she laughs she doesn't smile—do you know what I mean? Then her hair—it has lost its wonderful gloss. Of course, I know she is fretting about me; but that is so peculiar, too, for at times, as I have told you, she will implore me to go and leave her, and then perhaps only a few minutes later, she will wreathe her arms round my neck and say she cannot live without me. And I feel that there is a struggle going on within her, that she is only yielding slowly to the horrible influence—whatever it is—that she is herself when she begs me to go, but when she entreats me to stay—and it is then that her fascination is most intense—oh, I can't help remembering what she told me before we were married, and that word'—he lowered his voice—'the word "vampire"——'

He passed his hand over his brow that was wet with perspiration. 'But that's absurd, ridiculous,' he muttered; 'these fantastic beliefs have been exploded years ago. We live in the twentieth century.'

A pause ensued, then Vance said quietly, 'Mr Davenant, since you have taken me into your confidence, since you have found doctors of no avail, will you let me try to help you? I think I may be of some use—if it is not already too late. Should you agree, Mr Dexter and I will accompany you, as you have suggested, to Blackwick Castle as early as possible—by tonight's mail North. Under ordinary circumstances I should tell you as you value your life, not to return——'

Davenant shook his head. 'That is advice which I should never take,' he declared. 'I had already decided, under any circumstances, to travel North tonight. I am glad that you both will accompany me.'

And so it was decided. We settled to meet at the station, and presently Paul Davenant took his departure. Any other details that remained to be told he would put us in possession of during the course of the journey.

'A curious and most interesting case,' remarked Vance when we were alone. 'What do you make of it, Dexter?'

'I suppose,' I replied cautiously, 'that there is such a thing as vampirism even in these days of advanced civilization? I can understand the evil influence that a very old person may have upon a young one if they happen to be in constant intercourse—the worn-out tissue sapping healthy vitality for their own support. And there are certain people—I could think of several myself—who seem to depress one and undermine one's energies, quite unconsciously, of course, but one feels somehow that vitality has passed from oneself to them. And in this case, when the force is centuries old, expressing itself, in some mysterious way, through Davenant's wife, is it not feasible to believe that he may be physically affected by it, even though the whole thing is sheerly mental?'

'You think, then,' demanded Vance, 'that it is sheerly mental? Tell me, if that is so, how do you account for the marks on Davenant's throat?'

This was a question to which I found no reply, and though I pressed him for his views, Vance would not commit himself further just then.

Of our long journey to Scotland I need say nothing. We did not reach Blackwick Castle till late in the afternoon of the following day. The place was just as I had conceived it—as I have already described it. And a sense of gloom settled upon me as our car jolted us over the rough road that led through the Gorge of the Winds—a gloom that deepened when we penetrated into the vast cold hall of the castle.

Mrs Davenant, who had been informed by telegram of our arrival, received us cordially. She knew nothing of our actual mission, regarding us merely as friends of her husband's. She was most solicitous on his behalf, but there was something strained about her tone, and it made me feel vaguely uneasy. The impression that I got was that the woman was impelled to everything that she said or did by some force outside herself—but, of course, this was a conclusion that the circumstances I was aware of might easily have conduced to. In every other aspect she was charming, and she had an extraordinary fascination of appearance and manner that made me readily understand the force of a remark made by Davenant during our journey.

'I want to live for Jessica's sake. Get her away from Blackwick, Vance, and I feel that all will be well. I'd go through hell to have her restored to me—as she was.'

And now that I had seen Mrs Davenant I realized what he meant by those last words. Her fascination was stronger than ever, but it was not a natural fascination—not that of a normal woman, such as she had been. It was the fascination of a Circe, of a witch, of an enchantress—and as such was irresistible.

We had a strong proof of the evil within her soon after our arrival. It was a test that Vance had quietly prepared. Davenant had mentioned that no flowers grew at Blackwick, and Vance declared that we must take some with us as a present for the lady of the house. He purchased a bouquet of pure white roses at the little town where we left the train, for the motorcar has been sent to meet us.

Soon after our arrival he presented these to Mrs Davenant. She took them it seemed to me nervously, and hardly had her hand touched them before they fell to pieces, in a shower of crumpled petals, to the floor.

'We must act at once,' said Vance to me when we were descending to dinner that night. 'There must be no delay.'

'What are you afraid of?' I whispered.

'Davenant has been absent a week,' he replied grimly. 'He is stronger than when he went away, but not strong enough to survive the loss of more blood. He must be protected. There is danger tonight.'

'You mean from his wife?' I shuddered at the ghastliness of the suggestion.

'That is what time will show.' Vance turned to me and added a few words with intense earnestness. 'Mrs Davenant, Dexter, is at present hovering between two conditions. The evil thing has not yet completely mastered her—you remember what Davenant said, how she would beg him to go away and the next moment entreat him to stay? She has made a struggle, but she is gradually succumbing, and this last week, spent here alone, has strengthened the evil. And that is what I have got to fight, Dexter—it is to be a contest of will, a contest that will go on silently till one or the other obtains the mastery. If you watch, you may see. Should a change show itself in Mrs Davenant you will know that I have won.'

Thus I knew the direction in which my friend proposed to act. It was to be a war of his will against the mysterious power that had laid its curse upon the house of MacThane. Mrs Davenant must be released from the fatal charm that held her.

And I, knowing what was going on, was able to watch and understand. I realized that the silent contest had begun even while we ate dinner. Mrs Davenant ate practically nothing and seemed ill at ease; she fidgeted in her chair, talked a great deal, and laughed—it was the laugh without a smile, as Davenant had described it. And as soon as she was able to she withdrew.

Later, as we sat in the drawing-room, I could feel the clash of wills. The air in the room felt electric and heavy, charged with tremendous but invisible forces. And outside, round the castle, the wind whistled and shrieked and moaned—it was as if all the dead and gone MacThanes, a grim army, had collected to fight the battle of their race.

And all this while we four in the drawing-room were sitting and talking the ordinary commonplaces of after-dinner conversation! That was the extraordinary part of it—Paul Davenant suspected nothing, and I, who knew, had to play my part. But I hardly took my eyes from Jessica's face. When would the change come, or was it, indeed, too late!

At last Davenant rose and remarked that he was tired and would go to bed. There was no need for Jessica to hurry. We would sleep that night in his dressing-room and did not want to be disturbed.

And it was at that moment, as his lips met hers in a goodnight kiss, as she wreathed her enchantress arms about him, careless of our presence, her eyes gleaming hungrily, that the change came.

It came with a fierce and threatening shriek of wind, and a rattling of the casement, as if the horde of ghosts without was about to break in upon us. A long, quivering sigh escaped from Jessica's lips, her arms fell from her husband's shoulders, and she drew back, swaying a little from side to side.

'Paul,' she cried, and somehow the whole timbre of her voice was changed, 'what a wretch I've been to bring you back to Blackwick, ill as you are! But we'll go away, dear; yes, I'll go, too. Oh, will you take me away—take me away tomorrow?' She spoke with an intense earnestness—unconscious all the time of what had been happening to her. Long shudders were convulsing her frame. 'I don't know why I've wanted to stay here,' she kept repeating. 'I hate the place, really—it's evil—evil.'

Having heard these words I exulted, for surely Vance's success was assured. But I was to learn that the danger was not yet past.

Husband and wife separated, each going to their own room. I noticed the grateful, if mystified glance that Davenant threw at Vance, vaguely aware, as he must have been, that my friend was somehow responsible for what had happened. It was settled that plans for departure were to be discussed on the morrow.

'I have succeeded,' Vance said hurriedly, when we were alone, 'but the change may be a transitory. I must keep watch tonight. Go you to bed, Dexter, there is nothing that you can do.'

I obeyed—though I would sooner have kept watch, too—watch against a danger of which I had no understanding. I went to my room, a gloomy and sparsely furnished apartment, but I knew that it was quite impossible for me to think of sleeping. And so, dressed as I was, I went and sat by the open window, for now the wind that had raged round the castle had died down to a low moaning in the pinetrees—a whimpering of time-worn agony.

And it was as I sat thus that I became aware of a white figure that stole out from the castle by a door that I could not see, and, with hands clasped, ran swiftly across the terrace to the wood. I had but a momentary glance, but I felt convinced that the figure was that of Jessica Davenant.

And instinctively I knew that some great danger was imminent. It was, I think, the suggestion of despair conveyed by those clasped hands. At any rate, I did not hesitate. My window was some height from the ground, but the wall below was ivy-clad and afforded good foothold. The descent was quite easy. I achieved it, and was just in time to take up the pursuit in the right direction, which was into the thickness of the wood that clung to the slope of the hill.

I shall never forget that wild chase. There was just sufficient room to enable me to follow the rough path, which, luckily, since I had now lost sight of my quarry, was the only possible way that she could have taken; there were no intersecting tracks, and the wood was too thick on either side to permit of deviation.

And the wood seemed full of dreadful sounds—moaning and wailing and hideous laughter. The wind, of course, and the screaming of night birds—once I felt the fluttering of wings in close proximity to my face. But I could not rid myself of the thought that I, in my turn, was being pursued, that the forces of hell were combined against me.

The path came to an abrupt end on the border of the sombre lake that I have already mentioned. And now I realized that I was indeed only just in time, for before me, plunging knee deep in the water, I recognized the white-clad figure of the woman I had been pursuing. Hearing my footsteps, she turned her head, and then threw up her arms and screamed. Her red hair fell in heavy masses about her shoulders, and her face, as I saw it in that moment, was hardly human for the agony of remorse that it depicted.

'Go!' she screamed. 'For God's sake let me die!'

But I was by her side almost as she spoke. She struggled with me—sought vainly to tear herself from my clasp—implored me, with panting breath, to let her drown.

'It's the only way to save him!' she gasped. 'Don't you understand that I am a thing accursed? For it is I—I—who have sapped his life blood! I know it now, the truth has been revealed to me tonight! I am a vampire, without hope in this world or the next, so for his sake—for the sake of his unborn child—let me die—let me die!'

Was ever so terrible an appeal made? Yet I—what could I do? Gently I overcame her resistance and drew her back to shore. By the time I reached it she was lying a dead weight upon my arm. I laid her down upon a mossy bank, and, kneeling by her side, gazed intently into her face.

And then I knew that I had done well. For the face I looked upon was not that of Jessica the vampire, as I had seen it that afternoon, it was the face of Jessica, the woman whom Paul Davenant had loved.

And later Aylmer Vance had his tale to tell.

'I waited', he said, 'until I knew that Davenant was asleep, and then I stole into his room to watch by his bedside. And presently she came, as I guessed she would, the vampire, the accursed thing that has preyed upon the souls of her kin, making them like to herself when they too have passed into Shadowland, and gathering sustenance for her horrid task from the blood of those who are alien to her race. Paul's body and Jessica's soul—it is for one and the other, Dexter, that we have fought.

'You mean,' I hesitated, 'Zaida the witch?'

'Even so,' he agreed. 'Hers is the evil spirit that has fallen like a blight upon the house of MacThane. But now I think she may be exorcized for ever.'

'Tell me.'

'She came to Paul Davenant last night, as she must have done before, in the guise of his wife. You know that Jessica bears a strong resemblance to her ancestress. He opened his arms, but she was foiled of her prey, for I had taken my precautions; I had placed That upon Davenant's breast while he slept which robbed the vampire of her power of ill. She sped wailing from the room—a shadow—she who a minute before had looked at him with Jessica's eyes and spoken to him with Jessica's voice. Her red lips were Jessica's lips, and they were close to his when his eyes were opened and he saw her as she was—a hideous phantom of the corruption of the ages. And so the spell was removed, and she fled away to the place whence she had come—'

He paused. 'And now?' I inquired.

'Blackwick Castle must be razed to the ground,' he replied. 'That is the only way. Every stone of it, every brick, must be ground to powder and burnt with fire, for therein is the cause of all the evil. Davenant has consented.'

'And Mrs Davenant?'

'I think,' Vance answered cautiously, 'that all may be well with her. The curse will be removed with the destruction of the castle. She has not—thanks to you—perished under its influence. She was less guilty than she imagined—herself preyed upon rather than preying. But can't you understand her remorse when she realized, as she was bound to realize, the part she had played? And the knowledge of the child to come—its fatal inheritance—'

'I understand,' I muttered with a shudder. And then, under my breath, I whispered, 'Thank God!'

THE SUMACH

Ulric Daubeny

Ulric Evan Daubeny (1888–1922) was, like M.R. James, both a notable scholar-antiquary and a fine writer of ghost stories. His unjustly neglected collection, *The Elemental: Tales of the Supernormal and the Inexplicable*, was published by G. Routledge in 1919, five years after the same company issued Bram Stoker's *Dracula's Guest and Other Weird Stories* in a similar cheap format. Daubeny may well have been influenced by Stoker's classic collection, and 'The Sumach' is one of the best and most unusual tales in the entire vampiric genre. His non-fiction books in the antiquarian field were *Orchestral Wind Instruments, Ancient and Modern* (1920), *Ancient Cotswold Churches* (1921; published as an impressive quarto size on the same lines as M.R. James's later *Abbeys* and *Suffolk and Norfolk*), and *How to Choose Antiques* (1924). Daubeny might have blossomed into one of the greatest British writers of supernatural-horror fiction had he not been struck down by meningitis in his 34th year.

❦

'How red that Sumach is!'

Irene Barton murmured something commonplace, for to her the tree brought painful recollections. Her visitor, unconscious of this fact, proceeded to elaborate.

'Do you know, Irene, that tree gives me the creeps! I can't explain, except that it is not a nice tree, not a *good* tree. For instance, why should its leaves be red in August, when they are not supposed to turn until October?'

'What queer ideas you have, May! The tree is right enough, although its significance to me is sad. Poor Spot, you know; we buried him beneath it two days ago. Come and see his grave.'

The two women left the terrace, where this conversation had been taking place, and leisurely strolled across the lawn, at the end of which, in almost startling isolation, grew the Sumach. At least, Mrs Watcombe, who evinced so great an interest in the tree, questioned whether it actually was a Sumach, for the foliage was unusual, and the branches gnarled and twisted beyond recognition. Just now, the leaves were stained with splashes of dull crimson, but rather than droop, they had a bloated appearance, as if the luxuriance of the growth were not altogether healthy.

For several moments they stood regarding the pathetic little grave, and the silence was only broken when Mrs Watcombe darted beneath the tree, and came back with something in her hand.

'Irene, look at this dead thrush. Poor little thing! Such splendid plumage, yet it hardly weighs a sugar plum!'

Mrs Barton regarded it with wrinkled brows.

'I cannot understand what happens to the birds, May—unless someone lays poison. We continually find them dead about the garden, and usually beneath, or very near this tree.'

It is doubtful whether Mrs Watcombe listened. Her attention seemed to wander that morning, and she was studying the twisted branches of the Sumach with a thoughtful scrutiny.

'Curious that the leaves should turn at this time of year,' she murmured. 'It brings to mind poor Geraldine's illness. This tree had an extraordinary fascination for her, you know. It was quite scarlet then, yet that was only June, and it had barely finished shooting.'

'My dear May! You have red leaves on the brain this morning!' Irene retorted, uncertain whether to be irritated or amused. 'I can't think why you are so concerned about the colour. It is only the result of two days' excessive heat, for scarcely a leaf was touched, when I buried poor old Spot.'

The conversation seemed absurdly trivial, yet, Mrs Watcombe gone, Irene could not keep her mind from dwelling on her cousin's fatal illness. The news had reached them with the shock of the absolutely unexpected. Poor Geraldine, who had always been so strong, to have fallen victim to acute anaemia! It was almost unbelievable, that heart failure should have put an an end to her sweet young life, after a few days' ailing. Of course, the sad event had wrought a wonderful change for Irene and her husband, giving them, in place of a cramped surburban villa, this beautiful country home, Cleeve Grange. Everything for her was filled with the delight of novelty, for she had ruled as mistress over the charmed abode for only one short week. Hilary, her husband, was yet a stranger to the more intimate of its attractions, being detained in London by the winding-up of business affairs.

Several days elapsed, for the most part given solely to the keen pleasure of arranging and re-arranging the new home. As time went by, the crimson splashes on the Sumach faded, the leaves becoming green again, though drooping as if from want of moisture. Irene noticed this when she paid her daily visits to the pathetic little dog grave, trying to induce flowers to take root upon it, but do what she might, they invariably faded. Nothing, not even grass, would grow beneath the Sumach. Only death seemed to thrive there, she mused in a fleeting moment of depression, as she searched around for more dead birds. But none had fallen since the thrush, picked up by Mrs Watcombe.

One evening, the heat inside the house becoming insupportable, Irene wandered into the garden, her steps mechanically leading her to the little grave beneath the Sumach. In the uncertain moonlight, the twisted trunk and branches of the old tree were suggestive of a rustic seat, and feeling tired, she lifted herself into the natural bower, and lolled back, joyously inhaling the cool night air. Presently she dropped asleep, and in a curiously vivid manner, dreamt of Hilary; that he had completed his business in London, and was coming home. They met at evening, near the garden gate, and Hilary spread wide his arms, and eagerly folded them about her. Swiftly the dream began to change, assuming the characteristic of a nightmare. The sky grew strangely dark, the arms fiercely masterful, while the face which bent to kiss her neck was not that of her young husband: it was leering, wicked, gnarled like the trunk of some weather-beaten tree. Chilled with horror, Irene fought long and desperately against the vision, to be at last awakened by her own frightened whimpering. Yet returning consciousness did not immediately dissipate the nightmare. In imagination she was still held rigid by brutal arms, and it was only after a blind, half-waking struggle that she freed herself, and went speeding acros the lawn, towards the lighted doorway.

Next morning Mrs Watcombe called, and subjected her to a puzzled scrutiny.

'How pale you look Irene. Do you feel ill?'

'Ill! No, only a little languid. I find this hot weather very trying.'

Mrs Watcombe studied her with care, for the pallor of Irene's face was very marked. In contrast, a vivid spot of red showed on the slender neck, an inch or so below the ear. Intuitively a hand went up, as Irene turned to her friend in explanation.

'It feels so sore. I think I must have grazed the skin, last night, while sitting in the Sumach.'

'Sitting in the Sumach!' echoed Mrs Watcombe in surprise. 'How curious you should do that. Poor Geraldine used to do the same, just before she was taken ill, and yet at the last she was seized with a perfect horror of the tree. Goodness, but it is quite red again, this morning!'

Irene swung round in the direction of the tree, filled with a vague repugnance. Sure enough, the leaves no longer drooped, nor were they green. They had become flecked once more with crimson, and the growth had quite regained its former vigour.

'Eugh!' she breathed, hurriedly turning towards the house. 'It reminds me of a horrid nighmare. I have rather a head this morning; let's go in, and talk of something else!'

As the day advanced, the heat grew more oppressive, and night brought with it a curious stillness, the stillness which so often presages a heavy thunderstorm. No bird had offered up its evening hymn, no breeze came sufficient to stir a single leaf: everything was pervaded by the silence of expectancy.

The interval between dinner and bedtime is always a dreary one for those accustomed to companionship, and left all alone, Irene's restlessness momentarily increased. First the ceiling, then the very atmosphere seemed to weigh heavy upon her head. Although windows and doors were all flung wide, the airlessness of the house grew less and less endurable, until from sheer desperation she made her escape into the garden, where a sudden illumination of the horizon gave warning of the approaching storm. Feeling somewhat at a loss, she roamed aimlessly awhile, pausing sometimes to catch the echoes of distant thunder, until at last she found herself standing over Spot's desolate little grave. The sight struck her with a sense of utter loneliness, and the tears sprang to her eyes, in poignant longing for the companionship of her faithful pet.

Moved by she knew not what, Irene swung herself into the comfortable branches of the old Sumach, and soothed by the reposeful attitude, her head soon began to nod in slumber. Afterwards it was a doubtful memory whether she actually did sleep, or whether the whole experience was not a kind of waking nightmare. Something of the previous evening's dream returned to her, but this time with added horror; for it commenced with no pleasurable vision of her husband. Instead, relentless, stick-like arms immediately closed in upon her, their vice-like grip so tight that she could scarcely breathe. Down darted the awful head, rugged and lined by every sin, darting at the fair, white neck as a wild beast on its prey. The foul lips began to eat into her skin . . . She struggled desperately, madly, for to her swooning senses the very branches of the tree became endowed with active life, coiling unmercifully around her, tenaciously clinging to her limbs, and tearing at her dress. Pain at last spurred her to an heroic effort, the pain of something—perhaps a twig—digging deep into her unprotected neck. With a choking cry she freed herself, and nerved by a sudden burst of thunder, ran tottering towards the shelter of the house.

Having gained the cosy lounge-hall, Irene sank into an armchair, gasping hysterically for breath. Gusts of refreshing wind came through the open windows, but although the atmosphere rapidly grew less stagnant, an hour passed before she could make sufficient effort to crawl upstairs to bed. In her room, a further shock awaited her. The bloodless, drawn face reflected in the mirror was scarcely recognizable. The eyes lacked lustre, the lips were white, the skin hung flabby on the shrunken flesh, giving it a look of premature old age. A tiny trickle of dry blood, the solitary smudge of colour, stained the chalky pallor of her neck. Taking up a hand-glass, she examined this with momentary

concern. It was the old wound reopened, an angry-looking sore, almost like the bite of some small, or very sharp-toothed animal. It smarted painfully . . .

Mrs Watcombe, bursting into the breakfast room next morning, with suggestions of an expedition to the neighbouring town, was shocked at Irene's looks, and insisted on going at once to fetch the doctor. Mrs Watcombe fussed continually throughout the interview, and insisted on an examination of the scar upon Irene's neck. Patient and doctor had regarded this as a negligible detail, but finally the latter subjected it to a slightly puzzled scrutiny, advising that it should be kept bandaged. He suggested that Irene was suffering from anaemia, and would do well to keep as quiet as possible, building up her strength with food, open windows and a general selection of pills and tonics. But despite these comforting arrangements, no one was entirely satisfied. The doctor lacked something in assurance, Irene was certain that she could not really be anaemic, while Mrs Watcombe was obsessed by inward misgivings, perfectly indefinable, yet none the less disturbing. She left the house as a woman bent under a load of care. Passing up the lane, her glance lighted on the old Sumach, more crimson now, more flourishing in its growth than she had seen it since the time of Geraldine's fatal illness.

'I loathe that horrid old tree!' she murmured, then added, struck by a nameless premonition, 'Her husband ought to know. I shall wire to him at once.'

Irene, womanlike, put to use her enforced idleness, by instituting a rearrangement of the box-room, the only part of her new home which yet remained unexplored. Among the odds and ends of the rubbish to be thrown away, there was a little notebook, apparently unused. In idle curiosity, Irene picked it up, and was surprised to learn, from an inscription, that her cousin Geraldine had intended to use it as a diary. A date appeared—only a few days prior to the poor girl's death—but no entries had been made, though the first two pages of the book had certainly been removed. As Irene put it down, there fluttered to the ground a torn scrap of writing. She stooped, and continued stooping, breathlessly staring at the words that had been written by her cousin's hand—*Sumach fascinates m*──

In some unaccountable manner this applied to her. It was obvious what tree was meant, the old Sumach at the end of the lawn; and it fascinated her, Irene, though not until that moment had she openly recognized the fact. Searching hurriedly through the notebook, she discovered, near the end, a heap of torn paper, evidently the first two pages of a diary. She turned the pieces in eager haste. Most of them bore no more than one short word, or portions of a longer one, but a few bigger fragments proved more enlightening, and filled with nervous apprehension, she carried the book to her escritoire, and spent the remainder of the afternoon in trying to piece together the torn-up pages.

Meanwhile, Mrs Watcombe was worrying and fretting over Irene's unexpected illness. Her pallor, her listlessness, even the curious mark upon her neck, gave cause for positive alarm, so exactly did they correspond with symptoms exhibited by her cousin Geraldine, during the few days prior to her death. She wished that the village doctor, who had attended the earlier case, would return soon from his holiday, as his locum tenens seemed sadly wanting in that authoritative decision which is so consoling to patients, relatives, and friends. Feeling, as an old friend, responsible for the welfare of Irene, she wired to Hilary, telling him of the sudden illness, and advising him to return without delay.

The urgency of the telegram alarmed him, so much so that he left London by the next train, arriving at Cleeve Grange shortly after dark.

'Where is your mistress?' was his first enquiry, as the maid met him in the hall.

'Upstairs, Sir. She complained of feeling tired, and said she would go to bed.'

He hurried to her room, only to find it empty. He called, he rang for the servants; in a moment the whole house was astir, yet nowhere was Irene to be found. Deeming it possible that she might have gone to see Mrs Watcombe, Hilary was about to follow, when that lady herself was ushered in.

'I saw the lights of your cab——' she commenced, cutting short the sentence, as she met his questioning glance.

'Where is Irene?'

'Irene? My dear Hilary, is she not here?'

'No. We can't find her anywhere. I thought she might have been with you.'

For the space of half a second, Mrs Watcombe's face presented a picture of astonishment; then the expression changed to one of dismayed concern.

'She is in that tree! I'm certain of it! Hilary, we must fetch her in at once!'

Completely at a loss to understand, he followed the excited woman into the garden, stumbling blindly in her wake across the lawn. The darkness was intense, and a terrific wind beat them back as if with living hands. Irene's white dress at length became discernible, dimly thrown up against the pitchy background, and obscured in places by the twists and coils of the old Sumach. Between them they grasped the sleeping body, but the branches swung wildly in the gale, and to Hilary's confused imagination it was as if they had literally to tear it from the tree's embrace. At last they regained the shelter of the house, and laid their inanimate burden upon the sofa. She was quite unconscious, pale as death, and her face painfully contorted, as if with fear. The old wound on the neck, now bereft of bandages, had been reopened, and was wet with blood.

Hilary rushed off to fetch the doctor, while Mrs Watcombe and the servants carried Irene to her room. Several hours passed before she recovered consciousness, and during that time Hilary was gently but firmly excluded from the sickroom. Bewildered and disconsolate, he wandered restlessly about the house, until his attention was arrested by the unusual array of torn-up bits of paper on Irene's desk. He saw that she had been sorting out the pieces, and sticking them together as the sentences became complete. The work was barely half finished, yet what there was to read, struck him as exceedingly strange:

The seat in the old Sumach fascinates me. I find myself going back to it unconsciously, nay, even against my will. Oh, but the nightmare visions it always brings me! In them I seem to plumb the very depths of terror. Their memory preys upon my mind, and every day my strength grows less.

Dr H. speaks of anaemia. . .

That was as far as Irene had proceeded. Hardly knowing why he did so, Hilary resolved to complete the task, but the chill of early morning was in the air before it was finished. Cramped and stiff, he was pushing back his chair when a footstep sounded in the doorway, and Mrs Watcombe entered.

'Irene is better,' she volunteered immediately. 'She is sleeping naturally, and Doctor Thomson says there is no longer any immediate danger. The poor child is terribly weak and bloodless.'

'May—tell me—what is the meaning of all this? Why has Irene suddenly become so ill? I can't understand it!'

Mrs Watcombe's face was preternaturally grave.

'Even the doctor admits that he is puzzled,' she answered very quietly. 'The symptoms all point to a sudden and excessive loss of blood, though in cases of acute anaemia—'

'God! But—not like Geraldine? I can't believe it!'

'Neither can I. Oh, Hilary, you may think me mad, but I can't help feeling that there is some unknown, some awful influence at work. Irene was perfectly well three days ago, and it was the same with Geraldine before she was taken ill. The cases are so exactly similar . . .Irene was trying to tell me something about a diary, but the poor girl was too exhausted to make herself properly understood.'

'Diary? Geraldine's diary, do you think? She must mean that. I have just finished piecing it together, but frankly, I can't make head or tail of it!'

Mrs Watcombe rapidly scanned the writing, then studied it again with greater care. Finally she read the second part aloud.

'Listen, Hilary! This seems to me important.'

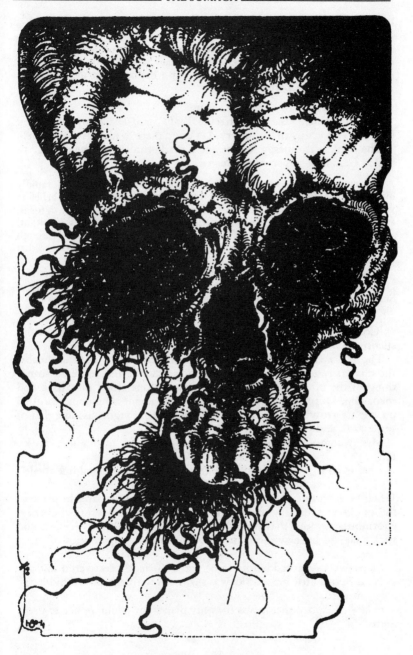

Dr H. speaks of anaemia. Pray heaven, he may be correct, for my thoughts sometimes move in a direction which foreshadows nothing short of lunacy— or so people would tell me, if I could bring myself to confide these things. I must fight alone, clinging to the knowledge that it is usual for anaemic persons to be obsessed by unhealthy fancies. If only I had not read those horribly suggestive words in Barrett . . .

'Barrett? What can she mean, May?'

'Wait a moment. Barrett? Barrett's *Traditions of the County*, perhaps. I have noticed a copy in the library. Let us go there; it may give the clue!'

The book was quickly found, and a marker indicated the passage to which Geraldine apparently referred.

At Cleeve, I was reminded of another of those traditions, so rapidly disappearing before the spread of education. It concerned the old belief in vampires, spirits of the evil dead, who by night, could assume a human form, and scour the countryside in search of victims. Suspected vampires, if caught, were buried with the mouth stuffed full of garlic, and a stake plunged through the heart, whereby they were rendered harmless, or, at least, confined to that one particular locality.

Some thirty years ago, an old man pointed out a tree which was said to have grown from such a stake. So far as I can recollect, it was an unusual variety of Sumach, and had been enclosed during a recent extension to the garden of the old Grange. . .

'Come outside,' said Mrs Watcombe, breaking a long and solemn silence. 'I want you to see that tree.'

The sky was suffused with the blush of early dawn, and the shrubs, the flowers, even the dew upon the grass caught and reflected something of the pink effulgence. The Sumach alone stood out, dark and menacing. During the night its leaves had become a hideous, mottled purple; its growth was oily, bloated, unnaturally vigorous, like that of some rank and poisonous weed.

Mrs Watcombe, looking from afar, spoke in frightened, husky tones.

'See, Hilary! It was exactly like that when—when Geraldine died!'

When evening fell, the end of the lawn was strangely bare. In place of the old tree, there lay an enormous heap of smouldering embers— enormous, because the Sumach had been too sodden with dark and sticky sap, to burn without the assistance of large quantities of other timber.

Many weeks elapsed before Irene was sufficiently recovered to walk as far as Spot's little grave. She was surprised to find it almost hidden in a bed of garlic.

Hilary explained that it was the only plant they could induce to grow there.

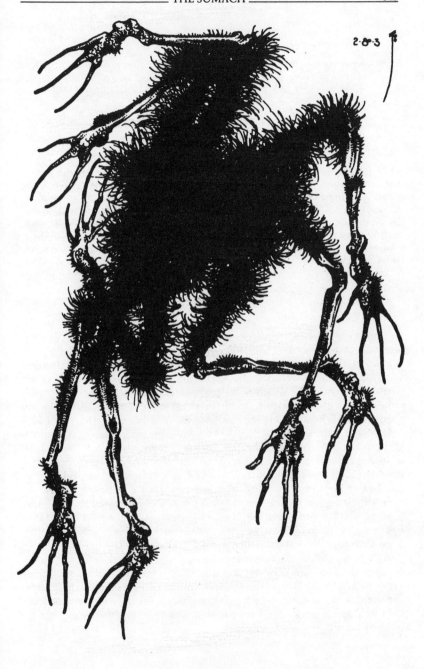

2·8·3

WAILING WELL

M. R. James

Although the doyen of British ghost story writers, Montague Rhodes James (1862–1936) was not particularly fond of *Dracula*, thinking it 'suffered by excess', aspects of vampirism turned up from time to time in his tales, notably 'Count Magnus' and 'An Episode of Cathedral History'. A later variation on the theme was manifest in 'Wailing Well', written for the Eton College troop of Boy Scouts (James became Provost of Eton in 1918) and read at their camp-fire at Worbarrow Bay in August 1927, 'with the result that several boys had a somewhat disturbed night as the scene of the story was quite close to Camp'.

IN THE year 19— there were two members of the Troop of Scouts attached to a famous school, named respectively Arthur Wilcox and Stanley Judkins. They were the same age, boarded in the same house, were in the same division, and naturally were members of the same patrol. They were so much alike in appearance as to cause anxiety and trouble, and even irritation, to the masters who came in contact with them. But oh how different were they in their inward man, or boy!

It was to Arthur Wilcox that the Head Master said, looking up with a smile as the boy entered chambers, 'Why, Wilcox, there will be a deficit in the prize fund if you stay here much longer! Here, take this handsomely bound copy of the *Life and Works of Bishop Ken*, and with it my hearty congratulations to yourself and your excellent parents.' It was Wilcox again, whom the Provost noticed as he passed through the playing fields, and, pausing for a moment, observed to the Vice-Provost, 'That lad has a remarkable brow!' 'Indeed, yes,' said the Vice-Provost. 'It denotes either genius or water on the brain.'

As a Scout, Wilcox secured every badge and distinction for which he competed. The Cookery Badge, the Map-making Badge, the Life-saving Badge, the Badge for picking up bits of newspaper, the Badge for not slamming the door when leaving pupil-room, and many others. Of the Life-saving Badge I may have a word to say when we come to treat of Stanley Judkins.

You cannot be surprised to hear that Mr Hope Jones added a special verse to each of his songs, in commendation of Arthur Wilcox, or that the Lower Master burst into tears when handing him the Good Conduct Medal in its handsome claret-coloured case: the medal which had been unanimously voted to him by the whole of Third Form. Unanimously, did I say? I am wrong. There was one dissentient, Judkins *mi.*, who said that he had excellent reasons for acting as he did. He shared, it seems, a room with his major. You cannot, again, wonder that in after years Arthur Wilcox was the first, and so far the only boy, to become Captain of both the School and of the Oppidans, or that the strain of carrying out the duties of both positions, coupled with the ordinary work of the school, was so severe that a complete rest for six months, followed by a voyage round the world, was pronounced an absolute necessity by the family doctor.

It would be a pleasant task to trace the steps by which he attained the giddy eminence he now occupies; but for the moment enough of Arthur Wilcox. Time presses, and we must turn to a very different matter; the career of Stanley Judkins—Judkins *ma*.

Stanley Judkins, like Arthur Wilcox, attracted the attention of the authorities; but in quite another fashion. It was to him that the Lower Master said, with no cheerful smile, 'What, again, Judkins? A very little persistence in this course of conduct, my boy, and you will have cause to regret that you ever entered this academy. There, take that, and that, and think yourself very lucky you don't get that and that!' It was Judkins, again, whom the Provost had cause to notice as he passed through the playing fields, when a cricket ball struck him with considerable force on the ankle, and a voice from a short way off cried, 'Thank you, cut-over!' 'I think', said the Provost, pausing for a moment to rub his ankle, 'that that boy had better fetch his cricket ball for himself!' 'Indeed, yes,' said the Vice-Provost, 'and if he comes within reach, I will do my best to fetch him something else.'

As a Scout, Stanley Judkins secured no badge save those which he was able to abstract from members of other patrols. In the cookery competition he was detected trying to introduce squibs into the Dutch oven of the next-door competitors. In the tailoring competion he succeeded in sewing two boys together very firmly, with disastrous effect when they tried to get up. For the Tidiness Badge he was disqualified, because, in the Midsummer schooltime, which chanced to be hot, he could not be dissuaded from sitting with his fingers in the ink: as he said, for coolness' sake. For one piece of paper which he picked up, he must have dropped at least six banana skins or orange peels. Aged women seeing him approaching would beg him with tears in their eyes not to carry their pails of water across the road. They knew too well what the result would inevitably be. But it was in the life-saving competition that Stanley Judkins's conduct was most blameable and had the most far-reaching effects. The practice, as you know, was to throw a selected lower boy, of suitable dimensions, fully dressed, with his hands and feet tied together, into the deepest part of Cuckoo Weir, and to time the Scout whose turn it was to rescue him. On every occasion when he was entered for this competition Stanley Judkins was seized, at the critical moment, with a severe fit of cramp, which caused him to roll on the ground and utter alarming cries. This naturally distracted the attention of those present from the boy in the water, and had it not been for the presence of Arthur Wilcox the death-roll would have been a heavy one. As it was, the Lower Master found it necessary to take a firm line and say that the competition must be discontinued. It was in vain that Mr Beasley Robinson represented to him that in five competitions only four lower boys had actually succumbed. The Lower Master said that he would be the last to interfere in any way with the work of the Scouts; but that three of these boys had been valued members of his choir, and both he and Dr Ley felt that the inconvenience caused by the losses outweighed the advantages of the competitions. Besides, the correspondence with the parents of these boys had become annoying, and even distressing: they were no longer satisfied with the printed form which he was in the habit of sending out, and more than one of them had actually visited Eton and taken up much of his valuable time with complaints. So the life-saving competition is now a thing of the past.

In short, Stanley Judkins was no credit to the Scouts, and there was talk on more than one occasion of informing him that his services were no longer required. This course was strongly advocated by Mr Lambart: but in the end milder counsels prevailed, and it was decided to give him another chance.

So it is that we find him at the beginning of the Midsummer Holidays of 19— at the Scouts' camp in the beautiful district of W (or X) in the country of D (or Y).

It was a lovely morning, and Stanley Judkins and one or two of his friends—for he still had friends—lay basking on the top of the down. Stanley was lying on his stomach with his chin propped on his hands, staring into the distance.

'I wonder what that place is,' he said.

'Which place?' said one of the others.

'That sort of clump in the middle of the field down there.'

'Oh, ah! How should I know what it is?'

'What do you want to know for?' said another.

'I don't know: I like the look of it. What's it called? Nobody got a map?' said Stanley. 'Call yourselves Scouts!'

'Here's a map all right,' said Wilfred Pipsqueak, ever resourceful, 'and there's the place marked on it. But it's inside the red ring. We can't go there.'

'Who cares about a red ring?' said Stanley. 'But it's got no name on your silly map.'

'Well, you can ask this old chap what it's called if you're so keen to find out.' 'This old chap' was an old shepherd who had come up and was standing behind them.

'Good morning, young gents,' he said, 'you've got a fine day for your doin's, ain't you?'

'Yes, thank you,' said Algernon de Montmorency, with native politeness. 'Can you tell us what that clump over there's called? And what's that thing inside it?'

'Course I can tell you,' said the shepherd. 'That's Wailin' Well, that is. But you ain't got no call to worry about that.'

'Is it a well in there?' said Algernon. 'Who uses it?'

The shepherd laughed. 'Bless you,' he said, 'there ain't from a man to a sheep in these parts uses Wailin' Well, nor haven't done all the years I've lived here.'

'Well, there'll be a record broken today, then,' said Stanley Judkins, 'because I shall go and get some water out of it for tea!'

'Sakes alive, young gentleman!' said the shepherd in a startled voice, 'don't you get to talkin' that way! Why, ain't your masters give you notice not to go by there? They'd ought to have done.'

'Yes, they have,' said Wilfred Pipsqueak.

'Shut up, you ass!' said Stanley Judkins. 'What's the matter with it? Isn't the water good? Anyhow, if it was boiled, it would be all right.'

'I don't know as there's anything much wrong with the water,' said the shepherd. 'All I know is, my old dog wouldn't go through that field, let alone me or anyone else that's got a morsel of brains in their heads.'

'More fool them,' said Stanley Judkins, at once rudely and ungrammatically. 'Who ever took any harm going there?' he added.

'Three women and a man,' said the shepherd gravely. 'Now just you listen to me. I know these 'ere parts and you don't, and I can tell you this much: for these ten years last past there ain't been a sheep fed in that field, nor a crop raised off of it—and it's good land, too. You can pretty well see from here what a state it's got into with brambles and suckers and trash of all kinds. You've got a glass, young gentleman,' he said to Wilfred Pipsqueak, 'you can tell with that anyway.'

'Yes,' said Wilfred, 'but I see there's tracks in it. Someone must go through it sometimes.'

'Tracks!' said the shepherd. 'I believe you! Four tracks: three women and a man.'

'What d'you mean, three women and a man?' said Stanley, turning over for the first time and looking at the shepherd (he had been talking with his back to him till this moment: he was an ill-mannered boy).

'Mean? Why, what I says: three women and a man.'

'Who are they?' asked Algernon. 'Why do they go there?'

'There's some p'r'aps could tell you who they *was*,' said the shepherd, 'but it was afore my time they come by their end. And why they goes there still is more than the children of men can tell: except I've heard they was all bad 'uns when they was alive.'

'By George, what a rum thing!' Algernon and Wilfred muttered: but Stanley was scornful and bitter.

'Why, you don't mean they're deaders? What rot! You must be a lot of fools to believe that. Who's ever seen them, I'd like to know?'

'*I've* seen 'em, young gentleman!' said the shepherd, 'seen 'em from nearby on that bit of down: and my old dog, if he could speak, he'd tell you he've seen 'em, same time. About four o'clock of the day it was, much such a day as this. I see 'em, each one of 'em, come peerin' out of the bushes and stand up, and work their way slow by them tracks towards the trees in the middle where the well is.'

'And what were they like? Do tell us!' said Algernon and Wilfred eagerly.

'Rags and bones, young gentlemen: all four of 'em: flutterin' rags and whitey bones. It seemed to me as if I could hear 'em clackin' as they got along. Very slow they went, and lookin' from side to side.'

'What were their faces like? Could you see?'

'They hadn't much to call faces,' said the shepherd, 'but I could seem to see as they had teeth.'

'Lor'!' said Wilfred, 'and what did they do when they got to the trees?'

'I can't tell you that, sir,' said the shepherd. 'I wasn't for stayin' in that place, and if I had been, I was bound to look to my old dog: he'd gone! Such a thing he never done before as leave me; but gone he had, and when I came up with him in the end, he was in that state he didn't know me, and was fit to fly at my throat. But I kep' talkin' to him, and after a bit he remembered my voice and came creepin' up like a child askin' pardon. I never want to see him like that again, nor yet no other dog.'

The dog, who had come up and was making friends all round, looked up at his master, and expressed agreement with what he was saying very fully.

The boys pondered for some moments on what they had heard: after which Wilfred said: 'And why's it called Wailing Well?'

'If you was round here at dusk of a winter's evening, you wouldn't want to ask why,' was all the shepherd said.

'Well, I don't believe a word of it,' said Stanley Judkins, 'and I'll go there next chance I get: blowed if I don't!'

'Then you won't be ruled by me?' said the shepherd. 'Nor yet by your masters as warned you off? Come now, young gentleman, you don't want for sense, I should say. What should I want tellin' you a pack of lies? It ain't sixpence to me anyone goin' in that field: but I wouldn't like to see a young chap snuffed out like in his prime.'

'I expect it's a lot more than sixpence to you,' said Stanley. 'I expect you've got a whisky still or something in there, and want to keep other people away. Rot I call it. Come on back, you boys.'

So they turned away. The two others said, 'Good evening' and 'Thank you' to the shepherd, but Stanley said nothing. The shepherd shrugged his shoulders and stood where he was, looking after them rather sadly.

On the way back to the camp there was great argument about it all, and Stanley was told as plainly as he could be told all the sorts of fools he would be if he went to the Wailing Well.

That evening, among other notices, Mr Beasley Robinson asked if all maps had got the red ring marked on them. 'Be particular,' he said, 'not to trespass inside it.'

Several voices—among them the sulky one of Stanley Judkins—said 'Why not, sir?'

'Because not,' said Mr Beasley Robinson, 'and if that isn't enough for you, I can't help it.' He turned and spoke to Mr Lambart in a low voice, and then said, 'I'll tell you this much: we've been asked to warn Scouts off that field. It's very good of the people to let us camp here at all, and the least we can do is to oblige them—I'm sure you'll agree to that.'

Everybody said, 'Yes, sir!' except Stanley Judkins, who was heard to mutter, 'Oblige them be blowed!'

Early in the afternoon of the next day, the following dialogue was heard. 'Wilcox, is all your tent there?'

'No, sir, Judkins isn't!'

'That boy is *the* most infernal nuisance ever invented! Where do you suppose he is?'

'I haven't an idea, sir.'

'Does anybody else know?'

'Sir, I shouldn't wonder if he'd gone to the Wailing Well.'

'Who's that? Pipsqueak? What's the Wailing Well?'

'Sir, it's that place in the field by—well, sir, it's in a clump of trees in a rough field.'

'D'you mean inside the red ring? Good heavens! What makes you think he's gone there?'

'Why, he was terribly keen to know about it yesterday, and we were talking to a shepherd man, and he told us a lot about it and advised us not to go there: but Judkins didn't believe him, and said he meant to go.'

'Young ass!' said Mr Hope Jones, 'did he take anything with him?'

'Yes, I think he took some rope and a can. We did tell him he'd be a fool to go.'

'Little brute! What the deuce does he mean by pinching stores like that! Well, come along, you three, we must see after him. Why can't people keep the simplest orders? What was it the man told you? No, don't wait, let's have it as we go along.'

And off they started—Algernon and Wilfred talking rapidly and the other two listening with growing concern. At last they reached that spur of down overlooking the field of which the shepherd had spoken the day before. It commanded the place completely; the well inside the clump of bent and gnarled Scotch firs was plainly visible, and so were the four tracks winding about among the thorns and rough growth.

It was a wonderful day of shimmering heat. The sea looked like a floor of metal. There was no breath of wind. They were all exhausted when they got to the top, and flung themselves down on the hot grass.

'Nothing to be seen of him yet,' said Mr Hope Jones, 'but we must stop here a bit. You're done up—not to speak of me. Keep a sharp look-out,' he went on after a moment, 'I thought I saw the bushes stir.'

'Yes,' said Wilcox, 'so did I. Look . . . no, that can't be him, It's somebody though, putting their head up, isn't it?'

'I thought it was, but I'm not sure.'

Silence for a moment. Then:

'That's him, sure enough,' said Wilcox, 'getting over the hedge on the far side. Don't you see? With a shiny thing. That's the can you said he had.'

'Yes, it's him, and he's making straight for the trees,' said Wilfred.

At this moment Algernon, who had been staring with all his might, broke into a scream.

'What's that on the track? On all fours—O, it's the woman. O, don't let me look at her! Don't let it happen!' And he rolled over, clutching at the grass and trying to bury his head in it.

'Stop that!' said Mr Hope Jones loudly—but it was no use. 'Look here,' he said, 'I must go down there. You stop here, Wilfred, and look after that boy. Wilcox, you run as hard as you can to the camp and get some help.'

They ran off, both of them. Wilfred was left alone with Algernon, and did his best to calm him, but indeed he was not much happier himself. From time to time he glanced down the hill and into the field. He saw Mr Hope Jones drawing nearer at a swift pace, and then, to his great surprise, he saw him stop, look up and round about him, and turn quickly off at an angle! What could be the reason? He looked at the field, and there he saw a terrible figure—something in ragged black—with whitish patches breaking out of it: the head, perched on a long thin neck, half hidden by a shapeless sort of blackened sun-bonnet. The creature was waving thin arms in the direction of the rescuer who was approaching, as if to ward him off: and between the two figures the air seemed to shake and shimmer as he had never seen it: and as he looked, he began himself to feel something of a waviness and confusion in his brain, which made him guess what might be the effect on someone within closer range of the influence. He looked away hastily, to see Stanley Judkins making his way pretty quickly towards the clump, and in proper Scout fashion; evidently picking his steps with care to avoid treading on snapping sticks or being caught by arms of brambles. Evidently, though he saw nothing, he suspected some sort of ambush, and was trying to go noiselessly. Wilfred saw all that, and he saw more, too. With a sudden and dreadful sinking at the heart, he caught sight of someone among the trees, waiting: and again of someone—another of the hideous black figures—working slowly along the track from another side of the field, looking from side to side, as the shepherd had described it. Worst of all, he saw a fourth—unmistakably a man this time—rising out of the bushes a few yards behind the wretched Stanley, and painfully, as it seemed, crawling into the track. On all sides the miserable victim was cut off.

Wilfred was at his wits' end. He rushed at Algernon and shook him. 'Get up,' he said. 'Yell! Yell as loud as you can. Oh, if we'd got a whistle!'

Algernon pulled himself together. 'There's one,' he said, 'Wilcox's: he must have dropped it.'

So one whistled, the other screamed. In the still air the sound carried. Stanley heard: he stopped: he turned round: and then indeed a cry was heard more piercing and dreadful than any that the boys on the hill could raise. It was too late. The crouched figure behind Stanley sprang at him and caught him about the waist. The dreadful one that was standing waving her arms waved them again, but in exultation. The one that was lurking among the trees shuffled forward, and she too stretched out her arms as if to clutch at something coming her way; and the other, farthest off, quickened her pace and came on, nodding gleefully. The boys took it all in in an instant of terrible silence, and hardly could they breathe as they watched the horrid struggle between the man and his victim. Stanley struck with his can, the only weapon he had. The rim of a broken black hat fell off the creature's head and showed a white skull with stains that might be wisps of hair. By this time one of the women had reached the pair, and was pulling at the rope that was coiled about Stanley's neck. Between them they overpowered him in a moment: the awful screaming ceased, and then the three passed within the circle of the clump of firs.

Yet for a moment it seemed as if rescue might come. Mr Hope Jones, striding quickly along, suddenly stopped, turned, seemed to rub his eyes, and then started running *towards* the field. More: the boys glanced behind them, and saw not only a troop of figures from the camp coming over the top of the next down, but the shepherd running up the slope of their own hill. They beckoned, they shouted, they ran a few yards towards him and then back again. He mended his pace.

Once more the boys looked towards the field. There was nothing. Or, was there something among the trees? Why was there a mist about the trees? Mr Hope Jones had scrambled over the hedge, and was plunging through the bushes.

The shepherd stood beside them, panting. They ran to him and clung to his arms. 'They've got him! In the trees!' was as much as they could say, over and over again.

'What? Do you tell me he've gone in there after all I said to him yesterday? Poor young thing! Poor young thing!' He would have said more, but other voices broke in. The rescuers from the camp had arrived. A few hasty words, and all were dashing down the hill.

They had just entered the field when they met Mr Hope Jones. Over his shoulder hung the corpse of Stanley Judkins. He had cut it from the branch to which he found it hanging, waving to and fro. There was not a drop of blood in the body.

On the following day Mr Hope Jones sallied forth with an axe and with the expressed intention of cutting down every tree in the clump, and of burning every bush in the field. He returned with a nasty cut in his leg and a broken axe-helve. Not a spark of fire could he light, and on no single tree could he make the least impression.

I have heard that the present population of the Wailing Well field consists of three women, a man, and a boy.

The shock experienced by Algernon de Montmorency and Wilfred Pipsqueak was severe. Both of them left the camp at once; and the occurrence undoubtedly cast a gloom—if but a passing one—on those who remained. One of the first to recover his spirits was Judkins *mi*.

Such, gentlemen, is the story of the career of Stanley Judkins, and of a portion of the career of Arthur Wilcox. It has, I believe, never been told before. If it has a moral, that moral is, I trust, obvious: if it has none, I do not well know how to help it.

ANOTHER SQUAW?

E. Heron-Allen

Edward Heron-Allen (1861–1943) was a notable scholar and marine biologist who published several books on his specialized subjects, violin-making, cheirosophy, and the local history of Selsey where he lived. In the First World War he was attached to Staff Intelligence. He remains an intriguing and rather mysterious figure, deserving of a full biography. He was a close acquaintance of Bram Stoker from the 1880s onwards and wrote a novel of psychic vampirism, *The Princess Daphne* (published in 1888). Much later he wrote a series of unusual horror tales under the pseudonym of Christopher Blayre, from the fictitious habitat of the University of Cosmopoli. These stories were collected as *The Purple Sapphire* (1921), expanded and reissued as *The Strange Papers of Dr Blayre* (1932). Four more Cosmopoli tales were privately printed by Heron-Allen in 1934, limited to only 100 copies, and entitled *Some Women at the University*. The 'blood is the life' motif runs strongly through the book, notably in the lengthy Stoker-inspired vampire story set in Austria, 'Zum Wildbad', and the equally memorable shorter tale reprinted here: 'Another Squaw?'

From *The Times*, 4th November, 19—
'On November 2nd, at the Marine Biological Station, Baxmouth, the result of an accident, *Jennifer Sidonia Pendeen, B.Sc.*, in her twenty-sixth year. Funeral at Polperro, Cornwall, on Monday, November 5th, at 2 p.m.'

IN THE concluding years of the nineteenth century, Bram Stoker, the efficient and justly celebrated manager of the Lyceum Theatre in the palmy days of Sir Henry Irving, and author of many works of fiction, the best-known of which at the present day is his Vampire novel *Dracula*, published a short story, entitled 'The Squaw', a horrible story, only redeemed by its utter impossibility and extravagantly exaggerated anthropomorphism.

In this story an American tourist, leaning over the battlements, or parapet, of the Schloss at Nuremberg, dislodges a large stone, which, falling into the moat below, strikes and kills the single kitten of a cat which happened to be lying at the foot of the keep. The frantic efforts of the mother cat to scale the wall and get at the murderer of her kitten are vividly described. Later in the day, when the tourist and his friends are visiting the Museum of Instruments of Torture, the cat has gained admission with them, after the manner of cats, and is malevolently prowling round the turret-room in which the 'Iron Maiden' is exhibited by the attendant, who, by pulling a lever, opens the 'Maiden', revealing the huge spikes which, when the 'Maiden' is closed upon the victim forced into it, stabs him in a score of vital spots. On this occasion, the lever having been pulled and the 'doors' being thus held open for the inspection of the inside by visitors, the tourist in Stoker's story questioning whether a full-grown man could be forced inside, insists upon entering the 'Maiden'. At that moment the cat, who has been watching her opportunity for revenge, springs at the attendant and claws at his eyes. The wretched man, maddened with pain, lets go the lever, the doors clang to upon the tourist, and he meets with a hideous death. As I have said, the impossible anthropomorphism of the cat robs the story of its ghastliness, and it was received (as it was intended to be) as an ingeniously gruesome effort at sensationalism.

The circumstances which I am about to record recalled this story to my mind; I record them as they happened, and must leave the reader of these lines to form his own conclusions.

One of my most brilliant pupils, and later my assistant in the Zoological Department, of the University of Cosmopoli, was Miss Jennifer Pendeen, a Cornish girl, who, having taken her science degree, became in turn demonstrator in my department, and, in due course, my assistant lecturer. Her special subject was fishes, and she was engaged, at the time of which I write, upon an intensive study of the oceanic angler-fishes, the Ceratioids, which inhabit the open ocean, living generally from about 500 to 2000 metres (250 to 1000 fathoms) below the surface. These fishes are, for the most part, uniformly blackish in colour, and their 'bait' (or 'lure') is a luminous bulb, which attracts their prey to within a catching distance. Their teeth, which are long, slender and very sharp, can be sloped inwards at will, with the result that when a fish gets caught between them it cannot get back, but must proceed into the stomach—after the manner of an awn of creeping grass. The angler-fish is fortunately (for itself) extremely distensible, and it can swallow and 'accommodate' fishes several times its own length and weight. Once seized by the teeth of the angler, the victim cannot escape, nor can the angler cast itself loose and reject its prey.

A salient and remarkable peculiarity of the angler is that all the free-swimming fish are females, the males being little parasitic dwarves, which live indissolubly attached to the females. As soon as the male is hatched, it seeks a female, to which it attaches itself—

anywhere where it can lay hold. In a short while the lips, tongue and teeth of the male 'fuse' with the skin of the female, and the two are thenceforth inseparably united. His mouth, being closed by the skin of the female, and, in due course, absorbed, the male can no longer feed himself, but is nourished by the bloodstream of the female, which reaches him through an anastosmosis of the blood system, which thus becomes continuous and common to both male and female—indeed, the alimentary canal of the male becomes vestigial and his stomach rudimentary, and he becomes a mere appendage to the female, receiving nourishment through capilliary veins in what used to be his snout. This condition of things is unique in the vertebrate animal kingdom. Instances are known of females three feet six inches in length whose parasitic husbands are no more than three inches long, and of females having two or more 'husbands' welded into, and parasitic upon them. They 'stick' where they first strike, anywhere—on the head, on the abdomen or by the tail, and live happily ever after with a wife who may be a thousand times as large as they are.

The reproduction of these fishes would appear to be brought about by an 'urge' at spawning time, effected by some *hormone* which causes the female to discharge her ova, which are immediately fertilized by the parasitic male—this is the only incident and object of his existence. Females have been caught without parasitic males, but the males have never been caught separately, which is not remarkable, seeing that they live in perpetual darkness, mostly at very low temperatures, and would seldom be retained by any net of large enough and strong enough mesh to capture the female.

It was to this remarkable group of fishes that Jennifer Pendeen was devoting her attention and studies at the time of which I am writing. Her Monograph upon the group, which it was my somewhat melancholy task to prepare for, and see through the press, after her tragic and mysterious death, is the outstanding and most notable contribution to the literature of the subject. Her great ambition, which, as we shall see, was ultimately realized, was to obtain a living specimen and to study its life-history.

The difficulties in the way of this seemed to be insurmountable, for it must be remembered that these fish swim about at depths of from 250 to 1000 fathoms. Now, taking the pressure of the atmosphere at sea-level to be fifteen pounds to the square inch and 33 feet of sea-water being equal to 30 inches of mercury, at a depth of 33 feet in the sea, the pressure would be two atmospheres, or 15 pounds; at 99 feet, 3 atmospheres, or 45 pounds to the square inch—and so on as one goes deeper. So, at 2000 fathoms, the pressure is of 360 atmospheres, i.e. 5,400 pounds (or 2.4 tons) to the square inch. The effect of decrease of pressure upon deep sea fish is well known. As the fish is drawn to the surface the decrease of pressure causes their swim bladders to expand, and after rising a certain distance they go on, as Sir John Murray put it, 'tumbling inwards', and they are killed by the distensions of their organs as the pressure becomes less and less. It has been found, however, that fishes brought up from moderate depths, to all appearances dead, can be revived by keeping them in 'compressing chambers', in which the pressure is not much less than that at which they were caught, and on gradually diminishing the pressure, their intercellular fluids have time to get into equilibrium, and the fish gradually recovers its normal functions and powers of movement.

This was the problem with which Jennifer Pendeen was confronted, and to it she devoted long-protracted and ingenious experiments, at first with fish from moderate depths, and gradually with specimens from deeper ocean strata, which she caused to be caught in copper cylinders, which could be hermetically closed by a 'messenger' (as it is called) sent down the line when the delicate instruments used in the experiments announced that a fish had entered the cylinder.

The opportunity, of which during the few years of her working life she had had a 'Pisgah-view', came at last when thé 'Deep Sea Exploration Expedition' was organized by the University of Cosmopoli, under the leadership of Captain John Satterley, R.N., who presented the rare phenomena of a naval officer of distinguished service record, who was not only an expert hydrographer (which might, at a stretch, have been expected), but also a keen marine biologist. He had even put in six months, when home on leave, at the Baxmouth Marine Biological Station, and the Lords of the Admiralty 'seconded' him for service with the Cosmopoli University Expedition at the request of the Senate. A Cornishman himself, and Jennifer Pendeen being the child of an old friend, though at first taking a somewhat humoristic view of her 'study', he gradually came round to an earnest interest in it.

Under their joint supervision a copper cylinder was constructed, tested for implosive and explosive pressure up to 90 atmospheres, open at both ends, save for hinged coverings—'lids'—of fine wire netting. This could be lowered to any depth, and the desired depth attained, the wire covers could be withdrawn, and at a given moment their place could be taken by copper covers, which closed the cylinder to all intents and purposes hermetically. The interior was heavily chromium-plated to withstand the action of sea water. An electrical appliance indicated on deck when any object above a certain size entered the cylinder, by weight and oscillation.

This cylinder trap was sent down 'baited' with a quantity of small fish, which, of course, were killed by the increasing pressure, but remained in the cylinder. These, it was anticipated, might attract larger 'denizens of the deep' when the wire ends were removed or opened. Time and again the cylinder was 'down' for various lengths of time and was hauled up again, nothing whatever having happened. Glass panels in the sides, protected by a slipping collar or band, enabled the observers to see whether any fish was inside, and frequently fishes (not *Ceratias*) came up in the cylinder, which were released, and exploded on the spot. A detailed account of their 'results' would not be germane to our subject, but they did fish up some very queer creatures.

At last the long-looked-for moment arrived—the presence of a large fish in the cylinder was indicated, and, as usual, the ends were closed and the cylinder hauled on deck. Inside it was a *Ceratias* some four feet long, and the cylinder was hurried home and placed in a large narrow tank filled with sea water, kept at an appropriate temperature, in the Marine Biological Laboratory at Baxmouth, where Jennifer Pendeen was waiting to receive it. By means of an ingenious apparatus in the nature of a pressure gauge, attachable to the cylinder, the *Ceratias* was carefully and gradually 'decompressed', and, as good luck would have it, it had kept and did keep itself alive with the corpses of the 'martyrs to science', which had been sent down in the cylinder as bait. In a much shorter time than Jennifer had anticipated, the *Ceratias* got into equilibrium with its surroundings and was let out into the tank, not, apparently, any the worse for its environment.

It became known in the laboratory as Jennifer's 'pet'. She had sole charge of it, and—a true Cornishwoman—she christened it 'Ysolde'. Attached immediately below its right pectoral fin was a perfectly formed and apparently happy—though undemonstrative—parasitic male. Him she christened 'Tristan'.

Remarkable testimony to the care, attention and efficiency, primarily of Jennifer Pendeen and generally of the staff of the Baxmouth Marine Laboratory, is afforded by the fact that this curious *menage* settled down, lived and flourished in the tank that it inhabited. At the end of a month Jennifer began to consider in all its bearings the biological experiment that she had in view; this was neither more nor less than to separate them: to excise Tristan, and, by an ingenious system of artificial feeding—if such a term may be permissible in the case of a fish whose mouth-parts and alimentary system have become vestigial—to keep him alive. The interest taken in the affair by the Zoological Department of the University was keen, and it was fully shared by the Director and staff of the Zoological Gardens and Aquarium of the town of Cosmopoli. Many were the conferences which Jennifer held with Sir George Amboyne, the Regius Professor of Medicine, and Michelson, the Prosecutor of the Zoo, both of whom, it may be said at once, were of opinion that the idea was fantastic, and its execution impossible, but Sir George went so far as to interest an eminent surgeon in the matter, who undertook to perform the operation under the direction and supervision of Michelson. Jennifer's theory was, that if skilfully

performed, so as not to injure any vital part of the fish, Ysolde would not suffer from the operation, and that Tristan might be kept alive—*ein toller Einfall*, as Burger, the Reader in German, put it.

The conditions and formalities imposed by the Vivisection Act of 1876 were scrupulously carried out and the necessary licence obtained, and one morning, when Tristan and Ysolde had inhabited their tank for about two months, the operation was performed in the circumstances above indicated. Ysolde was carefully 'repaired' and returned to her tank, and after a few hours of restlessness seemed none the worse for her divorce. The only change apparent in her was that she developed a nervousness that she had not hitherto exhibited, and seemed averse to allowing Jennifer to touch and 'tickle' her as she had been wont to do. As Jennifer put it: 'She does not trust me any more, and when I feed her I think she would like to snap at me—it would be rather awful if she got those recurved teeth of hers into my hand!'

With Tristan I regret to say that it was a different matter. For about twenty-four hours he showed signs, unmistakable, of life, lying on his side at the bottom of his little tank, but next day he equally unmistakably died, and received the decent interment due to another martyr of science.

Any student or biologist who is working at the Baxmouth Laboratory is given, on his (or her) arrival, a latch-key to the building, so that he can visit his work and observe its progress at any hour of the night as well as by day. By this means many biological experiments of great importance have been facilitated, the workers in many well-known instances spending their nights in the laboratory. Jennifer, who was at this time the guest of the Director and his wife, made it her practice, at least once in the night, to come down and see how Ysolde was getting on.

It was about three weeks after the *Ehescheidung* that the maid who brought her matutinal tea found that she was not in her room. An hour later she had not returned, though her clothes were as she left them overnight, and so the matter was reported to the Director. He assumed that Jennifer was in the tank-room as usual, but when she did not put in an appearance at breakfast time he went to look for her.

The spectacle that met his eyes was terrible. Clad in her pyjamas and a thin silk wrapper, Jennifer was lying huddled together at the bottom of the tank on the top of Ysolde. Summoning assistance, he lifted her out, and Ysolde came with her, very much alive and lashing out furiously. She had caught Jennifer by the forearm, as, evidently, she had leaned over the edge of the tank, and reached down to touch her. The formidable recurved teeth had met in Jennifer's arm; Ysolde could not have let go, *had she wished or striven to do so*, and Jennifer, encumbered and entangled in her wrapper, could not have struggled to the surface owing to the narrowness of the tank, and the fact that she was on the top of her captor. In the opinion of the doctor, who was summoned, she had been dead about five hours.

Another Squaw?

THE LIVING STONE

E. R. Punshon

Ernest Robertson Punshon (1872–1956) began work at the age of fourteen as a clerk in a London office. He soon tired of this trade and emigrated to Canada (like Algernon Blackwood, who headed west at the same time), intending to make his fortune growing wheat. This came to nothing, and for the next few years he wandered about Canada and the United States. After returning home by working a passage on a cattle boat, he began to write popular thrillers and never looked back. *Punch* described him as 'one of the most entertaining and readable of our sensational novelists because his characters really live and are not merely pegs from which a mystery depends'. Chiefly remembered now for his detective novels, he also contributed some fine weird tales to magazines which have never been reprinted. 'The Living Stone' appeared in the *Cornhill*, for September 1939 (in the same volume that carried M. R. James's 'Letters to a Child').

❧

Life sleeps in the stone, dreams in the plant, wakens in the animal.
Ancient Hindu saying

I

THERE was a general giggle.

The quaint little gentleman from London, beaming on them through his enormous horn-rimmed glasses, might be as learned as learned professors must always be, but fancy asking a question like that when the name of their little inn, 'The Missing Men', was the general jest all through this lonely Cornish district. Why, whenever any of the local inhabitants was missing from his own hearthside, here in the comfortable warm bar of 'The Missing Men' was the place to seek and generally to find. One or two of those present laboriously explained the point of the pleasantry, and the little professor listened gravely.

'I see,' he said.

It was the chair of comparative religion at the Great Southern University that he held, and though few there knew what comparative religion was, and probably none had even heard of his great work on

'Human Sacrifice' in which was traced the history of that dark, evil rite from early days—the days of Abraham and Isaac—down to the faint traces of it still surviving, as when the small boy in city streets asks for a penny for the guy he means presently to offer up in fire, or, more sinister, in the offering of the youth of the nation on the sacrificial altar of that new god, the State, yet all knew that awe and reverence are a professor's due. For a professor is a person of strange knowledge, and therefore of strange powers, since knowledge is always power.

But now they felt more at their ease, now that he had shown he shared their common humanity by asking so simple a question and needing to have so simple a pleasantry explained to him. The professor took the giggling in good part. He wondered how long the name had been in use. No one knew. Most thought name and inn were co-existent.

'I asked,' explained the professor, 'because I noticed on the map there's a lane near here that seems to be called "Missing Lane"'.

The jesting suddenly ceased, as abruptly as though those fatal words: 'Time, gentlemen, time,' had boomed out suddenly from behind the bar.

'I was wondering,' the professor explained, 'whether the inn took its name from the lane, or the lane from the inn.'

No one seemed to know. No one seemed to care. The conversation showed a tendency to revert to football pools, an engrossing if limited topic. The professor did not seem interested in football pools. He had arrived by car that afternoon from London, a late survival of the touring season since now it was dark and chilly November when motorist and hiker alike seek their repose. He took an opportunity of a pause, while all were wrapped in silent contemplation of the curious fact that others habitually won enormous prizes in the pools, but none of them ever did, to remark:

'I couldn't make out from the map where that lane led.'

'Well, it doesn't rightly lead nowheres in particular,' explained the landlord.

'Well, now, that's odd,' murmured the professor. 'If it goes no-where, why is it at all?'

No one seemed to know that either. It was just there. It had always been there. That was all. Went to the top of the hill, and, so to say, got lost there.

'Missing Lane, in fact,' mused the professor. 'Perhaps how it got its name. I suppose, if it goes nowhere, it's not often used?'

It began to appear that the lane was in fact very seldom used. Continued over the hill it would have provided a short and convenient way to the nearest market town. Only, somehow, no one seemed ever to have thought of that. Men working in the fields by which it ran used it sometimes, and, in the autumn, blackberrying parties, since the summit of the hill, were finally the lane lost itself, was famous for blackberries. But the blackberry pickers went always in parties, it seemed, and never stayed late.

'Not if they've sense, they don't,' said an old man who hitherto had hardly spoken. 'And if they do, maybe it's them that's missing or some of 'em.'

'Now grandpa,' interposed the landlord warningly.

'Thirty years ago,' said the old man, 'and never none to tell to this day what became of Polly Hill.'

'Wasn't there something in the paper the other day about a young woman who had disappeared from somewhere about here?' asked the professor.

'That would be Aggie, little Aggie Polton,' said someone else.

'Good-looking piece,' said the landlord. 'Lordy, when girls take themselves off, they have their own reasons. Flighty, that was Aggie.'

It appeared that Aggie had had something of a reputation. Most evenings, the tale went, she had a 'date' with one or other of the young men of the neighbourhood. On one occasion, a little time previously, there had been one of these 'dates' with the son of the local butcher. He had not been able to keep it. His mother had had suspicions, and naturally looked higher than poor little Aggie for her son, no matter how fascinating Aggie's blue eyes and curls might be. The general opinion was that Aggie had 'taken the huff', had been afraid of being laughed at, and had gone off to London, as she had often spoken of doing, in order to become one of those fascinating young ladies known as 'Nippies', whose portraits in the papers had aroused her mingled admiration and envy.

Only it was true no trace of her in London had as yet been found.

'No great loss, a girl like her, setting all the lads at odds,' said someone else. 'But I reckon Mr Phelps up at Tor Farm would give a deal to know what's become of "Beauty of Bolton Three."'

'What's that?' asked the professor.

He was told that 'Beauty of Bolton Three' was a prize bull, worth some two or three hundred pounds, perfect in every way, and so tame and peaceable that it was allowed to graze out in the fields without any special precautions being taken. It was always brought in at night, but the other evening, when a farm lad went to fetch it as usual, though at a later hour than was customary, it wasn't there. No sign of it. Nothing to show what had happened to it.

'Curious,' said the professor. 'Curious about the young lady who was mentioned just now. Curious, too, about Polly Hill thirty years ago. Curious again that in the Annual Register of sixty years back there's mention of a valuable stallion that vanished in this neighbourhood. Supposed to have been stolen by the groom, as he vanished himself next day.'

'That's sixty years gone,' said the landlord doubtfully. 'I wasn't born then,' and he had the air of suggesting that what had happened before he was born really didn't matter very much.

'Lot of interesting reading in the Annual Register,' observed the professor, 'and odd how often there is a mention of this neighbourhood at intervals of thirty years. Was Mr Phelps's bull in the field near the Hunting Stone? That stands at the top of Missing Lane, doesn't it?'

'That's right,' said the landlord, somewhat surprised at this display of local knowledge; 'but there's no mystery about the bull being missing. Worth a mort of money. 'Ticed away and hidden somewhere till he can be smuggled off to foreign parts.'

'Not so easy to 'tice away,' interposed the old man who had spoken of the missing Polly Hill of long ago, 'and someone got hurt, too; for there was blood on the Hunting Stone. I seen it myself and didn't stop to look for long, neither.'

'Why is it called the Hunting Stone?' asked the professor.

The landlord said he supposed it had always been called that. The professor asked if the stains supposed to be blood seen on the base of the Hunting Stone had been examined or analysed. No one had thought of having that done. There seemed no reason. It was mentioned that the only trace of the recently vanished Aggie, the girl with the fondness for making 'dates' and the ambition some day to become a 'Nippy', had been her handbag found near this same Hunting Stone. Probably her 'date' with the youthful heir of the local butcher had been made for the foot of Missing Lane. When he failed to keep it, she might well have wandered up the lane rather than go straight home, but what had happened to her after that was entirely a matter for conjecture.

The door opened and an elderly woman looked in.

'Our Tim here?' she asked. 'He's not been home.'

No one had seen her Tim and she went away grumblingly. The landlord winked at the professor.

'Out after rabbits,' he said, 'that's where her Tim is, and he'll be copped some day. But there's a mort of them up by that there Hunting Stone.'

The old man in the corner got up to go. In the doorway he turned: 'Tim's a fool if he goes after rabbits there,' he said, 'for if there's rabbits there, there's more than rabbits, too.'

He went out, and the landlord laughed, though a trifle uneasily.

'To hear him talk,' he said, 'there might be something queer about that there lump of granite what's been standing up on the hill ever since the Flood, so to say.'

'I think I'll have a look at it myself,' observed the professor, 'but not tonight.'

'No, I wouldn't tonight,' agreed the landlord.

II

It was in fact high noon before the professor next day walked slowly and warily up the Missing Lane that was hardly a lane at all but rather a rough track with fields on one side—the south—and the bare slope of the hill on the other, the north. Where the cultivated land ceased and the ground grew rough and bare with scattered blackberry bushes at intervals and many rabbit holes all around, stood the Hunting Stone, a huge upright oblong block of granite, standing on a sort of rough base. It was some eight or nine feet high and must have weighed many tons. On its face were carved signs that once may have been letters or symbols of some kind but that the wind and the rain of innumerable years had worn in part away. Reared by who could tell what strange distant tribe of men in what strange dawn of humanity, or by what pain or sacrifice in dragging that enormous weight from the distant quarry where it had been carved, all through the slow centuries it had stood on this bare hillside. Now at its base there sat a burly man in plus fours, smoking a pipe, and the professor nodded a greeting.

'Nice morning, chief inspector,' he said, 'but I wouldn't sit there if I were you.'

Chief Inspector Harris of Scotland Yard looked surprised, but got up all the same, for his was a disciplined mind and for all professors he had a proper respect.

'Why not?' he asked. 'It's firm enough. I thought I felt a tremor when I sat down, but it won't fall over just yet.'

The professor said: 'Know anything about a local lad called Tim something?'

'Reported missing,' said the chief inspector. 'You heard about that?'

'Yes,' said the professor.

'Maybe he had something to do with the "Beauty of Bolton Three" case,' observed the inspector musingly, 'but it's not so likely a smart, lively young girl like this Aggie Polton would mix up with cattle thieving.'

'No,' said the professor.

'Well, there you are,' said the chief inspector.

'Noticed anything about here?' asked the professor.

'Not a thing, except——' and he pointed to a strange, plainly marked trail on the ground as though something immensely heavy had passed that way. 'Looks like a steamroller has been by,' he remarked, 'only there can't have been, can there?'

'No,' said the professor. 'Noticed that?'

He pointed to a reddish-brown stain on the stone base just where the chief inspector had been sitting. The chief inspector shook his head. 'What is it?' he asked.

'I don't know,' said the professor, 'but I think it might be blood.'

He walked away a little distance and presently paused where the rabbit holes seemed most numerous in a low bank at a little distance. It was a fragment of a net he had picked up and he came back carrying it in his hand.

'Useful for snaring rabbits?' he suggested.

'Might be,' agreed the chief inspector. 'Why?'

'In the pub they seemed to think Tim was very likely out after rabbits,' the professor explained.

'Well then,' said the chief inspector. 'Don't think someone's kidnapped him, do you?'

'Not kidnapped, no,' said the professor.

The chief inspector strolled away and seated himself again on the base of the Hunting Stone. He got up hurriedly. He said: 'Gosh! I believe you're right.'

'What's that?' asked the professor, turning sharply.

'I thought I felt the thing move,' the chief inspector answered. 'When I sat down, I mean. A sort of movement, a tremor. As if it might topple over.' He put his hand against the stone and pushed. 'Seems firm enough,' he said.

The professor was looking at the sky. 'High noon,' he said. 'Just as well. No, I don't thing there's any chance of its toppling over.'

'Well, then,' said the chief inspector. He looked very worried and a trifle pale. He said: 'I'll swear I felt—something.' After a pause, during which the professor was silent, he added: 'If I didn't know I hadn't, I should think I had been drinking.'

'I think we'll go, shall we?' said the professor.

The chief inspector agreed, somewhat hurriedly. He was looking back over his shoulder as they walked away. He said: 'It must be the mist; it gives the thing a sort of swaying sort of look, sort of to and fro, if you know what I mean.'

'There isn't any mist,' said the professor.

He was walking very quickly. At times he almost ran.

The chief inspector said: 'What's the hurry?'

'I don't know,' answered the professor. He added presently: 'I think where you were sitting is where the victims were offered when that was a stone of sacrifice.'

'Ugh!' said the chief inspector. 'Enough to make anyone a bit jittery if they knew that.'

'Or even if they didn't,' said the professor. When they had come to the bottom of the lane, he said: 'I want you to get me a bullock, white, without spot or blemish.'

'Eh?' said the chief inspector. 'What's that?'

The professor explained. The chief inspector said firmly: 'That's plumb crazy.'

'Yes, I know,' said the professor.

'If it hadn't been for what I felt up there . . .' said the chief inspector.

'White from head to tail, without spot or blemish,' the professor repeated.

'Right-oh,' said the chief inspector. 'It's a screwy business,' he said 'I feel I want to report myself off my head.'

'You mean you want to report me,' said the professor grimly. 'I know. Only what happened to little Aggie Polton? Where is she? What's become of Mr Phelps's prize bull? Where's Tim who went up there snaring rabbits, and now it seems he isn't anywhere? And why almost every thirty years does the Annual Register report some mysterious disappearance in this district?'

'Oh, have it your own way,' said the chief inspector angrily. 'I don't believe a word of it, and what's more, I don't know where to get a what-is-it!—a white bullock without spot or blemish! We aren't cattle-dealers at the Yard.'

The professor gave him an address.

'Friend of mine,' he said. 'Big noise in the farming way. Ring him up. I asked him to see what he could do.'

The chief inspector went away to find a telephone. It was dusk when there arrived a lorry containing a fine young bullock, its hide snowy white, no spot or blemish on it from head to tail.

The professor looked it over carefully and seemed satisfied. Later on, as it drew towards midnight, by the light of the moon could have been seen the unusual sight of a learned professor and a chief inspector of Scotland Yard solemnly driving a snow-white ox up a steep and narrow lane.

It was a perfect night. The moonlight lay on the land like a faint and silvery sea, lending to all things a distant, wan enchantment. Not a breath of wind stirred. Not a living creature was abroad. It might have been a land from which all life had fled, and through it there passed slowly that small and strange procession—the snow-white bullock and the two men behind.

'Keep well back,' the professor whispered.

The chief inspector needed no such warning. He muttered presently: 'There's lots of rabbits here, but there's none about tonight.'

'They know,' the professor said.

Before them, plain in the white moonlight, the great stone showed, upright and waiting.

The chief inspector said: 'This moonlight plays queer tricks with a man's eyes.'

'So it does,' agreed the professor.

They walked on a little way. They were quite near now, or rather the bullock was quite near. The two men were some yards behind. The bullock paused and lowed uneasily and the sound seemed to travel far through the heavy silence of the moonlit night.

'I've got the jitters,' said the chief inspector. 'I've no drink taken all this day, but I could have sworn the stone was on the right-hand side of the lane.'

'So it was,' said the professor. He added: 'So it is.'

The chief inspector stood and stared.

'Well, it was on our left just now,' he said.

'So it was,' said the professor.

They stood still, The ox lowed again, a long low call. The professor took his companion by the arm. He said: 'We won't go any nearer.'

'No,' said the chief inspector. He said: 'What's that noise?'

'I think it's your teeth chattering,' said the professor. 'Or else it's mine.'

The ox moved on. Again it lowed. It stood still and then once more moved forward, very slowly, as if irresistibly impelled.

'Look,' screamed the professor.

They saw. In the pale moonlight they saw clearly. They saw the great stone as it were heave itself forward. Plainly they saw how it lifted itself from its base and propelled itself upon the approaching ox. Earth and sky were still, still and motionless were the two men, the ox was still as they, as the vast immobile block of that huge stone lifted itself, left its firm base, flung itself in great leaps upon the motionless bullock. The chief inspector turned and ran. The professor followed. They ran as they had never run before, as few indeed have ever run but they, since few but they have ever had such need for fearful speed. Once the chief inspector fell, and as he fell, he screamed, for he had felt something plucking at his ankle. It was only a bramble that had tripped him, but he was still screaming as he got to his feet and ran on again, nor indeed has he ever been quite the same man again.

Not till they were near the inn, not till lights showed close ahead, not till friendly human voices could be heard, did they cease that wild and dreadful flight.

When at last they were both safe in the professor's room at the inn, he said: 'I knew. At least I think I knew. But it's a different thing when you see it for yourself.'

'No one will believe us,' muttered the chief inspector. 'I don't think I believe it anymore myself. I thought it had me when that thing caught my ankle.' He said fiercely: 'What's it mean?'

'No one will believe us,' agreed the professor. 'Why should they? For how long, no one can even guess, but all through the centuries that thing stood there and was offered every day perhaps the blood of living victims, human victims, too, till at last, for the blood is the life, it began to have a life of its own, as evil as what caused that life, and when its worshippers no longer brought it victims then it began to seek them for itself, so to preserve with their blood the dim life the blood of others had begun to create within itself.'

'You mean the beastly thing grew alive?'

'I think it was wakening to life,' the professor answered.

The chief inspector went to the window and looked out into the palely lit night.

'I don't think I shall go to bed,' he said. 'I should dream—dream of that beastly thing making its way down here, crashing in the door or the walls—what could any man do against fifty tons of granite made animate?'

'It'll be safe tonight,' the professor answered. 'Safe and satiate. Satiate probably for another thirty years. Asleep again, the life within it. We won't risk another wakening though.' He motioned towards his luggage. 'There's enough high explosive there,' he said, 'to blow up half the hill. We'll wait till high noon.'

'No one will believe us,' the chief inspector repeated. 'I don't think I do quite myself. If I did, I think I should go mad.'

'We'll neither of us believe it,' agreed the professor. 'Safer not to.' After a time, he added: 'Not only in those days of the dawn of humanity have men made for themselves a god to destroy themselves.'

PRINCESS OF DARKNESS

Frederick Cowles

The final story in this anthology is a hitherto unpublished vampire story by the antiquary Frederick Cowles (1900–48). A Fellow of the Royal Society of Literature, he was a lifelong connoisseur and collector of ghost stories, 'from the ghost scenes in the Greek tragedies to the stories of Le Fanu and Richard Middleton; from Calmet's *Traité sur les Apparitions des Esprits* to the more recent learned works of Montague Summers; from Ennemoser's *History of Magic* to the ever-green thriller *Dracula*.' His two collections of ghost and horror stories, *The Horror of Abbot's Grange* (1936) and *The Night Wind Howls* (1938), are among the scarcest and most eagerly sought in the genre. He wrote several vampire tales, including 'The Vampire of Kaldenstein' and 'The Horror of Abbot's Grange' itself, both recently anthologized elsewhere. 'Princess of Darkness' was one of a number of supernatural stories destined for his third, and perhaps best, collection, *Fear Walks the Night*, which sadly was never published. It was inspired by a visit Cowles made to Budapest in July 1939. I am grateful to Mrs Doris Cowles for making it available for publication here.

I

IN THE spring of 1938 I was sent to Budapest on a rather delicate mission. For some years diplomatic circles, in at least five European countries, had been somewhat puzzled about a certain Princess Bessenyei who made sporadic appearances in the Hungarian capital, and was vaguely suspected of being involved in international espionage. The lady first attracted notice early in 1925 when she suddenly appeared in Budapest and just as suddenly departed after dazzling her admirers for little more than two months. Nearly a year passed before she was again seen in public and thereafter, at varying intervals, she was back in the capital for periods of from six weeks to three months at a time.

Lots of ugly rumours were whispered about the Princess. It was said that her departures from the city always coincided with the mysterious deaths of men who were reputed to have been her lovers. There were those who even asserted that a woman, strangely like the Princess, had been closely associated with Bela Kun, the notorious Communist leader, and had inspired many of the bloody orgies perpetrated by his regime. This suggestion was treated as idle gossip, for who could credit a story which linked such a proud aristocrat with the lowest of the vile criminals who, for a brief time, held in their incompetent hands the reins of government in Hungary?

No one could speak with any certainty of encountering the lady prior to 1925. The only facts one could accept with any degree of certainty were that the Princess was a member of a very ancient Hungarian family and that she appeared to have unlimited wealth at her disposal. Her claim to possess an estate on the borders of Transylvania was unquestioned as a place called Bessenyei appeared on the map. The story that she was a spy was difficult to believe as, so far as could be ascertained, Budapest was the only city she favoured with her presence. Yet the suggestion was taken seriously in certain quarters and my journey to Hungary must have been backed by some definite information. My task was simply to become acquainted with the Princess and to discover, if possible, something of her background.

Budapest, in the years between wars, was a favourite rendezvous for crooks of all types, as well as a very popular tourist resort. It was a lovable and romantic city and I remember, with nostalgic pleasure, the twinkling lights along the Danube, the great flood-lit statue of St Gellert, and the eternal Gypsy music throbbing through the night.

Istvan Zichy was one of our agents in those days and we had become fairly close friends during my many visits to his country. He was an attractive young man and, being a Count, moved in the best society. His greeting was very warm when he met me at the *Nyugati Pályaudvar*, and he chattered of trifling things as we drove to the *Dunapalota* where accommodation had been reserved for me. He became more serious in the privacy of my suite and I was surprised to find that he regarded my mission with some uneasiness.

'I don't like it, my friend,' he said. 'There is something uncanny about the woman, but it is all nonsense to suggest she is a spy. For myself I am of the opinion that she is thoroughly evil and a worshipper of the devil.' He made a quick sign of the Cross and, catching an involuntary smile on my face, continued. 'Ah! you laugh at me and think that Istvan grows superstitious. I am a Hungarian and I know that in this country the old beliefs die hard. What do we know of this Princess Bessenyei? For a few months she stays with us in Budapest and then back she goes to her castle near Arad—a castle which no one has ever visited and which, to my certain knowledge, is little more than a ruin. She leaves the city and immediately some young man who has enjoyed her favours dies in a strange fashion. Wait until you have seen the lady. I think you will find that cold shivers will go down your spine.'

'But,' I protested, 'I have been led to believe that the Princess is very beautiful.'

'Certainly she is lovely,' he replied. 'But I do not like her kind of beauty. A snake is a splendid thing—to those who like snakes. There is another queer point to which I must draw your attention. Why has this Princess no relatives to show? Often she speaks of her father but he never comes with her to Budapest, nor have I known of any person who has ever met him.'

'Relations can be an awful nuisance at times,' I laughed. 'Perhaps the lady prefers to keep hers in the background.'

'Possibly she prefers to keep a lot of other things in the background,' he replied. 'Well, my friend, I will help you all I can, but I do not envy you the job. Everything is arranged for you to meet the Princess tomorrow night and you can form your own conclusions. For myself I think that if she is a spy, the government for which she works is ruled over by a gentleman with horns on his head.'

II

The following evening, at the *Astoria*, I was presented to the Princess. Istvan had carefully paved the way for the encounter and I had been spoken of as a wealthy English nobleman visiting Hungary on my way to Constantinople.

It is not easy to describe the Princess nor to set down my first impression of her. She was a slim woman of medium height, with auburn hair and piercing green eyes. She appeared to be about thirty years of age, and her face and hands were so pale that they seemed quite bloodless, although her lips were unnaturally red. I noticed that the hand she extended for me to kiss was intensely cold and, when she smiled, sharp fang-like teeth were revealed. As the night advanced and I was able to examine the woman more closely, I became more and more uncertain about her. Although, when animated, her face was that of a young woman, in repose there was an indefinable air of age about it. Not a single wrinkle marred its loveliness and yet, in those odd moments, it was old in the way that a flawless piece of ivory may have been carved centuries ago. Then, whilst her eyes were definitely green when the light reflected upon them, in the shadow they appeared almost black.

For most of the time she kept up a lively flow of conversation, discussing all manner of topics from the international situation to the play then running at the *Nemzeti Szinház*. She ate nothing but a couple of peaches and drank only aerated water. This, I afterwards discovered, was her invariable practice, and no one had ever seen her eat a more substantial meal. The leader of the Gypsy orchestra seemed to avoid her as much as possible and, in his perambulations of the tables, seldom paused by our party. When he did he was careful to stand behind the Princess. Once she snapped a remark at him and I am sure I saw fear in the man's eyes.

During the next few days I encountered the Princess on several occasions and she always seemed pleased to see me. Within a week or so we were on fairly intimate terms and, to tell the truth, I found her very fascinating although, in some unaccountable way, I was afraid of her. One night we had been dancing at the *Hungaria* and I was taking her back to the flat she rented in one of the old palaces in Buda. We had just crossed the *Széchenyi Lánchid* when the taxi lurched and threw her against me. I put out my arm to steady her and she pressed herself against me, lifting her face with such obvious invitation in her eyes that I bent over and kissed her red lips. Her mouth opened and I felt her sharp teeth pierce my lower lip. It all happened in a moment and, just as quickly, she drew away from me with a long, satisfied sigh. Then she laughed softly. It was an unpleasant sound with no humour in it, and I felt that she was secretly gloating over gaining some purpose of her own. This impression was confirmed when we were parting and she said very quietly, 'Now you are mine for ever. I think you will dream of me tonight.'

I did dream about her and it was not a nice experience. As is my usual practice I read for about half an hour and then switched off the light and settled down to sleep. I suppose I must have dozed off for what followed could only have been a dream in spite of its seeming reality. I thought a ray of dull green light suddenly shone through the window and upon it, floating into the room, came the Princess Bessenyei. She was dressed in a long white robe, her teeth appeared abnormally long, and her eyes blazed like cold emeralds. I was powerless to stir or to utter one word, although I knew that those teeth would soon be fixed upon my throat. Closer she came, her mouth dripping with saliva in a most repulsive manner. She lifted the bed-clothes and then, like a snake darting upon its victim, she bent down to my neck. There was a sudden jar of metal upon bone, and I realized her teeth had struck the little silver crucifix which I always wear about my neck. With a bitter, frustrated cry she stood erect and I saw her pale face change in a most horrible manner. The cheeks sunk inwards, the eyes became hollow sockets, the mouth a gaping hole—I was gazing upon the ghastly head of a corpse. From this nightmare I awakened in a cold perspiration to find the window wide open and the curtains billowing in the breeze. I did not get to sleep again that night.

The following evening Istvan and I attended a gala performance at the Opera. The Princess was there with a party from the German Embassy. During the interval we went to the box to pay our respects and the first thing I noticed was that her mouth was disfigured by a thin white scar—a mark which might have been made by a thin piece of hot

metal. She observed my glance and, with a forced laugh, said something about being careless with a cigarette.

Nearly a week passed before we met again and then it was an accidental encounter in the *Allatkert*—the Budapest Zoological Garden. The park was almost deserted, for it was a chilly day, and I came upon the Princess by the house in which the Siberian wolves are kept. She had climbed inside the barrier and was stroking the animals through the bars of the cage. I was amazed to see the ferocious beasts behaving like huge dogs—grovelling at her touch and licking her hands.

'Be careful,' I exclaimed as I approached. 'Surely it is hardly safe to tempt them with such dainty morsels.'

'They will not hurt me,' she replied. 'I am used to wolves and know when they are dangerous.'

She swung herself through the rail and came to my side. For a few moments we stood looking at the animals and then I invited her to take some refreshment with me in the restaurant. She excused herself, saying she never ate between meals, but suggested she should sit with me whilst I drank a coffee. We went into the almost empty café and, sitting at a table against the wall, talked trivialities for a time. Suddenly she said, 'Tell me, are you a Catholic?' I admitted the fact and she went on, 'Then perhaps you have such a thing as a small cross or holy medal you would give me for a keepsake. Tomorrow I must go away and we may never meet again.'

'I have a little crucifix which I always wear,' I replied. 'But it has a sentimental value and I would not care to part with it. Let us go into the city and I will buy you a small souvenir of our friendship.'

'No,' she exclaimed rather pettishly. 'I want something that has a real personal association—something you wear. You see I have a fondness for you and would wish to remember these happy days.'

I surprised a hard gleam in those green eyes and knew that she was anxious to obtain possession of my cross and that nothing else would satisfy her. I also realized that the crucifix was my shield against some unknown danger and, without it, I should be at the mercy of a power I did not understand. As casually as possible I changed the subject and we chatted amiably for another ten or fifteen minutes. Then I escorted her to the gates where she called a taxi and held out her hand in farewell. As I kissed the cold fingers she whispered, 'You have refused my request, but the cross will not save you. You are mine for ever and I can afford to wait.' The red lips parted in a mirthless smile as she gave a sharp instruction to the driver and was borne away.

I was sufficiently disturbed by the events of the morning to seek out Istvan and recount them to him. He listened without comment as I told of the Princess's familiarity with the wolves and of her desire to possess my little crucifix. I also gave him a brief account of my unpleasant dream.

'It all confirms my suspicions,' he said when I had finished. 'This apparently attractive woman is not what she seems. If I were to tell you exactly what I believe her to be I am afraid it would tax your credulity. I am, however, convinced that, in your own interest, some immediate action must be taken to put a stop to something that is devilish. Will you do me the favour of telling your experiences to my friend Professor Otto Nemetz?'

'Do you mean the famous psychical investigator and the author of so many learned books and monographs on occult subjects?' I enquired.

'The very same. The Professor is very interested in our friend the Princess and may feel disposed to give you some surprising information regarding the lady.'

'I shall be delighted to meet Nemetz,' I replied. 'I have read many of his works and, if the man is only half as interesting as his writings, he should be a remarkable individual.'

'I promise that you will not be disappointed,' said Istvan.

III

My friend took me along to Otto Nemetz's apartment and, having performed the necessary introductions, pleaded another engagement and left me alone with my host. The Professor was utterly unlike what I had pictured him to be. Instead of the tall, scholarly man with a slightly sinister air which I had imagined, I found a small, rotund individual with merry twinkling eyes. When Istvan had departed Nemetz drew me over to the wide window and enthused about the wonderful vista of the Danube. It was certainly a marvellous scene from that fourth floor balcony—the silver ribbon of the stream far below, the Royal Palace and the Coronation church beyond, and, to the north, the blue heights of the encircling mountains.

Suddenly the Professor pulled me back into the room, closed the window, and said, 'Now let us get down to business.' He piloted me to a chair and, taking a bunch of keys from his pocket, unlocked a drawer in his desk. Carefully withdrawing a parcel wrapped in green baize, he removed the covering and placed a small oil-painting in my hands. It was a portrait of the Princess Bessenyei and the artist had caught, with uncanny skill, the wicked gleam of the green eyes and the bitter curl of the red lips.

'It is a remarkable likeness,' I exclaimed. 'Who is the artist?'

'You mean who *was* the artist. It was painted by Nicholas Erdösi and he, it may surprise you to know, died in 1502.'

'But that is impossible,' I protested somewhat feebly. 'It is certainly a portrait of the Princess Bessenyei but, according to your statement, it is over four hundred years old.'

'Exactly,' replied the Professor drawing his chair closer to mine and speaking in a low tone. 'That, in my opinion, is the age of the Princess. I believe that this woman has troubled the world for over four hundred years. Don't think me mad. Listen to what I have to say before you decide to dismiss by theories as fantastic dreams.'

He passed me the cigarettes and lit his own pipe before he continued.

'In parts of Hungary, more especially in the Transylvanian district, a belief in vampires stills exists. Throughout the centuries it has been held that certain persons can, by evil arts, retain a semblance of life within the tomb. I need only refer you to Johann Christofer Herenberg's *Philosophicae et Christianae Cogitationes de Vampiris* as proof of the fact that this belief has been seriously studied by learned men. The unholy dead nourish their bodies upon the blood of living men and women and, when this sustenance is available, can walk the world and behave like normal people. Time and distance mean nothing to the vampire and, after a period of quiet rest in the grave, it is capable of living like a human being for as long as six months at a time. In its lust for living blood it is inspired by a passion which often resembles love, and its victims are frequently wooed by an artful courtship. Usually the vampire does not care to be away from its home for a long period and, in fact, it cannot manage this unless it obtains the nourishment it requires. Yet, in the grave, it can retain the appearance of healthy life for hundreds of years providing it rises, from time to time, to drink human blood.

'It is a recognized fact that certain families in this part of Europe were, in the Middle Ages, brought under the vampire curse through their own criminal activities. The Bessenyeis were one of these. In the fifteenth century certain members of this family dabbled in the black arts and Prince Lóránd was the worst of them all. He undoubtedly sold his soul to the Evil One and initiated his daughter, the Princess Gizella, in all the foul rites of Satanism. She became the terror of the countryside—an avowed murderess who was eventually executed for her misdeeds in 1506. Unfortunately, having regard for her rank, her body was interred in the chapel of Bessenyei Castle. If it had been burned much trouble would have been saved, for I am convinced, that she and her father have been as active from the tomb as they were in life. At different times throughout the centuries this woman has appeared in the world, and she is the person you know as the Princess Bessenyei.'

'But surely such a tale is ridiculous,' I interrupted. 'I am prepared to swear that the Princess is a woman of flesh and blood, and I cannot believe that your theory will bear scientific investigation. After all this is the twentieth century.'

'She is certainly a creature of flesh and blood,' replied Nemetz. 'But that flesh and blood is over four centuries old. I know it all sounds like a medieval fantasy and yet I believe it to be true. I am so convinced that I am determined to prove my contention and, in doing so, to rid the world of a devilish evil. Hungarians are naturally superstitious and I should find it difficult to persuade any person in this country to give me the assistance I require. You are an Englishman and can help me if you will.'

'How is that possible?' I asked in some trepidation for, remembering the strange incidents connected with my short acquaintance with the Princess, I felt myself becoming convinced against my will.

'Come with me to the Castle of Bessenyei,' suggested the little Professor. 'I can guarantee you protection against the undead, but I do not promise that the sights I may reveal will be pleasant. You are, I take it, a man with good nerves and are not afraid of things which may live in your memory for ever.'

'I am not afraid of anything I can understand, but this is quite beyond me,' I replied. 'I have to find out all I can about the woman and, for this reason if for no other, I am prepared to help you even to the extent of accompanying you to Bessenyei.'

'Good,' cried Nemetz. 'No time must be wasted and we will start at nine o'clock in the morning. Meanwhile it may be as well for us to visit the *Országos Levéltár*—the department of State Archives—to see if we can obtain any information about the home of the Bessenyeis.'

He seized his hat and stick and presently we were hurrying along the *Horthy Miklos Ut*. By the bridge the Professor signalled a taxi which carried us across the river to Buda, by the Coronation church, to the modern building in the *Bécsikapu Tér* where all documents of the Hungarian State are housed. Soon we were closeted with a courteous official who, in the pleasant fashion of the country, produced a bottle of wine before he dealt with our enquiry.

'Yes,' he said. 'I have heard of the castle but, so far as I can recollect, it is situated in disputed territory. I will, however, let you have all the information that is available.' He rang a bell and instructed the subordinate, who answered the summons, to bring certain documents and maps. When these were before him he gave us the startling intelligence that the Bessenyei family, at least that branch of it which owned the castle, had become extinct in 1723.

'But', I said, 'there is certainly a Princess Bessenyei who is well known in Budapest society.'

'She probably comes from another branch of the family,' he replied. 'Bessenyei Castle, with its estates, seems to have become State property about the middle of the last century. The building can be little more than a picturesque ruin and I see from our records that a caretaker was maintained there until the outbreak of the last war. Since the Treaty of Trianon we have had no official connection with the estate which appears to be in territory still the subject of litigation. If you wish to visit the place you will encounter no difficulties, although I think it most unlikely that any custodian is on the premises. Certainly we have met no charges for maintenance during the past twenty or thirty years.'

Thanking him for his assistance we parted with mutual expressions of goodwill, and Nemetz and I returned to Pest.

IV

Punctually at nine o'clock the following day the professor was at my hotel. He came up to my suite and, spreading a map on the table, pointed out the road we had to follow.

'The actual distance,' he said, 'is little more than a hundred English miles. But I am afraid the latter part of the journey will be by bad roads and we cannot expect to arrive at our destination before late evening. It may be helpful if we can spend the night in the castle. Do you think you can face such an ordeal?'

'Having undertaken this adventure,' I replied, 'I am in your hands. If you think we should spend the night in the building I am quite agreeable.'

'Excellent! One more thing before we start. Are you wearing the crucifix about your neck?'

I showed him the cross on its thin silver chain and he gave a grunt of approval. He led me out to the waiting car which he was driving himself. I noticed two travelling cases in the back seat, also a small crowbar.

On the whole it was a pleasant drive with brief stops at Kecskemét and Szeged. At the latter place we had a meal and inspected the splendid votive church. From Makó the roads were little more than dusty tracks through cornfields and vineyards. At last we came to a gloomy forest and, upon the edge of it, was a Gypsy encampment. Nemetz pulled up and called out to one of the men, asking if he could direct us to the castle. The fellow came over to the car and appeared to be afraid to answer the question. On the Professor repeating his request the Gypsy burst into a torrent of words accompanied by urgent gestures. So far as I could make out the castle was in the forest, but it was only a deserted ruin. It was an evil place and we would be well advised to give it a wide berth. Nemetz laughed and said something about calling on the Princess. This remark served to increase the man's agitation and his incoherent warnings rang in our ears as we drove away.

'You see,' said my companion, 'even the Gypsies are afraid of the castle and know it to be the home of evil things.'

It was so dark under the trees that we had to switch on the headlights to enable us to see the way. After about a couple of miles there was a break in the trees and a pair of ruined columns, one still surmounted by a heraldic device, indicated the approach to a large house. In the distance we could see the outline of a tower, but the drive was overgrown and hardly distinguishable from the surrounding fields. Dusk was falling as we turned into the entrance and suddenly there was a blood-curdling howl and a gaunt grey wolf leaped from the shadows and bounded along at the side of the car. Nemetz applied the brakes, pulled out a revolver, and fired three rounds at the animal. At such short range he could hardly have failed to hit it. But, with a howl of rage, it reared up on its hind legs and then ran off among the trees. Then, from all over the forest, came the answering cries of a pack of wolves howling in anger.

Beyond the shattered gates the track led through a wilderness which must have originally been parkland. A few stunted trees hung above a reedy lake into which flowed the waters of a dark moat, which we crossed by a crumbling bridge.

As we neared the castle I could see that it was little more than a shell, with a round tower on the western side and, beyond it, a detached building which looked like a chapel. Drawing up before the main doorway the Professor handed me a powerful electric torch and, carrying a bag each, we climbed the broken steps.

'There is just a chance that there may be a caretaker in the place,' said Nemetz, 'although I think it most unlikely.' He pulled a chain which hung from a pillar and, far away inside the building, a bell tolled with a hollow sound. As its echoes died we heard the sound of shuffling footsteps and the heavy door swung open. On the threshold stood a tall man dressed in the dark costume of an old-fashioned retainer. He held a lighted candle in his hand and the light fell upon a bearded face in which the eyes glowed with a curious red glow. I confess that I was afraid and wished myself back in the pleasant comfort of the *Dunapalota*. But the Professor did not appear unduly alarmed.

'You are the custodian I presume?' he asked. The man gave a barely perceptible nod and Nemetz went on. 'We are two travellers who desire shelter for the night. Can it be arranged?'

'The accommodation is poor,' was the reply in a thin, fluting voice. 'But you are welcome to such as it is. Enter, gentlemen. Enter of your own free will and become the guests of Castle Bessenyei.'

He stood aside, holding the candle high, and we entered the building. The hall, which appeared to be in a tolerable state of repair, stank of damp and decay. A ragged tapestry fluttered on one wall, but the others were green with mildew. Our guide gave us little chance to examine our surroundings for, after slamming the door, he led the way up a wide staircase, along a narrow corridor on the first floor, and ushered us into a room at the end of it. It was apparently a large apartment and the feeble light of the candle revealed a bare floor, a heavy table, two chairs, and an oak settle.

'This is the best we can offer,' said the strange custodian. 'I trust you have food with you, for there is none in the castle. You will, I hope, find this better than a night spent in the forest.' With a soft chuckle he added, 'It is many years since last we entertained guests in Castle Bessenyei.'

'Can you light a fire?' demanded the Professor. ''The room is as cold as a tomb.'

'I regret there is no fuel in the castle,' was the reply. 'This is all we can provide—a roof over your heads and chairs in which you can await the dawn. Even a tomb is not so cold as the living believe.' As he spoke the howl of a wolf sounded from under the windows. With a muttered word of apology he grabbed the candle and hurried from the room, leaving us in the semi-darkness.

The door had hardly closed when Nemetz quietly opened it again and, beckoning me to follow, led the way along the passage to the head of the stairs. The old man was descending and his candle cast queer shadows on the damp walls. Moving with a strange gliding motion he hurried over to the heavy door and flung it open. At once a long grey shape bounded over the threshold and I started back in fear. But immediately, before our eyes, the wolf changed into a woman. It was the Princess Bessenyei. We heard the muttering of low conversation and then the woman raised her eyes and looked to where we were standing. The Professor pulled me back into the deeper shadow and we watched as the two figures below moved towards a door near the foot of the stairs and vanished through it. We waited a few moments and then silently crept back to our room.

'Now we know exactly where we stand,' said the Professor, driving home the rusty bolt on the door. 'The Princess is here and it is obvious that the custodian is not what he pretends to be. We must prepare ourselves for the night.'

From the first case he unpacked a portable electric lamp which was powerful enough to illuminate the sombre chamber. We saw that the dust of years covered the floor and the barred windows were festooned with cobwebs. A coat of arms was carved above the wide stone fireplace and this was repeated over each of the two windows. Nemetz then produced handfuls of garlic and spread the herb on the threshold of the rooms and on the window-sills. On the table he placed a pair of brass candle-sticks containing long yellow tapers which he lighted.

'We are now safe from direct attack,' he explained. 'For some reason the undead loathe the smell of garlic and it has always been considered a sure protection against their spells. The candles were blessed by the archbishop last Candlemas Day and, to make things doubly sure, I shall now sprinkle the room with holy water.'

He took a flask from his pocket and, reciting the prayer of the *Asperges*, sprayed drops of the blessed water into every corner of the apartment. We then drew the chairs up to the table and ate a light meal of sandwiches washed down with a bottle of seltzer water.

'It will be safe enough to sleep,' said the little man when we had finished our repast. 'But on no account must you attempt to leave the room or to open the door or windows.'

For a while we chatted of ordinary things which seemed ridiculously unreal in those sinister surroundings. But I was very tired and could feel my lids growing heavier. After a time I saw that my companion was finding it difficult to remain awake. Suddenly he slumped over the table and settled his head on his arm. I also must have fallen asleep and yet it seemed that I never closed my eyes. I became aware of a reddish glow which appeared to come from the fireplace and eventually resolved itself into minute particles of gleaming dust which danced in the light of the electric lamp. Gradually they took shape, misty at first and then more clearly defined until the Princess Bessenyei stood before me. Her green eyes were tender and inviting, and she beckoned me to follow her. I knew that I must remove the crucifix from my neck before I could rise from the chair. But I found it impossible to lift my hands—I was chained to the spot and could not move. The woman's face changed as she watched my fruitless efforts to obey her unspoken command. Angry frustration blazed from her eyes, her mouth twisted into a horrible dribbling leer, and she bared the white fangs of her teeth. Then the figure became blurred and a cloud of red dust hung in the light of the lamp before it faded away. The hungry cry of a wolf, echoing through the ruined castle, awakened me. Nemetz was already on his feet and he put his finger to his lips to enjoin silence. From beyond the door came the sibilant whisper of voices and then the wolf's howl rang out again.

'There is nothing to fear,' the Professor assured me. He went on to explain that the vampire frequently assumes the shape of a wolf and, in this guise, is able to satisfy its lust for blood. I suppose the even murmur of his voice must have lulled me off to sleep again. When I awakened next time it was morning and the sun blazed through the dirty windows. The little man was bending over a primus stove and the warm, friendly aroma of coffee pervaded the apartment.

V

We made a good breakfast, for Nemetz had brought a liberal supply of food. I noticed, however, that no meat was provided and this was explained when the Professor remarked that, in dealing with the occult, it was best to avoid flesh-meat. After the meal we packed everything back into the cases in readiness to carry them out to the car.

'The real business of our visit remains to be performed,' said my companion. 'The task we have set ourselves is to rid the world of this evil creature and we shall require all our courage if we are to succeed. God grant we do not fail.'

He opened the door and we were carrying our things into the passage when I stopped with a sudden exclamation. Just over the threshold, written in the dust on the floor, were the words, 'You are mine for ever.' Nothing I had experienced during my association with the Princess had affected me as did that strange message. I literally trembled with fear and it took all Nemetz's assurances to restore some of my self-control. Even then I would have backed out of the business if I could have done so honourably.

There was no sign of the old man we had seen on the previous evening and, in the cold light of day, the castle looked an utterly abandoned ruin. We peeped into some of the rooms on the ground floor and, apart from a few broken articles of antique furniture, they were quite empty. In what had evidently been the dining hall some of the carved panelling had been roughly ripped from the walls and birds were nesting in the crevices.

Before we packed the bags into the car Nemetz removed certain articles and placed them in his capacious pockets. These included a wooden crucifix, a wicked-looking dagger, a handful of garlic, and the bottle of holy water. Taking the crowbar in his hand he led the way towards the chapel.

The little building probably dated from the early fourteenth century and was graceful in design. The door opened to our touch and a wave of cold, dank air greeted us. The interior was filthy and littered with fallen masonry. A few fragments of coloured glass remained in the windows and there was a stone altar at the east end. The Professor mounted the steps and examined the slab. It was covered with the droppings of birds and, scraping some of the dirt away, he pointed to dark brown patches which stained the centre of the table. He also showed me that the five consecration crosses had been roughly obliterated and the receptacle for relics was empty.

'Here are the marks of unholy sacrifices,' he said, 'and proofs that this altar has been used for the wicked blasphemy of the Black Mass.'

At the back of the altar we found a flight of narrow steps leading down into the depths of the earth. At the bottom was a small door marked with the same coat of arms we had seen in the castle.

'Now comes the real test,' said Nemetz. 'This is the burial vault of the Bessenyei family and here we shall find the evidence we seek. Let us pray for strength to enable us to finish this awful business.'

Beside the desecrated altar we knelt and asked heaven to bless our efforts and to shield us from evil. Then the Professor led the way down the steps and tried the door of the vault. It was apparently secured, but the rusty lock soon gave way before the crowbar and the door swung inwards. With a wild shriek which froze the blood in our veins, something flapped out of the darkness and soared towards the roof of the chapel. It was only a great white owl but our nerves, keyed almost to breaking point, were badly shaken. Speaking for myself I would, at that moment, gladly have abandoned the task we had set ourselves. But the Professor soon recovered himself and, with a self-conscious laugh, directed the beam of his torch into the vault. A ghastly sight met our eyes. Coffins of all shapes and sizes were ranged in niches around the walls and most of them had been broken open. Here and there bones protruded and the floor was covered with fragments of human bodies, some of them with dried scraps of flesh still adhering. In the centre of the place two great leaden coffins stood side by side.

'These are the ones we want,' said the Professor advancing into the vault. 'The others are of no importance for we can see that their inmates have suffered the normal course of corruption.'

He placed the torch in my hands and motioned me to hold it so that the light fell upon the first of the two coffins. Then, with the crowbar, he prised the lid and found that it was not sealed in any way. He moved it a little so that he could get a grip on the edges. Evidently it was not so weighty as he had anticipated, for he lifted it off with comparative ease. There, before us in the leaden casket, was the body of the man we had taken to be the caretaker of the castle. He appeared to be sleeping and, in repose, the cruel lines of his mouth were set in an evil grin.

'Just as I suspected,' muttered Nemetz. 'This is Prince Lorand who is supposed to have died in the fifteenth century. You see for yourself how he lives in the grave and can arise when occasion demands. Now let us look at the other.'

We turned to the second coffin and, without any difficulty, the two of us lifted the lid and placed it on the floor. I was more or less prepared for the sight that met our gaze but, even so, it gave me a nasty shock. The light of the torch showed us the Princess Bessenyei to all intents and purposes resting quietly in the tomb. She could hardly be described as sleeping, for her wicked eyes were wide open and gleamed with mocking scorn. Looking upon that beautiful face it was hard to believe that this woman had roamed the earth for over four centuries and that the source of her immunity from death was the blood of the innocent people who became her victims. Yet I was convinced at last.

We turned back to the first coffin and the Professor drew his dagger. Whispering to me to hold the torch steady he raised his arm and plunged the weapon deep into the heart of the thing in the casket. An unearthly scream of agony came from the twisted lips, the body writhed in grotesque fashion for a few moments and then, before our eyes, it turned to dust. Nemetz, who seemed quite unmoved, put a few bulbs of garlic into the coffin and sprinkled it with holy water. We were bending to lift the lid when I dropped the torch and plunged the vault into darkness. Before I could retrieve it a burst of harsh laughter rang out. We both sprang round and there, framed in the narrow doorway and wrapped in a pale, phosphorescent glow, was the Princess with her

green eyes blazing with hellish anger. In a second the Professor had drawn his revolver and emptied it into the figure. He might have spared himself the trouble for the shots had no effect at all.

Lifting her hand in a commanding gesture which seemed to paralyse us into immobility, the Princess addressed us.

'You, Professor Nemetz,' she said, 'have taken my father from me and, for this, you shall pay the penalty. You have failed to destroy me and nothing can save you from my vengeance when the hour comes, for the undead do not forget.' Then turning to me she smiled a slow mysterious smile. 'There is no need for me to tell you again that you will be mine in the end. Your lips have touched mine and, although years may pass and seas may divide us, I shall come for you in my own good time.'

With these words she vanished from our sight. Power was suddenly restored to our limbs and we rushed up the steps into the chapel. There was no sign of the Princess but, with a hoot of derision and a flapping of wings, the great white owl swooped down and flew back into the vault.

The Professor seemed very badly shaken. 'Too late,' he groaned. 'Too late. I should have realized that she is too skilled in her evil arts to allow herself to be destroyed by the usual methods.'

We made our way back to the car and were soon driving through the forest. Nemetz hardly spoke a word. He drove as if trying desperately to escape from a pursuing terror and we were back in Budapest by the late afternoon. I gave him a stiff brandy in my room, but all life seemed to have gone out of him.

'I must again seriously warn you of the danger in which you stand,' he said before we parted. 'This creature has a passion for you which resembles, to some degree, the passion of violent love. It will never be content until you have become its victim—even if it has to wait many years. I can only urge you to protect yourself by every means in your power. I fear for you and I also fear for myself. The Princess has promised to have her revenge and I am convinced it will not be long before the attack comes. God be with you, my friend. If all is well I will call upon you in the morning.'

I never saw Professor Nemetz alive again. That same night he was killed in most brutal fashion. The authorities decided that some wild animal had gained access to the poor man's apartment, though how it was impossible to determine, for he was literally savaged to death. But I know how and why he died. I saw the glazed terror in his dead eyes and remembered the gaunt grey wolf of Bessenyei.

My turn will come. I feel safe with the little cross around my neck, but she will find some way of overcoming its power. I write down this story so that the truth may be known and perhaps, in God's good time, someone will be brave enough to again attempt the destruction of the undead. I leave this city with fear in my heart, for I know she will follow me to the ends of the earth.

Postscript by Dr Reginald Staines, Medical Officer in charge of Eastdown Mental Home, Devon.

The foregoing manuscript was written by Harvey Gorton, a former member of the Diplomatic Service, who was admitted to this institution on 10th November 1939. His was a case of psychosis, the chief feature of which was a fixed delusion that he was being hunted by the woman he called the Princess Bessenyei. Apart from this he was apparently normal and never caused any trouble. I found him a most cultured man and we often chatted together about the international situation. He was very perturbed about the war and seemed particularly anxious that Hungary, for which country he had a great affection, should not be drawn into the conflict. In the ordinary course of events I think we should have effected a complete cure within a few months.

On 2nd December, after a light fall of snow, he was walking in the grounds when he stumbled over the root of a tree and fell some five or six feet down an embankment, injuring his left shoulder. He was evidently in great pain and an x-ray revealed a fracture in a bad position at the upper end of the humerus. It was decided to give an anaesthetic for reduction. Gorton always wore a little crucifix at his neck and I noticed that, when the surgeon lifted it aside to enable him to examine the shoulder more carefully, the man became unduly agitated and protested that the cross must on no account be removed. We injected pentolthal into a vein in the arm and, as Gorton was becoming unconscious, the nurse, by some clumsy movement, broke the chain on which the cross was suspended and it fell to the floor. The patient was only out for about forty seconds and, when he was taken back to his room, the crucifix was apparently forgotten. Later he became very anxious about the loss and worked himself up into such a state that I gave instructions for it to be restored to him. Unfortunately the operating theatre had been swept and, although the cross had been found, it had been locked up in the desk of the Matron. She had gone off duty and it was impossible for us to secure the thing until she returned.

I tried to soothe Gorton, but he made a terrible fuss about the business and demanded that the desk should be broken open. As he seemed likely to become violent I gave him a strong sleeping draught as the best way out of the difficulty.

Later in the evening, having ascertained that the patient was sleeping soundly, I went over to the vicarage for an hour to discuss with the vicar's wife the formation of some First Aid classes. I had hardly settled down when the telephone rang and I was recalled to the Home.

The whole place was in confusion. My deputy, Doctor Snell, reported that, about five minutes after I had left, a woman, speaking with a foreign accent, had called at the Home and asked to see Gorton. She was shown into a waiting room whilst the nurse went to inform Snell of the request. He naturally said it was quite impossible for Gorton to be seen and the nurse, returning to inform the visitor, found the waiting-room empty. At that moment she heard a terrified scream and members of the staff, rushing upstairs, discovered the door of Gorton's room wide open. The poor wretch was lying half in and half out of bed and was already dead. When I came to examine the corpse I found that it was almost entirely drained of blood—a most difficult condition to describe or explain. The only wound on the body was a tiny double puncture in the throat.

ACKNOWLEDGEMENTS

FOR permission to print copyright material in this anthology grateful acknowledgements are made to the following:

A. P. Watt Ltd. and Mrs Sheila Reeves for 'The Singular Death of Morton' by Algernon Blackwood.

Mrs Doris Cowles for 'Princess of Darkness' by Frederick Cowles.

Every effort has been made to trace the owners of copyright. The editor and publishers apologize for any omissions.